AN INTRODUCTION TO MODERN EUROPEAN LITERATURE

Also by Martin Travers and published by Macmillan

THOMAS MANN

An Introduction to Modern European Literature

From Romanticism to Postmodernism

Martin Travers

First published 1998 by
MACMILLAN PRESS LTD
Houndmills, Basingstoke, Hampshire RG21 6XS
and London
Companies and representatives
throughout the world

ISBN 0–333–59453–3 hardcover
ISBN 0–333–59454–1 paperback

A catalogue record for this book is available
from the British Library.

This book is printed on paper suitable for recycling and
made from fully managed and sustained forest sources.

10   9   8   7   6   5   4   3   2   1
07 06 05 04 03 02 01 00 99 98

Typeset by EXPO Holdings, Malaysia

Printed in Hong Kong

Published in the United States of America 1998 by
ST. MARTIN'S PRESS, INC.,
Scholarly and Reference Division
175 Fifth Avenue, New York, N.Y. 10010

ISBN 0–312–17638–4 cloth
ISBN 0–312–17639–2 paperback

Contents

Preface

Modern European literature. But which Europe? Which literature? The shifting historical borders of the former admit of no easy classification. 'Europe', as a geographical, geopolitical reality, is a changing construct, the product of military and diplomatic struggles that have characterized its history for more than a thousand years. What we understand as 'European' has changed with the ages. It has traditionally included Iceland, in the North, and Greece, in the South, but not Turkey, or what is now known as Israel; while Russia, then the Soviet Union, and now Russia again, has hovered around the edges of the continent, politically and spatially important, its central state included, but its satellite minorities, such as Georgia and Armenia, often excluded.

In terms of the literary history of the continent, however, matters are less confounded. Culture may be the expression of the symbolic and moral values of an individual nation; but it is equally true that once a culture is exported, it enters into a complex but by no means mysterious relationship with cultures of other nations. Shared readerships, common literary markets, literary personalities, fashion, journals and publishers provide a network of influences in which certain authors, styles and genres become dominant, and others do not. It is for this reason that this introduction to modern European literature is structured around those schools or movements which have provided the nodal points for writers in Europe over the past two hundred years: Romanticism, Realism, Naturalism, Modernism, and Postmodernism, to which we must add (in a welcome departure from 'ismism') the literature of political engagement that emerged during the interwar years, between 1918 and 1945.

Certainly, we cannot claim that every writer of significance during this period belonged to a school or movement. British writers, in particular, have seemed (and seem) to share an abhorrence of labels, categories and classifications, and have often consciously held themselves distant from the trends of their age. I have, obviously, not attempted to allocate writers to a school or movement where such an allocation was clearly inappropriate. In the final analysis, noting, for example, that Tennyson wrote in the age of Realism tells us little about Realism and even less about

Tennyson. Focussing upon such schools or movements also serves to privilege certain nations, such as England, Germany and Italy (but most notably France, from which most of these movements originated), whilst relegating other nations, for example, Greece and the Scandinavian countries, to the cultural periphery. In writing this book, however, I have tried to remain aware of the invidious politics of cultural canonicity, consciously bringing into the picture (as far as space would permit) writers who are normally excluded from such studies, such as the great poet of Greek Romanticism, Dionysios Solomos, or (at other end of the temporal spectrum) the Serbian poet, Vasko Popa, and the Hungarian, László Nagy, whose works were not only central to the nations from which they came, but who also made an important contribution to the broad development of European literature during this period.

Nevertheless, the fact remains that many writers did see themselves as part of a larger movement, and framed both the theory and the practice of their work in terms of that movement. If we bear these caveats in mind, and others, such as the fact that many of the authors of whom we will speak occupied transitional positions between these movements (James Joyce, for example, who seems to straddle late Realism, Modernism and Postmodernism in his *Dubliners, Ulysses* and *Finnegans Wake,* respectively, or Flaubert, whose work traces the trajectory between Realism and Romantic Decadence), approaching European literature from the perspective of its major cultural formations allows us to identify the common projects that bound the major writers of each period together, to establish a comparative framework for their work. It also enables us to tie their creative writing to the wider philosophical and political issues that governed the historical periods of which they were a part. Adopting this perspective, we can see that Romanticism, for example, was not just the invention of Rousseau in Paris, the Schlegels in Berlin or Coleridge in London; it was a broad movement of ideas that was formed by, and helped form, European history between 1770 and 1848, which was a period of revolutionary change, propelled by the boundless energies, utopian expectations and almost monomaniacal presentations of self that informed literature and politics alike. The same might be said of Realism, Modernism, and Postmodernism: they are short-hand signatures for the intellectual paradigms in which successive stages of European culture have acquired their distinctive identities.

1
Romanticism

1 RADICAL ENERGY: THE CONTEXT OF EUROPEAN ROMANTICISM

'Nothing was dreamt of it but the regeneration of the human race', announced the English poet and critic, Robert Southey in 1824. He meant his words to apply to the French Revolution, but they might equally well describe that literary movement of which he himself was a central part: Romanticism. From Byron's act of self-sacrifice in the cause of the liberation of Greece, to Shelley's Promethean myth and the radical stage of Victor Hugo, Romanticism enjoyed a close, almost symbiotic relationship with the political changes of the age. The French Revolution, with its explosive mixture of revolutionary optimism and totalitarian cynicism, was certainly the most dramatic of these changes; but much else happened in the period between 1770 and 1830 to bring European society to a final break with its feudal past. The industrial revolution began to transform, initially technologically but then socially, continental Europe; nationalism and ethno-centricity emerged as political forces; and science established its potency through, for example, the discoveries of electricity and electro-magnetism. These changes and others, such as the spread of religious evangelicalism, and the rediscovery of rural life and peasant culture, produced a climate of 'reformation and change', which seemed to many, including the English radical, William Godwin, to augur a new period in human history.[1]

But it was the French Revolution that came to dominate the imagination of the age. Its achievements were undeniable. During the course of five momentous years, between 1789 and 1794, it dismantled the ramshackle (but no less oppressive) political apparatus of the *ancien régime*, abolished feudal rights and guild restrictions, rationalised fiscal and taxation systems, redrafted the relationship between Church and State, and, above all, enfranchised groups long deprived of political representation. The early energies that brought the Revolution into existence were celebrated throughout

Europe. The enthusiastic and often quoted lines by the major English Romantic poet, William Wordsworth – 'Bliss was it in that dawn to be alive/but to be young was very Heaven' – were echoed by an entire generation of youthful writers, who saw in the French Revolution a vindication of morality over ossified convention, justice over tyranny, nature over artifice. The initial reception was particularly positive in Germany. The leading member of the Jena school of German Romanticism, Friedrich Schlegel, viewed the Revolution as 'the greatest and most singular phenomenon in the history of states', a realisation of 'God's Empire on earth'; whilst his compatriot, Christoph Martin Wieland, welcomed it as the culmination of that 'beautiful, noble and happy state of being with which nature has endowed mankind'. None could escape its influence. As Heinrich Heine wrote, even 'the most isolated author, living in a distant corner of Germany, took part in the movement; sympathetically, even without fully understanding its political import'.[2]

The French Revolution was the first major political event of the modern period. Not only did it give birth to a notion of governmentality that merged (in striking anticipation of the mass political movements of the twentieth century) techno-rationality with populist notions of democracy and the needs of 'the people'; it also attempted to mobilise the electorate in the direction of the Revolution through propaganda and civic symbolism. This included not only a rewriting of the calendar (nominally beginning French history from 1792) but, in a more grandiose gesture, the replacement of traditional religion and the rites of the Church with a new civic faith, whose spiritual locus would be not God, but a state-inspired Supreme Being. The leaders of the French Revolution anticipated the political demagogues of the twentieth century in one further area: the practice of politics as a mysticism of power. This manifested itself in the moralistic and self-righteous tone of successive leaders from Danton to Robespierre, who increasingly came to see themselves as chosen ones, individual expressions of that anonymous totality, the popular will. The Romantics were fully justified in seeing their own aesthetic of self-expression and self-empowerment writ large in the grandiose style in which the Revolution was conducted. As the English poet Thomas de Quincey shrewdly observed, 'until the French Revolution, no nation in Christendom except England had any practical experience of popular rhetoric; any deliberative eloquence, for instance; any forensic eloquence that was made public; any democratic eloquence of the hustings; or any form whatever of public rhetoric'. Slogans such as 'the father-land', 'citizens', and 'liberty' were fashioned into an emotive dis-course, and used by successive revolutionary leaders to impart legitimacy to their aspirations for power. Robespierre, in particular, showed himself master of the rhetoric of political Romanticism. His famous speech 'On the Cult of the Supreme Being' (1794), with its emotive declaration and grandiose generalisations, conjured up the 'immortal events of our revolution' in a language that seemed to echo the hyperbolic idiom of the Romantic voice.[3]

The leaders of the French Revolution were driven by a moral mission, whose abstract principles they tried to put into concrete and immediate form. In the early days of the Revolution, these principles formed a charter, 'The Rights of Man', which received memorable formulation in the tract by the English political theorist, Thomas Paine. But Paine's influence was short-lived; as the Revolution progressed, his liberal-egalitarian credo gave way to the infinitely more abstract and impenetrable notion of the 'General Will' (*volonté générale*), whose source lay in the writings of the French pre-Romantic, Jean-Jacques Rousseau, and most notably in his influential political treatise, *The Social Contract* (1762). The 'General Will' was not an empirical reality, but a mystical ideal, a governing abstraction that helped legitimise acts of brutality against all who stood in the way of radical change. As the Revolution progressed, the ideals that were embodied in the Estates-General of 1787 soon degenerated into collective violence, first in the trial and execution of Louis XVI in 1793, and then through the Reign of Terror of the years 1793–1794, masterminded by the most ruthless of the Revolution's leaders: Maximilien Robespierre. Byron's later expression of repugnance with the Revolution: 'But France got drunk with blood to vomit crime' (voiced in the fourth canto of *Childe Harold's Pilgrimage*, 1818), graphically described the disaffection that began to spread throughout Europe. Those who initially supported the Revolution, such as Wordsworth and Coleridge, now came to reject all forms of revolutionary activity, redefining themselves in the process as in-tractable defenders of the 'social order'.[4]

It is only an apparent paradox that the energies unleashed by the French Revolution should find their supreme embodiment in the personality who would be responsible for its termination – Napoleon Bonaparte. For he was a child of the Revolution. At the age of twenty-four, he became the youngest general in French history, his meteoric rise made possible by the egalitarian policies of a revolutionary government that encouraged both personal and professional mobility, allowing for careers, as Napoleon himself described it, 'open to all talents, without distinctions of birth'. 'Mounting the throne', the French Romantic writer, François-René de Chateaubriand, noted later in his *Memoirs*, 'he seated the common people beside him. A proletarian monarch, he humiliated the kings and nobles in the ante-chambers; he levelled the ranks of society, not by lowering them but by raising them up'. It was fitting that Napoleon should be created Emperor of the French 'by grace of God', in a ceremony that took place in Notre Dame only ten years after the ceremonies in the same cathedral in honour of the goddess Reason. His *coup d'état* of 1799 put an end to the Revolution, but brought a style to politics that was as every bit as revolutionary as anything that had preceded it. His imperial ambitions transformed the cosmopolitan idealism of the French Revolution into a nationalist cause, and provided the springboard for a resurgence in the economic, political and, above all, military might of the French nation. Napoleon's achievements were many, and they went well beyond his momentous victories in Italy, Spain and Germany, which were made possible through the first example of mass mobilisation (*levée en masse*) in European history. Equally impressive were the internal administrative reforms carried through during his first period of rule between 1799 and 1804, known as The Consulate. These included the professionalisation of the state bureaucracy, the centralisation and rationalisation of the judiciary through the *Code napoléon*, and the restructuring of the French educational system. Such initiatives, taken together with the diplomatic coup of The Concordat (1801), which turned the Church in France into an institution of the state, transformed the unstable achievements of the French Revolution into a permanent form of governance. It is not surprising that many, including the great German philosopher Hegel, saw the French Emperor as the major figure of his age. After watching the conquering hero ride through the streets after the Battle of Jena, Hegel had little doubt that he was seeing a world-historical individual, indeed, 'the World Spirit on horseback'.[5]

To his supporters, Napoleon represented the necessary emergence of discipline out of the rampant and unchecked individualism unleashed by the French Revolution. But it was the imperial (and imperious) personality that won the hearts of his contemporaries. Bonaparte embodied many of the personal qualities that the Romantics were to idealise in their writings: charismatic leadership, disdain for traditional class distinctions and advocacy of an aristocracy of personal merit, sexual prowess and an aggressive self-confidence. He possessed, according to the French novelist Stendhal (who wrote not one but two studies of his hero) 'the energy necessary to shake the enormous mass of contracted habits' that had remained unaffected by the Revolution. The French Romantic, Alphonse Lamartine, held him for the essence of 'gloire! honneur! liberté!', sentiments reiterated by the Italian, Ugo Foscolo, in his ode, 'Bonaparte, liberator' (1796), and by the Swedish poet, Esaias Tegnér (the author of the epic *Frithiof's Saga*, 1825), who celebrated Napoleon's military prowess in the Russian campaign in his poem, 'Hero' (1813). Even after Napoleon had surrendered at Fontainebleau and had been despatched to Elba, the English critic, William Hazlitt, was still prepared to defend the former emperor in public, extolling him in his *Life of Napoleon Buonaparte* (1830) as a universal liberator, 'the child and champion of the French Revolution'.[6]

Napoleon met his nemesis on the fields of Waterloo. What followed him was a period of political reaction known as the Restoration. From 1815 onwards, the conservative, aristocratic, and largely Catholic values that had dominated pre-revolutionary Europe now found themselves back in favour, enshrined in the portentous protocols of the Congress of Vienna, signed in that year by the reigning monarchs of Austria, Russia and Prussia (the so-called Holy Alliance). Where the ideas of Rousseau had once reigned, now came those of Joseph de Maistre (*Essay on the Generative Principle of Political Constitutions*, 1814), and Edmund Burke, whose repudiation of the French Revolution in his *Reflections on the Revolution in France* (1790) ('a revolutionary book written against a revolution', as the young German poet, Novalis, shrewdly observed) gained increasing currency. Notions of liberty, equality and the rights of man now gave way to an emphasis upon order, consensus and community, the key terms of a new social and political ethos that would be combined 'with morality and religion; with the solidity of property; with peace and order; with civil and social manners'. Revolutionary stirrings were repressed by governments throughout Europe in a process of counter-revolution masterminded by the noted architect of repression, the Austrian Foreign

Minister, Prince Klemens von Metternich. His intervention into the
affairs of Italy in 1821, and of Spain in 1823, executed through a sophisticated police and spy network, retarded the development of
liberalism in those countries by decades, and gave succour to all
who longed for a restoration of traditional conservative values in
Europe. As Wordsworth's friend and colleague, Samuel Taylor
Coleridge wrote, by 1830 'the hand of providence ha[d] disciplined
all Europe into sobriety [...] by alternate blows and caresses'.[7]

But Napoleon's legacy could not be undone. He had ridden into
Italy in 1796 not as a conqueror but as a liberator, bringing with
him not only the techniques of modern warfare, but an ideology of
national self-determination that was to prove as effective as his
cannons and rifles. Even in those countries that had not been occupied by Napoleon's armies, such as Greece and Hungary, the modernising effect of his ideas was still felt, and served to support, in
Greece's case, its war of liberation against the Ottoman Empire. The
Germans, however, did not find Napoleon's intervention as inspiring. In 1799 and 1802 he had defeated their two largest states,
Austria and Prussia, in spectacular military victories. These victories enabled Bonaparte to break up the patchwork principalities that
had been a feature of German political life since the Holy Roman
Empire, and replace them in 1806 with a much more tightly-knit
organisation known as the Confederation of the Rhine. Under
Napoleon's protectorate, the German states became both more secularised and more centralised; feudal entitlements were largely
abolished, and educational and political institutions put on a
modern footing. Even quintessential Germans, such as Johann
Wolfgang von Goethe, were forced to admit that Napoleon was
'one of the most productive men that ever lived'. 'His destiny was
more brilliant' as the great poet noted later in a spirit of unqualified
admiration, 'than any the world had seen before him, or perhaps,
will ever see after him'.[8]

And yet Napoleon's success was also the cause of his undoing.
His dramatic victories over Austria and Prussia produced amongst
the defeated Germans an intense feeling of ethnic solidarity that
helped inspire their dramatic military resurgence. Nationalist
fervour was widespread; even the otherwise metaphysically-
inclined Romantics were affected by the rising tide of nationalism.
In their evocative descriptions of the German countryside, with its
arcane customs and superstitions, works such as Ludwig Tieck's
Minstrel Airs from the Swabian Past (1803), Ludwig Achim von

Arnim and Clemens Brentano's, *The Boy's Magic Horn* (1805–1808), and the Grimm brothers' *Fairy Stories* (*Kinder- und Hausmärchen*, 1812–1814), promoted those qualities of the German character that were most at odds with the rationalist-liberal traditions of nations such as England and, in particular, France. The philosopher, Johann Gottfried Herder, directed the attention of his countrymen to the existence of an indigenous literature in his two volumes of *Songs of the Folk* (1778–1779), evoking that uniquely German *Volksgeist*, which had traditionally manifested itself in superstition and popular literature. In the generation after Herder, the philosopher, Friedrich Schleiermacher, castigated the French for their lack of natural piety, and for treading the 'holiest ordinances under foot'; and the playwright, Heinrich von Kleist, in his historical drama, *The Battle of the Teutoburger Wald* (*Der Hermannschlacht*, 1808), transposed the Napoleonic invasion back into the Roman colonisation of Germany, at one point in the play exhorting his audience to take all measures 'to cleanse the fatherland from foreign tyranny'. More explicitly political were the writings of Johann Gottlieb Fichte, who argued in his 'Addresses to the German Nation' (1808), delivered in Berlin during the French occupation of that city, that Germany possessed a moral superiority over its enemies and a historical mission which would, one day, make it 'the regenerator and re-creator of the world'. In Fichte's writings, and in the writings of others, such as Adam Müller (*The Elements of State Policy*, 1809), the contours of a more aggressively nationalist ideology emerged, an ethos that valorised social duty over the rights of the individual, the norms of the community over personal self-gratification, and which celebrated that higher unity of nation and state, that 'spiritual community', which represented for many (including the otherwise otherworldly poet, Joseph Freiherr von Eichendorff) the fullest realisation of 'the mind and the soul of the people'.[9]

The Germans were not alone in inflecting their Romanticism through a rhetoric of national revival. Elsewhere in Europe, the rediscovery of national culture and custom merged with the Romantic project, to give a symbolic form to the former, and a political dynamism to the latter. In Italy, for example, the great poet, Giacomo Leopardi, began his career with his patriotic verse 'To Italy' (1818). Scandinavian writers were also awakened to the distinctive racial and cultural identities of their peoples. Major voices here included the Norwegian, Henrik Wergeland, who wrote the ambitious philosophical-religious epic, *Creation, Humanity and*

Messiah (1830); the Danish poet, Adam Oehlenschläger, whose poems 'The Golden Horns' and 'Midsummer Night's Play' (both 1802) draw on Scandinavian mythology; and the Swedish writer, Esaias Tegnér, whilst, in Finland, Elias Lönnrot's *Kalevala* (1835, expanded 1849) brought that nation into the forefront of European literature for the first time in its history. Not all of these works were unambiguously nationalistic: Wergeland's epic mythologising, for example, belongs to the world of the fantastic that would later be cultivated by the Dane, Hans Christian Andersen, in his *Fairy Tales* (1835–1848). But much of this literature is inspired by patriotic sentiment, even if such sentiment is disguised in the form of the folk-tale or historical parable. This is the case with the *Tales of Ensign Stål* (1848–1860) by the Finnish writer, Ludwig Runeberg, who offered his work to the public as a 'patriot song'; but even Lönnrot's *Kalevala*, which depicts the history of its people from the creation of the world to an unspecified present where light has conquered darkness, felt convinced that his task was to infuse 'the rising generation' with a sense of cultural community and historical mission by reminding it of the customs of its past, its folk traditions and military exploits.[10]

Behind this work of national recuperation lay a figure whose influence on European Romanticism was to remain unparalleled: Walter Scott. His enormous fictional output (which began with *Waverley* in 1814, and ended, more than thirty novels later, with *Castle Dangerous* in 1831) helped produce throughout Europe an apparently insatiable enthusiasm for folk antiquity, chivalry and antiquarian habit. Many regarded him as the Shakespeare of modern times, a writer who had brought the past back to live in the collective memory of the present. Goethe greeted his work with awe and admiration, divining in Scott's historical fiction an entirely original literary genre, 'a wholly new art, with laws of its own'. Certainly, the great Scottish novelist treated the folk-lore and customs of the past, and particularly the past of his own country, with sympathy and historical insight, allowing the values and psychology of his characters to emerge on their own terms. And yet, Scott's appropriation of the past was not as simple as it seemed to his many admirers. For, as Scott made clear in his first and greatest novel, *Waverley* (within the context of a detailed portrayal of the failed Scottish insurrection of 1745) the 'solitary and melancholy grandeur' of the past is worth retaining, but not at the expense of the present or the future. This is the wholly non-Romantic moral that Waverley, the young English protagonist of that novel, must learn to draw. In spite of his emotional commitment to the raw vitality of the Highland clan custom (and to the wild charm of his Scottish sweatheart), Scott's hero is brought to a crucial recognition: that 'real history' possesses a forward momentum which transcends individual volition, and which compels even the most idealistically inclined to expediency and compromise. In Scott's fiction, we near the end of Romanticism and approach the beginning of that new culture of moral restraint and *Realpolitik* that would eventually be called Realism.[11]

2 'THE WAY WITHIN': ROMANTICISM – GOALS AND PROGRAMME

Well before the French Revolution had effected its final break with the *ancien régime*, the aristocratic culture of eighteenth-century Europe, and the neo-classical aesthetic upon which it was based, had come under increasing attack. The forms of this criticism were varied, but all had their source in the rise of a new self-confident middle class, which wished to see its growing power and status reflected in the concerns of contemporary literature. On the eve of the industrial revolution in Europe, these needs were met both by an expanding and increasingly mercantile publishing industry, and by writers such as Samuel Richardson (*Pamela*, 1740–1741, and *Clarissa*, 1747–1748), George Lillo (*The London Merchant*, 1731), Denis Diderot (*Father of the Family*, 1758) and Gotthold Lessing (*Miss Sara Simpson*, 1755), who elevated the precocious moral world of the merchant classes to the status of high drama – the so-called 'bourgeois tragedy'. These novels and plays invested their characters with a particular *larmoyante* sense of self, a capacity for feeling ('sensibility' was the contemporary word in England; *Empfindsamkeit* in Germany), and a 'habit of virtue' (as Diderot termed it), which stood in sharp contrast to the self-seeking, vain and rapacious mentality of the aristocratic characters who also appeared in such literature. The Romantics were deeply influenced by such authors, as they were by the other great critic of the *ancien régime*: the French philosopher and social theorist, Jean-Jacques Rousseau. His political writings, *The Discourse on Inequality* (1755) and *The Social Contract* (1762), had helped prepare the way for the Revolution of 1789; but the impact of his literary work, *The New*

Héloïse (an epistolary novel on love and the sacrifice of love to duty, 1761) and *Emile* (a discursive novel extolling the value of natural education, 1762), was, if anything, even more dramatic. For here, Rousseau deepened the eighteenth-century cult of sensibility into a philosophy of personal interiority, a complex ethos which included a spiritualised view of nature, a rejection of social convention, and a valorisation of pure expressivity, values which were to become key terms in the aesthetic of Romanticism.[12]

This rediscovery of the irrational, deepened and legitimised through a new preoccupation with the metaphysics of death (exhibited, for example, in Edward Young's *The Complaint, or Night Thoughts on Life, Death and Immortality*, published serially between 1742 and 1745), through a renewed interest in racial traditions, and through the rediscovery of the art and culture of medieval Europe (approached under the rubric of 'The Gothic'), provided the framework in which a younger generation of writers came to define themselves as 'Romantic'. The term had long been used by the exponents of neo-classicism, but in a largely derogatory sense, as coterminous with the 'absurdities or incredible fictions' cultivated in certain Romance literatures (hence the derivation of the term), or, more positively, as a synonym for 'picturesque' in landscape painting. William Blake in England, and Friedrich Schlegel and Novalis in Germany were happy to embrace the alternative and oppositional values that these categories implied, deepening in their work the otherness associated with the 'Romantic' into a systematic aesthetic far removed from what they regarded as the trivialising discourse of the neo-classicists. The terms of that aesthetic emerged in a number of major essays and manifestos. They included, in Germany, Novalis' *Pollen* (1798), Friedrich Schlegel's 'Dialogue on Poetry' (1800), and his many 'Fragments', published between 1798 and 1800 in the journal *Athenäum*, and August Wilhelm Schlegel's *Lectures on Dramatic Art and Literature* (1809–1811); in England, Wordsworth and Coleridge's preface to the second edition of the *Lyrical Ballads* (1800), and Shelley's 'Defence of Poetry' (1821); in Italy, Giovanni Berchet's *The semiserious Letter* (1816), Pietro Borsieri's, 'Literary Adventures of a Day' (1816), and Alessandro Manzoni's *Letter on Romanticism* (1823), which self-consciously came out in defence of the new movement. In France, Madame de Staël's *On Literature* (1800), and *On Germany* (1810), Stendhal's *Racine and Shakespeare* (1823), and Victor Hugo's preface to *Cromwell* (1827) provided the key texts; whilst Mariano Larra's essay

'Literatura' (1836) belatedly brought Spain into the debate. Collectively these writings helped to produce a new cultural paradigm, which pitted spontaneity against deliberation, imagination against reason, the native against the foreign, inwardness against formalism, authenticity against convention, and energy against stasis. By 1823, these terms had formed themselves into a recognisable aesthetic, which could clearly be associated with a rising generation of writers whose work, as Stendhal noted, sought to explore 'the genre of fantasy and the mysteries of the soul'.[13]

There were, certainly, differences of emphasis and strategy here, dividing, for example, the more theoretically sophisticated but largely apolitical Germans (in their pre-nationalist mode) from the empirically inclined English Romantics, and the highly politicised Shelley and Hugo; and, as their publication dates suggest, the chronology of their emergence was both broad and non-synchronous, with England and Germany providing the inspiration behind the development of Romanticism in Italy, Spain and finally (and in spite of its pre-Romantic initiatives) France. The European Romantics, nevertheless, had much in common. They all emphasized the liberating potency of feeling and pure inwardness; they held to a radically new sense of the poetic mission, endowing the artist with an almost mystical status, feeling that personal vision alone could guarantee artistic integrity; and all converged on a rejection of the 'rules' of decorum and formal conservatism of the neo-classicists.

What the Romantics aspired to was a type of writing that was (and the paradox was central to the Romantic imagination) both more popular and more mystical. These goals were evident as early as 1798 in Wordsworth's and Coleridge's *Lyrical Ballads*. The two poets had set out to choose (as they noted in their famous preface) 'incidents and situations from common life, and to relate or describe them throughout [...] in a selection of language really used by men'. Such poems as 'Michael', 'The Brothers' and 'The Idiot Boy' conspicuously break with previous picturesque treatments of rural themes by focussing upon rural poverty and deprivation and by radically departing from the poetic diction in which such themes had traditionally been depicted. But as Wordsworth also noted in his preface, 'ordinary things should be presented to the mind in an unusual aspect', transformed by the poetic imagination, and made to reveal the ineffable mystery which resides even in the most common-place. These were sentiments that Coleridge, in particular, took to heart, giving expression in 'poems of fancy', such as 'The Rime of the Ancient Mariner' and 'Kubla Khan', to a unique and often disturbing poetry of visionary intensity.[14]

It was precisely this creative facility to merge the natural with the supernatural that constituted for Madame de Staël, the foremost exponent of Romanticism in France, the strength and originality of Romantic writing. In her *On Literature*, the French critic drew a famous distinction between 'the literature of the South', with its innate propensity towards formal perfection, high-minded nobility and the decorum of unmixed genres; and 'the literature of the North', which had traditionally combined the epic, the lyrical, the comic and the tragic, seeking to give voice to eternal concerns: the 'transience of life, veneration for the dead, [and the] glorification of their memory'. Romantic literature was, in short, metaphysical, moving in those realms of experience that lie above and below the surface of civilisation. For Madame de Staël and for other Romantic theorists, there were two authors, in particular, who embodied this literature of metaphysical depth: Shakespeare and Ossian. Friedrich Schlegel called Shakespeare the 'actual centre, the core of the Romantic imagination', who, in combining 'narrative, song and other forms' in his plays, had heroically broken with the neo-classical tyranny of genre; whilst the translations of Shakespeare's works into German by August Wilhelm Schlegel (Friedrich's brother) and Ludwig Tieck, which were published between 1797 and 1810, made Shakespeare a household name in Germany. In France, Stendhal traced his adherence to the Romantic cause back to his discovery of Shakespeare, whilst Madame de Staël was able to justify the Romantic's neglect of the rules by pointing to the 'varied inventions of [this] man of genius'. Wherever the Romantic spirit found theatrical expression, from Schiller to Hugo, it was the figure of Shakespeare, now cast in medieval guise, now in the radical garb of modernity, who provided the inspiration.[15]

But for many the great English playwright was but an emanation of a spirit that was even more fundamental to the Romantic imagination: the legendary Gaelic bard, Ossian. His verse, distilled from fragments of Celtic folklore, and brought back to life by the young scholar, James Macpherson, came to dominate the imagination of a generation sentimentally inclined to ethnic authenticity. It mattered little to this readership (pleasing 'persons of exquisite feelings of heart') that Ossian's verse, published by Macpherson as *Fragments of Ancient Poetry, collected in the Highlands of Scotland* (1760) (and

from 1765 largely as *The Poems of Ossian*) was the product of an en-
terprising minor poet, familiar with the emotive power of Gothic
melodrama and the mystique of the ancient epics. In a collective act
of self-deception, an entire generation read the *Fragments*, eagerly
intent on finding a northern equivalent to Homer, and a pedigree
for its obsession with the heroic, the simple, the arcane, and the
tribal. Such readers were (as Macpherson knew) emotionally committed to the mysteries and customs of their ancestors, as they had
existed in their pure form 'before those refinements of society had
taken place' to produce a civilisation devoid of 'human imagination
and passion'. The poems of Ossian were enthusiastically received
throughout Europe. They were translated into German in 1769, in
which form they influenced both Herder (*Letters regarding Ossian
and the Songs of ancient Peoples*, 1773) and Goethe (they play a
pivotal role in his *The Sorrows of Young Werther* of 1774), and into
French in 1760, becoming the basis of Mme de Staël's distinction
between the culture of the South, deemed to be formal and
superficial, and the rugged, mysterious and autochthonic art of the
Gothic North.[16]

Shakespeare and Ossian were not simply consummate artists;
they were also 'geniuses', intuitively at one with the deeper spiritual needs of their people. The notion of the Romantic artist as
genius was central to the self-image of this generation. Edward
Young did not invent the word, but his *Conjectures on Original
Composition* (1759), with its celebration of 'the native growth of
mind', and its consistent denigration of 'the soft fetters of easy imitation', helped to give a powerful resonance to the idea. In the
hands of subsequent Romantics, the notion of the artistic genius
came to acquire an almost religious significance. Shelley, for
example, in his 'Defence of Poetry', argued that the poet was a
prophet, being 'the author to others of the highest wisdom, pleasure, virtue and glory'. Even when artists were unconscious of their
high office, they remained, nevertheless, capable of expressing in
their work the most positive energies of their age. As Shelley noted
in the concluding, triumphalist lines of his essay: 'they are the
trumpets which sing to battle, and feel not what they inspire; the
influence which is moved not, but moves. Poets are the unacknowl-
edged legislators of the world'.[17]

Most Romantics viewed the empirical world simply as the starting point for a revolutionary process of creative transformation.
The name that gained common currency for this transforming

faculty was 'Imagination'. It was a mental facility which occupied for many a conceptual space somewhere between the aesthetic and the mystical. For Wordsworth, it was (as he noted in *The Prelude*) 'another name for absolute power/And clearest insight, amplitude of mind,/And Reason in her most exalted mood'. As he later confessed in a letter written at the height of his religious convictions, 'even in poetry it is the imaginative only, viz., that which is conversant [with] or turns upon infinity, that powerfully affects me'; adding 'all great poets are in this view powerful Religionists'. The most sophisticated definition was provided by Wordsworth's friend and colleague, Coleridge, who made in his *Biographia Literaria* (1817) a distinction between 'primary' and 'secondary' imagination: 'The primary imagination', Coleridge explained, 'I hold to be the living power and prime agent of all human perception, and as a repetition in the infinite mind of the eternal act of creation in the infinite I AM. The secondary I consider as an echo of the former, co-existing with the conscious will, yet still as identical with the primary in the kind of its agency, and differing only in degree, and in the mode of its operation. It dissolves, diffuses, dissipates, in order to re-create; or where this process is rendered impossible, yet still, at all events, it struggles to idealise and to unify. It is essentially *vital*, even as objects (as objects) are essentially fixed and dead'.[18]

As Coleridge's comments make clear, what the Romantics were trying to achieve was no less than an epistemological revolution, a radical renewal of the categories, both cognitive and perceptual, that had governed Western thinking for at least for two hundred years, since Descartes and the Rationalists. The terms in which that revolution was to be carried out were manifold. Friedrich Schlegel spoke of Romantic writing, which he termed 'Transcendental Poetry', as a synthesising imperative, capable of restoring that sense of totality that had been lost through the corrosive intellectualising of Enlightenment philosophy. Novalis was more specific about the cognitive faculty that would allow this merging of the objective and subjective spheres, calling it 'Magic Idealism'. This was a perspective capable of construing the universe as a system of analogies and interrelationships in which the human, the natural and the spiritual would coexist in a powerful symbolic relationship. As the poet explained in a fragment from the year 1798: 'Romanticising is no more than a qualitative empowerment [...] By giving a higher meaning to the quotidian, a mysterious aspect to the ordinary, to the familiar the dignity of the unfamiliar, to the finite the appearance of infinity, then I am romanticising it'. This is also how Blake conceived of the term: as a mystical power capable of transforming the phenomenal world, an intellectual energy whose potency the poet crystallised in his famous maxim from *The Marriage of Heaven and Hell* (1793): 'If the doors of perception were cleansed every thing would appear to man as it is, infinite'.[19]

In the place of the model of versification favoured by the neo-classicists, the Romantics invoked a poetic process that was both irrational and, ultimately, inexplicable, being the pure product of unmediated expressivity. Wordsworth, in his preface to the *Lyrical Ballads*, provided the most famous formulation of this process, when he described the poetic statement as a 'spontaneous overflow of powerful feelings'. Self-consciousness was seen as a hindrance to poetic creation. The successful poet, according to Keats, needed to possess a 'negative capability', a mental set that would allow him to remain in 'uncertainties, Mysteries, doubts, without any irritable reaching after fact & reason'. The poet, in short, had to surrender the self to the object world so that it might be understood from within. Shelley held a similar view, believing writing to be an activity of the unconscious mind, and, therefore, beyond rational control. As he noted in his 'Defence of Poetry', 'the mind in creation is as a fading coal, which some invisible influence, like an inconstant wind, awakens to transitory brightness: this power arises from within, like the colour of a flower which fades and changes as it is developed, and the conscious portions of our nature are unprophetic of its approach or its departure'.[20]

But achieving such a state of unreflective consciousness was not an unproblematical goal, as Friedrich Schiller knew. In his *Naive and Sentimental Poetry* (1795–1796), he argued that the modern (read Romantic) artist was positioned between a non-self-reflective, almost innocent intellectual disposition, and a more reflective, analytical attitude towards the self and the world. Poets who embodied the former type of consciousness Schiller called 'naive', adding 'we love in them the tacitly creative life, the serene spontaneity of their activity, existence in accordance with their own laws, the inner necessity, the eternal unity with themselves'. The latter type of poet he called 'sentimental'. These artists (and he included himself amongst their number) have lost that secure self-confidence in their mission. Poets of this type feel compelled to provide a theoretical justification for their activities; for them the mind 'is in motion, it is in tension, it wavers between conflicting feelings', it is forced to bear witness to a 'unity that has been disrupted by abstraction'. Schiller saw these configurations as antinomies, irreconcilable poles around which the modern mind was doomed, indefinitely, to circle. The German dramatist, Heinrich von Kleist, however, saw them as parallel paths to the same destination. As he argued in his parable 'On the Marionette Theatre' (1810), what is decisive is not self-consciousness or its absence, but the intensity with which each position is felt by the individual thinker; for 'grace [the perfect union of mind and body] appears purest in that human form which has either no consciousness or an infinite one, that is, in a puppet or in a god'. This would remain the ultimate goal of the Romantic dream: to give concrete form to the plenitude of consciousness, to find a literature that would give shape to the paradox of a nature made more natural through increased intellectual depth. This would be a literature which, once written, would constitute (in Kleist's uncompromising words) 'the last chapter in the history of the world'.[21]

3   SELF AND WORLD: THE LITERATURE OF ROMANTIC INDIVIDUALISM

At the very start of Romantic literature is the great 'I am', that assertion of personal identity that argues for the uniqueness of self, and the irreducibility of personality to moral or social convention. It is the most characteristic voice of the Romantic imagination. Rousseau gave it seminal expression in his epic of self-revelation, *The Confessions* (completed in 1770), and in later works, such as *The Reveries of a Solitary Walker* (published posthumously in 1782). In both texts, a form of secularised mysticism appears, whose channels are intense introspection and meditation, and whose product is a spiritual self-sufficiency that brackets out the external world entirely so that the hyper-sensitive Rousseau can exist fully in and for himself. The result is someone who finds himself, 'tranquil at the bottom of the gulf, a poor unfortunate mortal, but as undisturbed as God himself'. The tone of Rousseau's writing, an emotive combination of strident self-assertion and deeply-felt alienation, influenced an entire generation; but Romantic individualism found expression in many other ways: for example, in the rebellious assertiveness of Byron and Hugo; in the mystical intoxication of Blake and Novalis; and in the pantheistic identification with nature felt by Wordsworth, Lamartine and Eichendorff. These forms of subjectivity found concrete expression in the many types of hero and heroine who appear in Romantic writing: in Wordsworth's child of nature (see, for example, the 'Lucy' poems, but also the autobiographical *The Prelude*); in the rebel-martyr figure of Shelley's hero Prometheus; in noble outlaws, such as Karl Moor in Schiller's *The Outlaws* (1781); in Byron's multiple amoral outsiders, such as Childe Harold and Don Juan; and, finally, in the heroines of George Sand's fiction, those brave spirits, whose will to self-assertion eventually goes under, broken (as Sand herself noted in the preface to her novel, *Indiana*, 1832) in a 'ruthless combat with the reality of life'.[22]

Two types of hero came to particular prominence in Romantic literature: the introvert, whose highly developed sensibility and finely tuned self-consciousness made him or her a victim of an uncaring and unselfcritical society (the major examples here being Goethe's Werther, Benjamin Constant's Adolphe, and Ugo Foscolo's Jacopo Ortis); and the hero of pure extroversion, self-confident and dismissive of society's values, but also world-weary and sceptical (Byron's Don Juan, and Pushkin's Eugene Onegin were paradigmatic of this latter type). Of them all, it was Werther, the focus of Goethe's famous novel *The Sorrows of Young Werther* (1774), who made the greatest impact upon literary Europe. The obsessive nature of Werther's amorous fixation, the rhetorically persuasive nature of his *Weltschmerz*, and his freely and rationally chosen suicide affected a readership that was already predisposed to extremes of sentiment. Goethe's novel was the work of an original mind; but it also brought to fruition developments within the literature and thinking of pre-Romanticism. It drew upon the lachrymose emotionalism that had been a part of the representation of female subjectivity since Richardson's *Pamela*, and Lessing's *Miss Sara Simpson*, but which, from the mid-eighteenth century onwards, began to be usurped by male characters, such as the hero of Henry Mackenzie's *The Man of Feeling* (1771); it gave further substance to the romanticisation of death evident in Young's *Night Thoughts*, which was translated into German in 1751; and it gave a highly personal inflection to the 'natural' morality and 'back to nature' philosophy of Rousseau. These ideas and others were given memorable shape in Goethe's novel, making its hero a representative of his generation. As Thomas Carlyle (the foremost Anglophone commentator on German literature in the nineteenth

century) noted in his essay on Goethe, Werther's outpourings, emotionally sincere if intellectually naive, could be read as 'the cry of
that dim, rooted pain, under which all thoughtful men' in the age
of Romanticism were suffering.[23]

The Sorrows of Young Werther attained a cult following in Europe
(in France alone, it was published sixteen times between 1776 and
1799); its influence on the broad course of European Romanticism
was immense. Its brooding melancholia permeates Chateaubriand's
René (1802), in which the youthful hero seems not only to endure,
but positively to cultivate 'the emptiness of a lonely heart', giving
himself over without resistance to a *Weltschmerz* that is only par-
tially caused by his incestuous relationship with his sister; the
Italian, Ugo Foscolo used the same motif of the love-torn hero in his
Last letters of Jacopo Ortis (1802), but made his travails coterminous
with those of an Italy deprived of national heritage by Napoleon's
conquests; whilst Benjamin Constant added a twist to the theme in
his psychological novel, *Adolphe* (1816). Its hero has the ability,
which was later to be known as the *dédoublement constantien* (the
Constantian split-personality), both to suffer the anguish of emotional dislocation whilst enjoying, at the same time, the process
through which such pain is analysed, succumbing to the perversion
of 'a vanity which is only concerned with itself when recounting
the evil it has done'. All of these novels gave expression to the
many aspects of Wertherian introverted Romanticism: its insistence
upon the primacy of individual experience; its denigration of bourgeois order; its cultivation of suffering; its desire to lose the self in
nature, and its longing for the unattainable.[24]

In the hero of Constant's *Adolphe*, Romantic sentiment is no
longer naive, but forms the medium for a style of personal fashion-
ing, which seeks to distance the self from the offending emotions
that it is experiencing. The writer who explored, and, indeed, most
embodied this complex set of psychological dispositions was
George Gordon, Lord Byron. From his early verse, *Childe Harold's
Pilgrimage* (1812–1818), *The Corsair* (1814) and *Manfred* (1817),
through to his later masterpiece, *Don Juan* (1819–1824), the poet systematically built up a composite picture of the Byronic hero, a multiple persona which drew upon images of the aristocrat, the dandy,
the womaniser, the social and political outcast, and the rebel. That
feeling of estrangement (which verges upon self-pity) experienced
by Werther and his like has little place in Byron's poetry. Here,
suffering is transposed from alienation into a sense of aristocratic

superiority, which sees itself justified in creating its own set of values, albeit often confounding in the process (as Lara does, in the poem of the same name) 'good and ill/And half [mistaking] for fate the acts of will'. Byron's life was characterised by a restlessness that often finds expression in his semi-autobiographical heroes, such as the bandit in *The Corsair*, or the religious rebel in *Cain* (1821), who embody (as the poet himself did) moral transgression and a concern for personal integrity and the individual's right to self-determination. Both elements are combined in Byron's most famous hero, *Don Juan*. Here, in an extended picaresque poem (left unfinished at his death in 1824), Byron wrote a social and moral allegory, constructing a narrative which takes his hero from the exotic climes of Spain and Turkey to the familiar one of the *roué*'s London. In the process, Don Juan and his narrator give voice to what was popularly understood as the uniquely Byronic world-view, that set of values which combined carefree adventurism with a hard-headed pragmatism. In spite of its obvious bravura, however, Byron's *Don Juan* embodies a trenchant element of political satire, whose target is a Restoration Europe that has given itself over to military aggression and pompous religiosity, in a period described by Byron as a 'patent age of new inventions/For killing bodies, and for saving souls'. In the final analysis, to set against the widespread political and sexual hypocrisy that he saw around him, Byron offered to the public the achievement of a life lived from the source of self, and based upon a personal philosphy, which, in spite of the poet's sometimes histrionic projection of self, was concerned to give full voice to 'the hope, the fear, the jealous care/The exalted portion of the pain/And power of love'.[25]

The élan of Byron's verse, and the charisma of the author, impressed an entire generation of writers. In Spain, the major poet of this generation, José Espronceda, dealt with themes of transgression and rebellion in his two epic poems, *The Student of Salamanca* (1840), and the more metaphysically ambitious, although incomplete, *The Devilish World* (1841). Equally influenced by Byron was the major Czech Romantic, Karel Mácha, whose most famous poem, the epic *May* (1836), treats of incest and patricide, but also of the Byronic transcendence of crime through love and expiation. Byron's influence was particularly telling upon the two major Russian Romantics: Alexander Pushkin and Mikhail Lermontov. Pushkin's epic poem, *Eugene Onegin* (1833) is one of the great works of Russian literature. It depicts an individual who is isolated from society through guilt and superior intellect, and whose amoral progress through the world leaves him, in characteristic Romantic fashion, oscillating between the poles of *ennui*, solitude, amorous involvement, and exile. Pushkin subtitled his poem 'a novel in verse'. It was an apt description, not only because of the proportions of the poem (which consists of eight cantos, each containing some fifty fourteen-line stanzas), but also because of the focus of the work. Pushkin's poem details not only Onegin's personal development, but also the backwardness and sham cosmopolitanism of his contemporary Russia, with its polite society that feeds itself solely upon the 'reproduction of the vagaries of others, [and] fashionable words'.[26]

At one point in *Eugene Onegin*, the narrator makes the following generalisation: 'He who has lived and pondered cannot in his heart but despise people; he who has experienced emotions is disturbed by the phantom of irrevocable days, no longer feels fascination, is gnawed at by the serpent of memories and by repentance'. They were characteristic sentiments of late Romanticism, that twilight moment in the movement, which witnessed the claims of subjectivity and individualistic voluntarism give way to a quasi-Realist pessimism and cynicism regarding personal ideals. It was, once again, a Russian, Mikhail Lermontov, who provided the most memorable statement of this attitude. In his novel, *A Hero of our Time* (1840), Lermontov sets up the central terms of Romantic individualism: idealism, the refusal to compromise personal integrity, and the loss of the self in nature, only to deflate them through the cold, analytical gaze of the 'hero' of the novel, Pechorin. This character works not with, but on and through Romantic individualism. He sees it as a mere pose, something that is adopted by lesser mortals (such as the cadet, Grushnitsky), who wish to make 'a solemn display of uncommon emotions, exalted passions and exceptional sufferings. Their greatest pleasure in life is to create an effect, and romantic provincial ladies find them madly attractive'. Such characters, Pechorin notes, don the personae of Werther or Byron at will, toying with the affections of the loved one, fully realising that they are involved in nothing more than an elaborate game. Pechorin, for his part, has passed through such games, arriving at a personal philosophy that has exchanged ideals for a cynicism towards others and an honesty towards himself. As he concludes towards the end of the story: 'One just goes on living, out of curiosity, waiting for something new. It's absurd and annoying'.[27]

Sixty years on from *Werther*, Lermontov took the moral relativism and solipsism that resided at the heart of Romantic individualism to its logical conclusion. 'I've an insatiable craving inside me', notes the blasé Pechorin, at one point in the novel, 'that consumes everything and makes me regard the sufferings and joys of others only in their relationship to me, as food to sustain my spiritual powers'; 'I'm incapable of friendship'. Byron's heroes would not have put it quite so brutally, but subsequent figures in the pantheon of post-Romantic writing would. These included aristocratic exponents of amoral self-assertiveness, such as Raskolnikov in Dostoyevsky's *Crime and Punishment* (1866); the decadent poets (*poètes maudits*) of mid-nineteenth century France, notably Baudelaire and Rimbaud; the aesthetes of England, such as Oscar Wilde; and the iconoclastic German philosopher, Friedrich Nietzsche. All despised the claims of conventional morality and the bourgeois terrain from which it emerged, and all argued for the right to live, as Nietzsche put it, 'beyond good and evil', seeking in the intensity of their artistic visions that 'secret citadel' where the superior consciousness 'is set free from the crowd'. Lermontov had anticipated them all, and the movement to which they belonged: Romantic Decadence.[28]

4   REVOLT AND DECLARATION: ROMANTIC DRAMA

'Rouze up, O Young men of the New Age!', Blake had exhorted in his preface to his epic poem, *Milton* (1803–1808), and he was followed by a generation that infused into Romanticism the energies and missionary zeal of a religious revival. The young Goethe and Schiller were amongst its ranks, as were the French Romantics, Victor Hugo and Alexander Dumas, and also Shelley. They all embodied that heightened sense of self first celebrated by Rousseau (and given memorable shape through Goethe's hero, Werther, and Chateaubriand's René); but they balanced the introversion endemic to that mental set both with a competing set of more extrovert dispositions, and with a greater awareness of the public ambit of their work, often radicalising the momentum of Romantic individualism into a conscious oppositional ethos. This is particularly true of Shelley, who connected Romantic subjectivity and political radicalism both in his theoretical writing (most notably in *The Defence of Poetry*, 1821), and in verse works such as *Prometheus Unbound* (1820), a political allegory in which constrained humanity is pitted against arbitrary despotism, and whose eponymous hero, half saint, half political rebel, accepts his martyrdom in order to defy 'the deepest power of hell'.[29]

The political intent of Romantic individualism first emerged in the German Storm and Stress (*Sturm und Drang*) movement, whose poetry and plays provided a vehicle for the widespread feeling of antagonism to the social order of aristocratic Europe. The major works of the movement included Goethe's *Götz from Berlichingen*, (1773), Jakob Lenz's *The Tutor* (1774) and *The Soldiers* (1776), Friedrich Maximilian Klinger's *Storm and Stress* (1777) and Heinrich Wagner's *The Child Murderess* (1776). These plays dealt with extreme themes: murder and suicide, psychological obsessions and madness, seduction and incest, political tyranny and martyrdom. According to Lenz, who provided the most extensive statement of the movement's aesthetic in his *Remarks concerning the Stage* (1774), the Storm and Stress dramatists wished to produce a theatre that was both democratic and challenging, open to the raw energies of 'chaos', for there alone could 'freedom' be expected to flourish. In pursuit of their goals, they achieved two things: an innovatory dramaturgy, and a highly suggestive drama of political statement. On the stage, they broke with the major conventions of neo-classical drama: they ignored the traditional unities of time, place and action; they dealt with the problems of the middle classes rather than the aristocracy; they tended towards melodrama rather than tragedy; and they drew characters who were psychologically complex and morally ambiguous, hoping to shock their audiences out of their political complacency and slavish adherence to the status quo. Lenz's plays, in particular, are replete with covert politics, *The Soldiers* demonstrating the double standards and sexual rapacity of an aristocratic class that continued to insist on its honour, even as it had become 'hardened to every kind of debauchery and infidelity'. Like Beaumarchais in France, writing at exactly the same time (*The Marriage of Figaro*, 1784), Lenz sought to make his political point in an satirical-ethical way, disclosing in his plays the vices and the abuses 'which disguise themselves in a thousand ways beneath the mask of our dominant customs'.[30]

The restless dynamism of the Storm and Stress movement provided inspiration for many of the major German playwrights of this period, such as Friedrich Schiller (*The Outlaws*, 1781, *Wallenstein*, 1799, and *Maria Stuart*, 1800), Johann Wolfgang von Goethe (*Egmont*, 1788, and *Faust* I and II, 1808 and 1832), and Heinrich von

Kleist (*Penthesilea*, 1808, and *Prince Friedrich of Homburg*, 1810, published in 1821). Their work reflects the vitality and acerbic morality
of the Storm and Stress school, but integrates those energies into a
formally more coherent and intellectually more complex type of
drama, which reveals a greater sense for the impingement of ethical
and religious values upon life. Schiller's *The Outlaws* is a case in
point. Many of his contemporaries viewed the reversal of natural
filial ties depicted in the play, and its radical questioning of political authority, as 'a terrifying spectacle of the most deplorable
human misery, of the deepest confusions, of the most terrible vice'.
Certainly, the hero's assertion: 'I could blow the trumpet of rebellion throughout the realm of nature' touched an important nerve
in pre-revolutionary Europe. And yet *The Outlaws* is far from unambiguously libertarian; the motifs of familial deceit and deception, of honour and chivalry, around which the play revolves,
ultimately anchor it in a pre-political terrain, and its denouement
(which sees the robbers' leader, Karl, surrendering to the law, re-
signed to his execution) clearly leaves the established order intact,
indeed, inviolable. The same could be said of Schiller's later play,
Maria Stuart, which focuses upon conflicts between duty and conscience, and between individual integrity and the greater needs of
the state, which it dramatises in terms of the personal contest
between Elizabeth and Mary for the crown of England. Mary loses
both her claim to the throne and her life, but, in doing so, confirms
her moral superiority over Elizabeth. The triumphant Queen must
continue to live in the shadow of her more idealistic sister, her
name 'abhorred for all eternity'.[31]

Schiller's concern to read political struggle in terms of moral
conflict is evident in all of his historical dramas, including *Don
Carlos* (1787), and his final play, *William Tell* (1804). Writing the
latter, Schiller had the example of Goethe's *Egmont* before him,
which likewise focuses upon the efforts of a small nation (in this
case Holland) to free itself from foreign tyranny. Schiller chose a
popular hero, Tell, as the catalyst for his Swiss rebellion; Goethe's
hero is an aristocrat, whose political motives have their origins in a
personal philosophy of self-affirmation, which coincides, at this historical juncture, with the needs of his countrymen. Egmont freely
commits himself to the cause, knowing it will lead to his death. But
for the world-historical individual, there is no choice. As he explains in a famous image: 'Our destiny is like the sun; invisible
spirits whip up time's swift horses, away with its light chariot they

run, and all we can do is take courage, hold the reins in a firm grip, and keep the wheels clear of the rocks on the one hand, the precipice on the other'.[32]

Egmont is a charismatic figure, who seeks to direct fate through force of personality; instinct takes precedence over judgement, emotion over reason, and ideals over the needs of *Realpolitik*. He prefers to risk destruction and self-destruction rather than inhibit his natural commitment to the moment. As such, he is a typical product of the Romantic imagination, which consistently celebrated autotelic energy and *élan* over the Enlightenment values of moderation and self-restraint. Goethe gave fuller expression to this type of personality in his verse drama, *Faust*. Appearing as a fragment in 1790 (subsequently known as the *Urfaust*), and expanded into two parts, published in 1808 and 1832, Goethe's work gives mythic form to the spirit of revolt that inspired much Romantic thinking. Faust is the archetypal rebel, the overreacher, prepared to sell his soul to the Devil in return for knowledge unbounded. He is the quintessential product of the Germanic *Sturm und Drang* mentality: a restless figure, bent on escaping from 'the damnable, bricked-in, cabined hole' of conventional wisdom, tradition and shallow rationality, determined to embrace new experience irrespective of the consequences to body and soul. In the second part of *Faust*, Goethe, now in his post-Romantic phase, sought to redeem the amoral vitalism of his hero by allowing Faust to embrace Christian salvation. But in *Faust I*, Goethe's hero embarks on a spiritual journey unchecked by moral scruple or religious censure. No door is closed, no path obstructed: 'the fruits of pain or pleasure', 'sweet triumph's lure, or disappointment's wrath' are all accepted in the cause of the boundless expansion of self-knowledge and self-realisation.[33]

The workings of the irrational mind also fascinated the German playwright and short story writer, Heinrich von Kleist. In 1801, at the age of twenty-four, he had come to the sudden realisation (subsequently known as his 'Kant crisis') that reason plays no part in human affairs, but is simply a veneer beneath which lie the real forces that drive the world: irrational fears, phobias, fantasies and uncontrollable sexual urges. The 'terror' that Kleist experienced on that occasion left a dark trace throughout all his work: the short stories 'Michael Kohlhaas', 'The Marquise of O...', and 'The Earthquake in Chile' (published, together with others, as *Stories* in 1810–1811), and plays such as *The Family Schroffenstein* (1803), *Penthesilea* and *Prince Friedrich of Homburg*. All give a picture of a world that is propelled by currents of senseless violence and demonic energy, and which is held together (if at all) purely by superannuated codes of ethics and dynastic honour. In *Penthesilea*, however, there is nothing to check the profound and destructive forces that Kleist regarded as endemic to human nature. The play deals with the clash between Achilles, and his Greek warriors, and the Amazons during the Trojan war. Kleist expands the element of martial contestation found in earlier treatments of this classical subject into a highly-charged depiction of physical rapacity and sexual struggle. Through twenty-four dramatic scenes, the emotions of the two protagonists – lust, the desire to master the other and the desire for self-surrender – go through a number of permutations, reaching in the end violent climax, in which distinctions between eros and thanatos, love and death, dramatically merge. As Penthesilea graphically asserts over the body of the vanquished beloved foe: 'A kiss, a bite – how cheek by jowl/they are, and when you love straight from the heart/the greedy mouth so easily mistakes/one for the other'.[34]

The dark obsessions of German Romantic drama (and the Shakespearean model in which most of it originated) attracted playwrights throughout Europe. In France, Benjamin Constant expressed his admiration for Schiller in his *Reflections on the Tragedy of Wallenstein* (1809), praising the refound Shakespearian vitality that he saw embodied in Schiller's work. Constant's feelings were shared by other French dramatists, such as Victor Hugo (*Hernani*, 1830 and *Ruy Blas*, 1838), Alfred de Musset (*Lorenzaccio*, 1835), Alfred de Vigny (*Chatterton*, 1835), and Alexandre Dumas (*Henry III*, 1829, and *Antony*, 1831). All hoped to re-create French drama on the basis of a more vital theatrical tradition. As Hugo had argued in his famous preface to *Cromwell* (1827), if French theatre were to be revitalised, the dramatist would have to abandon the Classical unities of time, place and manner, which had dominated the stage since Racine, and embrace a dramaturgy that would blend 'in a single breath the grotesque and the sublime, the terrible and the farcical, tragedy and comedy', modes that he saw as fulfilling the aesthetic needs of the 'modern period'. Hugo's next play, *Hernani* (which became a *succès de scandale* on its first performance in 1830), provided the most noted example of this new drama. Set in the sixteenth-century court of the Spanish king, Don Carlos, the play is a historical costume drama characterised by intrigue, amorous involvement, and power politics, in which spectacle and scenic pageantry are exploited to the full. Its eponymous hero, true to Romantic theory, is both a revolutionary and an outlaw, 'a bandit whom the gallows will claim'. And yet, it is Hernani alone who provides a source of moral credibility in the play, holding to a notion of honour and personal valour, for which he is prepared to die rather than compromise. His death and the death of his beloved, who enters a pact of suicide, is depicted as confirmation of the Rousseauistic axiom that true morality can only be found beyond, never within the social realm.[35]

French theatre in the Romantic period was able to exploit a native talent for psychological drama. Its focus upon the complications of desire, the tensions between duty and natural morality, and the call of the self to dissolution in death was also taken up by the Spanish dramatists of this period, playwrights such as Mariano José de Larra (*Macías*, 1834), Angel de Saavedra, Duque de Rivas (*Don Alvaro and the Force of Destiny*, 1835), Antonio García Gutiérrez (*The Troubadour*, 1836), Juan Eugenio Hartzenbusch (*The Lovers of Teruel*, 1837), and José Zorrilla (*Don Juan Tenorio*, 1844). These plays reflected the French flair for the exotic and the *outré*, for elaborate stage settings and historicising contexts, but infused into their stories of amorous intrigue and outraged honour a sense of Byronic transgression often absent in the work of their French counterparts.

Elsewhere in Europe, in countries distant from mainstream Romanticism, writers were able to draw upon an alternative idiom, one that had its origins in folk and mythic tradition. This was the case in Poland, where Adam Mickiewicz combined patriotism and historical mythologising in his plays and epic verse. Mickiewicz was the leading voice amongst the Polish Romantics, although others, such as Juliusz Slowacki (*Kordian*, 1834, and *Mezepa*, 1840, both epic historical dramas), and Zygmunt Krasiński (*The Undivine Comedy*, 1835, and *Psalms of the Future*, 1845, enlarged 1848), also produced writing that was characteristic of the uniquely visionary quality of Polish Romanticism. Mickiewicz's major works were verse dramas: *Konrad Wallenrod* (1828), and the great epic written from exile in Paris that helped give shape to the spirit of revolt growing in his country against Russian domination: *Master Thaddeus* (1834). In Hungary, Sándor Petöfi was perhaps the most original spirit, with his *Poems* (1844), the folk-song epic, *János, the Hero* (1844), and a host of poems of individual brilliance such as 'The Poets of the Nineteenth Century' (1847), and the patriotic 'National Song' (1848), although Petöfi had learnt much from Mihály Vörösmarty, whose epics, *The Flight of Zalan* (1823), and *Csongor and Tünde* (1831) also sought to unite patriotism with Romanticism.

These writers demonstrated that the claims of Romantic individualism, its rebelliousness and assertive defence of natural morality, could be transferred to the national realm, and could take the sufferings and afflictions of a people as its subject matter as well as those of the alienated poet or romantic outsider. It was, perhaps, fitting that it should be the Greek poet and dramatist, Dionysios Solomos, the leading member of the Romantic movement in that country, who should find the most immediate use for the Romantic rhetoric of revolt and declaration. Greece had long been the object of veneration for Western poets, its traditions and customs apostrophised and re-interpreted for centuries to suit the mytho-poetical needs of mainstream European culture. Now, at the moment of its greatest need, in the midst of its war of liberation against Turkey, Greece found a writer capable of mobilising both indigenous tradition and the fashionable ideas of Romantic Europe for the use of its people. In poems such as 'Hymn to Liberty' (1823), 'The Cretan' (1833), and, above all, in *The Free Besieged*, written in three drafts between 1830 and 1844, Solomos demonstrated that persecution and oppression were not simply metaphors for sensibilities no longer at home in the modern world, but were concrete realities, under which a nation was labouring, seeking to defend itself against extinction. The inward struggles depicted by a generation of Romantic dramatists were here turned outward into armed struggle and self-sacrifice. It is this ethos of national militancy that Solomos celebrated in *The Free Besieged*, a poem written in praise of those who give their lives in a spirit of self-sacrifice at the siege of Missolonghi, defending their homes and cities, but even in death emerging from their martyrdom 'unvanquished'.[36]

5   'ALL THINGS ARE SENTIENT': ROMANTIC NATURE POETRY

The Romantics rejected the ideas of the Enlightenment, believing that the philosophy of materialism and the principle of scientific rationality necessarily led to a mechanistic and reductionist model of human nature, which had no place for the spiritual or the transcendent. Instead, Romantic writers looked to nature, contact with which, they believed, would restore to the individual a sense of the

interdependence of living things and a feeling for the organic evolution of life. Certainly, this focus was neither new nor original.
Pre-Romantic writers such as James Thomson (*The Seasons*,
1726–1730), Thomas Gray ('Elegy written in a Country Churchyard',
1750) and Oliver Goldsmith (*The Deserted Village*, 1770), had also
written important poems, invoking nature to different purposes.
Goldsmith, for example, used natural custom in his poem as a
model of the historical harmony that has been destroyed by industrialisation; whilst Gray focused upon the plight of human nature
locked into the rites of passage of birth and death. But it was not
until the Romantics proper that nature came to acquire a certain
privileged ontology: it alone could put man and woman in contact
with authentic experience. As Gérard de Nerval, the French trans-
lator of Goethe's *Faust,* and author of *The Chimera* (1854), asked:
'How have I been able to live so long outside Nature without identifying myself with it? Everything lives, everything moves, everything corresponds; the magnetic rays, emanating either from myself
or from others cross the infinite chain of created things unimpeded;
it is a transparent network which covers the world, and its slender
threads communicate themselves by degrees to the planets and
stars. Captive now upon earth, I commune with choirs of stars who
share in my joys and sorrows'.[37]

In Romantic literature, nature possessed a complex symbolic ambience, which ranged from the indeterminate atmospheric verse
(*Stimmungskunst*) of the German poet, Eichendorff, through to the
pantheistic sensibilities of Wordsworth, and the ecstatic poetry of
Novalis and Blake, who saw in nature 'Imagination itself'. Certainly,
poets such as Byron and Alfred de Vigny held to a cosmopolitan
irony that did not lend itself to rural mysticisms of any sort. Vigny
(an early forerunner of the 'poètes maudits') looked, as Baudelaire
would later do, to the unique excesses of the city for his stimulation. But they were exceptions: the great majority of Romantic
writers would have agreed with Bernadin de Saint-Pierre, whose
popular idyll, *Paul and Virginia* (1787), showed how contact with
nature both simplified social relations and ennobled personal
morality, allowing all who found themselves in this state of natural
grace to enjoy 'the pleasures of love and the blessings of equality'.
Even, Leopardi, who saw in nature a darker, more mysterious
force, posited nature, in his famous poem 'The Infinite' (1819), as a
medium through which the sentient self could make contact with
'Eternity,/The ages that are dead, and the living present'. A similar

transfiguration of nature took place in the work of Alfred de Musset (see, for example, 'The Night' cycle, 1835–1840) and Adolphe de Lamartine, whose *Meditations* (1820) (a volume that marked the beginning of Romantic poetry in France) infused into nature emotions of loss, transience and mutability.[38]

A similar pathos pervades much of the nature poetry of the German Romantic, Eichendorff, but is without the erotic complicity that links the poetic self and nature in Lamartine (and which emerges most clearly in 'The Valley' – 'But it is nature herself who invites you there and whom you love'). In poems such as 'Departure', 'Twilight', 'Longing' and 'Forest Loneliness' (all published in *Poems*, 1837), and also in his noted novella *From the Life of a Ne'er-do-well* (1826), Eichendorff endowed nature with qualities that are both more spiritual and more ethereal. In these works, the author celebrated nature as a God-given part of creation, whose purpose may be obscure, but which is divinable nevertheless through intuition and self-surrender, but only to those prepared for loneliness and isolation. In this respect, Eichendorff came close to that type of faith represented by the German Romantic theologian, Schleiermacher, who asseverated that religious understanding of the world lay neither in thoughts and actions, but in perception and feeling, in that constant openness to the movement of the 'World-Spirit' in nature and in man.[39]

In England, the major poets responded to nature in different ways. Keats wrote a number of famous odes, such as 'Ode to a Nightingale', 'Ode on a Grecian Urn' and 'To Autumn' (all published in 1820), in which nature functioned both as a symbol of a higher realm and as a cornucopia of fecundity; Shelley wrote nature into his own version of Neoplatonism in poems such as 'Hymn to Intellectual Beauty' and 'Mont Blanc' (both written in 1816), where he spoke of the communion between that 'unseen power' of nature and the 'human mind', which (as in the latter poem) holds, sometimes with delight, sometimes with trepidation, 'an unremitting interchange/With the clear universe of things around'; whilst Coleridge celebrated 'animated nature' in his verse, likening (in one famous simile) the sensibility of the poet to an 'Eolian harp' (in the poem of the same name, composed in 1795), which, although passive in itself, is nevertheless attuned to the 'intellectual breeze' that radiates from Nature, bringing God and the Spirit into the hearts of men.[40]

As we know from his poem 'Dejection' (1802), Coleridge, the intellectual, was unable to sustain the naive empathy necessary for a successful symbiosis between animated mind and inanimate nature, and looked to his friend and collaborator on the *Lyrical Ballads* (1798), Wordsworth, to complete a task that they had jointly conceived. Both had been in the vanguard of a poetic revolution that had sought to reinvigorate poetry by infusing it with the diction and speech patterns of ordinary language. Certainly, they had not been alone in this project. The greatest Scottish poet of the Romantic period, Robert Burns, had also striven to find a voice for the people in his *Poems, Chiefly Written in the Scottish Dialect* (1786, expanded in 1793). Burns developed in this volume a unique style capable of locating philosophic import in apparent banality, of seeing, for example, in the straightened circumstances of a mouse, an existential predicament that brings reader, poet, and animal alike into 'Nature's social union'.[41]

Wordsworth and Burns had much in common. Both described the pressures and exigencies of rural life, and both returned to an indigenous ballad form of folk literature, in order to free their subject matter from the easy pastoralism of the neo-classical tradition, which John Ruskin and others repudiated – Ruskin particularly through his notion of the 'pathetic fallacy'. And yet there were important differences between these two great poets of common life, which lay largely in that sense for the spiritual immanence of nature that pervades almost all of Wordsworth's verse. It is evident in poems such as 'The Idiot Boy', 'We are seven', and the Lucy poems (1800), where quotidian realism is transfigured by a natural piety existing in characters and poet alike; and more substantially in poems such as 'Expostulation and Reply' and 'Lines composed a few miles above Tintern Abbey' (both 1798), where a more reflective version of the poet's religious humanism becomes evident. Wordsworth had remained largely unaffected by the German tradition of *Naturphilosopie* that had so affected Coleridge, but had come to his own personal version of pantheism early in his life, when he had learned to view nature both as a source of spiritual delight, and as a medium through which the self might be made whole again through contact with a higher realm. 'Tintern Abbey' (an extended conversation poem in blank-verse) is his most important nature poem. Here he fuses the 'sense sublime' of the visionary poet, capable of speculating on memory, identity and the formation of self, with a more down-to-earth temperament, which never loses sight of the concrete world, but remains committed to those 'little, nameless, unremembered, acts/Of kindness and of love' that serve as the ultimate reference points of the poet's vision. Set against the mytho-poetising of Novalis, or the narcissism of a poet such as Lamartine, where observation of nature is often the pretext for the articulation of failed desire, poems such as 'Tintern Abbey' lead the reader to the unquestionable presence of the spiritual in the real, and the permanent and constantly renewable option of grace.[42]

For Wordsworth, the inner self, as revealed through contact with nature, possessed both a visionary potency and an organic form, capable of developing through time. This is how it manifests itself in *The Prelude* (begun in 1799, but only published posthumously in 1850). The poem charts Wordsworth's evolution as a poet and as a man. It shows how the later achievements of his artistic self grew out of the raw potential of his character in youth and boyhood. In *The Prelude*, nature provides not only the content of Wordsworth's vision of self, but also its form, for character here is not something static or determined by external circumstance; it is a growing reality, a process whose end product is a fully formed totality, 'the discipline/And consummation of a Poet's mind'. In *The Prelude*, self and world enjoy a symbiotic relationship, made possible through an openness to experience and to the spiritual component of the world, to that higher reality that the sensitive soul can reach through dream and imagination, that 'plastic power' which lies within. Once that pact has been made, the union of consciousness and external reality (that synthesis longed for by the Romantic mind) comes close to realisation; the poet no longer appropriates, but becomes part of nature, flowing with a 'stream' whose course, beset by obstacles and impediments, will nevertheless ultimately reach its final goal: 'Faith in life endless, the sustaining thought/Of human Being, Eternity, and God'.[43]

6   THE DARKER SELF: ROMANTIC GOTHIC

Wordsworth sought to make contact with a higher realm by transfiguring the natural world. Coleridge nurtured similar goals, but even in his earliest poetry, a darker, less transcendent quality is apparent, whose ambit is not mystery as the spiritually ineffable, but the para-normal, the macabre, in short, Otherness. These qualities are evident in one of his most famous poems, with which the *Lyrical Ballads* opens: 'The Rime of the Ancient Mariner' (1798). It

tells the story of an errant sailor, who, in killing an albatross, con-
demns his crew to death, and himself to perpetual damnation. He
becomes compelled to wander the world, obsessively repeating his
tale – with his 'strange power of speech' – to anyone who will
listen. Coleridge's poem is an allegory which speaks, not of a
happy union between nature and mankind, or of personality restored to unity through contact with organic life, but of transgression, of guilt, of the eruption of the irrational into rational
discourse, of (as Coleridge himself later explained) the pervasive
dark presence of 'supernatural agency' in human affairs.[44]

It is certainly no coincidence that it should have been Coleridge
(that acolyte of German culture), rather than Wordsworth, who
took an interest in the occult. The consequences of religious transgression for our spiritual health, the moral dangers of intellectual
over-reaching, and the tenuous distinction between the natural and
supernatural, were themes that attracted an entire generation of
German Romantics, from Novalis and Kleist through to Goethe,
whose *Faust I* and *II* struggle both to explicate and contain those
experiences and ideas that lie beyond existing realms of knowledge. The genre that leant itself most readily to this Romantic obsession with otherness was the German *Märchen* (the adult
fairy-story). Its most noted examples were Ludwig Tieck's 'The
Blond Eckbert' (1797), Friedrich Fouqué's 'Undine' (1811), Adelbert
von Chamisso's *Peter Schlemihl's Miraculous Story* (1814), Clemens
Brentano's 'The Story of Honest Casper and Fair Annie' (1817),
Achim von Arnim's 'The Mad Invalid of Fort Ratonneau' (1818)
and a host of stories by E.T.A. Hoffmann, the most important being
'The Sandman' (1816), 'Councillor Krespel' (1818), 'The Mines at
Falun' (1819) and the novella, *The Golden Pot* (1814). Writing in
1799, Novalis called the *Märchen* 'a dream-scape, an ensemble of
fantastic things and events, without logical connection. A musical
fantasy, nature itself'. Indeed, magical acts and unreal characters
abound in the genre: the chameleon witch in Tieck's 'The Blond
Eckbert'; the ghostly miner in Hoffmann's 'The Mines at Falun',
and the living shadow in Chamisso's 'Peter Schlemihl' are some
of the most memorable. These characters often function as
Doppelgänger, being the darker alter egos of otherwise normal
people, objective correlatives of those subconscious parts of the
psyche that must not be allowed to see the light of day. These
shadowy creatures move in a landscape somewhere between the
recognisable terrain of everyday existence, and that other realm

whose contours are formed by fear, suspicion and madness. Their existence proves, as Clara says in Hoffmann's 'The Sandman', that 'in cheerful, careless hearts there too may [...] dwell the presentiment of a dark power which strives to ruin us within our own selves'.[45]

The *Märchen* represents the dark side of the German Romantic vision. In it, the love of nature and natural solitude that was extolled, for example, by Eichendorff, and that feeling for the wonder and mystery of the world, which is so evident in the poetry of Novalis, are deprived of their innocence, and made to reveal the irrational and demonic potential that exists at their centre. Tieck's famous 'The Blond Eckbert' is a case in point. The story takes some of the classic features of the fairy story: the benevolent witch, anthropomorphised animals, and a love between a knight (Eckbert) and a peasant girl (Bertha), but develops them into a sombre tale of trust betrayed, secrets repressed, friends suspected, in a skilfully written narrative, whose ambience is increasingly one of guilt and crime. The grim disclosure that Eckbert has been guilty not only of murder but also, unwittingly, of incest leaves the hero (and, possibly, the reader) in typical *Märchen* fashion, 'numbed and bewildered', unable to distinguish between truth and fantasy.[46]

In giving shape to their perceptions of the darker side of human nature, the authors of the *Märchen* were able to draw upon a popular tradition of writing that had developed throughout the eighteenth and into the early nineteenth century: the Gothic novel. Early examples of the genre, such as Horace Walpole's *The Castle of Otranto* (1764), William Beckford's *Vathek* (1786), Ann Radcliffe's *The Mysteries of Udolpho* (1794), and M.G. Lewis's *The Monk* (1796), mobilised all those qualities of fictional fabulation that were inimical to Enlightenment thought: a belief in the supernatural, the cultivation of ambience and mood, a nostalgia for the medieval, and plots structured around enigma and mystery, which often included sensationalist violence. In her novel *Northanger Abbey* (1818), Jane Austen satirised Gothic literature on account of its unhealthy focus on 'darkness impenetrable' and 'horror', finding such values contrary to the 'laws of the land and the manners of the age' of an early eighteenth century England governed by good sense and decorum. Jane Austen would not (or could not) recognise that Gothic writing clearly performed a function for its contemporary readership, in providing a vehicle for the exploration of excess and taboo, and for indirect critical commentary upon the 'empty pomp and hidden power' that characterised the political and sexual culture of the *ancien régime*.[47]

The Gothic also influenced the English Romantics. Shelley drew upon its heightened rhetoric, not only in poems such as 'Queen Mab' (1813), where 'tainted sepulchres', 'putrefaction's breath', and 'loathsomeness and ruin' are evoked, but also in his more mature works such as 'Prometheus Unbound' (1820), where the Gothic penchant for graphic violence lends a particularly visceral intensity to the sufferings of the fallen Titan, who must undergo his gruesome ordeal, passively watching 'Heaven's winged hound', while 'His beak in poison not his own, tears up/My heart'. Byron likewise used similar iconography, modelling many of his demonic heroes on the familiar Gothic villain who, like the Giaour (in the poem of the same name) possesses a 'dark and unearthly' scowl, in which 'lurks that nameless spell/Which speaks, itself unspeakable,/A spirit yet unquell'd and high'. Keats drew upon Gothic imagery in his 'The Eve of St. Agnes' (1819), and in 'La Belle Dame sans Merci' (1820), both of which exhibit a distinctive medievalism, and an attraction (as in the latter poem) for 'death-pale' apparitions, who surface to remind poet and hero alike of the transitoriness of love, but also of its dangers. Finally, Blake used the Gothic for quite different purposes in *The First Book of Urizen* (1794) and *Jerusalem* (written between 1804 and 1820). In these poems, Blake gave voice to a pessimistic vision of a swiftly industrialising England, where factories and mills have become inhuman vehicles of subjugation and terror, bringing all who come under their dominion to a living death, forced to live under the 'loud sounding hammer of destruction'. In such a landscape, all are victims of Gothic horror, forced to surrender dignity and freedom, living in a land where 'Los's Furnaces howl loud, living, self moving.'[48]

The most memorable use of the Gothic tradition was, however, made by Mary Shelley in her novel, *Frankenstein* (1818). It is a remarkable text for many reasons, not least because it was written by a woman. Prior to its publication, Gothic writers had described women largely in passive terms, as the guileless victims of male rapacity. In many respects, this view of woman mirrored in exaggerated form the predicament of femininity within the Romantic imagination itself, which tended to construe the female as the object rather than the subject of desire, the goal of Romantic obsession rather than its producer, a symbol both of earthly perfection but also of a distant corporality, whose mystique and unattainability gave rise to that characteristic Romantic emotion of immeasurable longing (known in German as *Sehnsucht*). For many Romantic writers, the female formed the centre of a poetics of loss: Lamartine had his Julie Charles, Novalis his Sophie, and Nerval his Sylvie. Certainly, attempts were made to provide women with their own position of speech: Friedrich Schlegel made one such attempt in his fragmentary and incomplete novel, *Lucinde* (1799), in which he describes the ideal marriage of two free souls, Julius and Lucinde, who are united in a relationship that combines 'spiritual desire and sensual bliss'. Written clearly under the influence of Rousseau's notion of natural morality, *Lucinde* posits its two protagonists as free agents, who are able to produce a heightened communion of mind and body, returning through their physical love to that 'golden age of innocence' that the Romantics longed for. But even here, at the moment of her greatest equality, the Romantic heroine remains a distant figure, a positive otherness, now angel, now earth mother, a creature who ultimately can only find her happiness in the serenity of the male.[49]

Mary Shelley intervened into this framework, not by writing a 'woman's novel' (as Madame de Staël had done in her *Corinne*, 1807, and as George Sand would later do in *Indiana*, 1832, and *Lélia*, 1833), but by taking possession of a form that had, with the exception of Ann Radcliffe's *The Mysteries of Udolpho*, traditionally been written by men. She also injected into her narrative a critique of two of the most dominant male archetypes of the Romantic imagination: Faust and Prometheus. These two figures stand for those who would seek (as Shelley explained in her introduction to the novel) to 'mock the stupendous mechanism of the Creator of the world', by seeking to push knowledge and power beyond their natural and moral limitations. In this sense, she meant her novel to be read both as a critique of the triumphalist and arrogant nature of scientific rationalism (she targets in her introduction the new and disturbing energy of electricity), and of Romanticism itself. In celebrating genius and unbridled creativity, the latter has (Shelley implies) entirely forgotten the modest origins of art in human experience, seeking, as the unhappy Frankenstein retrospectively laments regarding himself, 'to become greater than nature will allow'. The monster that Shelley constructs in her novel is pure Gothic. Assembled from the 'degraded and wasted' human remains culled from the local churchyard, he is from the moment of his birth regarded even by his creator with 'horror and disgust', a 'demoniacal corpse'. Left to wander the world, travelling from bucolic Switzerland to the bleak Arctic, abandoned and despised, he gives himself over to a life defined by 'carnage and misery', revenging himself on those he deems to have betrayed him.[50]

But Shelley also makes it clear that the monster possesses a soul; and in the closing stages of her narrative, she adds to the ethical conservatism with which she has sustained the moral allegory of her story so far an important component of social reformism, projecting the monster now as much the victim of evil as its perpetrator. In the final scene of the novel, the monster learns to speak of his persecution and defilement, explaining that he has been 'wrenched by misery to vice and hatred', degraded by 'crime [...] beneath the meanest animal', by an uncomprehending and uncaring world. His artificial creation may have been an affront to the laws of nature and religious piety; but the greater crime, Mary Shelley concludes (drawing upon the reformist zeal of her father William Godwin, whose novel *Caleb Williams*, published in 1794, came to similar conclusions) is the one shared by all: the corruption of original innocence, a lack of sympathy for one marked by difference and estrangement, and a refusal to take responsibility for crimes that are of our own making.[51]

7   'HYMNS TO THE NIGHT': THE LONGING FOR TRANSCENDENCE

In his 'Auguries of Innocence' (1789), William Blake exhorted his readers 'to see a World in a Grain of Sand/And Heaven in a Wild Flower,/Hold Infinity in the Palm of your Hand/And Eternity in an Hour'. In spite of their inherent mysticism, Blake's lines were the product of a mind that enjoyed a natural vitality and energy, and was fully committed to the tangibility of the world. In other Romantic poets, experience of nature involved a more passive facility, an opening, almost surrender of self to a higher, transcendent reality. This will to dissolution reappears throughout Romantic writing. It is evident in the religious lyrics of the great Polish Romantic, Adam Mickiewicz, and in those of the Dane, B.S. Ingemann, whose *Morning and Evening Songs* (1839) represent one of the high points of Scandinavian Romanticism. It is pre-eminently evident in the work of Ugo Foscolo (*Sepulchral Verses*, 1807), and in that of Giacomo Leopardi (*Songs*, 1831), the two foremost representatives of the Romantic movement in Italy. Both were poets of the night, explorers of the depths, anxieties and mysteries that lie beyond the provenance of the daylight world. Leopardi, in particular, in poems such as 'The Infinite', 'The Evening after the Holy Day' (both 1819), and 'To Himself' (1833), identified with this mentality, giving voice in his verse to a powerful sense of existential dread occasioned by the 'unearthly silences, and endless space' that seemed forever to surround him. This is poetry permeated by a fear of a universe irretrievably obscure and inaccessible to moral scrutiny. It offers nothing to either man or poet, both of whom, like the hopeful traveller, in the poem 'The Setting of the Moon' (1837), must conclude their life's journey in despair: for 'in the night,/ Where through the dark we come/The gods have set a sign for us, the tomb'. The Greek poet, Solomos, offered a similar homily to the poetics of the night in his remarkable poem, 'The Shark' (1848). Here, the merging of self into nature is not conducted through wise passivity, but through an act of apparently irredeemable violence (the death of a young British soldier killed by a shark in the waters of the Aegean). In spite of the grim realism of the poem's subject, Solomos persists with the Romantic insistence that the experiencing self can only reach fruition through the dissolution of identity. And as the beast of prey takes its victim, Solomos offers us neither tragedy nor pity, but a glimpse into the mind of an individual forced suddenly to come to terms with life and death, in one moment of pure knowledge, when 'a light flashed like lightning and the youth knew himself'.[52]

The seminal text in this literature of dark transcendence was Novalis's *Hymns to the Night* (written in 1789 and published in the *Athenaeum*, edited by the Schlegels, in 1800). In his *Bildungsroman* (novel of self-formation and personal development) *Henry from Ofterdingen* (published posthumously in 1802), Novalis extolled the value of earthly achievement, depicting the quest of the young Henry for ideal love and spiritual fulfilment (represented in the novel by Mathilde, but, on a more symbolical level, by the ethereal blue flower of Romantic mythology). The earlier *Hymns to the Night*, however, gives expression to a quite different vision of the world. The poem tells of Novalis's attempt to make contact with his loved one, the diseased Sophie; she has left this world for a higher realm that can only be reached by those prepared to embrace darkness and death as positive values. *Hymns to the Night* is a work of unrelieved interiority which, in six short paeans (some in prose poems, some in rhyming verse) describes the poet's journey from light into darkness, from earth-bound existence to ethereal spirituality. Around this quest, Novalis spins a condemnation of Enlightenment thinking and scientific rationality, which have destroyed that sympathetic bond between the individual and nature that Novalis saw as existing in the golden age of our past. This is the central theme of the *Hymns*, and in the fifth in the series the poet looks back in a rare moment of mythic retrospection to the prehistory of mankind, where all lived in a 'holy intoxication' produced by the animistic immanence of spirit in nature. That world is historically past but, as he argues in the third Hymn, it can be recreated in our minds if we replace 'the chains of light', those mental habits of a calculating, quantifying rationality, with a greater feeling for the ineffable in all its forms: shadows, the subterranean, dreams, in short, the night. What is required is an intellectual leap, a breakthrough (*Durchbruch*) to a higher realm. Novalis leaves the ultimate destination of his journey unclear, and intentionally so: it is meant to combine the spiritual and the natural, the earthly and the heavenly, that which can be possessed and that which must remain forever an object of that dominant Romantic emotion, *Sehnsucht*. The *Hymns*, accordingly, move back and forth between these realms, hovering around a fixed point of yearning, which is the product of a restless will that seeks to see the distinction between dream and reality finally overcome.[53]

At the centre of Novalis's work lies a paradox central to the Romantic imagination: for the self to reach a higher plane it must dissolve precisely those faculties that provide for its definition: rationality, self-consciousness, the ego. In this inversion of values, death becomes life, and the undefinable workings of mood and temperament the sole source of true knowledge. Linking the two realms was the goal of such Romantic writers as Hoffmann and Tieck, and Coleridge, whose deranged hero in 'The Ancient Mariner', can be read as a mediator between earth and hell. There were other prophets of the night, such as Etienne Pivert de Sénancour, the author of *Obermann*, and the anonymous author of the *Nightwatch of Bonaventura* (both 1804). Both interpret the need for transcendence as an obsession; not as a medium of spiritual transfiguration, but as a psychological problem that can leave the conscious self (as the hero of Sénancour's novel attests) 'lost in the abyss' of an 'inquietude' that is as pervasive as it is irredeemable. These writers were aware of the limitations of Romantic self-consciousness, and as such anticipated two figures who would effectively bring Romantic optimism to an end: Thomas de Quincey and Gérard de Nerval. De Quincey's most famous work, *Confessions of an English Opium-Eater* (1822, enlarged edition 1856) is an autobiographical account of his experiments with opium, and clearly draws upon Coleridge's famous poem *Kubla Khan* (written in 1797, but not published until 1816), which likewise linked poetic fantasy to the use of drugs. Like Coleridge's poem, De Quincey's work is also ambiguous in its attitude to opium, oscillating between moral condemnation and a celebration of the transforming capacity of the drug. His hallucinations, graphically described and framed within the urban context of modern London, hover between vision and terror, as the author moves between dreams of his loved ones and nightmares that conjure up unfamiliar beasts and transform lakes into mosaics of suffering human faces. These are experiences which liberate de Quincey from conventional notions of selfhood, but also leave him 'agitated, writhing, throbbing, palpitating, shattered', physically and mentally broken, and finally prepared to renounce the temptations of Romantic transport.[54]

Almost half a century separates Novalis from Gérard de Nerval. Like Novalis, Nerval also sought to distance himself from the stultifying tradition of Enlightenment rationalism, and came close to the Magic Idealism of his German forerunner. His philosophy is evident in poems such as 'Gilded Verses' (1845), where he reminds the 'free-thinking man' that in 'Each flower is a soul blossoming in nature;/ In metal there dwells a mystery of love;/ "Everything is sentient!" And everything has power upon you'. This was pure Novalis, but what came after was not. Nerval is a late figure in French Romanticism, but an important one: his translations of Goethe and Heine were responsible for popularising the work of those authors, and of German Romanticism, in general, in France. His own publications extended from the early impressionistic travelogue, *Voyage to the Orient* (1851), through to the poetry of *Chimeras* (published in 1854, which contains the famous poem of fantasy, 'El Desdichado'), and the story *Sylvia* (1853), whose mock-heroic reconstruction of an idealised French countryside reveals the growing presence of the Realist movement. In all of these works, the mentally unstable poet had crossed genres, played with the reader's expectation of form and style, and produced a world dominated sometimes by fantasy, sometimes by clear realism. As Nerval tells us in his letters, such works were products of a mind liberated through 'illusion, paradox, [and] the presumption of all those things that are enemies of good sense'.[55]

In his final work, *Aurélia* (published in Nerval's last year, 1855) the poet intensified the Romantic optic to the point where the fusion of dream and reality is no longer a Romantic metaphor, but signals an irreversible process of mental derangement. *Aurélia* has neither story nor plot, nor protagonists beyond the first person subject of the narrative. Time, space and sequence are likewise left unspecified, as Nerval moves around Paris, seeking to make sense of his experiences, retreating to one mental hospital after another. This is the record of a voyage into the night, whose starting point: 'Our dreams are a second life', is one that would have been familiar to Blake, Novalis and all who sought a higher reality in dream or the transports of religious visions. But *Aurélia* speaks not of dream but of nightmare, and although the personal obsession which initiates the narrative (the death of the loved one) appears throughout Romantic literature, Nerval's account of the psychological effects of that obsession is unique in nineteenth-century literature. Nerval's journey charts a 'descent into hell', into a world dominated by animistic fantasies, delusions of grandeur, schizophrenia and simple 'terror'. With *Aurélia*, we have reached the end of the tradition of epistemological utopianism that found its earliest and most memorable form in Novalis. The nocturnal vision projected by the German poet had belonged to the realm of gentle sleep, had opened the riches of the unconscious, had served as a metaphor for infinity. By the time Nerval enters a similar region, Romanticism has lost both its optimism and its *naïveté*; the Other that the demented narrator of Nerval's narrative encounters is part of his deeper self, but hostile, and, as the century turns the corner to the modern age, is subject to the new scientific discourses of psychology and medical pathology. This is where Nerval leaves us: at the end of the trajectory of Romantic idealism. As the hero explains at one moment of rare clarity: 'born in days of revolutions and storms, when every belief was broken [...] for us it is very difficult, when we feel the need of it, to resurrect that mystic edifice already built in their ready hearts by the innocent and simple'. Within this context, on the eve of the triumph of positivism and utilitarianism, the Romantic impulse cannot survive; fantasy has become an historical impossibility, and 'ignorance cannot be learned'.[56]

8 LITERATURE IN THE AGE OF ROMANTICISM: A CHRONOLOGY

1759, Young, *Conjectures on Original Composition*.
1760, Macpherson, *Fragments of Ancient Poetry, collected in the Highlands of Scotland* (Poems of 'Ossian').
1761, Rousseau, *La Nouvelle Héloïse* (The New Héloïse).
1764, Walpole, *The Castle of Otranto*.
1765, Percy, *Reliques of Ancient English Poetry*.
1765–1770, Rousseau, *Confessions* [publ. 1783].
1771, Klopstock, *Oden* (Odes).
1772–1776, Rousseau, *Les Rêveries du promeneur solitaire* (Reveries of a Solitary Walker) [publ. 1782].
1773, Herder, *Von deutscher Art und Kunst* (On the German Mind and German Art).
1774, Goethe, *Die Leiden des jungen Werthers* (The Sorrows of Young Werther).
1776, Lenz, *Die Soldaten* (The Soldiers).
1777, Klinger, *Sturm und Drang* (Storm and Stress).
1778–1779, Herder, *Volkslieder* (Songs of the Folk).
1781, Schiller, *Die Räuber* (The Outlaws).
1784, Beaumarchais, *Le Mariage de Figaro* (The Marriage of Figaro).
1786, Burns, *Poems Chiefly Written in the Scottish Dialect*.
1787, Bernardin de Saint-Pierre, *Paul et Virginie* (Paul and Virginia).
1788, Goethe, *Egmont*.
1789, Blake, *Songs of Innocence*.
1790, Burns, 'Tam O'Shanter'.
1792, Karamzin, *Bednaya Liza* (Poor Liza).
1794, Blake, *Songs of Experience*.
1794, Godwin, *Caleb Williams*.
1795–1796, Schiller, *Über naive und sentimentalische Dichtung* (On Naive and Sentimental Poetry).
1795, Schiller, *Briefe über die ästhetische Erziehung des Menschen* (Letters on the Aesthetic Education of Man).
1796, Jean Paul, *Des Quintus Fixlein Leben* (Life of Quintus Fixlein).
1796, Coleridge, *Poems on various Subjects*.
1797, Tieck, 'Märchen vom blonden Eckbert' ('The Blond Eckbert').
1797, Coleridge, *Kubla Khan* [publ. 1816].
1797–1799, Hölderin, *Hyperion*.
1798, Wordsworth and Coleridge, *Lyrical Ballads*.
1798, Novalis, *Blütenstaub* (Pollen).
1798–1800, Friedrich Schlegel, *Athenäum Fragmente* (Atheneum Fragments).
1799, Friedrich Schlegel, *Lucinde*.
1800, Wordsworth, Preface to second edition of *Lyrical Ballads*.
1800, Novalis, *Hymnen an die Nacht* (Hymns to the Night).
1800, de Staël, *De la littérature* (On Literature).
1801, Southey, *Thalaba the Destroyer*.
1801, Chateaubriand, *Atala*.

1802, Chateaubriand, *René*.

1802, Coleridge, 'Dejection'.

1802, Novalis, *Heinrich von Ofterdingen* (Henry from Ofterdingen).

1802, Foscolo, *Le ultime lettere di Jacopo Ortis* (The Last Letters of Jacopo Ortis).

1804, Sénancour, *Obermann*.

1804, Anon., *Nachtwachen des Bonaventura* (The Nightwatch of Bonaventura).

1805, Wordsworth, *The Prelude* (full manuscript published in 1850).

1805–1808, Arnim and Brentano, *Des Knaben Wunderhorn* (The Boy's Magic Horn).

1807, Foscolo, *Dei Sepolcri* (Sepulchral Verses).

1807, Constant, *Adolphe* [publ. 1816].

1808, Kleist, *Penthesilea*.

1808, Goethe, *Faust*, Part I.

1808–1809, August Schlegel, 'Vorlesungen über dramatische Kunst und Literatur' ('Lectures on Dramatic Art and Literature') [publ. 1809–1811].

1810, de Staël, *De l'Allemagne* (On Germany).

1810, Kleist, 'Über das Marionettentheater' ('On the Marionette Theatre').

1811, Bilderdijk, *Kort verhaal van eene aenmerklijke luchtreis* (Brief Account of a Remarkable Air Voyage).

1811, Fouqué, *Undine*.

1812–1814, J. and W. Grimm, *Kinder- und Hausmärchen* (Fairy Tales).

1812–1818, Byron, *Childe Harold's Pilgrimage*.

1813, Shelley, *Queen Mab*.

1814, Austen, *Mansfield Park*.

1814, Chamisso, 'Peter Schlemihls wundersame Geschichte' ('Peter Schlemihl's Miraculous Story').

1814, Scott, *Waverley*.

1814, Hoffmann, *Der goldne Topf* (The Golden Pot).

1815, Scott, *Guy Mannering*.

1815, Uhland, *Die Gedichte* (Poems).

1816, Berchet, 'Lettera semiseria di Grisostomo al suo figliuolo' ('The Semiserious Letter from Chrysostom to his Son').

1817, Keats, *Poems*.

1817, Byron, *Manfred*.

1818, Mary Shelley, *Frankenstein*.

1818, T.L. Peacock, *Nightmare Abbey*.

1818, Jane Austen, *Northanger Abbey*.

1818, John Keats, *Endymion*.

1819, Eichendorff, *Das Marmorbild* (The Marble Image).

1819–1821, Leopardi, *Idill* (Idylls).

1819–1824, Byron, *Don Juan*.

1820, Keats, *Lamia, Isabella, the Eve of St. Agnes and Other Poems*.

1820, Lamartine, *Méditations poétiques* (Poetic Meditations).

1821, Shelley, *Adonais*.

1821, Shelley, 'The Defence of Poetry' [publ. 1840].

1822, De Quincey, *Confessions of an English Opium-Eater* [enlarged 1856].

1823, Manzoni, 'Sul romanticismo' ('On Romanticism').

1823, Solomos, 'Ymnos Eis Tin Eleftherian' ('Hymn to Liberty').

1823, Lamartine, *Nouvelles méditations poétiques* (New Poetical Meditations).

1823, Stendhal, *Racine et Shakespeare* (Racine and Shakespeare) [revised 1825].

1825, Tegnér, *Frithiofs Saga*.

1825, Vörösmarty, *Zalán Futása* (The Flight of Zalan).

1826, Hölderlin, *Gedichte* (Poetry).

1826, Eichendorff, *Aus dem Leben eines Taugenichts* (From the Life of a Ne'er-do-well).

1826, Vigny, *Poèmes antiques et modernes* (Modern and Ancient poems).

1826–1828, Hugo, *Odes et Ballades* (Odes and Ballades).

1827, Heine, *Buch der Lieder* (Book of Songs).

1827, Hugo, *Cromwell*.

1828, Carlyle, 'Essay on Goethe'.

1828, Guerrazzi, *La battaglia di Benevento* (Manfred; The Battle of Benevento).

1830, Musset, *Contes d'Espagne et d'Italie* (Stories of Spain and Italy).

1830, Hugo, *Hernani*.

1830, Wergeland, *Skabelsen, Mannesket og Messias* (Creation, Humanity and Messiah).

1830–1844, Solomos, *Oi Eleftheroi Poliorkimenoi* (The Free Besieged) [publ. 1859].

1831, Hugo, *Notre-Dame de Paris* (The Hunchback of Notre Dame).

1831, Pushkin, *Boris Godunov*.

1831, Leopardi, *Canti* (Songs).

1832–1851, Almquist, *Törnrosens bok* (Book of the Thorn and the Rose).

1832, Goethe, *Faust*, Part II.

1832, Sand, *Indiana*.

1832, Runeberg, *Elgskyttarne* (The Elkshooters).

1833, Pushkin, *Yevgeny Onegin* (Eugene Onegin).

1834, Mickiewicz, *Pan Tadeusz* (Master Thaddeus).

1834, Rivas, *El moro expósito* (The Foundling Moor).

1834, Musset, *Lorenzaccio*.

1834, Larra, *Maciás*.

1835, Gautier, *Mademoiselle de Maupin*.

1835, Krasinski, *Nieboska komedia* (The Undivine Comedy).

1835, Lönnrot, *Kalevala* [enlarged 1849].

1835, Rivas, *Don Alvaro o la fuerza del sino* (Don Alvaro and the Force of Destiny).

1835–1848, Andersen, *Eventyr* (Fairy Tales).

1836, Mácha, *Máj* (May).

1836, Larra, 'Literatura' ('Literature').

1836, Garcia Gutiérrez, *El Trovador* (The Troubador).

1836, Vigny, *Chatterton*.

1836, Musset, *La Confession d'un enfant du siècle* (Confessions of a Child of our Age).

1837–1843, Balzac, *Illusions perdues* (Lost Illusions).

1837, Eichendorff, *Gedichte* (Poems).

1837, Hartzenbusch, *Los amantes de Teruel* (The Lovers of Teruel).

1839, B.S. Ingemann, *Morgen- og Aften-sange* (Morning and Evening Songs).

1840, Espronceda, *El estudiante de Salamanca* (The Student of Salamanca).

1840, Lermontov, *Geroi nashego vremeni* (A Hero of our Time).

1840, Wergeland, 'Jan van Huysum's Blomsterstykke' ('Jan van Huysum's Flower-piece').

1841, Espronceda, *El diablo mundo* (The Devilish World).

1844, Petöfi, *Versek* (Poems).

2
Realism and Naturalism

1 'FORCE AND MATTER': THE CONTEXT OF EUROPEAN REALISM

In 1821, John Keats died; in 1822, Shelley; in 1824, Byron; Ugo Foscolo in 1827; in 1829, Friedrich Schlegel; Constant in 1830; Leopardi in 1837; Pushkin in 1837; in 1841, Lermontov. All dead, and for diverse reasons, which included tuberculosis (Keats), military combat (Byron), duelling (Lermontov), and boredom (Foscolo). Their tragedies were private ones, but they contained an important symbolic significance: by 1840 the movement to which they had all lent their exuberant talents was over, its energies dissipated, its idealism now redundant in a new cultural climate that valorised science over art, fact over fantasy, immanence over transcendence; in short, Realism over Romanticism. Even before that date, the death knell of the Romantic movement had been sounded by some of its erstwhile adherents. William Wordsworth was one of them. As early as 1800, the architect of the *Lyrical Ballads,* who had attempted to produce a theory of poetry that endeavoured, by returning to 'the ordinary language of ordinary men', to effect a final break with the elitist diction of neo-classicism, had begun to write poetry that modified both the political radicalism and the pantheistic sentiment of his early verse. The errant energy of his youthful writing was now to be held in check, as in his 'Ode to Duty' (1807), by a newly won moral conscience, that 'stern Daughter of the Voice of God', whose presence would come to dominate all of Wordsworth's later verse. A similar trajectory was followed by Southey and Coleridge, in England; Chateaubriand, in France; and Friedrich Schlegel and Goethe, in Germany: all expressed a nostalgia for the religion-based consensus of pre-revolutionary Europe, and all moved towards a more 'mature' acceptance of the status quo, elaborating, in works such as Coleridge's *On the Constitution of the Church and State* (1830) and Schlegel's *Philosophy of Life* (1828), philosophies that sought to reconcile the individual with God and country, with society and the state.

As German Romanticism's most trenchant critic Heinrich Heine noted in his acerbic *The Romantic School in Germany* (1836), by 1830 a movement that had once been libertarian and expansionist in its goals had degenerated into a 'Neo-German-Religious-Patriotic Art', whose intellectual values were those of the Roman Catholic Church and whose *raison d'être* lay in providing a quasi-mystical legitimation of the Austrian and Prussian states.[1]

The historical factors that brought about this transition from Romanticism to Realism were diverse. In political terms, the most notable was the return of a period of reaction in European politics known as the Restoration (on account of the return of the aristocracy, in the form of Louis XVIII, to the French throne). Its values – conservative, aristocratic, Catholic and pre-revolutionary – were enshrined in the protocols of the Congress of Vienna of 1815, ratified by the reigning monarchs of Austria, Russia and Prussia. Where the ideas of Rousseau and Paine had once reigned, now came those of Joseph de Maistre and Edmund Burke. In his *Reflections on the Revolution in France* (1790), the latter had accused the perpetrators of the French Revolution of 'personal self-sufficiency and arrogance', condemning their lack of respect for those institutions – Church, Family and Throne – which give solidity and purpose to the lives of individuals and nations alike. Notions of liberty, equality and the rights of man came to be replaced in Europe by a new focus upon order, consensus and community. Action soon followed rhetoric. Throughout the continent, indications of revolutionary stirring were repressed by governments in a systematic process of reaction, largely orchestrated by the Austrian foreign minister, Prince Klemens von Metternich. He masterminded the suppression of liberal movements in Italy and in Portugal in 1821, and presided over the restoration of the monarchy in Spain in 1823. Metternich's promise of 'peace and order' (*Ruhe und Ordnung*) became the motto for an increasingly conservative political intelligentsia (as the equation of 'matter and force', coined by the materialist philosopher, Ludwig Büchner, provided a catch-phrase for the scientific community). On the basis of Metternich's policies, there emerged a Holy Alliance between Austria, Prussia and Russia, who, proclaiming themselves defenders of a Christian faith threatened by post-Enlightenment atheism, enforced a gospel of obedience upon their intimidated subjects.[2]

These efforts found support and theoretical legitimation not only in the writings of traditional conservative thinkers such as Burke and de Maistre, but in the work of a new generation of political philosophers and historians, who grafted on to earlier vindications of absolutist forms of government a modern, evolutionary quality that allowed 'might' to be equated with 'right'. This is particularly true of the German thinkers of this era. They ranged from the military historian, Carl von Clausewitz, who, in his textbook *On War* (1832), formulated the famous dictum 'War is a mere continuation of policy [politics] by other means', through to the philosopher, Georg Wilhelm Friedrich Hegel (*The Philosophy of Right*, 1821), and the historians, Heinrich von Treitschke and Leopold von Ranke. Ranke and Treitschke, in particular, combined their goal to grasp history as it actually was (*wie es eigentlich gewesen*) with a firm belief in the world-historical mission of the German nation, convinced that it was the historian's task to 'create in the hearts of his readers, *joy in the Fatherland*'. These historians were the exponents of *Realpolitik*, an ethos that argued for the supremacy of the state and the nation in both internal and external affairs. *Realpolitik* guided the policies of many politicians in the age of Realism, statesmen such as Guizot in France, Cavour in Italy, and, above all, Bismarck in Prussia. The latter's philosophy of 'blood and iron' represented the most successful manifestation of this ethos of uncompromising pragmatism. Through its implementation, the industrial prowess and military might of Germany increased dramatically in the space of barely two decades, transforming that country from a disunited constellation of semi-medieval principalities into one of the most dynamic and self-confident nations of the modern period.[3]

The values that underscored the ethos of *Realpolitik*: a scepticism regarding ideals and an acceptance of force and power as ineluctable realities in private and political life, were reflected in the literature of this period, most notably in the historical novel. Walter Scott had established the popularity of the genre in the early part of the century with novels such as *Waverley* (1814) and *Guy Mannering* (1815). The success of these novels had helped reawaken national identity in many countries throughout Europe, in Spain, for example, where an entire body of literature (known as *costumbrismo*) came into existence around depictions of local customs, values and traditions. Noted examples included Mariano José de Larra's *The King's Page* (1834), Patricio de la Escosura's *Neither King nor Rook* (1835) and Enrique Gil y Carrasco's *The Master of Bembibre* (1844). The great historical novels of the Realist period, however, such as Stendhal's *The Charterhouse of Parma* (1839), Alessandro

Manzoni's, *The Betrothed* (1827, second definitive edition 1840–1842), and Leo Tolstoy's *War and Peace* (1863–1869), are both more cosmopolitan and more pessimistic in their bearing, and give voice to a greater feel for the randomness of events and for the absence of moral direction in history. This mood is particularly evident in Manzoni's epic novel. Set in a mid-seventeenth-century Lombardy suffering under the yoke of Spanish rule, *The Betrothed* describes, in the greatest detail and with the greatest compassion for the two principal protagonists, the village lovers, Renzo and Lucia, a society dominated by avarice, sexual rapacity and political thuggery. In such a world, life has little worth and little meaning. The two lovers survive, through the timely solicitations of Father Cristoforo, but Manzoni's Hobbesian moral is clear: the political realm is dominated by power and by the anarchic powers of darkness. Even 'the most prudent and innocent conduct' is not sufficient to guarantee survival; and Manzoni concludes his novel with an exhortation aimed at protagonists and reader alike: look to God, for He alone can provide a path through and out of history.[4]

The novels of Stendhal and Tolstoy have a more contemporary setting: the Napoleonic period, towards the end of the Emperor's push for control of Europe. The young hero of Stendhal's *The Charterhouse of Parma* is Fabrizio, who, in journeying from the chaotic battlefield of Waterloo to the political tyranny of the state of Parma (and then to final incarceration), learns, through a series of complicated personal and political imbroglios, that the post-Napoleonic period is governed by a 'horror of enthusiasm and spirit', and by a calculating pragmatism that is, ultimately, without regard for life or ideals. Tolstoy's vision in *War and Peace* is less bleak, and his canvas is broader, but even here the scope for individual action is limited. The novel depicts the titanic struggle of his country against Napoleon's Grand Army in the period between 1805 and 1812 and, against the background, the more personal trials and achievements of a number of individuals and families. Tolstoy joins the two realms, allowing his characters to move in and out of history, describing a process that sometimes involves personal tragedy (as in the death of Prince Andrew on the fields of Schöngraben), but at other times becomes the condition for self-realisation (as is the case with Pierre Bezukhov, a seeker after true knowledge). Throughout his novel, Tolstoy raises fundamental questions about the relationship between free will and determinism, about the role of the individual in history, and about the very nature of historical change, complex issues that the author addresses directly in his famous second epilogue to the novel. In this, he argues that history cannot be reduced to a series of objective laws or subjective acts of will, but is a complex and frequently irrational process, whose determining mode depends upon the perspective and experience of the individual observer. In the final analysis, action and inaction may produce the same results; all the individual can do is to embrace (as Tolstoy does in his novel) epic irony, that facility to accommodate oneself to 'a freedom that does not exist, and to recognise a dependence of which we are not conscious'.[5]

Although the revolutionary energies unleashed by the French Revolution soon dissolved in the cold light of Restoration Europe, the class that the Revolution had brought to power in 1789, the bourgeoisie, continued to grow in strength throughout the nineteenth century, taking advantage of a new political climate in which wealth and property became the sole criteria for political office and social status. This class increasingly consolidated its position of power within the state through successive revolutions in France, in 1830 and 1848, in Italy, in 1860, and in Spain, in 1868; of all the major European nations, Germany alone failed to stage a successful bourgeois revolution, its attempt in 1848 foundering on strong opposition from the army and monarchy. The values that this new ruling elite embodied: plutocratic power-broking, mistrust of the intelligentsia, and an assertive ethos of moral self-righteousness that combined religious probity and myopic materialism, were frequently mocked in the literature of the period, through comic figures such as Joseph Prudhomme, César Birotteau and Podsnap (from works by Henri Monnier, Balzac and Dickens, respectively). The 'hard wrathful and sordid nature' of the ethos they embodied was consciously satirised in novels such as Balzac's *Lost Illusions* (1837–1843), and Dicken's *Hard Times* (1854). But that the bourgeoisie was a dynamic force in world history, none, not even their detractors, such as Karl Marx, could deny. It was (ironically, perhaps) Marx who provided one of the most noted homilies of that class. In his *Communist Manifesto* (1848), he described how the bourgeoisie had once been a revolutionary force, how it had torn asunder 'the motley feudal ties' that had bound man to his 'natural superiors', and destroyed those 'most heavenly ecstasies of religious fervour, of chivalrous enthusiasm, of philistine sentimentalism' that had prevailed in Europe before 1789. This superannuated aristocratic class had now largely disappeared from the world stage, and a new ruling elite of industrial magnates and international bankers had arrived in its place, figures such as Rothschild and Krupp in Germany, Peugeot and Dollfuss in France, and Brunel and Fairbairn in England. These were the new masters of Europe, ruthless in asserting their interests not only over the landed aristocracy, but also over those of that other new class of the modern age: the proletariat. The latter, Marx believed, held the key to the future; but in the meantime it would be forced to cope with the most sombre of realities of this emerging capitalist society: the fact that its labour was worth nothing more than it would fetch on an open and uncaring market.[6]

The rise to power of the bourgeoisie possessed both a material base, which lay in the discovery of new methods of manufacture and of new forms of energy, and an ideological one. As the captains of industry grew in importance and self-confidence, they were accompanied by a growing number of philosophers, sociologists and political economists who sought to provide an intellectual legitimacy for their activities. Some such as David Ricardo and J.B. Say celebrated the market economy and the importance of entrepreneurial initiative, defending its right to function on its own *laissez-faire* terms, independently of state control; others, such as Jeremy Bentham, emphasised the desirability of a quantitative and material assessment of individual and social happiness, arguing for a doctrine of pure Utilitarianism; whilst others still, such as Samuel Smiles, in his inspirational manual, *Self-Help* (1859), working on a more popular level, sought to elaborate a Victorian version of the Protestant ethic, built around the solid values of 'common sense, attention, application, and perseverance'. Others still attempted to locate the driving energies of the capitalist mentality not in history or in personal morality, but in the natural laws of biology, those processes of natural selection and struggle, to which all species (it was felt) were subject. The terms of this conflictual model had originally been stated in Charles Darwin's *The Origin of Species* (1859). Darwin had attempted there to account for the evolutionary nature of animal species in terms of their ability to adapt to their natural environments. He had offered his views within the context of a long-standing debate within the natural sciences and had not sought to apply them to the social or political sphere. For Herbert Spencer, however, Darwin's views had an obvious relevance to human affairs. In his magnum opus, *Principles of Sociology* (1876–1896), he argued that societies and individuals were dominated by exactly the same internal laws of development as natural phenomena, being locked into 'struggles for existence' that no one could avoid. Many will go under in this process (Spencer clinically observed) but those in whom the power of self-preservation is dominant will emerge victorious, made stronger and more re-sourceful by their ordeals, becoming members of an ever-evolving society, whose course is continually renewed by 'the survival of the fittest'.[7]

The evolutionary fatalism of Spencer's social Darwinism was rejected by many who were forced to witness the material impact of *laissez-faire* liberalism upon the working people of Europe. Robert Southey was one such witness. In 1808, he visited Birmingham, and left his impression of its factories and work places: 'My head aches with the multiplicity of infernal noises, and my eyes with the light of infernal fires, – I may add, my heart also, at the sight of so many human beings employed in infernal occupations, and looking as if they were never destined for any thing better. Our earth was designed to be a seminary for young angels, but the devil has certainly fixed upon this spot for his own nursery-garden and hot-house'. Southey's words were echoed by others equally appalled both by the poverty and misery that they saw in large cities, and by what they perceived to be the callous indifference of the social theorists of the liberal school, such as Spencer, David Ricardo and Thomas Robert Malthus, to the grim nature of life in industrial England. Malthus, in particular, whose *An Essay on the Principle of Population* (1803) construed poverty as an unavoidable consequence of an expanding population and a contracting food supply, could find nothing in his theories to gainsay the continuation of such misery. To counteract the fatalism and quietism of the liberal-capitalist position, works such as Harriet Martineau's *Poor Laws and Paupers Illustrated* (1833), Thomas Carlyle's *Past and Present* (1843), and Henry Mayhew's *London's Labour and London's Poor* (1849–1862) appeared, documenting the plight of London's underclass, in the hope of awakening the conscience of their middle-class readership to the sorry situation of the poor and destitute. Friedrich Engels, in his *The Condition of the Working-Class in England* (1845), however, went beyond the emotive humanism evinced in the majority of these 'condition of England' studies. What Engels was looking for was not analysis, but remedy, and in his later writings he came to align himself with the tradition of radical socialism (soon to be called Communism), whose most sophisticated exponent was the radical political economist, Karl Marx. Marx had consistently argued, from his early humanist 1844 *Manuscripts* through to the 'scientific' critiques, *The German Ideology* (1846), *Critique of Political Economy* (1859), and, finally, *Capital* (1867), that the injustices of the capitalist system could not be remedied by moral critique or social welfare, but only through the political awakening of the proletariat. Once this had reached full consciousness of itself as the driving force of history, it would (Marx argued) automatically abolish the capitalist system. Marx's historical materialism (a combination of Darwin's evolutionary thinking, English economic theory and French Utopian socialism) provided both a model of sociological analysis and an imperative to political engagement for an entire generation of European political thinkers. Marx inspired figures as diverse as August Bebel and Karl Kautsky in Germany, Antonio Labriola in Italy, and Jean Jaurès in France. These great thinkers of the Social Democratic movement in Europe sought to marry, under the banner of revisionism, Marxist theory to a party-political pragmatism, hoping in the process (in Jaurès' words) to 'translate and incorporate the ideal of humanity into reality and history'.[8]

The literary response to the rise of industrial society was without the philosophical baggage of Marxism, but possessed, nevertheless, its own political acumen. Novels that engaged with contemporary social themes included, in England, Benjamin Disraeli's *Sybil, or, The Two Nations* (1845), Elizabeth Gaskell's *Mary Barton* (1848), and *North and South* (1855), Dickens's *Hard Times* (1854), and George Eliot's *Felix Holt* (1866); in France, Victor Hugo's *Les Misérables* (1862), J-K Huysmans' *The Vatard Sisters* (1879), Emile Zola's *L'Assommoir* (1877), and his *Germinal* (1885); in Germany, Gerhart Hauptmann's play, *The Weavers* (1892) and (with a focus upon colonial exploitation) the remarkable Dutch novel, *Max Havelaar* (1860) by Multatuli. These were all works of social conscience, which took to heart the plight of the dispossessed and the impoverished, the outcast and the persecuted. Certainly, there were differences of emphasis and style; the aristocratic Disraeli, with his social panacea of *noblesse oblige*, would have rubbed shoulders uncomfortably with that social historian of prostitutes and criminals, Zola; and likewise, the comic satire of Dickens would have meant little to the politically engaged young Gerhart Hauptmann, for whom the exploitation of the Silesian weavers was no laughing matter. But this literature shared a common trajectory, which was of its age; away from imagination and a utopian construction of the world through dream and fantasy, and towards a recognition, however reluctant, of the importance of material factors in human affairs. These writers describe the impingements, intellectual, moral and material, against which all must struggle and most must fail, their 'lamentations and tears' captured both objectively and, as in the work of Elizabeth Gaskell, often with genuine compassion.[9]

There was, however, a second body of literature whose engagement with the social sphere was certainly more oblique but, in its own way, equally effective. It included, in England, the writing of a group of artists and poets known as the Pre-Raphaelites: Dante Gabriel Rossetti (*Poems*, 1870), Christina Rossetti, *Goblin Market* (1862) and William Morris, *The Earthly Paradise* (1868–1870); and some of the work written by major poets such as Tennyson (*Poems*, 1830 and 1832) and Robert Browning (*The Ring and the Book*, 1869). This literature often evinced a nostalgia for a pre-modern, medieval past, whose values, spiritual, authentic and ornate, it juxtaposed to the 'philistinism of modern society', whose drive to standardisation and mass production these writers thoroughly rejected and even (as in the later writing of William Morris) politically repudiated. A similar critique was launched by writers in France such as Théophile Gautier (*Mademoiselle de Maupin*, 1835), Charles Baudelaire (*The Flowers of Evil*, 1857) and Stéphane Mallarmé, ('The Afternoon of a Faun', 1876), and by a group of poets known as the Parnassians, whose most notable names were Charles Leconte de Lisle (*Ancient Poems*, 1852), and Théodore de Banville (*Funambulist Odes*, 1857). Under the rubric of 'art for art's sake' (*l'art pour l'art*), these writers confronted the cultural and intellectual inanities of their *nouveau riche* public with an aesthetic of formal self-sufficiency, which denied all utility to the work of art, but stressed instead its transitory beauty and its contact with a higher realm. Their goal was to float free (as Gautier noted in his preface to *Mademoiselle de Maupin*) of the 'progressive, moralising, [and] palingenesic' tendencies of a society that had committed itself to material progress and consumerism.[10]

In spite of their aristocratic distance from the social realm, these advocates of aesthetic purity also bore witness to the problems of the modern age. Baudelaire's writing, in particular, such as *The Flowers of Evil*, and the prose works, *Artificial Paradise* (1860) and *Paris Spleen* (1869), reflects the ambiguous empowerments of urban existence, describing a world that is criss-crossed by criminals, the homeless and other denizens of a city 'where/everything – horror too – is magical'. It is a 'city gorged with dreams', its reality is a *sur*-reality, where ghost and vagrant, prostitute and nurse, exchange identities under its pallid gloom. Baudelaire's Paris, oscillating between fantasy and squalor, beauty and corruption, would have been hardly recognisable to Dickens; but it possesses the same elemental energies, transfiguring and destroying, which are found in Dickens's London or Dostoyevsky's Saint Petersburg, or in the cities described by the other great Realist writers. The poet's world is as amoral as it is indecipherable, except to the poet alive to the 'correspondences' that exist between the material and immaterial realms. In the city-scapes of Baudelaire, Realism (understood in the broadest sense of the term) emerges both as a style, a dispassionate and, at times, clinical rendering of the travails of disorientated interiority, and as a sombre pessimism regarding absolute values, religious, moral and personal. Coming to terms with the city produced in Baudelaire a spiritual emptiness and a lack of purpose that the poet called *ennui*. It was an emotion, vague but intense, that would become for many the sickness of the age.[11]

2   'ALL IS TRUE': THE AESTHETIC OF LITERARY REALISM

'The ideal is gone, lyricism has run dry. We are soberer. A severe, pitiless concern for truth, the most modern form of empiricism, has penetrated even into art', noted the critic, Charles Augustin Sainte-Beuve in 1857, writing, in effect, a valediction for the Romantic movement in France and Europe. What came in the place of that movement was a type of literature that aimed to integrate the external world into the text, breaking both with the visionary impetus of the Romantic writer, and with his confidence in the primacy of self. The emergence of Realism as a distinct literary discourse took place without the elaborate metaphysical and aesthetic deliberations that had accompanied the rise of Romanticism. When Balzac asserted in the opening pages of his novel, *Old Goriot* (1834), in an act of narrative self-justification: 'All is true' (words significantly uttered in the new *lingua franca* of scientific and philosophic prose, English) he was expressing not only the central tenet of the Realist aesthetic: its concern for verisimilitude, for probability, and for 'close observation and the careful reproduction of minute detail and local colour' (as the author went on to explain), but also the modest pre-theoretical nature of its artistic ambit: the world is simply there; we need only open our eyes to see and describe it.[12]

Not only Balzac but also those that followed him stressed the epistemological innocence of the Realist aesthetic. The operative terms of Romantic literature: 'imagination', 'fantasy', and 'dream', with which poets as diverse as Novalis, Coleridge and Blake had attempted to unite the objective and the subjective spheres, found their equivalents in the infinitely more passive mechanisms of 'reflection', 'mirror', and 'reproduction', terms which appeared wherever Realism required a theoretical defence. George Eliot, for example (who was an early adherent to the Realist movement, and a defender of its moral probity), declared in an interlude in *Adam Bede* (1859) that her aim in writing that novel had been 'to give no more than a faithful account of men and things as they have mirrored themselves in my mind'. These were sentiments echoed by many writers, such as Anthony Trollope, who typified his novels (*Barchester Towers*, 1857, and *The Last Chronicle of Barset*, 1867) as 'Realistic' because they embodied 'truth of description, truth of character'; whilst Stendhal, that most individualist of writers, and an author with at least one foot in the Romantic school, could, in one famous passage in his *Scarlet and Black* (1830), describe the novel itself simply as 'a mirror journeying down the high road'. Even George Sand, whose early novels *Indiana* (1832) and *Lélia* (1833) possess a clear social, and even feminist message, reached towards the metaphor of mimetic compliance in order to justify the critical focus of her work. As Sand argued in her preface to the first edition of *Indiana*, what she was trying to do in her fiction was neither to proselytise nor to provoke, but simply describe contemporary domestic *mores*. If such *mores* seemed to be entirely repressive of female identity and ambitions that was not her fault. For as she explained: 'the writer is no more than a mirror that reflects [such injustices], a machine that traces them; and he owes no one apologies if his prints are exact and his images faithful'.[13]

Many, however, felt liberated by the Realists' concern for objective truth and by their engagement with the modern world. The Danish scholar and critic, George Brandes, was one such person. He was the foremost spokesman of the Realist movement in his country, and responsible for inspiring writers throughout Scandinavia, such as the playwright Bjørnstjerne Bjørnson (*The Editor*, 1874, and *Beyond our Power*, 1883), and the novelist Alexander Kielland (*Working People*, 1881), to broaden the focus of their work, and look outwards towards Europe for the great issues of the day, rather than inwards, towards parochial or purely national concerns.

In his major studies, *Main Currents in Nineteenth-Century Literature* (first published in 1871), and *The Men of the Modern Breakthrough* (1883), Brandes launched himself into a 'struggle for freedom and modern enlightenment', into whose cause he enlisted writers of the Realist school, and most notably the great Norwegian dramatist, Henrik Ibsen. In Ibsen, Brandes found an author who was committed to the 'new life that will rise out of social convulsions'. His plays were (Brandes noted in enthusiastic words)s 'in contact with the fundamental ideas of the age', and hence will live forever; for 'the modern is not the ephemeral, but the flame of life itself, the vital spark, the soul of an age.'[14]

Realism, regarded both as a style of writing and as a preference for certain types of subject matter, became the dominant literary mode in mid-nineteenth-century Europe. It is apparent even in the work of writers who held themselves distant from the theoretical debates and controversies that the new literary discourse gave rise to. They include some of the greatest novelists of the age: Balzac, Flaubert and Maupassant, in France; Dostoyevsky, Tolstoy, Turgenev and Gogol, in Russia; Manzoni and Verga, in Italy; Keller, Stifter and Fontane, in German-speaking countries; through to Pérez Galdós and Pereda, in Spain; and Dickens, George Eliot and Trollope, in England. For these writers, the Romanticism espoused by the preceding generation was at best redundant, at worst a distracting irrelevance in an era faced by an entirely new set of social, political and ethical challenges. To depict these, the writer had to move away from the focus upon self and subjectivity, and acquire a greater sense of compassion and understanding for those who live in the mundane world. In this respect, at least, George Eliot spoke for many in her essay on the pre-Romantic poet, Edward Young (author of *Night Thoughts on Life, Death and Immortality*, 1742–1745). Young, she argued, embodied the worst aspects of the Romantic taste for fantasy and self-absorption, which preferred an 'imaginary journey amongst the stars' to the realities of the here and now. 'That impiety towards the present and the visible' meant that Young was incapable of 'moral emotion', that facility to divine the spiritual depths that lie hidden in the affections and feelings of ordinary people, a realm that Eliot had committed herself to exploring in her own fiction. Such reservations regarding the limitations of the Romantic mind, with its tenuous grasp on the world of recognisable reality, were shared by all the major Realist writers; even Balzac (whose novels indisputably exude their own extravagant energy) criticised the prevailing taste for melodrama, for those extravagant situations and 'terrible sensations' that the reading public had come to expect in the wake of popularised Romanticism.[15]

Few Realist writers sought to ground their writing in a consciously formulated 'Realist' aesthetic, although there were exceptions. George Eliot (once again) wrote a substantial justification for Realism in her review of the writings of the art historian and critic, John Ruskin, whom she saw as expounding 'the doctrine that all truth and beauty are to be attained by a humble and faithful study of nature, and not by substituting vague forms, bred by imagination on the mists of feeling, in place of definite, substantial reality'. The German novelist, Theodor Fontane, came to similar conclusions in his 1853 essay 'Our Lyric and Epic Poetry since 1848', as did the Spanish writer Benito Pérez Galdós, who saw in Realism the sole literary form capable of capturing 'the present-day social situation with all its confusion and nervous disquietude'. Even Thomas Hardy, whose epic novels of character and environment (such as *Tess of the d'Urbervilles*, 1891, *Jude the Obscure*, 1895) seem to possess a timeless tragic dimension, also committed himself to a form of Realism, albeit one that could 'distinguish truths which are temporary from truths which are eternal, the accidental from the essential, accuracies as to custom and ceremony from accuracies as to the perennial procedure of humanity'.[16]

The most systematic attempts to formulate a theory of Realism came, however, from France. And it is significant that from the very first the movement was associated with the pictorial arts, and not philosophy, which had been (particularly in Germany, but also in England, through Coleridge) the discipline that had underpinned Romanticism. For Realism was essentially epistemological rather than metaphysical in its ambit; it was concerned with perspective, ways of viewing the world, rather than with speculations about God, death and the meaning of life. So much is clear in the first theoretical formulation of Realism, which came from the pen of the critic, Jules Husson (otherwise known as Champfleury). Written in defence of the work of the painter Gustave Courbet (whose paintings, exhibited in a private collection in 1855, had shocked a Parisian public accustomed to the conservative Salon style of Classicists or the sentimental idealisations of the Romantics), Champfleury's manifesto drew attention to the modest goals of Courbet's art: its simple aim to 'represent the customs, the ideas, the appearance of [his] times', without prejudice or value judgement. As the critic later argued in a collection of essays simply titled *Realism* (1857), Courbet had extended the range of great art by including in his paintings figures normally deemed unworthy of artistic treatment. Captives of misery, socially outcast and common in appearance, such lowly figures attain in Courbet's paintings (and the critic is thinking here of works such as 'The Funeral at Ornans', 1850) not only a dignity and vitality which transfigures their poverty, but also a representative value that transforms them into agents of Courbet's 'tactile allegory' (*allégorie réelle*). By focussing upon the here and now, and upon the materials that surround us in the ordinary world, Realism has made possible, Champfleury contended, the expansion of the aesthetic into the social.[17]

Champfleury's enthusiasm, however, was not shared by all. There were many detractors from the Realist ethos, and none more enigmatic than Gustave Flaubert. His position with regard to, and within, the Realist movement is a paradoxical one: his novel *Madame Bovary* (1857) embodies many of the classic traits of the Realist style: narrative objectivity, a focus upon the banal and quotidian, an accurate reconstruction of *milieu*, and, above all, a fundamental pessimism regarding the ability of the individual to assert him (and, more particularly, her) self in the face of an uncomprehending and indifferent world. And yet, Flaubert repeatedly distanced himself from the Realist movement, rejecting it on account of its 'materialism' and populist tendencies. Equally dismissive was the poet Baudelaire who, in his famous review of *Madame Bovary*, a novel praised for its *transfiguration* of reality, called Realism 'a degrading insult flung in the face of all analytical writers, a vague and over flexible term applied by indiscriminate minds to the minute description of detail rather than to a new method of literary creation'. The reservations of Baudelaire and Flaubert (uncompromisingly élitist in their aesthetic standards) were, however, balanced by expressions of support for the Realist project from other French writers, who felt artistically liberated by Realism, and stressed the new possibilities unleashed by the widening scope of subject matter that growing urbanisation and industrialisation had made possible. For writers such as Edmond and Jules de Goncourt, Guy de Maupassant and Émile Zola, the Realist (or, as it was soon to be named, the Naturalist) novel provided an exemplary medium in which a 'social examination' of contemporary society might, through 'analysis and psychological research', be carried out, allowing the novel to reach the status of 'contemporary moral history'. With the Realist novel (the Goncourts concluded), literature had finally come to undertake 'the studies and obligations of science'.[18]

The Goncourts' reference to science was neither incidental nor accidental. The Romantics had based their conceptual framework on the German Idealism of Kant, Schelling and Schleiermacher, who had largely construed the world as the product of hermeneutic interpretation, the result of the active and creative agency of self. The Realists, however, looked to an entirely different set of thinkers, not philosophers but sociologists, economists, psychologists, architects of the new 'sciences humaines', who believed not in the ethereal workings of subjectivity but in the mechanical, the deterministic, and the quantifiable. The most influential figures were Auguste Comte (sociology), Charles Darwin (evolutionary theory), Thomas Huxley (eugenics), Karl Marx (political economy) and Hippolyte Taine (intellectual history). In France, it was Comte who provided the most conspicuous paradigm: Positivism. In his *Course in Positivist Philosophy* (1830–1842), he wrote fulsomely about the victorious march of science, which had come to replace firstly theology and then metaphysics as the dominant mode of knowledge in the Western world. Comte's insistence that true, 'Positive' knowledge can only be based on observable facts, on 'natural laws, the discovery of which, and their reduction to the least possible number, is the aim and end of all our efforts', received further elaboration through Ernest Renan and Hippolyte Taine, who showed how the Positive method could be applied to the realm of ideas and matters as intangible as culture and art. In his famous introduction to *A History of English Literature* (4 vols, 1863–1864), Taine argued that a work of literature could be explained by reference to three conditioning factors: the racial identity of the author (*la race*), his social, political and geographical environment (*le milieu*), and the historical juncture at which he wrote (*le moment*). Here, environmental determinism, which had been an assumption throughout Comte's work, was developed into a full-blown methodology. Taine's assertion that 'vice and virtue are products like vitriol and sugar' became a catchphrase for a generation of writers seeking to distance themselves from the idealism of the Romantic tradition.[19]

Almost all the great novelists of the nineteenth century came within the ambit of this new scientific spirit, none more so than Balzac. As he made clear in the preface to his novel sequence *The Human Comedy* (published between 1830 and 1847), Balzac hoped to reproduce in the area of literature the insights won by contemporary scientists, such as Geoffroi Saint-Hilaire and Charles Bonnet, in the areas of zoology and natural history. Just as they had classified the animal kingdom into a taxonomy of types, so too would Balzac attempt to classify the 'human animal', detailing how it behaves within the social sphere, following 'the rudiments of the great law of Self for Self, which lies at the root of *Unity of Plan*', and which organises all animal life around urges of self-preservation, self-aggrandizement and material acquisition. In carrying out these scientific goals, the novelist becomes (Balzac assures us, alluding to his own project) not only a 'narrator of the dramas of private life, an archaeologist of social furniture, a cataloguer of professions, [and] a registrar of good and evil', but also an analyst and discloser of the 'causes' that bring these 'social effects' into being.[20]

Other novelists influenced by scientific thinking included George Eliot, Theodor Fontane and Ivan Turgenev. The attitude of Eliot to the growth of scientism and to its application to the social sphere was complex and by no means entirely positive. She remained alive throughout her life to the potentially destabilising effect of scientific theory upon religious and ethical values. Nevertheless, Eliot was also able to appreciate the importance of the work carried out by scientists and naturalists, for example Charles Lyell (*Principles of Geology*, 1830–1833), whose organicist methodology she saw as demonstrating 'the working of laws by which the earth has become adapted for the habitation of man', a reading that was to influence the way Eliot described her characters and how they relate to their environments. Fontane's greatest influence was Ludwig Feuerbach. The latter's anthropological theology (formulated in *The Essence of Christianity*, 1841), which took its cue not from ideas or spiritual values but 'from the *opposite* of thought, from Matter, from existence, from the senses', formed a central part of Fontane's own humanism and an essential part of his Realist art. The Russian Realist, Turgenev, on the other hand, took the contrary path, away from the empiricist humanism of Eliot and Fontane, towards a darker, less optimistic encounter with the new scientific spirit of the age. His mentor was Vissarion Belinsky, the major viaduct in mid-nineteenth-century Russia for Western ideas, an exponent of 'science, progress, humanity, [and] civilisation'. Turgenev, however, became increasingly disaffected with the cult of scientific inquiry, believing, as he made clear in his famous novel, *Fathers and Sons* (1862), that the rationalist-analytical ethos had degenerated into an arro-

gant and nihilistic credo, which was being used by Russian youth
(such as the hero of that novel, Bazarov) to support its destructive
campaign against tradition and natural piety.[21]

No such doubts, however, beset the French writer, Émile Zola.
His work represents the most ambitious attempt made in the nineteenth century to combine literature with scientific inquiry. In his
extended novel series, the *Rougon-Macquart* cycle (published
between 1871 and 1893), Zola set out not only to paint a detailed
picture of life in the Second Empire (much as Balzac had done for
Restoration France), but also to demonstrate his faith in a fundamentally new way of conceptualising behaviour and human character. Zola took his cue from the French behaviourist, Claude
Bernard, who had argued in his *Introduction to the Study of
Experimental Medicine* (1865) that psychology should be seen not
only as a mental process, but also as an expression of physiology,
being a product of the biological and genetic make-up of the individual. Such theories, it is true, were not new (Taine had elaborated
his own views on environmental determinism several years
earlier). What was original was the demonstrated quality of
Bernard's work: its detailing of the personal and medical connections between social generality and the specificity of individual
behaviour, which combine, according to Bernard, to make possible
a composite science of 'physiology, pathology and therapeutics'.
Out of this methodology, Zola developed his 'experimental novel',
the terms of which he outlined in the famous preface to the second
edition of his *Thérèse Raquin* (1867), and in essays such as *The
Experimental Novel* (1880). Here we learn that great novelists, such
as Balzac, do not simply 'photograph' reality, but seek to uncover
the deeper causes, rules and laws which govern behaviour. As Zola
explains: for the novelist, 'the whole operation consists in taking
facts from nature, then studying the mechanisms of the data by
acting on them through a modification of circumstances and environment without ever departing from the laws of nature. At
the end, there is knowledge, scientific knowledge, of man in his
individual and social action'.[22]

Zola's Naturalist method represented the culmination of the
Realist aesthetic in the nineteenth century. The clinical objectivity of
his writing, and the focus upon previously taboo areas of experi-
ence, influenced an entire generation of writers, from Gerhart
Hauptmann (*Before Sunrise*, 1889) in Germany, through to George
Gissing (*New Grub Street*, 1891) in England, Henrik Ibsen (*Ghosts*,

1882) in Norway, and August Strindberg (*The Father*, 1887) in Sweden. In their work, Realism elides into a complex social philosophy, deterministic, Darwinistic, and fatalistic. The growing dominance of the social sphere over the personal, a process that the great Realist novelists charted in France, England and Russia, has now been fully internalised by characters whose very psychological coherence and sense of self have been destroyed by the irremediable effects of syphilis, alcoholism or genetic weakness. As Strindberg noted with respect to his own problematical creations: 'living in a period of transition more feverishly hysterical than its predecessor', these 'heroes', 'vacillating, disintegrated', 'scraps of humanity', the products of a cheap and debased culture, no longer possess the heroic grandeur of Julien Sorel or Emma Bovary (who at least harboured the desire to be individuals), but face the world convinced from the very start of the hopeless nature of human action and the redundancy of all ideals, social, political and ethical. With such characters, we reach the end of the Realist trajectory, and the beginning of a new one, called Modernism. Its major exponents, such as Thomas Mann, Marcel Proust and Virginia Woolf, will attempt, modestly and not without philosophical reservations, to re-invest the individual with a modicum of self-determination and intellectual self-sufficiency, reclaiming in their work the viability of subjective experience out of the apparently unfathomable depths into which it had been placed a generation before by the exponents of the Naturalist method.[23]

3 'LOST ILLUSIONS': REALISM AND THE EXPERIENCE OF THE CITY

The Realist project begins and ends with the experience of the city. Real or imagined, delimiting or exhilarating, complex or monolithic, the city dominated the imagination of almost every writer in the nineteenth century. Balzac had Paris, sometimes evoked as the site of Darwinian struggle, sometimes as that 'shining world' of prosperity and rewards, whose bounty the youthful Rastignac (hero of *Old Goriot*) commits himself to possessing, even by sexual force (and whose criminal underworld had been explored, even celebrated by Eugène Sue in his best-selling *The Mysteries of Paris*, 1843). Dostoyevsky felt haunted by the infinitely more sinister, almost Kafkaesque world of St. Petersburg, 'the most abstract, the most deviously-minded, city on this terrestrial sphere of ours', whose dark corners and labyrinthine ways (moral and geographical) he explored in *Letters from the Underground* (1864) and *Crime and Punishment* (1866). Dickens had London, a world of sombre contrast between poverty and wealth, destitution and achievement; but also a pulsating metropolis, a commercial, administrative and industrial centre, and part of the 'mighty course of civilisation and improvement' that defined progress in the nineteenth century. And Jan Neruda (the most accomplished Czech novelist of this period) explored the city of Prague, caught somewhere in time between the medieval period and early modernity, in his *Tales of the Little Quarter* (1878). Even in those novels set in the countryside or in the provinces, such as Flaubert's *Madame Bovary* and Fontane's *Effi Briest*, the city is often present, not as a material reality, but as a set of internalised values, dreams, wish-fulfilments and fantasies. These heroines, such as Effi in Fontane's novel, are fired by 'a deep longing' to escape from the limitations of patriarchal conservative society, wishing to flee to the city, in whose cosmopolitanism and exotic culture they dimly glimpse the chance for autonomy and self-realisation.[24]

The Realist novelist could hardly have avoided confrontation with the city. Between 1802 (the year of publication of Novalis's *Henry from Ofterdingen*, and Coleridge's 'Dejection'), and 1881 (the year in which Flaubert published his last novel, *Bouvard and Pécuchet*), the major cities of Europe went through a process of massive and unparalleled expansion: London grew from a population of 864 000 to 3.3 million; Paris, from 547 000 to 2.2 million; and Berlin, from 183 000 to 1.1 million. With these increases came a plethora of industrial, social, and medical problems, whose impact upon the social fabric of the nation seriously threatened to undermine the ethical and political communality of societies that had (as Ferdinand Tönnies argued in his *Community and Society*, 1887) broken with the traditional ties of pre-modern Europe without finding an alternative source of order and legitimation. In England, it was Dickens who engaged most directly with the problems associated with the changing social and physical environment of a swiftly urbanising nation. Dickens's attitude to the city was a complex and, ultimately, ambiguous one. He shared the concern of humanists such as Godwin and Carlyle with the factory poor and the destitute, focussing, in particular, upon the *Lumpenproletariat*, those dark figures of Victorian life, who, living on the edge of society, subsisted either on crime or charity. He also documented how the 'labouring classes' (upon whose energies, after all, England's rapid industrial transformation had been based) were treated with scant respect, forced to lead abject lives amidst 'foul smells, disgusting habitations, bad workshops and workshop customs, want of light, air, and water, the absence of all easy means of decency and health'. In *Oliver Twist* (1838) and *Bleak House* (1853), Dickens injected into his account of urban poverty a tactile immediacy, a feel for the colours, smells, and sounds of deprivation, which was to make him famous throughout Europe, and encourage writers as diverse as Maupassant and Dostoyevksy to acknowledge him as the master of urban Realism. But, as *Hard Times* (1854) demonstrated, Dickens was also aware of the political, social and even intellectual causes of this deprivation. The novel is a bitter satire upon the ethos of Utilitarianism, but also (by implication at least) upon the profit motive, increasing industrialisation and the mindless accumulation of wealth upon which the economy of nineteenth-century England was based. Uncaring in its impact and rigid in its application, *laissez-faire* liberalism had produced an industrial system both inhuman and chaotic, its curious combination of functionalism and anarchy writ large in the 'wilderness of smoke and brick', that 'dense formless jumble' which oppresses the inhabitants of Coketown.[25]

And yet even here all is not loss; for running in tandem with Dickens's bleak analysis of industrialised England was both a recognition of the importance of modernisation, and an admiration for its material achievements, evident in the new buildings, roads and railways that were coming to dominate the urban landscape. This is less obvious in *Hard Times* (whose focus is not London but the monotonous industrial North), but it forms an essential element of novels such as *Dombey and Son* (1848) and *Our Mutual Friend* (1865). The former, in particular, retrieves the city as the place of dynamic movement, of progress, whose material advances Dickens welcomed even as he despaired of their human cost to society. None can resist those vital energies that exist at the 'heart of this great change'; those 'throbbing currents' of the new age: electricity, the railway and entrepreneurial zeal. They disrupt and displace, but provide, nevertheless, the city with 'its life's blood', without which the modern world cannot live or prosper.[26]

The city opened up possibilities for some, as it closed them down for others, providing the social site for that evolutionary struggle

that Herbert Spencer and others saw as an inescapable component
of the life process. And this is how Balzac depicted his Paris of the
Second Empire (French society between 1815 and 1848) in his compendious *Human Comedy*: not as Dickens had done, as an industrial,
urban reality which put human kind and human values in danger
simply through the expansion of its internal logic, but as a sphere
of moral and immoral action, the source of a bewildering array of
ethical, financial and sexual challenges that the individual must
meet if he or she is not to go under. Like other great Realist novelists, Balzac also described his city with detail and accuracy, believing in the determining nature of the material environment to which
he tied his characters (as in the description of Grandet's house in
Eugénie Grandet, 1833) in a process of symbolic symbiosis; but his
gaze (as his near contemporaries, the brothers Goncourt observed)
was also capable of penetrating beneath the surface of urban
society, of uncovering its underlying values and mores: 'the fact
beneath the word, the anarchy of unbridled interests beneath the
apparent order in the competition of talents'. Balzac's world was
that of nascent bourgeois France, which witnessed 'abuses replaced
by influences, privileges by more privileges, [and] equality before
the law annihilated by inequality before'; in other words, the a-
ristocracy of birth replaced by the plutocracy of money. Balzac was
both the semi-official historian of this society, and one of its
greatest admirers.[27]

The focus upon wealth, the struggle for its acquisition, and the
moral sacrifices that must be made in the process, appears in each
of the subdivisions into which Balzac divided his novelistic output:
'scenes from private life', 'scenes from provincial life', 'scenes from
Parisian life', 'scenes from political life', 'scenes from military life',
and 'scenes from country life'. This was a sequence of novels,
written in a style that captured the forward momentum of city life,
its bustle and barely containable energy, with verve and empathy,
and which, read in conjunction with his 'philosophical studies' and
'analytical studies', provided a picture of life in nineteenth-century
France which the Marxist philosopher, Friedrich Engels (amongst
others) held to be 'superior to all purely historical accounts of the
period'. The most noted novels in the series: *Eugénie Grandet* (1833),
Old Goriot, Lost Illusions (1837–1843) and *Cousine Bette* (1847), articulate their own version of *Realpolitik*, seen now not as the political or
military ethos of *force majeure*, but as a form of moral pragmatism in
the social and personal spheres. As the criminal Vautrin advises in

Old Goriot: 'Paris, you see, is like a forest in the New World, where you have to deal with a score of varieties of savages – Illinois and Hurans, who live on the proceeds of their social hunting'. It is a lesson that all of Balzac's heroes must learn, such as Lucien de Rubempré in the aptly named *Lost Illusions*, who comes to Paris dreaming of art, to discover that nothing (written or made) has value beyond its market price: lyrical poetry must needs survive as journalism. Lucien recognises the new rules of the game, but fails, ultimately, to master them, returning to his provincial origins in a mood of despair that brings him to the brink of suicide. Where de Rubempré fails, the young Eugene de Rastignac, the hero of *Old Goriot*, succeeds. As a witness to misplaced paternal love and daughterly avariciousness, he soon learns that simple moral virtues are out of place in a world that prizes status over duty, wealth over faith, and social extravagance over honour. In the famous last scene of the novel, looking out beyond the fresh grave of Goriot to the glittering night-scape of Paris, Balzac's young hero commits himself, in a gesture of typical bravado, to mastering this society, winning from her, through an act of 'pillage', the rewards that she has to offer.[28]

Balzac and Dickens provided the two poles around which the connection between the novel and society was formed in the nineteenth century. Writers such as William Makepeace Thackeray (*Vanity Fair*, 1848), Anthony Trollope (*The Way We Live Now*, 1875) and George Meredith (*The Egoist*, 1879), in England; Wilhelm Raabe (*Chronicle of Sparrow Lane*, 1857) and Gustav Freytag (*Debit and Credit*, 1855), in Germany; and Pérez Galdós (*Fortunata and Jacinta*, 1887), Leopoldo Alas (*La Regenta*, 1885) and Eça de Queiróz (*The Maias*, 1888), in Spain and Portugal, followed Dickens and Balzac in exploring the political and financial *mores* of their times. Their novels highlight the complex relationship between property, marriage and social advancement in the age of the amoral careerist and *parvenu*. And yet, for all the complications that define the personal and social tensions evoked in these novels (complications frequently reflected in their convoluted plot structures and elaborate character networks), the social problems that these texts explored were (so to speak) of a linear rather than a vertical nature; they exist upon the surface of a world whose values, fought over, disputed and contested, belong, nevertheless, to the clear-cut priorities of money, power and sex. Elsewhere, however, in the nineteenth-century novel, the city provided the context for the emergence of a set of deeper, more obscure values, which dwelt not on the centre stage of bourgeois society, but in its wings. The novelists who engaged with these values focussed not upon the material component of urban culture, but upon its effect upon personal identity, and when they spoke about the loss of illusions, they were referring not to the failure of an individual to secure his or her place in the world, but to that widespread feeling of alienation and disorientation that was coming to dominate the modern consciousness. Dickens had given glimpses of this structure of feeling in his depictions of the criminals, social outcasts and problematic natures who circulate in a shadowy way throughout his corpus; Baudelaire likewise had seen a certain majesty in the 'poetry of evil' that emanated from the *demi-monde* of his native Paris, whose sordid inclinations he had transformed through a highly personal aesthetic of symbolic correspondences. But it is only in the work of the three great Russian Realists, Ivan Turgenev, Nikolai Gogol and Fyodor Dostoyevsky that (in Baudelaire's words) 'man approaches his bestial metamorphosis', banned from the moral city to re-emerge on the edges of society as criminal, madman or saint.[29]

Turgenev's *Fathers and Sons* focusses upon a character who represents this particular direction within European Realism: the young nihilist, Yevgeny Bazarov. He is a representative of new Russian youth; confrontational, analytic and aggressive, he lives his life in 'the absolute and ruthless repudiation' of existing social norms, dismissive of all form of authority, personal and intellectual. Certainly, the notion of generational conflict was not new to the Realist novel. The major Hungarian novelist of this period, András Fáy, had written precisely about this theme in his epic study of social manners, *The House of Bélteky* (1832). Turgenev's interests are, however, philosophical rather than domestic. Set at a critical moment in Russian history, when medieval serfdom is giving way to modern liberalism, *Fathers and Sons* uses the figure of Bazarov, and his clash with the paternalistic conservative Nikolai Kirsanov, to dramatise the tensions and contradictions within the Russian propertied classes. The latter are caught between delusions of grandeur and a debilitating perception of their own worthlessness; between spirituality and rationality; between a commitment to progress and an innate scepticism regarding the value of all material works. The result is a peculiar form of inertia and spiritual turpitude, a mental set that came to be identified with one Russian protagonist, above all: the character Oblomov from the novel of the same name by Ivan Alexander Goncharov, published in 1859. But long before Goncharov's novel arrived on the scene, the same vagaries of the Russian soul had been depicted in the epic allegorical masterpiece, *Dead Souls* (1842), by Gogol. The title refers to the names of deceased serfs that the grasping hero of the novel, Chichikov, acquires in order to bolster the financial assets of his own estate. But the novel (left incomplete at Gogol's death) uses this Realist cue purely as a pretext for an extensive description, executed in exuberant and fantastic detail, of the individuals, classes and functionaries who thrived in the rural Russia of autocratic Tsar Nicholas I, and of the greed, cynicism, and ignorance that are the dominant values in that society. Many of the events described in Gogol's novel border upon the absurd, and, as such, represent an extension of the peculiar logic of disembodied consciousness that the author first explored in 'Diary of a Madman' (1835), 'The Nose' (1836) and 'The Overcoat' (1842). These stories introduce a new type of hero into European literature. The characters in these stories belong to the underworld of the self; the anonymous hero of the 'Diary of a Madman' calls himself an 'absolute *nobody*', and he means the term to be understood not only in social terms, but existentially, as a definition of a personality that lacks any sense of continuity of self. They define themselves purely through negativities: madness, pain and (as in the case of Akaky Akakievich in 'The Coat'), that 'feeling of dread' which borders upon the psychotic, often leaving the world as they enter it, without real identity, their downfalls or deaths left unobserved and unremembered.[30]

Gogol's stories sketch the contours of a type of alienated subjectivity that would only be fully developed in the novels of the greatest Russian Realist: Fyodor Dostoyevsky. The moral relativism, intellectual nihilism and psychological insecurities explored by Turgenev and Gogol in their fiction found in Dostoyevsky's *Crime and Punishment* (1866), *The Idiot* (1869), *The Devils* (1871), and *The Brothers Karamazov* (1880) their most systematic treatment. The problems faced by the anonymous protagonist of the early *Letters from the Underground* (1864) is typical of the plight that confronts all of Dostoyevsky's heroes. He is 'a man of the nineteenth century', the product of an urban culture (in this case St. Petersburg), in which the firm convictions of an older rural past have given way amongst many of its inhabitants to insecurity, introversion and aboulia. A radical non-conformist, the man from the underground rejects all attempts to alleviate his misery. Degradation is the key note in the self-image of this figure, which he drains to the full, enjoying that 'pleasure in a consciousness of his self-abasement', cultivating those 'unsatisfied wishes that for ever penetrate inwards.'[31]

At one point in his confessional narrative, the man from the underground explains his personal philosophy: 'I wish, in particular, to try whether one can *ever* be really open with oneself – *ever* be really fearless of any item of truth.' The issue of the ethical consequences not only of truth-saying but also of truth-doing informs Dostoyevsky's entire *oeuvre*. It characterises the dialectic the author sets up between sin and expiation, in *Crime and Punishment*, between social dejection and moral idealism, in *The Idiot*, or between atheism and the emotional need for spiritual transcendence, as explored in *The Brothers Karamazov*. All of these novels chart a path through a world dominated by the darkness created by scientific rationalism and ethical nihilism. But they do not leave us there; as with Nietzsche and Kierkegaard (with whom he had clear affinities), Dostoyevsky often compels his characters and his readers to confront darkness that they may recognise the minimal existence of light. In this sense, his novels, in spite of their apparent pessimism, possess a positive core: they are attempts to win through (against the obvious lessons of Realism) to a new vision of a mankind, one which will see it re-born out of its sufferings and its despair, prepared to meet the future, open to the possibilities of 'gradual regeneration' and of 'initiation into a new unknown life'.[32]

4   THE LIMITS OF SUBJECTIVITY: THE (FEMALE) SELF AND THE REALIST NOVEL

By 1815, the Napoleonic era had come to an end, and with it the period of revolutionary turmoil in European politics. In the age that was to follow, the radical politics of the *sans culottes* would give way to stability and order, military expansionism to religion, rampant individualism to *Realpolitik*, and a *rapprochement* would take place between a striving self-assertive bourgeois class and a precariously restored aristocracy. The closest observer of this age of transition was also the first major novelist of the Realist movement: Henri Beyle, known as Stendhal. In his *The Charterhouse of Parma* (1839), Stendhal had depicted the historical transformation of the Napoleonic era, sketching the political and military events that had helped bring that age to an end. In his most famous novel, *Scarlet and Black* (1830), he engages with the same theme, not directly, but, symbolically, through the fate of the hero of that novel, the young *parvenu*, Julien Sorel. Sorel is one of the great representative characters of the early nineteenth century: with his elemental energy and force of personality, he clearly looks back both to the Byronic hero of European Romanticism, and to the revolutionary *élan* embodied in the French revolutionaries and Napoleon. That age has, however (as Sorel soon realises), irrevocably gone. The dominant values now emanate not from the imperious and charismatic Emperor, but from the calculating statesmanship of Metternich and his ilk. Sorel becomes accordingly a child of his times, socially mobile, cynical, and manipulative, donning the black of the ecclesiastical cassock over the scarlet of the soldier, giving full rein to those 'transports of the most unbridled ambition', which propel him out of his *petit bourgeois* background and into the new world of social privilege and aristocratic favour.[33]

Sorel lives between the two poles of Romantic self-assertiveness and cynical Realism, without ever reconciling them. In spite of his own mercurial rise, he ultimately becomes a victim both of the irrational and unpremeditated assertiveness that adheres to the former mode (and which is exemplified in his attempted murder of his former mistress), and of the moral relativism of the latter, where notions such as sincerity and play-acting, truth and fiction, have become irretrievably intertwined. Even as his execution approaches, Stendhal's hero remains unable to see that the 'charlatanism' and 'hypocrisy' (with which he claims to have been surrounded throughout his life) are, in fact, facets of his own personality, products of a careerist mind that has sought to reach its objectives not only through the exercise of will-power and sexual charm, but also (as Madame de Renal laconically notes) by making 'use of phrases from novels', the other source of Sorel's rhetorical assertion of self.[34]

Julien Sorel awaits his execution and dies in a spirit of defiance, refusing all offers of mediation, viewing himself as a victim of that 'middle-class aristocracy', which has become the new ruling class in post-revolutionary France. In spite of his chosen tragic mode, Sorel does, however, come to understand that in the age of Realism, Romantic individualism is no longer capable of negotiating the limits that society imposes upon all acts of self-assertion. In this respect, at least, Stendhal's hero anticipated the plight of many who would follow him, and who would likewise find themselves on the

wrong side of history, or on the wrong side of an increasingly dog-
matic bourgeois society: artists, criminals and women. Women, in
particular, found that the libertarian political ethos espoused by
men during the revolutionary period meant quite the opposite
when applied in the domestic sphere. As Stendhal noted elsewhere,
women in post-revolutionary France were victims of educational
and cultural 'ignorance', and unable to escape through legal and
moral restraint from unhappy marriages held together by 'fear of
hellfire and religious sentiments'. Their predicament was to form a
recurring point of focus in many of the most notable novels of the
nineteenth century: George Sand's *Indiana* (1832), Carl Almquist's
Sara Videbeck (1839), Charlotte Brontë's *Jane Eyre* (1847), Gustave
Flaubert's *Madame Bovary* (1857), Leo Tolstoy's *Anna Karenina*
(1877), Luigi Capuana's *Giacinta* (1879, revised 1885), Benito Pérez
Galdós' *Fortunata and Jacinta* (1887), Thomas Hardy's *Tess of the
d'Urbervilles* (1891), Theodor Fontane's *Effi Briest* (1895), and
Frederik van Eeden's *The Deeps of Deliverance* (1900). These novels
raise issues which go well beyond the domestic sphere, with its
necessarily narrow focus upon courtship, marriage, and property,
to engage with matters that centre on the rights and possibilities of
the individual for intellectual and emotional self-realisation in a
period that increasingly seemed to legitimise conservative values
and the status quo. Some of these novels were penned in a spirit of
revolt against such values. George Sand, for example, spoke in the
1832 preface to her *Indiana* of the 'powerful instinct of protest'
against patriarchal power, which led her to pit her heroine against
'the injustice and barbarity of those laws which still govern women
in marriage, in the family, and in society'. Sand continued to write
in defiance of such laws, celebrating the noble efforts of her female
protagonists, 'the powers of [whose] souls are drained in the ruthless combat with the reality of life'.[35]

And yet, the final message of *Indiana* is a conservative one: the
heroine of Sand's novel survives by replacing one husband with
another, resolving her sexual crisis by marrying the man who has
helped free her from matrimonial control. In offering the reader
such an ending, Sand leaves the institution of patriarchy both un-
explained and intact. This is also the final effect of Brontë's *Jane
Eyre*, and Pérez Galdós' *Fortunata and Jacinta* (which, together with
Leopoldo Alas' *La Regenta*, formed the pinnacle of Realism in
Spain). *Jane Eyre* disperses its feminine consciousness across not
one but two female protagonists: Jane Eyre herself, who is an

orphan, and displaced thus from social centrality; and the 'mad woman in the attic', who is the lawful wife of Mr Rochester, but unable to play out her domestic role in his life. In the end, Jane comes to bridge these inclusive-exclusive notions of female identity, becoming (almost literally) a part of her new, but blind husband, encumbered with the duty of mediating between him and the world, a task which she fulfils without 'painful shame or damping humiliation'. Fortunata and Jacinta, in Pérez Galdós' novel, likewise represent two alternative models of female identity: Fortunata is a girl of the people, warm, spontaneous, an earth mother; Jacinta, middle-class, closed to experience, and infertile. What they have in common is their affiliation to the spoilt, but self-confident bourgeois, Juanito Santa Cruz, Jacinta's husband and Fortunata's lover. The novel revolves around this triangular relationship, and around the moral, familial and legal complications that it engenders. Fortunata never escapes the social stigma of her origins, and the restraining bonds of society are as clear in this novel as they are in the other great Realist novels of the nineteenth century; but Fortunata does finally find acceptance on her own terms, her transgressions tolerated by a conservative Catholic Spain where motherhood and the nurturing values of traditional femininity are invested with a quasi-religious mystique. As her husband Maxi explains at the end of the novel, after Jacinta's burial, it is nature, not society, which is the final arbiter of human destiny, that 'grand mother and teacher who rectifies the errors of those of her children who go astray'.[36]

Other heroines in the Realist novel experienced the confrontation between the potency of femininity and the containing nature of bourgeois morality with a greater, even tragic intensity. The social and ethical terms of this confrontation were most fully explored in Tolstoy's *Anna Karenina*, and Fontane's *Effi Briest*. The protagonists of these novels represent two divergent modes of female subjectivity: Effi is a confused mixture of naive romanticism and proprietorial pragmatism, who embraces the liberating potential of marriage to an older husband of status and wealth in a confused mixture of 'love of pleasure and ambition'. Anna is a more substantial personality, self-questioning and self-liberating, and possessed by a greater sense of her personal identity. Where the two converge is not only in the personal sources of their misery (which they seek to survive through adultery), but in the ways that they come, at the end of their sorry tales, to internalise the patriarchal values that they have spent the greater part of their lives either consciously (Anna) or unconsciously (Effi) struggling against. What Effi and Anna must learn is that ethical values and social customs, embedded in religious, political and family institutions are not simply minor obstacles to be overcome through a wilful and self-confident assertion of self, but are institutions which confine and, ultimately, define individual agency. Effi does eventually come to understand that the search for personal happiness is a form of egotistical utopianism, because it neglects 'that *something* which forms society': in this case, a Prussian code of honour that compels Effi's husband, Instetten, to revenge himself on his wife's ex-lover, and on his wife and child, six years after the brief act of adultery, entered into out of boredom and marital neglect, has taken place; whilst Anna finds herself forced into suicide, dying as the result of a similar categorical imperative, whose source lies in the reification of the notion of the family and familial duty, which she has offended by leaving husband and child, and whose observance constitutes (Tolstoy leads us to believe) 'the meaning of life and human relations'. Anna Karenina must die, and with full consciousness of a guilt that raises the bonds of marriage to a religious mystery that cannot be questioned.[37]

The heroine of Flaubert's *Madame Bovary* also dies after a life spent in unsuccessful adultery, her claims to independence and identity left unrecognised by an estranged husband and a community intoxicated on *Schadenfreude*. Emma Bovary has neither the innocent charm of Effi Briest, nor the moral stature of Anna Karenina; she is *petit bourgeois*: a product of provincial France, a doctor's wife, whose ambitions and fantasies have been nurtured on popular romance and sentimental fabulation. The limits imposed on the liberation of her sexuality emanate not from the rigid ethics of Prussian aristocracy, nor from the religious ties of Tolstoy's holy family, but from the banal restrictions of country life: from grass roots puritanism, common jealousy and gossip. And yet, Emma is one of the few female protagonists of the nineteenth century novel to possess genuine psychological depth, enjoying an intensity of lived emotion that allows her to transcend both her intellectual shortcomings and the banalities that surround her. Every turn of her inner life, from her frustrations and feelings of impotence to her transports of amorous delight, are registered with nuance and subtlety by Flaubert's famous narrative *impassibilité*, which creates the impression that we have unmediated access to the inner life of the character. Emma's external world is reconstituted with equal technical proficiency. In the novels of Fontane and Tolstoy, the bourgeois world confronts the heroine as an hypertrophied set of rules, whose unimpeachable integrity is consolidated through their abstract ethereality; in *Madame Bovary*, the bourgeois ethos is reconstituted as a material culture, a stultifying regime of personal habit, public ritual and political custom. Flaubert charts the oppressive nature of this world, from the 'fumes of nausea' which emanate from the gross gastronomic dimensions of Emma's domestic life, to the 'sombre monotony' and pomposity of the Annual Show, whose achievements range from grandiloquent celebrations of France's industrial might to the more prosaic presentation of livestock. Emma, in the end, does die, becoming a victim of the quixotic, but not inauthentic, nature of her desires and complicated wish-fulfilments; but her failure casts as much doubt upon the largely male world that surrounds her, as it does upon her own personality, a fact that the public prosecutor, who brought Flaubert to court on account of offending public decency in his novel, would have recognised. For, in spite of Flaubert's innate pessimism and his Olympian distance from his characters, his novel constitutes an argument for the moral necessity of revolt, even as it asserts the inevitability of its failure.[38]

5   INTEGRATION AND COMMUNITY: POETIC REALISM AND THE *BILDUNGSROMAN*

As our discussion of *Anna Karenina*, *Madame Bovary* and *Effi Briest* indicated, the Realist novel had as its focus the dissolution of the religious, moral and familial structures that had traditionally bonded individuals together. These novels gave expression to the centrifugal forces of the period, which they invested, not in classes or institutions, but in individuals whose desires, dreams and energies they offered as emblematic for the historical trend of the era. Not all Realists, however, accepted that trend, or sought to represent its corrosive moral thrust in their work. In Germany, a counter-movement was taking place, known as Poetic Realism. Its exponents argued that the Realist novel did not have to restrict itself to representations of alienation and distance, or entirely feature individuals torn through doubt, homelessness and sexual frustration, and prone to suicide, but could equally deal with integration and consensus, and with characters prepared to follow social custom and tradition, happy souls who recognise within themselves (in the words of Instetten in *Effi Briest*) 'what has got to be done'. For such writers, the external world exists, not as the brute objectivity that Emma Bovary vainly strives against, caught as she is within the bleak environment of provincial France, but as a living reality that both moulds and is moulded by the individual in a process founded, as the Poetic Realist, Gustav Freytag, argued, upon 'the secure basis of ethical feelings'.[39]

Germany, it is true, also had novelists who wrote about personal dislocation and social alienation: the work of Karl Ferdinand Gutzkow (*The Woman who Doubted*, 1835), Jeremias Gotthelf (*The Black Spider*, 1842), and Otto Ludwig (*Between Heaven and Earth*, 1856) often communicates the pessimism and the same feel for social disintegration that can be found in the French and Russian Realists. But the Poetic Realists were more representative of the German literature of this period. Characteristically, they focussed not upon the urban, cosmopolitan context of the mainstream Realist novel, but upon the more parochial world of the small town or the village, where they hoped to find a source for stable political and moral values. In the work of its minor adherents, such as Karl Spitta, Alexander Weill and Joseph Rank, Poetic Realism produced a type of sentimental writing known as *Biedermeier*, but in the more substantial literature of the period, in Goethe's novel *Elective Affinities* (1809), Grillparzer's play *Dream, a Life* (1834), Karl Immermann's *The Disciples* (1836), and Mörike's *Poems* (1838), for example, Poetic Realism promoted a more tangible philosophy, one which directed the individual away from the pains and confusions of city life, and towards the more manageable private sphere of home and domesticity. There, the individual, freed from the travails of history, could cultivate the small joys of life, enjoy (as Mörike countenanced in his famous poem, 'On a Lamp') the 'laughter' and the 'gentle spirit/Of gravity' that dwells within the simplest things and simplest events.[40]

Poetic Realism remained largely tangential to the main development of European Realism, although it found an echo in other countries, notably in Scandinavia, where writers such as Bjørnstjerne Bjørnson (*The Fisher Maiden*, 1868) and Jonas Lie (*The Family at Gilje*, 1883) combined a certain pastoralism with sharply observed studies of peasant and middle-class Norwegian life; in Finland, where Alexsis Kivi came to national prominence through his epic novel of rural life, *Seven Brothers* (1870) and in Holland, with the sharply drawn vignettes of social life penned by Nicolaas Beets,

Camera Obscura (1839). Poetic Realism did, however, give an impetus to one of the most important novelistic forms of the nineteenth century: the *Bildungsroman* (novel of personal development). Some of its major examples included Theodor Storm's *Immensee* (1851), Adalbert Stifter's *Indian Summer* (1857), and Gottfried Keller's *Green Henry* (1855; revised 1880). These novels countermanded the centrifugal trends evident in French, Russian and, to a lesser extent, English Realism. Not dissonance and alienation, but integration and moral maturity form the focus of this writing, and where the *Bildungsroman* authors dealt with the conflict between individual and society, they did so in order to resolve it at a higher level in the final phases of their narratives. As the critic and philosopher, Wilhelm Dilthey, was later to note, in the *Bildungsroman* 'life's dissonances and conflicts of life appear as transitions to be withstood by the individual on his way towards maturity and harmony'. One of the earliest examples of the genre was Goethe's *Wilhelm Meister*, which appeared in two volumes over a period of thirty years: *Wilhelm Meister's Years of Apprenticeship* (1796), and *Wilhelm Meister's Travels* (1821; revised 1829). The early novel, in particular, is structured around a series of rites of passage, initiations, awakenings, lessons, and experiences, which the young hero and aspiring actor must pass through if he is to reach maturity, and which initially halt, but then expedite, his journey through life. In the process, Wilhelm must overcome not only external obstacles, but internal ones as well: an intellectual self-sufficiency and egotism that allows him to acquire cultural attainment but not a balanced attitude to himself and others. It is only at the end of his journey that he proves able to unite the objective and subjective spheres, attaining that capacity for 'sympathy, love and orderly free activity', which (Goethe's narrator assures us) is 'the highest form to which man can develop'.[41]

Goethe's *Wilhelm Meister* is a moral allegory rather than a novel: its roots lie in the schematic symbolism of German Romanticism rather than in the material engagements of Realism. This imbalance is rectified in the two major *Bildungsromane* that followed Goethe's early model: Stifter's *Indian Summer*, and Keller's *Green Henry*. On the surface, both novels espouse the moral direction of the *Biedermeier* movement: a belief in mental balance and self-restraint, a concern for justice, a love of simplicity, and a commitment to practical application in one's immediate circle. Taken together, such values provide, as Stifter noted in the foreword to his collection of short stories, *Precious Stones* (1853), 'that gentle law that guides the human race'. Stifter regarded it as self-evident that such an ethos would exclude 'powerful movements of the soul, the terrible eruption of anger, the desire for revenge, the inflamed spirit that presses for action, tears down, effects change, destroys, and in its agitation often surrenders its own life', indeed, that entire gamut of highly-charged emotions that provided the staple diet of the Realist novel in England and France. In the place of such destructive (and self-destructive) passions, Stifter countenanced a greater feeling for the stability of the object world, for the spiritual integrity of nature, and for human artefacts, both domestic and aesthetic, whose facticity does not confront the individual in the spirit of determining otherness (as it does in *Madame Bovary*), but reflects both human values and human intentionality. It is amongst such values that the protagonists of Stifter's most famous novel, *Indian Summer*, move. The novel's young hero, Heinrich Drendorf, learns through a series of life experiences to appreciate the immanence of the rational in the real, and to recognise the presence of moral qualities in even the most mundane actions and events. The completion of Drendorf's spiritual journey is marked both by his acceptance into the home of his aristocratic mentor, von Risach, and by his marriage to Nathalie, an event which, in unifying the physical and spiritual in his nature, helps Risach see that there is an 'order within ourselves', which may remain hidden but can never be lost.[42]

Stifter's novel is a semi-utopian idyll; as a narrative it possesses a chronological shape, a forward momentum; but as an intellectual statement it remains curiously static, initiating no new values, developing no new arguments, eschewing surprises, tension and suspense, fixing all attention on the perpetual here and now through repetition and the development of a number of key *leitmotifs*. The Realism that it gives voice to is a transcendental Realism which views (following Goethe's famous sentiments) everything transitory as a parable. The smallest things are valued in Stifter's novel because they, as much as the larger ones, derive their value from their fixed place in the cosmic order. Keller's *Green Henry* (subtitled 'a novel of development') also expresses that 'outgoing love for everything that has come about and lasts, a love which honours the rightness and the significance of every thing and which feels the connection and the depth of the world'; but here the element of struggle that was missing in Stifter's serene work comes to the fore. For its hero is a problematic and divided individual, self-conscious and aware of his limitations both as a man and as a putative artist. His achievements are both fewer and won with greater pain. Keller describes the trials and tribulations of Henry with clear autobiographical sympathy, until he reaches that point in his quest, where, his artistic ambitions abandoned, and his relationships ruined through accident and poor judgement, Keller's hero finds the consummation of his life in a return to a minor administrative post with the State. Here amidst the calming atmosphere of the German countryside, he learns to carry out his humble duty 'with modest but manifold effect, living in peace and quiet', alone but content. His reward is not the perfection of sensibility that the heroes of other novels in the genre achieve, but the attainment of self-consciousness, which he now exercises in the form of a retrospective analysis of his life.[43]

The *Bildungsroman* was not the sole property of German writers; in England, Dickens (*David Copperfield*, 1850, and *Great Expectations*, 1861), George Meredith (*The Ordeal of Richard Feverel*, 1859, revised 1878) and Samuel Butler (*The Way of all Flesh*, written between 1872 and 1884), all brought elements of the genre into their work, as did Flaubert (albeit in a largely ironic fashion) in his second novel, *Sentimental Education* (1869). In England, the uniquely ethical world-view that underscored the *Bildungsroman* found its most convincing representation in the novels of Jane Austen (*Sense and Sensibility*, 1811, *Pride and Prejudice*, 1813, and *Mansfield Park*, 1814). On the surface, these novels appear to move within the familiar terrain of Poetic Realism: the domestic sphere, romance and marriage, the small town and rural setting, a world that is largely motivated by the familiar ethos of 'elegance, propriety, regularity, [and] harmony', values which allow personal relationships and the paths of courtship to be negotiated around the twin poles of personal attraction and social standing. But that Austen's poetic Realism was part of a deeper moral and even political world-view is evident from *Mansfield Park*. Here she makes it quite apparent that the concern for manners and decorum that she had extolled throughout her writing is not simply a trivial matter of polite observance, but forms that very bedrock of ethical life ('moral taste', her narrator calls it), without which a civilised nation such as England cannot survive. As Austen's novel demonstrates, those who mock such conventions (as Mary and Henry Crawford do through their play), seriously endanger the legitimacy of traditional society, and at a point in history when 'noise, disorder, and impropriety' (the disturbing side effects of an increasingly urbanising England) are posing the most serious threat to law, order and social stability. The observance of form, Austen finally tells us in *Mansfield Park*, is not just a social duty; it has become a political necessity.[44]

Jane Austen's conservatism was essentially defensive in nature; it was intended (as Edmund Burke's had been) to bolster the traditional ties of pre-revolutionary Europe against the destabilising influences of *laissez-faire* capitalism and political radicalism, whose amoral energies were threatening to open a Pandora's box of social discontent and unrest. For George Eliot, writing half a century after Austen, such changes had become *faits accomplis*. In her major novels, *Adam Bede* (1859), *Felix Holt* (1866) and *Middlemarch* (1872), she analysed the effect of these changes and others (such as the displacement of religion by scientific positivism) upon personal relationships. Eliot had written her own version of a *Bildungsroman* in *Mill on the Floss* (1860), in which she had sought to demonstrate that in human affairs 'the highest striving is after ascertainment of a unity which shall bind the smallest things with the greatest'. The same integrationist philosophy underscores her most ambitious novel, *Middlemarch*, but the unity to be attained here is not one between the humble and the mighty (the story unfolds almost exclusively within the middle-class community of Middlemarch), but between the conflicting philosophies and lifestyles that exist within this provincial world, ranging from Tertius Lydgate's scientific optimism to Rosamond Vincy's self-satisfied materialism, and Casaubon's arid High Toryism. At the centre of the novel is Dorothea Brooke. She learns through her contact with these individuals to abandon the abstract designs that she had held for world betterment (and which she hoped to further by marrying the Reverend Casaubon), and embrace a more modest but eminently more serviceable attitude to the world. Through the formation of Dorothea, Eliot gives voice to her conviction that a moral life is only achievable through the individual's experience of community: not the specific community of mid-nineteenth-century Victorian society, but community as a principle, as a form of social and ethical organisation capable of mediating between desire and duty, between the practical achievements of the phenomenal world, including scientific ones, and the more mysterious, but no less real, needs of the spiritual realm: between, in short, Realism and Idealism. Linking these two worlds is Dorothea's achievement, and that of George Eliot, whose insistence upon the importance of 'great feelings' and 'great faith' was won against her experience of the precarious nature of ideals in the age of Realism.[45]

6   THE PROBLEM OF ACTION: DRAMA IN THE AGE OF REALISM

The individual in the age of Realism had little scope for heroic action; the options (it seemed to be) were integration or exclusion, constructive participation or unredeemable alienation, marriage or suicide. Nowhere was the impossibility of heroic action more evident than in the theatre. From the drama of historical pessimism of Georg Büchner in the 1830s to the plays of personal crisis and social impasse of Ibsen and Chekhov at the end of the century, drama in the age of Realism gave itself over to an analysis of the insecurity, introspection, confusion and discomfort of a generation increasingly unable to avail itself of a stable world-view. There were, certainly, exceptions to this rule. Playwrights such as Eugène Scribe and Georges Feydeau in France, and Dion Boucicault and T.W. Robertson in England, did not worry about such metaphysical matters. They felt no qualms about celebrating the entrepreneurial energy and aggressive self-confidence evinced by the bourgeois class in the financial, political or domestic spheres. That is not to argue that plays such as Scribe's *The School for Politicians* (1833), Robertson's *Society* (1865) and Feydeau's *Hotel Paradiso* (1894) were uncritical of their subject matter. On the contrary, these plays brought to the fore the hypocrisy, sexual duplicity and amoral careerism that were a part of private and professional ethics in the age of industry and empire, a satirical perspective most evident in the popular Austrian playwrights, Ferdinand Raimund (*The Girl from the Fairy World or the Peasant as Millionaire*, 1826) and Johann Nestroy (*A Man Full of Nothing*, 1844); but they did so by translating the inner contradictions and moral shortcomings of this world into vaudeville or bedroom farce, or (at the other end of the spectrum) by inflating the personal drama of the treated situation into melodrama. These were the 'well-made plays' (*pièces bien faites*) of nineteenth-century theatre; tightly constructed dramatic units with complex plots, witty dialogue, suspense and surprise, executed with a care for *mise-en-scène* and illusionist detail. They drew successive generations of audiences into the private lives of public figures, and into the uncritical acceptance of a world that possessed a solidity and a totality that was made even more real by the shoddy nature of its power politics and sexual mores.

The dominant trend of nineteenth-century drama followed, however, a quite different trajectory, one that charted a growing distance between certain forms of subjectivity and the social sphere. This distance is evident in the work of the Austrian playwright, Franz Grillparzer, and of the German, Friedrich Hebbel. With their classical topoi and measured metrical form, Grillparzer's major plays (*Sappho*, 1818, *Hero and Leander*, 1831, and *Dream, a Life*, 1834) clearly look back to the Classical drama of Goethe and Schiller, whose heroes and heroines likewise find themselves torn between the competing claims of art and life, sensuality and the spirit, reason and instinct. What Grillparzer adds to the work of these earlier masters is a greater sense of the isolation of the self, which he deepens (as in *Libussa*, published posthumously in 1872) into an almost existential despair for those who 'lose the context of total-ity', in whom 'the voice of the heart speaks no more'. Such pes-simism is even more marked in the work of Hebbel, most notably in *Judith* (1840), *Maria Magdalena* (1846) and *Agnes Bernauer* (1851). Hebbel underpinned his dramatic output with essays such *My View of Drama* (1843), in which he speculated upon the problematic rela-tionship between the individual and history in an age characterised by 'the gradual disintegration of the religious and political forms of the world'. Hebbel explored the personal implications of this process of disintegration in his historical plays, *Judith* (1840), *Herod and Mariamne* (1846) and *Agnes Bernauer* (1852), whose female pro-tagonists must struggle against the abstract march of history in full knowledge of the hopelessness of their tasks. Hebbel's most famous play, *Maria Magdalena*, sketches the consequences of this predica-ment within the more recognisable domestic terrain of family duty, personal honour, right and wrong. The protagonists of this play represent distinct ethical positions: Master Anton (Maria's father) holds to the superannuated ethos of patriarchal morality, whose uncompromising values he exercises with 'a clenched fist'; whilst the son, Karl, and Maria's suitor, Leonard, are representatives of the new generation, 'Realists', for whom 'being reasonable' means abandoning all moral positions when necessary. Maria is caught between these two diverging codes, and, unable to effect a compro-mise between them, commits suicide. Her death is offered as proof of the impasse that bourgeois custom has reached in the age of po-litical pragmatism and fiscal utilitarianism. The concluding words of the play – Anton's despairing: 'I don't understand the world any more', gave voice to the concerns of a entire generation (and it would have included Hebbel) for whom Realism meant not the advent of new values, but disorientation and nihilism.[46]

Hebbel's world-view was deeply pessimistic; but it was, at least, articulated within a framework that posited some higher historical sense to individual suffering, examples of which could be read as evidence of the Hegelian 'cunning of reason' at work in the world. For Georg Büchner, history possessed no such sense or reason, and its cunning lay not in the agency of unforeseen providence but in the malicious exercise of its own inherent and unfathomable irrationality. Büchner was the leading dramatist of the *Vormärz* movement (so called because of its role in preparing the political insurrection of March 1848), whose emancipatory cause he promulgated through his tract, *The Hessian Courier* (1834). Like Ludwig Börne, Karl Gutzkow and, initially, Heinrich Heine (representatives of a cultural-political group known as Young Germany), Büchner combined an early form of socialism with a militant belief in liberal and democratic politics. Büchner's plays, however, the historical drama, *Danton's Death* (1835), the romantic comedy, *Leonce and Lena*, and the domestic-social tragedy, *Woyzeck* (both 1836), reveal little faith in the merits of political activism. On the contrary, these plays are marked by a deep-seated conviction that history is a random process, that personal action is futile, that (as Büchner put it in a letter of 1833) 'individuals [are] but froth on the waves, greatness a mere coincidence, the mastery of geniuses a dance of puppets, a ridiculous struggle against an iron law that can at best be recognised, but never mastered'. The action of *Danton's Death* bears out this pessimism. It follows its hero, one of the seminal figures of the French Revolution, from his disillusionment with the conduct of the Revolution to a world-weary cynicism. Tired of the machinations of power, and convinced of the essential futility of all political action, Danton chooses death on the guillotine rather than continue with the charade of revolutionary idealism. His parting words, 'the world is chaos, nothingness its due messiah', sounds a note of nihilism that, in the work of Dostoyevsky and Nietzsche, would become increasingly strident through the nineteenth century.[47]

Büchner's scepticism regarding the power of ideals to influence human affairs is further evident in his final play, *Woyzeck*. The focus now is no longer upon the experiences of world-historical individuals such as Danton and Robespierre, but upon those of a lowly soldier, cuckolded husband and part-time object of scientific experiment. Woyzeck is a victim both of circumstance and of a personality that is the plaything of uncontrollable energies and fears, suspicions and insecurities, which launch him down a path of emotional excess. His process of derangement is made even more effective by the 'open form' of the play which, in dispensing with conventional divisions between acts and scenes, condenses the action into a dramatically short time-span. In an act bloody and irrational, Woyzeck kills his common-law wife for being unfaithful; but in spite of the enormity of his act, he alone in the play seems to possess authenticity, for his animal passion and his primitive vision of 'men and women, man and beast', however incoherently expressed, stand out, in their intensity of self-expression, against the spurious rational-Idealist model of man that is pompously mouthed by the representatives of authority in the play.[48]

'Why does this "decrepit society of today"', Büchner asked in a letter of 1836, continue to exist? 'Its entire life consists solely in attempts to escape the most appalling boredom. May it die out – that's the only new experience it is capable of having.' The major direction of drama in the nineteenth century deepened Büchner's sense of an ending into a virtual eschatology of bourgeois society. This was notably the case in the work of the two most powerful dramatists of the Realist age: Anton Chekhov and Henrik Ibsen. Ibsen, in particular, sought to disclose the atrophy and hypocrisy that he saw at the centre of bourgeois society; in plays, such as *Pillars of Society* (1877), *A Doll's House* (1879) and *An Enemy of the People* (1882), he showed how the high moral image cultivated by the business community, the patriarchal family and the press, served to hide the deep-seated realities (of the profit motive, exploitation of women, and the invasion of personal liberty) upon which such institutions were, respectively, based. This theme of the contrast between noble appearance and deep-seated decadence was given a more literal inflection in *Ghosts* (1882) and *Hedda Gabler* (1891). Oswald Alving's syphilis, in the former play, and Hedda's unwelcome pregnancy, in the latter, act as signifiers of a more general malaise besetting those characters and, by extension, the social class to which they belong. In this world, unpalatable realities are repressed, and forced to emerge (in an almost Freudian way) through channels that are dangerous to the health of individual and society alike, returning to haunt those (like Mrs Alving in *Ghosts*) who 'are so pitifully afraid of the light'. Some do escape this claustrophobic world, such as

Nora in *A Doll's House*, who leaves husband and children, unprepared to accept the straitjacket of the institution of marriage. The sculptor, Arnold Rubek, in Ibsen's final play, *When We Dead Awaken* (1899), likewise has become 'completely free and independent' of the moral inhibitions and repressive social conventions of his native land. Yet even here, where artistic achievement has permitted a transfiguration of quotidian attachment and earthly duty, Ibsen foregrounds the inescapable realities of disillusionment and frustration. Despite the achievements of his life, Rubek can not rid himself of the feeling that the artistic vocation is 'empty and hollow', and 'fundamentally meaningless'. With his erstwhile model, Irena, Rubek chooses to end his life with a final grand gesture, disappearing into the stormy mountain peaks of his native Norway, seeking a death that will finally liberate him from his past.[49]

Ibsen's work is pervaded by a sense of an ending, and by an intimation of new forces, political, economic and social, that are emerging to hasten the demise of bourgeois society. Engstrand in *The Ghosts* (self-seeking, street-wise and ruthless), represents these forces, being an early harbinger of a type of personality who will only fully emerge in those political and social revolutions of the twentieth century. The dramatist who most sharply caught this mood of decline was Anton Chekhov. His *The Cherry Orchard* (1904) comes towards the end of nineteenth-century Realism, as it did towards the end of a rich period of dramatic achievement for the author. In his *The Seagull* (1896), *Uncle Vanya* (1898) and *Three Sisters* (1901), Chekhov had dealt, in a complex mixture of irony and humour, with characters adrift in a world that had lost its traditional bearings. *Three Sisters*, for example, (perhaps the most famous of these plays) paints a picture of a family martyred by a collective awareness of its own impotence. Dominated by their memory of past glory, and feeling unable to go forward into the future, the sisters fall victim to the 'rot of boredom', a state of spiritual atrophy which replaces ideals and action by habit, loneliness and silence. The spiritual collapse suffered by Chekhov's characters in *Three Sisters* is the result of a purely personal predicament: the female protagonists of the play find the prospect of an unhappy marriage, or, even (the implication is) of a happy one, a poor solution to their intellectual and spiritual needs. In *The Cherry Orchard*, the same predicament takes on an historical significance. The play depicts the plight of an aristocratic family, which finds itself unable to respond to the threat posed to the continuing existence of its ancestral home (and to the orchard which constitutes the sentimental core of the property) by the spirit of economic rationalism that has taken hold of modern Russia. In this new world, tradition and continuity have been forced to give way both to the fiscal pragmatism of the *nouveaux riches*, represented by the businessman, Lopakhin, and to a socialist meliorism, espoused here by the student radical, Trofimov. Caught between historical forces which they cannot master and only dimly comprehend, the aristocratic proprietors of the crumbling estate finally succumb not only to the economic realities with which they are faced, but to an 'oppressive sense of emptiness' that renders them incapable of action. With *The Cherry Orchard*, Chekhov brought the European stage to a point from which it could not return. Subsequent dramatists, in the Modernist and Postmodernist periods, would further develop Chekhov's perceptions, delineating characters who would increasingly find themselves forced into passivity towards history and their own fates.[50]

7 THE LITERARY LABORATORY: NATURALISM

Although Realist writers rejected the social, political and moral content of the bourgeois world-view, they largely retained the central epistemological tenet upon which it was based: scientific objectivity, or the aspiration to reproduce the external integrity of the world without recourse to subjective interpretation. Few Realist writers, however, sought to put this assumption on any theoretical basis, being content simply to assert the value of the mimetic principle, or embody it in their work. For this reason, Emile Zola is both an exception to the *modus operandi* of the Realist school, and yet its greatest theoretical exponent. From his early preface to the second edition of *Thérèse Raquin* (published in 1867) through to his lengthy essay, *The Experimental Novel* (1880), Zola sought to persuade the public of the scientific, analytical and disinterested nature of his literary project. He did this by aligning his work with that of the physiologist, Claude Bernard, who had attempted in his *Introduction to the Study of Experimental Medicine* (1865) to deduce social behaviour from certain physiological 'facts' of human nature. Zola took two things from Bernard: firstly, a deterministic model of human behaviour, the conviction, as he noted in his famous preface to *Thérèse Raquin*, that 'people [are] completely dominated by their nerves and blood, [and are] without free will, drawn into each

action of their lives by the inexorable laws of their physical nature';
and secondly, a strictly experimental methodology, which placed
hereditarily determined individuals, such as the two protagonists
of this novel, Thérèse and her lover, Laurent, within certain highly
charged situations (here an unhappy marriage and an adulterous
relationship), so that 'the profound modifications of an organism
subjected to the pressure of environments and circumstances'
might be judged. As Zola made clear, this was a project that forced
him to override the inhibiting concerns of 'morality and literary
decency'.[51]

Zola's concept of 'naturalistic evolution', which posited a causal
connection between biology and individual behaviour, formed the
central principle around which his *magnum opus*, the Rougon-
Macquart series turned. Published in twenty volumes between 1871
and 1893, Zola's novel sequence offers an epic picture of private and
public life in France during the Second Empire (1848–1870), linking
the treatment of matters as diverse as alcoholism (*L'Assommoir*, literally *The Gin Shop*, 1877), industrial confrontation (*Germinal*, 1885),
and prostitution (*Nana*, 1880), through the genealogy of two blood-
related families: the upper-middle class Rougons and the proletarian Macquarts. In spite of their different social standing, the
members of the family are equal victims of their genetic destinies,
forced to pay for the sins committed by their predecessors, propelled through depravity and corruption, violence and sensuality
by hereditary traits over which they have no control. The character
Nana (in the novel of the same name) typifies their predicament. She
is born into poverty and moral destitution, and into a world that is
subject to the 'filth of promiscuity, [and] to the progressive neglect
of decent feelings'. She has beauty and a resilient spirit, but this can
take her no further that the vaudevilles of Paris and the bedrooms of
its brothels. Nana becomes 'that Golden Creature, blind as brute
force', whose animal sensuality moves between an earthy sympathy
for the downtrodden and the innocent, and a destructive antipathy
towards the men in her life, to whom she responds with a mixture
of fear and hatred. In Zola's deterministic model, where biology is
destiny, Nana remains unable to purge herself of 'the poison that
she [has] assimilated in the gutters', ending her brief life, prostrate
with disease, her face and body reduced through a terminal illness
to 'a heap of matter and blood'.[52]

Zola's controversial writings were immensely influential upon
the course of European fiction. In France, J-K Huysmans (*Marthe*,

1876, and *The Vatard Sisters*, 1879), and Guy de Maupassant (*Boule de suif*, 1880); in England, George Gissing (*Workers in the Dawn*, 1880, and *New Grub Street*, 1891) and George Moore (*Esther Waters*, 1894); in Denmark, Herman Bang, (*Generations without Hope*, 1880); in Norway, Alexander Kielland, *Garman & Wörse*, 1880); in Spain, Leopoldo Alas, (*La Regenta*, 1885); in Hungary, Lajos Tolnai, (*Dark World*, 1894); in Holland, Louis Couperus's *Eline Vere* (1889); and in Finland, Minna Canth (*A Working-Class Wife*, 1885), adopted, to varying degrees, Zolaesque preoccupations: the focus upon the milieu of the socially deprived or the criminal; the depiction of tabooed subject matter, such as incest, alcoholism and prostitution; the assumption of environmental and biological determinism; and the employment of documentary and journalistic materials to validate the social authenticity of the account. Some, such as Tennyson, were appalled at the amoral and salacious nature of the Naturalist method, accusing its practitioners of 'wallowing in the troughs of Zolaism'; others, such as the Italian critic, Francesco de Sanctis (*Study of Zola*, 1878), and the Spanish writer, Emilia Pardo Bazán ('The burning Question', 1882) felt liberated by its techniques and themes, as if the final restrictions to a complete literary engagement with the world had been removed. That the Naturalist method could be applied to situations urban and rural was demonstrated by the Italian novelist, and the leading representative of the *verismo* movement, Giovanni Verga. In his stories, *Little Novels of Sicily* (1880), and in his major novel, *The House by the Medlar Tree* (1881), Verga depicted characters who were (as the author explained in his preface to the novel) 'defeated by life', victims both of the harsh natural environment of their native land and of instincts, rapacious and unforgiving, from which they prove unable to free themselves. In Germany, writers such as Gerhart Hauptmann, Arno Holz, Heinrich and Julius Hart, and Paul Ernst saw in Naturalism a belated opportunity for their culture to regain contact with the mainstream tradition of European Realism. Johannes Schlaf and Arno Holz, in particular, were enthusiasts, supplying the most original theoretical defence of the Naturalist text, which they cryptically defined as 'Art = Nature minus x'. In jointly authored stories such as 'Papa Hamlet' (1889), they elaborated their own 'telegram style' (*Sekundenstil*), seeking to capture the minute intonations and conversational idiom of colloquial speech. The result, according to the reviewer, M.G. Conrad, was an entirely original literature which, in focussing purely on 'the unmediated, brittle and strident' nature of its subject matter (in 'Papa Hamlet', the pathetic decline of a superannuated actor), offered the reader access to the 'tragic banality' of everyday life.[53]

It was, however, Gerhart Hauptmann and the Swedish playwright, August Strindberg, who made the most effective use of the Naturalist method. Hauptmann's first play, *Before Sunrise*, used the Naturalist method to remarkable effect; its use of dialect and colloquial speech, graphic references to bodily functions, and its unremitting biological fatalism (which posits hereditary traits, in this case, alcoholism, as ineluctable determinations of personal fate) outraged audiences during the play's first performances in 1889. It preached a simple message: youthful idealism (represented by the two lovers of the play, Helene and Loth) cannot survive in a world where even the well-meaning believe that 'belief, love, hope, and all that' is pure 'rot'. Hauptmann's subsequent plays, notably *Lonely People* (1892), *The Weavers* (1892), and *Rose Bernd* (1903), also dealt with the failure of individual idealism in a world governed by the crushing discourse of scientific determinism and moral cynicism. In *The Weavers*, which tells of a revolt of Silesian weavers in 1848, social determinism and political repression come to form an unholy union. Hauptmann treats the claims of the weavers for humane work conditions and basic rights with sympathy, describing their personal misery from within, using their own language and admittedly unsophisticated world-view (even more attenuated in the dialect version of the play, *De Waber*) to produce an image of an entire class and an entire community in crisis. Hauptmann affirms the right of the weavers to rebellion, even as he asserts the impossibility of their position: in the final analysis, they learn (as every protagonist in a Naturalist play must learn) that 'law and justice and righteousness' are pure chimera, ideals that cannot withstand the realities of political injustice and military repression.[54]

If Hauptmann's Naturalism looks outwards, to political confrontation and revolt, a direction further developed in his *Florian Geyer* (1896), the plays of August Strindberg look inward, into internecine struggles for psychic dominance and sexual control fought out within the domestic sphere. This terrain would have been familiar to the audiences of Ibsen and Chekhov; Ibsen's *A Doll's House*, in particular, gained notoriety throughout Europe for its uncompromising treatment of a husband-wife relationship. But Strindberg brings the subterranean tensions explored by these earlier dramatists to the surface, eschewing the moral problematising of Ibsen and the gentle quietism of Chekhov in favour of a dramatic reconstruction of persecution complexes, unconfinable obsessions and cynical and naked power politics. His aim was to create a theatre devoted (as he wrote in 1888) to 'the strong and cruel struggles' that constituted (for the Nietzschean-inspired Swede) 'the joy of life'. Strindberg's conflictual world-view finds its most memorable dramatisation in the plays *The Father* (1887) and *Miss Julie* (1889). In the former, he deals with one of the major preoccupations of the Realist novel: the emancipation of woman from patriarchal control. Flaubert, Tolstoy, and Fontane, amongst others, had dealt with this theme, using it to explore those tensions that they saw as endemic to nineteenth-century European society. Here, in *The Father*, a play written towards the end of the period of bourgeois legitimacy in Europe, the world of patriarchal control is imploding from within, its pretensions to dominance undermined by the 'new woman' of the age, represented here by the Captain's wife, Laura. She is the driving force of the play: articulate, self-confident, she alone knows the true facts of the paternity of their child (custody of whom she is determined to win). She exploits this knowledge, slowly pushing her husband over the edge into madness and committing, in the process, an act of 'innocent murder' that the law cannot recognise and only nature can sanction.[55]

Both the captain and his wife live by the ethos of 'eat or be eaten'. As Laura says: 'what has all this life and death struggle been about except power'. That gender power resides in sexual conquest is the theme of *Miss Julie*; but here the conflictual animus that drove the earlier play is supplemented by a social and (potentially, at least) a political dimension. The play centres on the attraction felt by the aristocratic Julie for Jean, the footman. The latter is a character rare in European literature: a member of the lower orders, whose nature (vulgar, brutal and erotically dynamic) is here allowed to triumph (as it was not with Zola's working-class heroes, such as Nana) over a superior social class. Jean takes sexual possession of Julie, who succumbs, as she realises, to 'the attraction the weak feel for the strong'. His conquest represents the victory not only of a new class, but of a new breed of person, whose values (held incoherently perhaps but with force) combine a neo-Darwinistic belief in the survival of the fittest with a simplified Nietzscheanism that recognises no moral order beyond that constructed through self-assertion. In *Miss Julie*, drama has moved beyond the terrain of the bourgeois sphere altogether, to a world where individual confronts individual, man confronts woman, servant confronts master in a spirit of bitter and irreconcilable hostility. Strindberg's plays, written at the end of the Realist tradition proper, bring us into the era of modernity, and hint darkly at a future that will see human behaviour first analysed, and then motivated, by forces and energies that are irredeemably irrational, and violently so.[56]

8   LITERATURE IN THE AGE OF REALISM: A CHRONOLOGY

1827, Grabbe, *Scherz, Satire, Ironie, und tieferer Bedeutung* (Jest, Satire, Irony and deeper Significance).
1827, Manzoni, *I promessi sposi* (The Betrothed) [revised 1840–1842].
1829, Goethe, *Wilhelm Meisters Wanderjahre* (Wilhelm Meister's Travels).
1830, Stendhal, *Le Rouge et le noir* (The Scarlet and Black).
1832, Fáy, *A Bélteky ház* (The House of Bélteky).
1832, Pellico, *Le mei prigioni* (My Prisons).
1833, Balzac, *Eugénie Grandet*.
1833, Scribe, *Bernard et Raton* (The School for Politicians).
1834, Grillparzer, *Traum, ein Leben* (Dream, a Life).
1834, Balzac, *Le Père Goriot* (Old Goriot).
1835, Gogol, *Mirgorod*.
1835, Escosura, *Ni rey ni Roque* (Neither King nor Rook).
1835, Gutzkow, *Wally, die Zweifelerin* (The Woman who Doubted).
1835, Büchner, *Dantons Tod* (Danton's Death).
1836, Büchner, *Woyzeck*.
1837–1843, Balzac, *Les Illusions perdues* (Lost Illusions).
1838, Dickens, *Oliver Twist*.
1838, Mörike, *Gedichte* (Poems).
1839, Almquist, *Det går an* (Sara Videbeck).
1839, Stendhal, *La Chartreuse de Parme* (The Charterhouse of Parma).
1842, Gogol, *Mertvyye Dushi* (Dead Souls).
1842, Gotthelf, *Die schwarze Spinne* (The Black Spider).
1842, Balzac, Foreword to *The Human Comedy*.
1843, Sue, *Les Mystères de Paris* (The Mysteries of Paris).
1844, Gil Y Carrasco, *El Señor de Bembibre* (The Master of Bembibre).
1844, Hebbel, *Maria Magdalena*.
1845, Disraeli, *Sybil, or, The Two Nations*,
1845, Eötvös, *A falu jegyzöje* (The Village Notary).
1847, Emily Brontë, *Wuthering Heights*.
1847, Charlotte Brontë, *Jane Eyre*.
1848, Gaskell, *Mary Barton*.
1848, Dickens, *Dombey and Son*.
1848, Thackeray, *Vanity Fair*.
1850, Tennyson, 'In Memoriam'.
1851, Storm, *Immensee*.
1853, Stifter, *Bunte Steine* (Precious Stones).

1854, Dickens, *Hard Times*.
1855, Keller, *Der grüne Heinrich* (Green Henry) [revised 1879–1880].
1855, Freytag, *Soll und Haben* (Debit and Credit).
1855, Gaskell, *North and South*.
1855, Nerval, *Aurélia*.
1856, Ludwig, *Zwischen Himmel und Erde* (Between Heaven and Earth) [revised 1862].
1857, Raabe, *Die Chronik der Sperlingsgasse* (Chronicle of Sparrow Lane).
1857, Flaubert, *Madame Bovary*.
1857, Champfleury, *Le Réalisme* (Realism).
1857, Baudelaire, *Les Fleurs du mal* (The Flowers of Evil).
1857, Stifter, *Der Nachsommer* (Indian Summer).
1857, George Eliot, 'Worldliness and Other-Worldliness: the Poet Young'.
1857, Bjørnson, 'Synnøve Solbakken'.
1858, Nievo, *Le confessioni di un Italiano* (The Castle of Fratta) [publ. 1867].
1859, Eliot, *Adam Bede*.
1859, Goncharov, *Oblomov*.
1860, Madách, *Az ember tragédiája* (The Tragedy of Man).
1860, Baudelaire, *Les Paradis artificiels* (Artificial Paradise).
1860, Collins, *The Woman in White*.
1862, Turgenev, *Otsy i deti* (Fathers and Sons).
1862, Hugo, *Les Misérables*.
1862, Christina Rossetti, *Goblin Market and Other Poems*.
1863–1869, Tolstoy, *Voyna i mir* (War and Peace).
1864, Dostoyevsky, *Zapiski iz podpolya* (Letters from the Underground).
1864, Goncourt brothers, *Germinie Lacerteux*.
1866, Dostoyevsky, *Prestupleniye i nakazaniye* (Crime and Punishment).
1866, Eliot, *Felix Holt*.
1867, Zola, *Thérèse Raquin*.
1868–1870, William Morris, *The Earthly Paradise*.
1868, Bjørnson, *Fiskerjenten* (The Fisher Maiden).
1869, Robert Browning,*The Ring and the Book*.
1869, Flaubert, *L'Education sentimentale* (Sentimental Education).
1870, Dante Gabriel Rossetti, *Poems*.
1870, Kivi, *Seitsemän veljestä* (Seven Brothers).
1870, Pérez Galdós, 'Observaciones sobre la novela contemporánea en España' ('Observations on the Contemporary Novel in Spain').
1871–1872, Eliot, *Middlemarch*.
1872, Butler, *Erewhon*.
1875, Trollope, *The Way We Live Now*.
1876, Pérez Galdós, *Doña Perfecta* (Lady Perfecta).
1877, Tolstoy, *Anna Karenina*.
1877, Zola, *L'Assommoir* (The Gin Shop).
1878, Neruda, *Povídky malostranské* (Tales of the Little Quarter).
1878, de Sanctis, *Studio supra Emilio Zola* (Study of Emile Zola).
1879, Capuana, *Giacinta*.
1879, Huysmans, *Les Soeurs Vatard* (The Vatard Sisters).
1879, Meredith, *The Egoist*.
1879, Ibsen, *Et Dukkehjem* (A Doll's House).

1880, Zola, *Le Roman expérimental* (The Experimental Novel).
1881, Verga, *Vita dei campi* (Little Novels of Sicily).
1880, Maupassant, 'Boule de suif'.
1880, Thomson, *The City of Dreadful Night and Other Poems*.
1880, Dostoyevsky, *Brat'ya Karamazovy* (The Brothers Karamazov).
1880, Verga, *I Malavoglia* (The House by the Medlar Tree).
1881, Flaubert, *Bouvard et Pécuchet*.
1882, Ibsen, *Gengangere* (Ghosts) [perf. 1891].
1882, Pardo Bazán, 'La cuestión palpitante' ('The Burning Question').
1883, Brandes, *Det moderne Gjennembrudsmaend* (The Men of the Modern Breakthrough).
1883, Lie, *Familjen paa Gilje* (The Family at Gilje).
1884, Butler, *The Way of all Flesh* [publ. 1903].
1884–1885, Alas ('Clarín'), *La regenta*.
1885, Canth, *Työmiehen vaimo* (A Working-Class Wife).
1885, Zola, *Germinal*.
1886, Pardo Bazán, *Los pazos de Ulloa* (The Son of the Bondswoman).
1887, Pérez Galdós, *Fortunata y Jacinta* (Fortunata and Jacinta).
1887, Strindberg, *Fadren* (The Father).
1887, Fontane, *Irrungen, Wirrungen* (Trials and Tribulations).
1888, Eça de Queróz, *Os Maias* (The Maias).
1889, Strindberg, *Fröken Julie* (Miss Julie).
1889, Hauptmann, *Vor Sonnenaufgang* (Before Sunrise).
1889, Holz and Schlaf, 'Papa Hamlet'.
1891, Gissing, *New Grub Street*.
1891, Hardy, *Tess of the d'Urbervilles*.
1892, Hauptmann, *Die Weber* (The Weavers).
1894, Moore, *Esther Waters*.
1894, Feydeau, *L'Hôtel du Libre-Echange*. (Hotel Paradiso).
1894, Asnyk, *Nad glebiami* (Over the Depths).
1895, Fontane, *Effi Briest*.
1895, Hardy, *Jude the Obscure*.
1896, Sinkiewicz, *Quo Vadis*?
1899, Ibsen, *Nar vi døde vaagner* (When We Dead Awaken).
1901, Chekhov, *Tri Sestry* (Three Sisters).
1904, Chekhov, *Vishnyovy sad* (The Cherry Orchard).

3
Modernism

1 'THE WILL TO THE END': THE CONTEXT OF EUROPEAN MODERNISM

In 1851, Charles Kingsley, cleric and popular novelist (*Westward Ho!*, 1855, and *The Water Babies*, 1863), visited the Great Exhibition in London, where the showcase of the century had been organised for British and European technology. The visit gave him occasion to speculate upon the material achievements of the nineteenth century: 'If these forefathers of ours could rise from their graves this day', he later declaimed in a sermon to his parishioners, 'they would be inclined to see in our hospitals, in our railroads, in the achievements of our physical science, confirmation of that old superstition of theirs, proofs of the kingdom of God, realisations of the gifts which Christ received for men, vaster than any of which they had dreamed.' In one sense, Kingsley was fully justified in viewing the nineteenth century as an era of prosperity and completion. Between 1800 and 1850, the population of Europe grew from 180 million to 226 million, industrial capacity more than quadrupled, life expectancy increased, and major electoral reforms were undertaken in Britain, in 1832, and in France, in 1848. Such evidence of 'progress' (a key term in the self-image of this generation) seemed to bear out Kingsley's quasi-religious enthusiasm, and lent support to others, such as the poet, Samuel Taylor Coleridge, who could, in spite of the growing asceticism of his life and person, still approach the energies and achievements of England's mercantile class 'under the strongest impression of awe, and admiration akin to wonder'.[1]

Such euphoria did not, however, outlast the century. By 1900, a defensive and pessimistic mood had set in amongst many of the erstwhile pundits of progress. Not only had the negative impact of industrial and technological change upon the physical and moral constituency of the nation come increasingly under focus, in works such as William Booth's *In Darkest England, and the Way Out* (1890), and Charles Booth's *Life and Labour of the People in London* (1889–1902), but the very ethos of *laissez-faire* liberalism, which had underpinned these changes, was beginning to seem to many a rigid, indeed repressive form of governance. These critics of industrial England were justified in feeling cynical about the values of Victorian society. For by the end of the nineteenth century, the ideals and utopian wish-fulfilment that had fired the revolutions of 1789, 1830 and 1848, had given way to a calculating pragmatism amongst successive liberal governments in Europe, many of which had sought to consolidate their political hegemony through alignments with the more flexible elements of the landed aristocracy (creating, for example, parties such as the National-Liberals in Germany). The result was the creation of a ruling élite, economically open, but politically closed, and fully prepared to use the techniques of the modern state to contain those groups that challenged its ascendancy. The events of the Paris Commune of 1871, in which more than 30,000 workers and disaffected soldiers lost their lives in a single 'bloody week', provided one instance of the ruthless determinism of reconstituted liberalism, as did the anti-socialist laws promulgated by a liberal-conservative alliance under Bismarck in Germany between 1878 and 1890. One event, in particular, came to form a test case for the moral probity of statist liberalism: the trial of Alfred Dreyfus. Falsely sentenced to life imprisonment in 1894, the Jewish army officer Dreyfus became the most conspicuous victim of the Third French Republic (founded in 1875), his case, the most glaring proof that a progressive liberal state was fully prepared to align itself with the traditional power centres of the Army, Church and Aristocracy, in order to defend its interests. After spending six years in prison, Dreyfus did finally receive justice, but only after intense agitation by the socialist deputy, Jean Jaurès, and the Naturalist writer, Emile Zola. The latter's polemical broadsheet, 'I accuse!', drew attention to the double standards that prevailed within the French nation, which made much of its high cultural achievements and political tolerance, but which continued (as Zola argued) to 'exploit patriotism for works of hatred'.[2]

But it was in the colonial sphere that the moral duplicity of Western liberal governments became most blatant. Between 1830 and 1900, every major European power launched itself into imperial expansion: England added to its already considerable Empire

Egypt (in 1882), Kenya (1890) and Uganda (1894); France acquired Algeria (1848) and Indochina (1858); Italy, Eritrea (1896); Belgium, the Congo (1885); and Portugal, Mozambique (1897). The governance of these colonies brought to light the darker side of the liberal ethos. Earlier talk of the rights of man, of liberty, fraternity and equality, a rhetoric that had inspired liberalism in its early days, now gave way to a new focus in the colonial fiction of, for example, John Buchan, upon 'the white man's duty', 'the gift of responsibility' and 'the fulfilment of [the] task' facing the colonising powers. That such words served to mask economic calculation and political expediency was recognised by many; not only by the emerging generation of Marxist analysts, such as Rosa Luxemburg (*The Accumulation of Capital*, 1913), but also by writers such as Rudyard Kipling (*Barrack Room Ballads*, 1892, and *Kim*, 1901) and Joseph Conrad (*Lord Jim*, 1900, and *Heart of Darkness*, 1902), who saw in the colonial 'mission' not just heroic endeavour (although this indisputably forms an essential component of Kipling's ideology), but exploitation and 'the devil of violence, and the devil of greed'.[3]

Liberalism, and that constellation of values with which it had become associated: Utilitarianism, economic individualism, and the notion of the survival of the fittest, had attracted critics throughout the nineteenth century. Figures as diverse as Carlyle and Ruskin, in England, and Baudelaire and Flaubert, in France, had decried the philistine nature of its culture, and its deadening influence upon the creative life of the individual, its destructive effect (in Carlyle's emotive words) upon those 'primary, unmodified forces and energies of man, the mysterious springs of Love, and Fear, and Wonder, of Enthusiasm, Poetry, Religion'. By the end of the century that critique had acquired a greater concern with the ethical and, increasingly, political tensions within the liberal-bourgeois tradition. This concern is evident in the work of writers such as Anatole France (see, for example, the novel series *The History of our Age*, published 1896–1901), Carl Sternheim, whose plays, such as *Schippel, the Bourgeois* (1913), satirised the manners of the *nouveau riche* in Germany; and the Irish playwright, and perhaps the most important dramatist of social conscience between Ibsen and Brecht, George Bernard Shaw. In his many plays and prefaces, Shaw held up to ridicule the 'gratuitous millennium' promoted by liberal ideology, whilst in plays such as *Major Barbara* (1905), *Man and Superman* (performed 1905), *John Bull's Other Island* (1907) and *Heartbreak House* (1920), he drew attention to the existence of poverty, socialism, nationalism and female emancipation as forces poised to demolish the complacency of the established political order.[4]

In England, one author, in particular, sought to explicate the inner dislocations within the liberal ethos: E.M. Forster. Born in 1879, (as he later noted) at 'the fag end of Victorian Liberalism', Forster remained aware throughout his life of the strengths and limitations of the *laissez-faire* world-view that had prevailed in his country since the beginning of the nineteenth century. In many of his novels, such as *The Longest Journey* (1907), and *A Passage to India* (1924), and in his essays, he sought to explore the Janus-faced nature of the liberal ethos: the fact that its admirable insistence upon freedom and the right to individual self-determination in the personal sphere stood at odds with the harshness of its business ethnic, whose uncompromising economic rationalism had culminated in the 'capitalist jungle' of modern society. Forster explored these antinomies most effectively in *Howards End* (1910). The novel deals with the tensions between mercantile opportunism and cultural sensibility in Edwardian society. Forster's message to these two groups, represented in the novel by Mr Wilcox and the Schlegel sisters, respectively, is 'only connect'; for the sake of political harmony and national self-interest (the novel was written against the backdrop of the strengthening power of Germany) the liberal bourgeoisie should merge the two defining features of its ideology: its humanism and respect for the creative life, and its financial and business pragmatism. Forster's novel seeks to affect a marriage (quite literally) between these two factions, who must not only overcome the internal divisions within their ranks, but also resist the 'continual flux' and 'eternal formlessness' of a modern world dominated by rampant urbanism, technological advancement and social dislocations (represented in the novel by the social climbing of the lowly Leonard Bast, and the feminine independence of Helen Schlegel). Forster's optimism, however, gives way in the end to apocalyptic gloom, as, in the midst of personal rapprochement, the characters become aware of a 'red dust' creeping slowly towards the haven of the family home: it is a symbol of those inexorable forces of dissolution, against which traditional alignments in family and state will, ultimately, prove helpless.[5]

What Forster had identified in *Howards End* was, in fact, not simply an impasse within a particular political ideology, or a crisis within a particular class, but the emergence of a configuration of social, political and economic changes that we know as Modernity.

Certainly, the forces that Forster identified in his novel were not new. From the very beginning of the century, it had become increasingly evident that traditional agrarian Europe was being rapidly replaced by a new type of society founded on urban, pluralistic, and materialist values, at a pace driven by technological change. Between 1870 and 1914, that process, starting in England, spread first to France and Belgium and then to Germany and Italy, gathering a startling momentum. During this period, transportation was radically improved through the invention of the electric locomotive (1879) and Daimler's internal-combustion engine; the potential for communication expanded through Bell's telephone (1876) and Marconi's wireless (1896); and industrial production was put on a modern footing through the increasing use of the American-inspired assembly line process. The social impact of these changes caused widespread consternation. In Germany, the sociologist, Ferdinand Tönnies, in his *Community and Society* (1887), described how the materialist, atomistic and self-interested priorities of a triumphant capitalist economy were undermining the spiritual and consensus-based values of older pre-mercantile Germany, producing a type of social organisation that was 'transitory and superficial', a 'mechanical aggregate and artefact'. In France, Emile Durkheim argued in his *Suicide* (1897) that modern society, lacking any 'limiting authority' or shared values, had a tendency to produce rootless and directionless citizens (he called them 'anomic'), who were increasingly linking their sense of self-worth to material acquisition, and were reacting to sudden economic deprivation with helplessness and despair. A similar prognosis was offered by Max Weber in the concluding pages of his *The Protestant Ethic and the Spirit of Capitalism* (1905). Here, Weber showed how the ethos of economic individualism, which had once performed a positive and emancipatory role, had degenerated into the stultifying orthodoxy of economic rationalism and bureaucratic statism. Those caught within this nullity, 'specialists without spirit, sensualists without heart', were dominated by routine and mechanical habit, unable to escape (in Weber's famous metaphor) from an 'iron cage' of their own making.[6]

Registering the subjective impact of these changes provided one of the pressing tasks for the literature of this period. German writers, in particular, living in a land experiencing the traumas of rapid industrial and technological expansion, revealed a pained awareness of the personal dislocations occasioned by modernity.

This is the theme of Thomas Mann's first novel, *Buddenbrooks* (1901), which tells how a once strong and self-confident mercantile family declines into bankruptcy and moral dissolution because it is unable to adapt to the grasping and arrogant materialist ethos that has come to reign in the new Germany. Only those, such as the *arriviste* family, the Hagenströms, who are 'free from the fetters of tradition and ancestral piety', are able to flourish in the cut-throat world of modern commerce, as if in vindication of the social-Darwinistic mentality that is the order of the day. The hero of Rainer Maria Rilke's *The Notebook of Malte Laurids Brigge* (1910) is similarly alienated from the modern world. Here, the crisis of modernity is registered on an internal and psychological, rather than on a social or cultural level. Experience of modernity appears in Rilke's novel as pure dislocation, an invasion of the senses through urban noise, squalor and speed, whose impact brings Brigge (a Danish poet living in Paris) close to the 'outlined edge of terror' that lies beneath the surface of life in the modern city. The disfiguration of consciousness that Brigge registers in Rilke's novel is also charted in Hermann Hesse's *Steppenwolf* (1927), but from an epic perspective capable of relating this particular mental configuration to a crisis within the history of the modern age, and to a generation which has lost 'the feeling for itself, for the self-evident, for all morals, for being safe and innocent'. As Harry Haller, the eponymous hero of the story, an introspective, asocial *Einzelgänger*, discovers: the secure world of the past has gone, and with it those rules which allowed us to distinguish between reality and illusion, the natural and the supernatural, sanity and madness. If we are to maintain these distinctions (Haller concludes) we must adjust to an elaborate 'game', whose rules are obscure and whose purpose is, ultimately, unknowable.[7]

These novels are permeated by an unmistakably apocalyptic mood, 'a constantly swelling unrest', a feeling, as the Austrian novelist Stefan Zweig noted in his autobiography, that the internal pressures that had accumulated in the years between 1870 and 1910 were now seeking 'violent release'. Evidence for this was provided by the growing diplomatic tensions between the major European powers, who launched themselves from 1905 (the date of the first Moroccan crisis) onwards into acts of increasing belligerence and displays of military might. Power politics between Germany-Austria, on the one side, and England-France (the so-called *Entente Cordiale*), on the other, deepened into an openly confrontational stance over Bosnia, in 1908, in Morocco, for the second time, in 1911, and, finally, over Serbia, in 1914. All this took place against the background of England's declining, and Germany's expanding, economic and industrial strength, of a major realignment of the status of these nations as world powers, and amidst clear signs that the impending competition for colonies would bring about a brutal and uncompromising conflict.[8]

A sense of an ending pervades the entire literature of the pre-war period. It is evident even in the work of more traditional writers, such as the English poets, A.E. Housman (*A Shropshire Lad*, 1896), Thomas Hardy (*Satires of Circumstance, Lyrics and Reveries*, 1914), and the Georgian poets, Edward Thomas and Rupert Brooke. All give voice to a gentle melancholia, to a nostalgia for a 'land of lost content' that hovers just beyond the consciousness, in a dimly remembered past. But their work also contains a distinct under-current of impending catastrophe, and it is this terminal mood that links them with mainstream modernist writers such as Italo Svevo, Robert Musil and Thomas Mann. Mann's *Death in Venice* (1912), in particular, captures that sense of crisis that was endemic to this period. The experiences that the hero of that novel, Gustav von Aschenbach, goes through, from moral and erotic dissolution to psychological self-delusion, are part of a personal crisis, but they are also tied by Mann to the nervous and debilitating atmosphere that gripped Europe in those years of diplomatic uncertainty and 'menace' prior to the First World War.[9]

Amongst a younger generation of writers that 'will to the end' that Nietzsche had identified as the defining trait of *fin de siècle* Europe was even stronger. It is to be seen in the work of the German Expressionists, who cultivated an *Untergangsstimmung* (mood of decline or destruction). This comes to the fore in the work of the young Austrian poet, Georg Trakl (*Poems*, 1913, *Sebastian in a Dream*, 1915), whose hermetic, indeed, quasi-surreal lyrics deli-cately hint at the presence of an indecipherable menace existing behind the phenomenal world of nature and things. This sense of an ending appeared more explicitly in Jakob van Hoddis's poem 'End of the World' (1911), which playfully announces the tragi-comic demise of bourgeois culture, and in the brutally apocalyptic poem 'War' (1911) by Georg Heym, which conjures up, in the midst of a despairing urban vision, the Moloch of war, who 'stands in the dusk, immense and unknown,/and the moon he crushes in his black hand'. The Italian Futurists were even more categorical. They embraced the Nietzschean 'will to an end' openly, celebrating the purifying conflagration of war, which, they felt, could alone purge Europe of the stultifying conventions of an atrophied bourgeois culture. As the leader of the group, Filippo Marinetti, declared in 'The Founding and Manifesto of Futurism' (1909), war was 'the world's only hygiene', 'militarism, patriotism, the destructive gesture of freedom-bringers, beautiful ideas worth dying for'; and he went on, in his 'Technical Manifesto of Futurist Literature' (1912), to compare a 'trench bristling with bayonets to an orchestra, a machine gun to a fatal woman', in an aesthetic paradigm that elevated violence to the level of erotic fantasy and determined aggression to an artistic practice. It is here, perhaps, in the Futurists' technocratic blueprint for the future, written barely two years before the cataclysm of the First World War, and in the first decade of a century that would attempt to undo, in the most brutal terms, the effects of liberal modernity, that energy and destruction, rebirth and annihilation, become fused into the most damaging of all modernist discourses: a playful nihilism.[10]

2   MODERNISM: BETWEEN EXPERIMENTATION AND TRADITION

Modernity called forth a mode of feeling that seemed alive to, indeed, seemed deliberately to cultivate the urgency of the moment. It is not surprising, therefore, that time, and the relationship between consciousness and time, formed a focus for much of the speculative writing of the period. Such concerns appear in the philosophy of Wilhelm Dilthey ('Ideas concerning a descriptive and analytical Psychology', 1894), and Henri Bergson (*Matter and Memory*, 1896, and *Creative Evolution*, 1907), and in science, particularly the physics of Ernst Mach (*Contributions to the Analysis of Sensations*, 1886) and Albert Einstein ('The Foundations of the General Theory of Relativity', 1916). All stress the importance of perspective, the circumscribed ontology of the material world and the defining agency of subjectivity, frequently anchoring that subjectivity in a revitalised notion of current temporality ('the now'), merging past and future in a process of heightened perception, in which (in the words of Bergson's enigmatic, indeed almost mystical language) 'our consciousness sums up for us whole periods of the inner history of things'.[11]

The literary culture of the period also took its name from this valorisation of immediacy (what Wyndham Lewis was later to describe as a 'philosophy of *psychological time*'), and not, as previous
movements in the arts such as Romanticism and Realism had done,
from a specific aesthetic theory. It was called Modernism. Although
the notion of 'the modern' found its way into a number of cultural
studies in the late nineteenth century, for example Georg Brandes'
Men of the Modern Breakthrough (1883) and Samuel Lublinski's
Assessing the Moderns (1904), 'modernism' as a recognisable literary
mode did not gain currency until the 1920s, when it found favour
amongst writers and scholars trying to make sense of a new type of
literature that represented not only aesthetic novelty and innova-
tion, but also (for many) obscurity and 'the divorce of advanced
contemporary poetry from the common-sense standards of ordinary intelligence'.[12]

But the spirit of Modernism had been evident long before
that date, both in the work produced by a number of individual
writers, and in the iconoclastic energies displayed by a generation
of younger artists, many of whom belonged to small and highly
radical cultural formations that are collectively known as the
Avant-Garde. The Avant-Garde manifested itself throughout
Europe: in Russia, there was Constructivism; in Italy, Futurism; in
Germany, Expressionism; Britain had both Imagism and Vorticism;
France and Belgium, Surrealism; and Dada's infectious energies
crossed the boundaries of Switzerland, Germany and France. These
were all theoretically sophisticated, cosmopolitan groupings, but all
revealed traits of their national origins: the Constructivists were a
product of the Russian Revolution; the Expressionists were able to
draw on the *Märchen* tradition of German Romanticism; whilst the
French Surrealists could trace their ancestry to the psychological
obsessions and fantasy worlds of Gérard de Nerval and Lautréamont.
Nevertheless, there were important convergences, which allows us
to think of them as individual contributions to the multiple phenomena of Modernism. They shared, for example, an irreverent
and provocative attitude towards high art and its pretentious consumerism. The catch-cry was 'épater le bourgeois' (or *Bürgershreck*,
in German), an iconoclastic strategy of provocation, antagonism,
and dissension, which possessed both a social (soon to become political), and a linguistic dimension. As the German Expressionist,
Ferdinand Hardekopf, explained (to those of his middle-class readership that dared to listen): 'our psychology will scandalise you.

Our syntax will asphyxiate you. We will observe your great confusions with a smile, observing them analytically and with premonition.' The German-Swiss movement, Dada, founded in 1916 by Hans Arp, Tristan Tzara, Hugo Ball and Richard Huelsenbeck, represented the acme of this mentality. From the vantage point of their *Cabaret Voltaire* in Zurich, they debunked, satirised, parodied and lambasted high cultural institutions and their representatives. The Dadaists sought to provoke and antagonise, to 'destroy the drawers of the brain and those of social organisation: to sow demoralisation everywhere, and throw heaven's hand into hell'. As Tzara explained: 'The beginnings of Dada were not the beginnings of an art, but those of a disgust.' Gestures of outrage, of targeted disgust, permeated the Avant-Garde. Alfred Jarry's play *King Ubu* (1896), a pre-Dadaistic parody of *Oedipus Rex*, opens with the exclamation, 'Shit!'. A similar scatological irreverence is evident in Bertold Brecht's play, *Baal* (1918, published 1922), whose quasi-mythic celebration of sensuality and physical corruption was clearly influenced by the highly volatile and aggressive anti-establishmentarianism that was typical of the Avant-Garde mentality.[13]

The tactics of the Avant-Garde may have seemed nihilistic; but they were put into the service of a goal that was essentially constructive: the regaining of an authentic base for European culture. Routes to that goal were diverse. Many, particularly in Germany, followed Nietzsche in returning to a revitalised notion of the primitive and the animalistic. Gottfried Benn apostrophised such forces in his ecstatic essay, 'Primal Vision' (1926), where he spoke of his own attempts to summon up through incantatory means the primeval layers of his being: 'I sniffed in masks, I rattled in runes, I dove into daemons with sleep-craving brutality, with mythical instincts, in the anteverbal, instinctual threat of prehistoric neura.' Benn's colleagues in the Expressionist movement might have been more restrained in their primitivism (Benn's eventually brought him into the National Socialist camp), but they too possessed their own mysticism of self. Formed around journals such as *Der Sturm* (The Storm, 1910–1932), edited by Herwarth Walden, *Die Aktion* (Action, 1911–1932), edited by Franz Pfempfert, and the *Die weißen Blätter* (The White Pages, 1913–1921), edited by Franz Blei and René Schickelé, Expressionism was governed by a visionary intensity whose voice was exhortation and invocation. As the poet Otto Flake asserted in 1915: 'We are the moderns: it is we who recognise the vital, animal, dynamic facts of life.' What Expressionists such as

Ernst Toller, Franz Werfel, Georg Heym and Georg Kaiser hoped to
achieve was nothing less than a 'break-through' to a new cultural
medium, a type of art that would allow emotion in all its forms
(suffering, visionary, despairing or ecstatic) to express itself beyond
the constraints of imposed form and the restraints of moral inhibi-
tion. The external world was to be posited ('expressed') as an emanation of the internal world of the poet. As Kasimir Edschmid
(*Verses, Hymns and Songs*, 1911) asserted in one of the key manifestos of the movement: '[the Expressionist artist] doesn't see, he
envisions. He doesn't depict, he experiences. He doesn't reproduce,
he fashions. He doesn't take, he searches. Now the chain of facts
exists no more: factories, houses, disease, whores, tumult and
hunger. Now there is only the vision of these.'[14]

Less visionary, but with an equal stress upon the rejuvenating
energies of the irrational, was the English movement, Vorticism.
Its leading light was Wyndham Lewis, a charismatic figure characteristic of Avant-Garde eclecticism, who combined the formulation of theoretical manifestos and the elaboration of speculative
philosophies with painting, design and novel writing (*Tarr*, 1918).
But Lewis's main contribution to the formation of an Avant-Garde
in England lay in his editorship (in conjunction with the American
poet, Ezra Pound) of the short-lived journal, *Blast* (1914–1915).
Here Lewis lambasted the inherited culture of the nineteenth
century, and in trenchant expletives, from which none were excluded: 'BLAST- years 1837 to 1900/curse Abysmal inexcusable
middle-class/(also Aristocracy and Proletariat) ... WRING THE
NECK OF all sick inventions born in that/progressive white
wake'. In the place of this pusillanimous complacency, the
Vorticists propounded a vitalistic philosophy, half Bergsonian,
half Italian Futurist, whose focus was the 'Vortex' of a present
shorn of all illusions and ideals: 'we wish the Past and Future
with us', Lewis announced in the first issue of *Blast* (June 1914),
'the Past to mop up our melancholy, the Future to absorb our
troublesome optimism'. Into this vision of pure immediacy, the
Vorticists sought to draw all who found themselves both fearful
and excited by the advent of modernity. As a movement, it did
not outlast the outbreak of the First World War, in which one of
its leading supporters, the French sculptor Henri Gaudier-
Brzeska, died, forced to bear witness, perhaps, to the fact that the
reality of martial apocalypse is frequently less rewarding than the
theory.[15]

The French Surrealists, founded as a group by André Breton in 1924, and dissolved soon after 1930, were without the ecstatic mentality of the German Expressionists or the violent self-assertiveness of the English Vorticists, but they too sought to give form to the dynamic workings of personal psychology. If Nietzsche dominated the thinking of the Expressionists (his presence is evident in their rhapsodic and often hyperbolic positions of speech, and in the nihilism that frequently invades their world-view), it was Freud (the analyst of dreams and other epiphenomenona of the unconscious) who acted as the presiding spirit of the Surrealist project. His influence is evident in the first Surrealist manifesto of 1924, in which, with a mock seriousness, Breton attempted a lexical definition of his aesthetic: 'SURREALISM, n. Psychic automatism in its pure state, by which one proposes to express – verbally, by means of the written word, or in any other manner – the actual functioning of thought, [...] in the absence of any control exercised by reason, exempt from any aesthetic or moral concern'. The Surrealists evinced a belief in 'certain forms of previously neglected associations, in the omnipotence of dream, in the disinterested play of thought', through whose channels they hoped to effect (as Breton later explained) 'the future transformation of those two seemingly contradictory states, dream and reality, into a sort of absolute reality, of surreality, so to speak'. The literary effect of these ambitions was varied. The members of the movement, Breton, Louis Aragon, Paul Eluard, Philippe Soupault and Robert Desnos, experimented with dream analysis, hypnosis, and automatic writing (*écriture automatique*). Much ephemera was produced through this process: poem-objects, collages, posters, exhibition catalogues; but also major work, poetry such as Eluard's *The Underside of Life or the Human Pyramid* and *Capital of Sorrow* (both 1926), and, with a greater typographical radicalism, Breton and Soupault's *Magnetic Fields* (1920). This is a poetry whose elliptical syntax and improbable juxtaposition of imagery forces the reader to make connections between areas of experience and facets of the phenomenal world previously unconnected. Such devices were also used by Breton in his novel *Nadja* (1928) (a mixture of reportage and urban fantasy) which centres around the author's amorous fixation with a stranger, and in Raymond Queneau's *The Bark Tree* (1933), a work of metafictional playfulness and existential parody, which seeks to open up a 'tridimensional reality', forcing the reader to suspend the conventions of philosophical and literary sense.[16]

Above all, Surrealists sought to open up the deeper workings of the mind into a dialogue with the world. Louis Aragon, in particular, insisted upon this greater mission of the Surrealist project: to foster a 'sense of the marvellous suffusing everyday existence'. As he noted in the preface to his most famous work, *Paris Peasant* (1926): 'each day the modern sense of existence becomes subtly altered. A mythology ravels and unravels'. To appreciate this modern mythology (here the city of Paris going through a process of rapid topographical change), we must rid ourselves of 'those hemp-seeds of the imagination' which consign the fantastic and surreal to the private world of dreams, and prevent us from recognising the 'admirable gardens of absurd beliefs, forebodings, obsessions and frenzies', which are a distinctive and common feature of the modern experience. Aragon's exhortation, that we should collapse the private and public realms into a single optic, was taken up by one of the most remarkable voices in the Surrealist movement: Antonin Artaud. In his plans for a Theatre of Cruelty (as formulated in *The Theatre and its Double*, 1938), Artaud sought to evolve a dramatic method based on the 'idea of culture-in-action', a dramaturgy which would allow him to abolish the distinction between ritual and reality, theatre and street. Here, performer and spectator alike would follow a 'language half-way between gesture and thought', giving themselves over to a drama of excess, in an effort to transform their inner wishes, fantasies and phobias into public spectacle. The result (Artaud contended) would be a theatre that would 'allow the public to liberate within itself the magical liberties of dreams which it can only recognise when they are imprinted with terror and cruelty'.[17]

The radical energies of the Avant-Garde emerged most clearly, however, in the texture of their writing. As Marinetti explained in his manifesto of 1913, the Futurists were seeking nothing less than a 'typographical revolution', which would give vent to an 'essential and synthetic lyricism, imagination without strings, and words-in-freedom'. The conventions of the page were to be redrawn, syntax dismantled, typefaces dislocated, to allow the written line to form a 'chain of pictorial sensations and analogies' that would cut across the artificial divide between the text as a semantic unit and the text as *objet d'art*. A similar tack was taken by the Dadaists. From the very beginning, Tzara, Huelsenbeck and Arp had sought to exploit the potential of their writing, combining (in their performances at the *Cabaret Voltaire*) song, mime, declaration and nonsense verse, to produce what they called the 'simultaneous poem' (*poème simultané*). Such poems were not for publication, but the spirit of this work reappeared in Arp's later volumes of poetry, *The Cloud Pump, One Bird in Three* and *The Swallow's Testicle* (all published in 1920), and (in a more structured way) in individual poems such as Hugo Ball's 'Karawane' (1917) and Kurt Schwitters 'Anna Blume' (1919). Such poems exploit the free semantic play of language, allowing the reader (as Schwitters noted in 1924) to 'evaluate word against word, concept against concept, within the context of verbal association'. The procedures and techniques of such verse strikingly anticipated the 'concrete poetry' written by Ernst Jandl and Eugen Gomringer later in the century.[18]

The Avant-Garde represented the most radical and (some might say) the most progressive wing of literary Modernism. And yet the iconoclastic energies of its work had only a limited impact upon the major writers of this period, those whom we now regard as main-stream Modernists such as Virginia Woolf, D.H. Lawrence and W.B Yeats, in England and Ireland; Marcel Proust and André Gide, in France; Thomas Mann, Robert Musil and Franz Kafka, in German-speaking Europe; and Italo Svevo, in Italy. Although many of these writers were impressed by the innovatory nature of the Avant-Garde project, and appreciated its youthful energies, they were also convinced of the need to absorb these energies into the traditions of their respective literary cultures. Virginia Woolf, for example, one of the first commentators on Modernism in England, as well as one of its first exponents, was impressed by the achievements of French Post-Impressionist school, seeing in the 1910 London exhibition of its works clear evidence that 'human character [had] changed' in the Western world. Woolf had, nevertheless, misgivings about the wider impact of the Avant-Garde revolution upon the 'very foundations and rules of literary society', and held herself apart from its more radical developments. T.S. Eliot (born in America, but a British citizen from 1927) showed the same ambivalence towards the Avant-Garde movement. He was happy to acknowledge his debt to Jules Laforgue and Tristan Corbière, leading voices in the French Symbolist movement (an early version of the French Avant-Garde), whose startling imagery and ironic urbanity influenced Eliot's first book of published verse, *Prufrock and Other Observations* (1917). And yet, like Woolf, Eliot was aware of the need to channel such disruptive energies into a productive relationship with existing literary forms, to incorporate them into a larger design. As he argued in his important essay, 'Tradition and the Individual Talent' (1920), the writer is unlikely to produce a genuine piece of writing unless he or she 'lives in what is not merely the present, but the present moment of the past', that community of knowledge and values that constitutes a culture. And, in what was clearly a critical rejoinder to those amongst the Avant-Garde who had mocked and pilloried high-cultural attainments, Eliot advocates both a greater conservatism and a simple lesson in cultural modesty: the poet 'must be aware that the mind of Europe – the mind of his own country – a mind which he learns in time to be much more important than his own private mind – is a mind which changes, and that this change is a development which abandons nothing *en route*, which does not superannuate either Shakespeare, or Homer, or the rock drawing of the Magdalenian draughtsmen'. A similar balancing act between Avant-Garde radicalism and conservative tradition was made by Thomas Mann. As he frequently admitted, his intellectual outlook was formed by the late neo-Romanticism of Wagner, Schopenhauer and Nietzsche (and perhaps more locally by the *Jugendstil* of *fin de siècle* Munich). And yet throughout his early work, most notably in *Buddenbrooks* (1901), *Tristan* and *Tonio Kröger* (both 1903), Mann treated the claims of artistic sensibility in a sympathetic but, ultimately, ironic fashion, relativising them against the more stable values that he saw emanating from the family or, more generally, from the positive features of bourgeois society itself, such as health and sociability.[19]

The goal of the mainstream Modernists was, in short, the absorption of novelty into custom; they sought not the destruction of the latter, but the retention of its vital elements to enrich the traditions of their respective literary cultures. Eliot showed how this was to be achieved in the poetry of his maturity, such as *The Waste Land* (1922). Here, the formal moment of Avant-Garde iconoclasm is exploited, but within a context alive to the mythic and religious structures which underscore the flow of history. An even more extensive attempt to exploit Avant-Garde techniques for Modernist purposes was made by James Joyce in his epic novel, *Ulysses* (1922). Joyce drew upon both the French Symbolist tradition and the language games of Dada and Apollinaire, producing a complex text of shifting narrative positions and typographies that would have been familiar to any exponent of the Avant-Garde. But Joyce gives unity to his work by framing these diverse techniques within a larger narrative adapted from the Greek epic poem of the *Odyssey*, and in such a way that the individual details of his novel can always be related to the larger underlying pattern. In a similar vein, Kafka availed himself of many of the techniques and themes of the German Expressionists, taking over not only the allegorising mode they favoured, but also their focus upon the obsessive nature of character and their interest in the psychic effects of generational conflict. These are all themes in Kafka's work, particularly the stories, 'The Metamorphosis' (1915), 'The Judgement' (1916) and 'A Hunger Artist' (1922). And yet these themes, and Kafka's own pre-Surrealist optic, are given a depth rarely present in the Expressionist genre. The reasons for this lie both in the personal intensity with which they are infused (whose sources were racial, psychological and familial) and in Kafka's exploitation of the Cabbalist tradition whose spiritual depths allowed the author to translate (as his friend and colleague Max Brod perceptively noted) the individual case into 'the eternal, the transcendental'. In the work of main-stream modernists such as Kafka and Joyce, the dislocations and challenges posed by modernity are registered, but also, at the same time, overcome, integrated into aesthetic totalities and larger patterns of meaning, which, ultimately, prove capable of capturing 'this varying, this unknown and uncircumscribed spirit, whatever aberration or complexity it may display', which Virginia Woolf, at least, regarded as the ultimate achievement of the Modernist ethos.[20]

3   THE LITERATURE OF AESTHETIC REVIVAL: SYMBOLISM AND DECADENCE

Even at the moment of its greatest triumph, voices had been raised against the Realist-Naturalist aesthetic; against, as the English critic, Arthur Symons noted, its slavish adherence to 'exteriority', its uncritical acceptance of the unmediated *données* of the world beyond the self. In France, Baudelaire dismissed Realism as 'a word, a banner, *a joke*', and even Flaubert, whose *Madame Bovary* (1857) was thought by many to be one of the great Realist novels of the age, rejected it as 'materialist' and populist. In his later works (the novel *Salammbô*, 1862, the drama-narrative *The Temptation of Saint Anthony*, 1874, and the stories 'The Legend of Saint Julian, Hospitaller' and 'Herodia', both 1877), Flaubert moved away from his earlier Realist style, towards a style which was both more erotic and more violent; indeed, towards an aesthetic which combined the two modes, confusing their boundaries through fantasy and parable. This new direction in Flaubert's writing is evident in *Salammbô*, whose narrative consists of a series of brutal and exotic *tableaux*, which are formed around the historical melodrama of the Mercenary Revolt against Carthage (just after the first Punic war). In spite of its antiquarian detail, however, Flaubert's novel is really concerned with the larger-than-life passions embodied in Salammbô, and in the men who come into contact with her. A similar sensuality is evident in *The Temptation of Saint Anthony*, and in the stories published as *Three Tales*. Both works draw us into a world of lasciviousness, cruelty, and unbridled egotism, and reveal a distinct macabre feel for the aestheticisation of suffering and death.[21]

Flaubert's late work formed a central part of a movement in the arts known as Romantic Decadence. The writers of Romantic Decadence sought to explore those areas of experience, illicit, marginal and exotic, which had not only been neglected by the majority of Realist writers, but had been positively prohibited by the publishers and journals of conservative France. As Flaubert and Baudelaire had discovered in 1866 (the year in which they were both tried for offending public decency) the moral-judicial limits on poetic licence were severe. Writing which attempted to push back the conventions of literary taste was forced into the shadow-world of private circulation and illicit publication. This was the case with one of the seminal texts of Romantic Decadence: *The Songs of Maldoror*, written by the twenty-two-year-old Comte de Lautréamont (*nom de plume* of Isidore Ducasse), between 1868 and 1869 and published in 1874. Composed in six long cantos, *The Songs of Maldoror* detail the epic picaresque voyage of its hero through a world of evil and deviant malpractices, from Vampirism to sexual initiation. The tone of the text is one of sustained hallucination, and its ambit one that moves between myth and personal fantasy, as it details the vision of 'man acting in all his stupidity, perverting souls by any means possible'. In its heightened sensationalism and macabre imagination, *The Songs of Maldoror* deliberately flaunted bourgeois standards, both moral and aesthetic. But the greatest shock to public sensibility came from the most iconoclastic of the *poètes maudits* (decadent poets, named thus after the title of a volume of essays published by Paul Verlaine in 1884): Arthur Rimbaud. Younger still than Lautréamont, Rimbaud developed his *oeuvre* around a sustained confrontation with the *mores* of (what he regarded as) a culturally bankrupt and atrophied society. His major works – 'The Drunken Boat' (1871), *Illuminations* (written in 1872, but not published until 1886) and *A Season in Hell* (1873) – give voice to a rhapsodic, almost visionary engagement with reality. In a famous letter written in 1871, Rimbaud announced that his ambition was 'to arrive at the unknown by the disordering of *all the senses*'. His work reflects this goal: extended narratives written largely in free verse combine religious, mythic and supernatural discourses with the profane (and sometimes obscene) iconography of the modern city. And throughout, Rimbaud withholds from the reader any clear idea of the enunciating subject: there is no lyrical self, no clear position of speech, simply a multitude of voices responding in pain, anger and delight to the needs of 'a soul that is almost dead to goodness, in which the light rises severe as funereal tapers'. And yet the much vaunted amorality of Rimbaud's vision (an image sustained by his own aesthetic self-stylisation amongst the Bohemian groups of Paris) served to obscure the deep sense of sin and longing for redemption that is also discernible in his work, particularly in *A Season in Hell*. In this volume, the ecstatic epiphanies of the *Illuminations* give way to painful introspection and confession, almost as if the poet is assessing the final fruits, psychological and moral, of the journey made through derangement and the experience of evil. Fatigue and despair are the key themes here, and a new note of spiritual vulnerability: 'I cannot defend myself! – I am hidden and I am not hidden/The flame rises again with its damned soul'.[22]

Rimbaud positioned the poet (in the words of his contemporary, Nietzsche) 'beyond good and evil', conceiving him as a denizen of a world where all may be experienced and forgiven, for the sake of a deeper penetration of those realms that lie beyond rational consciousness and moral acceptance. Both Rimbaud's exhortations and his example were followed by many from within the Decadent school. Barbey d'Aurevilly's tales, *The Diaboliques* (1874), half-detective fiction, half-horror, figure incestuous priests and sorcery in their diverse narratives; whilst Villiers de l'Isle-Adam's *Cruel Tales* (1883) and, most notably, his enigmatic play, *Axël* (1890), promoted a number of vices, obscure and less obscure. But the novel that transformed the Decadent position into a conscious and recognisable stance was Joris-Karl Huysmans' *Against Nature* (1884). In Huysmans' novel, we leave the street-wise youth-culture that Rimbaud had spun around the outcast, criminal and

Lumpenproletariat in his poetry, and enter the realm of aristocratic panache, of that key figure in *fin de siècle* Europe: the Dandy. Although no less amoral or hedonistic, Decadence here does not simply constitute a critique of bourgeois morality; it forms its replacement, providing a self-conscious counter-ethos, which sets against that functional Utilitarianism much beloved of the progressive liberal spirit, an inward-looking, sensation-seeking culture, whose ultimate goal is not material acquisition or social utility, but the capturing of 'erudite fancies, complicated nightmares, suave and sinister visions'. The aristocratic hero of the novel, Des Esseintes, is afflicted with the *mal du siècle*, that combination of boredom and satiety that Baudelaire and those that followed him called *ennui*. The victim of an over-developed sensibility, of a brain 'shaken and sharpened and rendered almost clairvoyant by neurosis', Huysmans' hero tries to rid himself of the commonplace banalities of late nineteenth-century commercial life, by giving himself over to a systematic cultivation of the senses, with the aid of exotic flowers, potent liquors, bizarre pets and an arcane library. In Des Esseintes's world, nature and artifice are transposed, imagination substituted for reality, and ethical norms relativised and displaced by those of an obsessive individualism that accepts no external check upon the exercise of its own privileged rights.[23]

Decadence became the dominant aesthetic of *fin de siècle* Europe. Arthur Symons called it 'a new and beautiful and interesting disease'; Paul Verlaine provided the first poetic use of the term in his poem 'Languor' (from the volume *Of Old and Late*, 1884), whilst Gautier supplied its most complete definition in his famous preface (written in 1868) to Baudelaire's *Flowers of Evil*, where he defined Decadence as 'the necessary but fatal idiom of those peoples and civilisations in which artificial life has replaced natural life and has brought forth within men obscure desires'. Walter Pater provided the *locus classicus* for the English Decadent position in his work of art history, *The Renaissance* (1873). Here, in the conclusion to his study, Pater argued that the individual must break the bounds of habit, but can only do so by remaining alive to those moments in which 'the greatest number of vital forces unite in their purest energy'. At such times of heightened sensibility, the mind and the emotions become transfigured, transported to a higher realm. 'To burn always with this hard, gemlike flame, to maintain [this] ecstasy, is success in life.' An entire generation, from Algernon Charles Swinburne to Oscar

Wilde, agreed. It was Wilde who provided the most vital example of the new sensibility. He achieved this not so much in his plays (*Lady Windermere's Fan*, 1892, *A Woman of No Importance*, 1893, and *The Importance of Being Ernest*, 1895), where he playfully teased aristocratic society for its double standards, role-playing and shallow sense of values, but in his sole novel, *The Picture of Dorian Gray* (1890). The hero of this novel attempts to arrest the decay of years by means both magical and amoral, but fails, physically wasted and morally repentant. In spite of its strangely pessimistic and somewhat moralising conclusion, the novel devotes much space to a celebration of a 'new Hedonism', often dwelling in loving detail upon the body culture and the cult of youth that was at the centre of the ethos of Romantic Decadence. Wilde achieved fame through his plays, and notoriety through his life; but his rare theoretical pronouncements on art are equally important, for in them he broke not only with the aesthetic desiderata of the Realist-Naturalist school, but with an entire tradition that sought to subject art to moralistic criteria. By reversing that equation ('the morality of art consists in the perfect use of an imperfect medium'), Wilde provided a succinct formulation of the aestheticism that underscored his personal outlook, whilst pointing the way forward for writers such as D.H. Lawrence, André Gide and Thomas Mann. These mainstream Modernists would later take such insights as their starting point, exploring in their work that pained (but often liberating) relationship between ethical transgression and individual self-fulfilment that Wilde had charted a generation earlier.[24]

The distance between the Decadence of Huysmans and the ethereal spirituality of the Symbolist poets, particularly of their guiding light, Stéphane Mallarmé, may seem great. But important affinities did exist: both groups viewed the aesthetic vocation with an almost religious intensity; both treated the phenomenal world purely as an extension of the perceiving self; and both were convinced that personal experience should be dislocated from habit and convention. Symbolism had its origins in poetry of the Parnassian school, a group of poets centred around the figure of the enigmatic Leconte de Lisle, whose promulgation of an 'art for art's sake' (*l'art pour l'art*) became the catch-phrase for this generation. They published their work in the esoteric journal *The Contemporary Parnassian* (three volumes: 1866, 1871, and 1876), where they expressed their characteristic aristocratic disdain for the common themes and bourgeois predicaments explored by Realist writers, and for the heroic and often lachrymose rhetoric favoured by French Romantic writers such as Hugo and Lamartine. In their insistence upon formal rigour and purity of diction, the Parnassians shared a common project with the Symbolists, who sought to remove poetry from the banalities of the everyday world and the politics of the literary market place. The Symbolists, however, deepened the Parnassian aesthetic into a poetics of heightened obscurity. Symbolist poets such as Mallarmé employed images that were often arcane and esoteric, but which could act (precisely because of their hermeneutic inaccessibility) as signs of higher realms of being and consciousness. It was the literary critic, Jean Moréas, whose 'Literary Manifesto of the Symbolist School' (published in 1886) supplied the public with an account of the Symbolist school, but it was Mallarmé who provided the movement with its theoretical justification. In his letters and essays, Mallarmé argued that the Symbolist poem should cultivate connotation rather than denotation, should 'retain only the suggestiveness of things', in an endeavour to capture that pristine world beyond language, whose secrets have opened themselves to music but never before to literature. It was within this rarefied realm of unmediated significance that Mallarmé wished the poet to move, creating an ideal text where (and the paradox was central to the Symbolist aesthetic) 'everything will be hesitation, disposition of parts, their alternations and their relationships – all this contributing to the rhythmic totality, which will be the very silence of the poem'.[25]

Mallarmé's output was slim (the major texts are 'The Afternoon of a Faun', 1876, *Several Sonnets*, including the famous 'The virginal, living and beautiful day', 1885, and *A Dice Throw*, 1897); but it was precisely the paucity of his writing that testified to his eclectic vision, and to his desire to refine the nature of poetic language to the point where it would prove capable of registering the 'image emanating from the reveries which things arouse in us'. Mallarmé's work, formally elliptical and semantically polyvalent, might best be understood as the poetic analogue of philosophical idealism; the mental states that he evokes (as in 'The Afternoon of a Faun') are the products of the indistinct workings of memory and dream, possessing a nebulous ontology that exists somewhere between memory and longing, between reality and wish-fulfilment. They are, in short, like the nymphs and the natural world that envelops the faun, timeless representatives of 'the visible, calm and artificial breath/Of inspiration'.[26]

Mallarmé was the still point around which the Symbolist movement turned, his leadership being assured both through the uncompromising integrity of his verse and through the magisterial presence of his personality. The other major Symbolists were Leconte de Lisle (*Antique Poems*, 1852), Paul Verlaine (*Gallant Festivals*, 1869, and *Wisdom*, 1881), Tristan Corbière (*Yellow Loves*, 1873), Jules Laforgue (*Complaints*, 1885) and Maurice Maeterlinck (*Pelléas and Mélisande*, 1892). The poetic idiom of these poets was wide, ranging from the late-Romantic intoxication that pervades Maeterlinck's play, through to the miniature conversation pieces of Verlaine, with their wistful evocations of the fleeting moment (see, for example, the famous 'Clair de Lune', 1869). In the more robust colloquial verse of Corbière and Laforgue, the use of argot, playful irony and polyphonic textuality, evident in, for example, Laforgue's *Complaints*, combined to produce some of the first examples of *vers libre* (verse free of metrical norms and rhyme) in modern poetry, allowing the Symbolist idiom to acquire a distinctive Modernist voice.

The impact of the Symbolist idiom on European literature was enormous. In England, Swinburne wrote, in the three volumes of his *Poems and Ballads* (1866, 1878, and 1889), a poetry, languorous and brooding, but also probing in its challenges to Victorian taboos on sexuality and death; whilst Pater expanded the classic statement of the Symbolist credo in *The Renaissance* into his *Bildungsroman*, *Marius the Epicurean* (1885), whose early Roman hero strives towards 'the very highest achievement: the unclouded and receptive soul' that was for Pater the *terminus ad quem* of all intellectual endeavour. Equally convinced of the mystical potency of the moment was the Czech poet, Otokar Březine (*Mysterious Expanses*, 1895), and Gerald Manley Hopkins ('The Wreck of the Deutschland', 1875). The Jesuit priest may not have sympathised with everything espoused by the French Symbolists, and yet, in his theory of 'inscape' he produced a theory of poetic inspiration that paralleled the Symbolist (and, later, Joycean) notion of the epiphany. Like them, Hopkins saw in heightened consciousness the same 'moulding force which succeeds in asserting itself over the resistance of cumbersome or restraining matter', and which leads to the distilling of an experience in a single image or symbol. That the poet saw in this intensity of experience proof of the immanence of God only serves to establish his connection with the French movement, many of whose members (such as Huysmans) were to discover a religious vocation towards the end of their literary careers.[27]

In Italy, Germany, Spain, and Russia, Symbolism interacted with the native literatures of those nations to produce a distinctive version of early Modernism. In Russia, Symbolism was the dominant literary movement in the years between 1890 and 1910, being formed by individuals such as Alexander Blok (*Verses about the Beautiful Lady*, 1904) and Andrey Bely (*Ashes* and *The Urn*, both 1909). In his early verse, Blok, who analysed the origins of his aesthetic in 'On the Present State of Russian Symbolism' (1910), drew out the mystical potential of the French tradition, fusing the feel of poets such as Mallarmé and Verlaine for mood and ambience with the traditional Russian adoration of sanctified femininity. Later, in his most famous poem, 'The Twelve' (1918), which likens a group of Russian revolutionaries to Christ's disciples, Blok's visionary Symbolism came to acquire the intensity of political messianism in a poem that transmutes the Revolution into an event of spiritual renewal. Spain and Portugal also possessed their indigenous Symbolist poets, in the shape of Gustavo Adolfo Bécquer (*Verse*, 1871), and Fernando Pessoa. Pessoa's poetry, in particular, took Symbolism into the discourse of Modernism proper, exploiting multiple personae to give voice to the many shades of introspection and stoicism that characterise his writing. In Italy, Gabriele D'Annunzio published poetry (*Early Spring*, 1879, and *Poetic Intermezzo*, 1883), and novels (*The Child of Pleasure*, 1889, and *The Triumph of Death*, 1895), which combined the Symbolist appreciation of colour and music with a Decadent craving for extreme sensuality. D'Annunzio, however, soon turned introspection into a more assertive idiom; in volumes such as *Alcyone* (1903), and in the third volume of the incomplete series titled *Praises of the Sky, of the Sea, of the Earth, and of Heroes*, he made contact with a Nietzschean vitalism, where sensual display acquires a more virile pose. The same transition was made by the Swedish poet, Werner von Heidenstam (*Poems*, 1895, and *New Poems*, 1915), and the German, Stefan George. George, in particular (a disciple of Mallarmé), subjected the Symbolist heritage to a firmer discipline, in which strict metrical form fused with a celebration of the values of hierarchy and order. These are the values that emerge out of *The Seventh Ring* (1907), and *The Star of the Circle* (1914). George appears in this verse as a quasi-Messianic figure, the chosen one, the magister who 'breaks the chains, and sweeping away the ruins/Imposes order, bringing back those who have run away/Into an eternal state of justice'. In this poetry, we come to the end of the Symbolist moment; born under the sign of Nietzsche's superman, George's verse seeks to transcend the hypertrophic aestheticism of the French school, replacing its ethereal dissipation with a new, more Germanic ethos, founded on respect for the charismatic personality, on self-discipline and on a rigour of mind and body, on values that hover somewhere between neo-classicism and ceremonial ritual.[28]

4   HEARTS OF DARKNESS: THE SELF AS OTHER

Underwriting the poetics of the Symbolist creed was the conviction that individual identity was a fragmented and discontinuous thing, the self a meeting place for conflicting desires and intellectual contradictions. The Symbolist poet, Jules Laforgue, for example, declared himself (in the first of his 'Sundays' poems, 1887) a 'poor pale and paltry individual/Who doesn't believe in his Self except at his lost moments'. His contemporary, Arthur Rimbaud, put it even more forcefully in a letter written in 1871, where he attested: 'It is a mistake to say: I think. One ought to say: I am thought [...] I is someone else' (literally: 'I is an other'). These were sentiments shared by many Modernist writers, including D.H. Lawrence. Writing in 1914, he warned his sympathetic readers that the notion of the stable personality was simply no longer tenable. As he explained in a letter (whose very grammar seems to reflect Lawrence's psychological relativism): 'You mustn't look in my novel for the old stable ego of the character. There is another ego, according to whose action the individual is unrecognisable, and passes through, as it were, allotropic states which it needs a deeper sense than any we've been used to exercise, to discover are states of the same radically-unchanged single element.'[29]

The writers of this period were supported in their belief in the manifold plurality and complexity of individual identity by a number of philosophical investigations into the nature and workings of the unconscious. As early as 1869, Eduard von Hartmann had published his *Philosophy of the Unconscious*, which influenced writers throughout Europe. But it was the work of Nietzsche and Freud that made the greatest impact. In spite of their radically diverging perspectives (existential-philosophical, in the former case, psychoanalytic-scientistic, in the latter), both posited the existence of a residual, darker self within the human psyche ('the primary man', according to Nietzsche), whose Dionysian energies, excessive and unindividuated, belong to the realm of '*dream* and *intoxication*'. As if to stress the otherness of such energies, Freud grouped them together under the name of 'das Es' (the Id, literally 'the It'), identifying them as that 'dark, inaccessible part of our personality'. As Freud explained, this element of our personality can only be approached through metaphor or analogy: 'we call it chaos, a cauldron full of seething excitations [...] it is filled with energy reaching it from the instincts, but is has no organisation, produces no collective will, but only a striving to bring about the satisfaction of the instinctual needs subject to the observance of the pleasure principle'.[30]

The notion that the self is both fragmented and morally ambiguous informs the fiction of many of the major writers of the Modernist period, from Joseph Conrad through to Franz Kafka, Luigi Pirandello and Robert Musil. The theme appears as early as 1886, in Robert Louis Stevenson's popular novel, *The Strange Case of Dr Jekyll and Mr Hyde*. The figure of the split personality had been familiar to the writers of the German Romantic *Märchen*, such as Tieck and Hoffmann, who had used the *Doppelgänger* device to give concrete shape to that duality of personality with which their heroes were often afflicted. Stevenson retains this device, but refracts it through the more contemporary and infinitely more sinister discourse of medical experimentation; and what are unleashed here are not creative urges, capable of transforming banality into a world of fantasy, but rapacity, cruelty and murder. Stevenson's story is a cautionary one, aimed both at those who cherish an optimism in a scientifically engineered future, and at the *fin de siècle* aesthetes, whose longing for ever more novel sensations and for a life enjoyed beyond the constraints of conscience and custom culminates here, not in the refinement of personality or artistic creation, but in 'delirium', in that 'cold thrill of terror' that attends Hyde as he stalks London during the moments of his bestial transformation.[31]

At one point in Stevenson's tale, Dr Jekyll makes reference to the 'unknown' nature of the creature that he has unleashed within himself; 'the state of my own knowledge', he confesses, 'does not pass beyond that point' of simple recognition: the psychic forces that create evil resist categorisation. Joseph Conrad came to a similar conclusion in his *Heart of Darkness* (1902). Set in the Belgian Congo at the height of its imperialist exploitation, Conrad's story provides an early study of the ethos of colonialism that the author was to explore further, with varying emphases upon the political, in later novels such as *The Nigger of Narcissus* (1897), *Lord Jim* (1900) and *Nostromo* (1904). The story tells of the journey of the central character, Marlowe, into the heart of Africa, and can clearly, on one level, be seen as a critique of the bankruptcy of 'moral purpose' that adhered to the imperialist mission in the nineteenth century. But the darkness that Marlowe finds is as much spiritual as political, as becomes evident in his encounter with Kurtz. The latter, an enigmatic station manager, has surrendered himself to the 'heavy, mute spell of the wilderness', and in the process has abandoned all standards of decency in favour of a barbaric life twisted by 'forgotten and brutal instincts, [memories] of gratified and monstrous passions'. As Marlowe discovers, in the face of such horror, conventional language, those 'familiar, vague sounds exchanged on every waking day of life', proves quite useless. The darkness that is the self-as-other cannot be described, but only invoked in metaphors, which will perhaps speak to the initiated, but will remain to others (such as Kurtz's fiancée) forever inaccessible.[32]

In Conrad's story, the conventional self, sociable, practical and rational, confronts its opposite in incredulity and incomprehension, But that the two realms of reason and unreason are intimately, if obscurely connected, Conrad leaves us in little doubt, evoking in the final words of his tale that 'tranquil waterway' which allows light and darkness to flow, quite literally, into one another. Stevenson, in his story, also makes it quite clear that there is a deep connection between criminality and normalcy; the former not only dwells within the latter, but supports and, indeed, makes it possible. This was a theme explored by the Austrian, Robert Musil, in his first novel, *The Confusions of Young Törless* (1906). Here, those dark urges that Conrad had attempted to delineate within the alien climes of an African jungle are located within the very heart of respectable society: in a military academy run for the sons of Austria's prosperous middle-classes. During his education here, Musil's young hero learns that behind the façade of academic and social respectability (which is maintained by his teachers and parents alike) exists a quite different world, one which possesses a raw and entirely amoral animality that governs all but is never acknowledged. Törless is initiated into this world by two co-boarders, Beineberg and Reiting, who have chosen one of their colleagues, the abject Basini, as an object for systematic and sadistic mistreatment. What Törless learns through these experiences, into the increasing homo-eroticism of which he is ultimately drawn, is that normalcy contains its own pathology, that 'between those people whose lives move in an orderly way between office and family', and the others, 'the outcasts, the blood-stained, the debauched and filthy', there was a bridge, 'and not only that, but that the frontiers of their lives secretly marched together and the line could be crossed at any moment'.[33]

That the fluidity of self has its psychological as well as its moral origins appears as a central tenet in the work of the German poet, Gottfried Benn. In an essay written in 1920, Benn had argued that the modern self could no longer be thought of as coherent or unified; it is, on the contrary, an inherently unstable, fractured thing, surviving on 'loss, frigidity, isolation from the centre, [being] without psychological continuity, without biography, without a centrally viewed history'. Both in his poetry (*Rubble*, 1924, *Narcosis* and *Split,* both 1925), and in his Rönne cycle of short stories (1915-1916), Benn depicted characters lacking recognisable inner life, motivation, or consistency, being, like the hero of 'The Conquest', so dominated by external forces and stronger personalities that their very physical existence seems transitory and incidental. This loss of self into literal and metaphorical nothingness is the reality (Benn argues) that generations of humanists have tried to ignore. The protagonist of the final story of the series, 'The Birthday', takes it upon himself to put the record straight: 'What is the path that mankind has trodden until now?', he asks in the concluding lines of the story. 'It wanted to establish order in something that should have remained a game. But in the end it did remain a game, for nothing was real. Was *he* real? No; he was a hotch-potch of possibilities; that's what he was.'[34]

That the self is something at base artificial, a social fiction of indeterminate status, was a tenet held by many Modernist writers, including the most famous Italian playwright of this period, Luigi Pirandello. In his plays, *The Rules of the Game* (1918), *Six Characters in Search of an Author* (1921), and *Henry IV* (1922), Pirandello sought to find a form that would capture 'the multiple personality of everyone corresponding to the possibilities of being to be found in each of us'. In *Henry IV*, he deals with a character who has apparently convinced himself that he is the incarnation of a Hapsburg king, and assembles around him a retinue to support him in this allusion. But that this is no conventional madness, Pirandello demonstrates in his denouement, where the 'mad' king reveals that his imperial role has been the product of a *'conscious* madness', part of an elaborate charade masterminded in order to revenge himself upon friends and family. That such a tactic might itself be the product of a genuine insanity is one of the tantalising possibilities muted in the final scene of the play. In Pirandello's most famous play, *Six Characters in Search of an Author*, the author developed this theme even further. The entire play takes place in the space between illusion and reality, the stage and the real world, with actors playing at being actors, caught in the act of rehearsing one of Pirandello's plays by a group by six characters whose dramatic status forever hovers between fiction and reality. The protagonists of the play act out their 'real-life' melodrama on the stage, convinced that the theatrical medium is 'less real perhaps, but truer!'. The result is a play, whose playful self-referentiality and wilful blurring of the boundaries between art and life strikingly anticipate the Absurdist direction that drama was to take later in the century.[35]

A more sinister account of what happens when the individual is stripped of the traditional defining categories of personhood is provided in the work of the great German-speaking Jewish-Czech writer, Franz Kafka. In his stories, Kafka explored the predicament of those who are forced to bend their personalities to the point where they become unrecognisable as individuals. This is the fate, for example, of the protagonists of 'In the Penal Colony' (1919) and 'The Hunger Artist' (1922). The 'heroes' of these stories find themselves reduced to pure passivity, not only literally (by an executioner's machine and by a cage, respectively), but also psychologically, in terms of their personal identities, as they are forced to internalise the alien legal and cultural norms of their 'superiors'. In his letters and diaries, Kafka expressed the deep sense of alienation that he felt both from his family (particularly from his father) and from the stultifying routines of the monotonous work ethic that he was compelled, as a minor clerk in an insurance company, to experience on a daily basis. Kafka's most famous story, 'The Metamorphosis' (1915), dramatises this sense of alienation. It charts the guilt, insecurity and growing inferiority complex experienced by Gregor, the son of a middle-class but impoverished family, who awakens one morning to find himself metamorphosed into an insect. Inwardly unchanged, and deeply sensitive to his plight, Gregor finds first his status, and then his very physical presence, gradually disowned by his family. He is finally reduced to the status of 'an enemy' by his loved ones, who impatiently attend the death of the insect-son, disposing of his remains in the domestic rubbish bin.[36]

Kafka's stories are structured around a tension between the repressive banality of the ordinary world and the introspective pain of those who feel themselves excluded from such a world (although it is also true that certain of Kafka's characters, such as the hunger artist, seem to cultivate their outsider status). Kafka's novels – *America* (written 1911–1914, but not published until 1927), *The Trial* (1915, published in 1925) and *The Castle* (1922, published in unfinished form in 1926) – explore this tension further, describing the attempts of their shared hero, Joseph K., to find recognition and a secure place in the world. Throughout Kafka's novels, the irrational appears not simply as an aberration of individual psychology, but as a generalisable *modus operandi*, as a system of values that defines the very nature of existence. In this world, events often seem to float free of time and logic, possessing an openness and unfathomability that produces in Kafka's characters (and often in the reader) a heightened sense of dislocation that borders upon terror. This is certainly the feeling that pervades *The Trial*. Its hero, Joseph K., finds himself arrested one day without prior warning, and by non-uniformed individuals who present no authority or warrant. Convinced in a quixotic way of the essentially rational nature of the law, Kafka's hero spends the entire novel searching for 'a clear answer' to his predicament, trying to wrest logic and rational purpose out of a judicial system that not only refuses to explain itself but remains wilfully impervious to scrutiny. The quest is a hopeless one. The novel concludes with Joseph K. succumbing to the judgement that has been passed upon him, and accepting a guilt that has no apparent foundations. In the final grim scene, he willingly participates in his own abject execution, viewing the knife that will end his life as a part of that 'ceremonial of courtesy' which he has spent his entire case admiring, seeking to join.[37]

5 MEMORY, TIME AND CONSCIOUSNESS: MODERNISM AND THE EPISTEMOLOGICAL 'BREAKTHROUGH'

Musil's hero, young Törless, in the midst of the cruelties he witnesses in his cadet school, experiences an epistemological crisis in his life, which takes the form of a radical questioning of the categories used by his 'conscious mind' to make sense of the world. 'It was the failure of language', he realises, 'that caused him anguish'; mere 'words' cannot grasp those stirrings of the consciousness that slip between the gaps of discourse, and which lie 'somewhere between experience and comprehension'. This focus upon knowledge, and the difficulties of achieving adequate forms for its articulation and representation, formed a central problematic within Modernist literature. Hugo von Hofmannstahl provided an early discussion of the theme in his 'The Letter of Lord Chandos' (1902). In this fictional letter, the young English aristocrat Lord Chandos tells his friend and mentor, Francis Bacon, of his sudden loss of faith in the ability of language to mediate between his consciousness and the world. No longer believing in the enticing myth of simple representation, Chandos succumbs to a process of mental dislocation, which brings him close to madness: 'For me everything disintegrated into parts, those parts again into parts', he tells Bacon, at one critical juncture. 'No longer would anything let itself be encompassed by one idea. Single words floated round me; they congealed into eyes which stared at me and into which I was forced to stare back – whirlpools which gave me vertigo and, reeling incessantly, led into the void.' Other Modernist writers, such as Franz Kafka, experienced similar crises. In the midst of writing his novel, *The Trial*, he too became aware of a radical disjunction between self and language. It was, as he explained in a letter of that year, 1914, an experience that left him on the point of despair: 'I write differently from what I speak, I speak differently from what I think, I think differently from the way I ought to think, and so it all proceeds into deepest darkness.'[38]

But what oppressed some, liberated others. Virginia Woolf, writing in 1919, also recognised that the perceiving self, when deprived of those traditional categories of perception used to filter and order experience, could easily fall prey to the 'myriad impressions – trivial, fantastic [and] evanescent' which descend on the mind like 'incessant showers of innumerable atoms' during our daily lives. But Woolf was also, at the same time, confident that the texture of these experiences could be captured, transposed into a 'pattern, however disconnected and incoherent', and made to return as an aesthetic structure. Woolf followed this trajectory in her own novels (*Mrs Dalloway*, 1925, *To the Lighthouse*, 1927, and *The Waves*, 1931), in which she attempted to find a form capable of capturing the 'fertility and fluency' of the artistic response to life. What she created in the process was a 'stream of consciousness' technique, a process of narration that replaces the omniscient narration of the Realist novel with a discourse reflective of the musings, wish-fulfilments and psychological projections of her characters. In *To the Lighthouse*, this technique allows Woolf to dramatise (so to speak) from within the two conflicting perspectives around which the novel rotates: the masculine principle, rational, empirical and assertive in its demands on the present, and represented by Mr Ramsey; and the feminine, embodied in Mrs Ramsey, which, whilst remaining open to the pressures of the unconscious, is nevertheless capable of divining 'a coherence in things, a stability', and has a greater feel for the permanence of the moment, whose ambit is 'that still space that lies about the heart of things'. Mediating between the two is the painter, Lily Briscoe. After Mrs Ramsey's death, she succeeds in reaching a symbiosis between the external preoccupations of Mr Ramsey and the internal values of Mrs Ramsey. She is able to achieve this, not simply because she is an artist, but because she is able to objectify in her aesthetic vision of life what had remained mystical inwardness in Mrs Ramsey. Consciousness can only grasp life as flux and indeterminacy; but becoming conscious of that consciousness, as Lily Briscoe does in her final 'vision' (which allows her to complete her painting as the Ramsey family finally reach the lighthouse) makes it possible for imagination and art, and the values of inner life, in general, to transcend their limitations and meet reality on its own terms.[39]

Leonard Woolf called *To the Lighthouse* a 'psychological poem', feeling that, as an exploration of the processes of the mind, it remained unsurpassed in Virginia's work. Her concern with time, memory and consciousness appear in a more self-conscious fashion in the work of other writers of this period, such as Italo Svevo's *Confessions of Zeno* (1923), and Thomas Mann's *The Magic Mountain* (1924). The former novel, written in the form of an extended dialogue between the hero and his psychoanalyst, has a greater epic sweep than any of Woolf's novels. It lays bare the foibles, psychological, sexual and financial, of the eccentric and highly self-conscious Zeno against the backdrop of the crisis of the European bourgeoisie on the eve of the First World War. In telling his story, Svevo's self-deprecating hero draws our attention to the unreliable nature of his memory, which rearranges the past, 'analysing the mass of truths and falsehoods' of his life to suit the needs of the present, effectively obscuring all distinctions between recollection and fabrication. This relationship between time, memory and personal identity is also explored by Thomas Mann in *The Magic Mountain*. The title refers to a Swiss sanatorium to which the guileless

Bürger, Hans Castorp, has come to visit a sick relative. Once arrived, he finds he cannot leave, spellbound by the many fascinating characters who have come to the mountain. The latter ostensibly seek health; but (as Mann's epic novel shows) these representatives of the European aristocracy and *haute bourgeoisie* have brought with them to the sanatorium a spiritual malaise that is far more potent than their physical afflictions: a lack of moral values, spiritual anomie, and, in the figures of Settembrini and Naphta, a political and philosophical extremism which offers the hero of the novel the beggar's choice of shallow rationalism or profound irrationalism. On Mann's magic mountain there are no absolutes of time, space, or selfhood, except one: 'the billow, the lion's jaws, and the sea': death. It exists as a metaphysical presence throughout Mann's novel, a vacuum waiting to be filled by the inmates of this privileged world, and by all adrift in the sphere of modernity, who may find the idea of a permanent solution, of any solution, to their personal crises, fatally seductive.[40]

As Mann makes clear in *The Magic Mountain* (which ends with its hero sacrificing himself as a combatant in the First World War) the challenges posed by modernity to the psychological and moral health of the individual cannot be overcome by the tentative and partial solutions that Hans Castorp grasps in that novel. What the individual must attain is a perspective capable of absorbing dislocations of identity and consciousness into a coherent and structured grid. This is precisely the achievement of the hero of Marcel Proust's epic novel, *Remembrance of Things Past* (published in nine separate but interconnecting parts between 1913 and 1927). The theme of the novel is the recovery of the past through memory. As such, Proust's novel had a remarkable parallel in Alain-Fournier's *The Lost Domain* (1913), which likewise dealt with the evolution of personality through time, and with attempts to reach a past whose contours seem to exist just beyond the reach of recollection. But there are important differences between the two novels, which lie not simply in the scope of Proust's work but, above all, in its theoretical sophistication. For at the centre of Proust's description of the personal and psychological growth of his hero exists an extended exploration into the form and nature of consciousness, and into the ways that are open to it for regaining contact with the past. The key (as the hero discovers in one trivial moment of taking tea) is involuntary memory: that mechanism of the mind that alone is capable of reactivating, through a chance taste or smell, those intangible

experiences which are 'more fragile but more enduring, more un-
substantial, more persistent, more faithful' than the concrete memories that make up our conscious self. But, as Proust makes quite
clear, such involuntary associations need to be ordered into a
formal pattern if they are to reveal their true importance. Life is
lived in terms of its experiential intensity, as insight and revelation;
but it can only be made to offer up its deepest secrets when it is
grasped as an aesthetic whole, as a pattern existing at the centre of
apparent confusion and anarchy. As Marcel notes in the final pages
of the novel, 'this life that we live in half-darkness can be illumined,
this life that at every moment we distort can be restored to its true
pristine shape' through the agency of the creative mind. It is only
the aesthetic will to form (Proust concludes) that can show us the
way out of the confusions and disorders of modernity. [41]

The novels of the great Irish Modernist, James Joyce (notably *A
Portrait of the Artist as a Young Man*, 1916, and *Ulysses*, 1922), likewise focus on themes related to memory, time and consciousness.
Joyce first explored such themes in *Portrait of the Artist* (and in the
earlier draft of that novel, *Stephen Hero*) through his depiction of
the young Stephen Dedalus, who struggles against family, country
and religion in furtherance of his artistic vocation. But that consciousness (even artistic consciousness) has its limits in the age of
modernity, Joyce made clear in his subsequent novel, *Ulysses*. The
main character here is again the precocious Dedalus; but now the
fledgling artist is seen simply as one personality amongst many, in
a kaleidoscope of figures drawn from the urban environment of
modern Dublin. In this highly wrought, polyphonic, symbolically
textured novel, Joyce attempts to describe a single day in the life of
this city, reconstructing its social, political, and even culinary and
sexual *mores*, with a concern for detail that reveals the author's
training in the Realist-Naturalist tradition. During the course of his
peregrinations, the young hero of the novel charts an unsteady path
through the often oppressive physicality of this world, now de-
pressed, now liberated, now bemused, now enlightened by his recurring experiences, but never entirely able to escape from the
plethora of details and events that surrounds him, that 'ineluctable
modality of the visible', which holds both his actions and his consciousness in check. [42]

In the final analysis, the plenitude that Joyce constructs on the
surface of his vast novel is held in check, not by Stephen's vacillating grasp of the world, but by the impressive formal structure of

the novel which, through an elaborate system of repetition, cross-referencing and transposition, allows the apparently fragmented nature of the experiences undergone by Stephen and others (such as Leopold Bloom and his wife, Molly) to cohere into a pattern. Further securing the coherence of the novel are the frequent references to, and parallels with, Homer's *Odyssey*, which bestow upon the minutiae of Joyce's narrative an archetypal significance. In this way Joyce succeeds in bringing to a close the aleatory nature of the journey that the errant Bloom and Dedalus have embarked upon, bringing the several figures that they represent: father and son, the *petit bourgeois* and the artist, body and mind, together in a final act of symbolic reconciliation. But the novel does not end here. Consciousness may be contained within form, but it can also be released through the sheer intensity of its articulation. And this is where Joyce leaves us, not with the would-be artist Dedalus nor with the myopic Leopold Bloom, but with his wife, Molly. Bloom's wife has been, perhaps, a marginal figure so far in the novel; but it is she who alone proves capable of overcoming the Modernist impasse of restrictive self-consciousness, giving voice in the extended soliloquy, with which the novel ends, to the sheer joy and plenitude of lived life, to 'that awful deep-down torrent O and the sea the sea crimson sometimes like fire and the glorious sunsets and the figtrees in the Alameda gardens yes'.[43]

6   LIBIDO AND BODY CULTURE: SEXUALITY IN THE MODERNIST NOVEL

That sexuality is not simply a matter of psychic disposition or physiological need but a complex personal medium, through which social norms and ethical values are challenged and even displaced, was a fact explored in many of the major novels of the nineteenth century, such as Thackeray's *Vanity Fair* (1848), Flaubert's *Madame Bovary* (1857), Tolstoy's *Anna Karenina*, (1877) and Fontane's *Effi Briest* (1895). These novels engaged with the nature of female sexuality in patriarchal society, adumbrating the fate of women in whose quest for self-fulfilment could be read a broader (if indirect) treatment of the predicament of attenuated subjectivity in the increasingly power-oriented and unselfcritical society of late nineteenth-century bourgeois Europe. The duplicity and double standards that lay at the core of male-female relationships in this

period, particularly as they emerged through the institution of marriage, also engaged the interests of early Modernist writers such as
Frank Wedekind in plays (*Spring's Awakening*, 1891, *Earth Spirit*,
1895, and *Pandora's Box*, 1904), which detail the demonic, but also
liberating, power of eroticism, and Arthur Schnitzler, whose
studies of the domestic *mores* of *fin de siècle* Vienna (the plays
Anatol, 1893, and the dramatic dialogues, *Merry-Go-Round*, 1897)
sought to disclose the provisional and self-interested nature of
the sexual behaviour of polite Viennese society. In this world of
deception and self-deception, the notion of an 'absolutely irre-
proachable life' is shown to be an ideal that none seem to follow,
but all employ as a rhetorical device, seeking to dissimulate the un-
restrained egotism of their life-styles.[44]

The characters who circulate on Schnitzler's carousel negotiate
their sexual relationships through gamesmanship and self-
conscious theatricality, and with a mixture of coyness and panache
that serves to diffuse the animosity and hostility existing as a sub-
current beneath this process of mutual, but civilised, exploitation.
In Strindberg's *The Father* (1887) and in Kokoschka's *Murderer, the
Hope of Women* (1907), however, latent aggression between man and
woman is forced to the surface in a spirit of intense and irrevocable
hostility. These plays give voice to a more dynamic notion of
female sexuality, which they depict as self-assured, rapacious and
uncompromising, and fully capable of adapting masculine techniques to its own ends. Kokoschka's play, in particular, which uses
all the dramaturgic devices of the Expressionist stage, struck its
contemporaries as a powerful allegory upon the theme of sexual
struggle. Its two protagonists are depicted as elemental parts of the
'devouring life' process of attraction and repulsion, whose *raison
d'être* seems to be (as if in some grotesque parody of the Wagnerian
Liebestod theme) union with the other through the other's annihilation and dismemberment.[45]

The plays of Strindberg and Kokoschka posed in the most radical
way questions that were to reappear throughout Modernist literature, questions relating to the relationship between sexuality and
power, to the nature of sexual deviance, and to the relevance of
marriage as an institution. Answers to such questions were diverse.
The French writer, Colette, in novels such as *The Vagabond* (1910),
and *Chéri* and *The Last of Chéri* (1920 and 1926), described the efforts
of women caught within, but also struggling against, the imposition of simplistic roles such as the mistress, the *rouée* and the *femme*

fatale. In the place of such clichés, Colette's heroines ('practical women of the world', such as Léa, in the *Chéri* novels) seek to enjoy the native sensuality that is their birthright, not rejecting the world of the male, but aware of its limitations, financial and erotic. That such female self-confidence could be seen as a threat to masculine identity was clearly demonstrated by the example of the French novelist and playwright, Henri de Montherlant. His novel tetralogy (*The Girls*, 1936, *Pity for Women*, 1936, *Demon of Good*, 1937, and *The Lepers*, 1939) constitutes a sustained attack upon femininity and female behaviour. Montherlant's narrating hero, the artist, Pierre Costals, is the mouthpiece for Montherlant's misogyny. He views femininity as a force that will not only challenge and disrupt, but, ultimately, undermine what is distinctively masculine within the male. Whereas Colette's heroines come to a compromise with male society (but largely on their own terms), Costals sees the divisions between male and female as unbridgeable. Contact is only possible at the level of sexual exploitation and control; all other options, including 'the state of being loved' are 'suitable only to women, animals and children'. Costals' indifference, and, indeed, cruelty to his female suitors had its sources both in the author's much vaunted quasi-Nietzschean notion of *dominio* (in which the other is both tamed and possessed), but also in a fear of the 'muddled, confused, impure, two-sided' nature of the modern condition, which threatens the viability of all absolute values, as it does the coherence of male identity.[46]

Fear for the masculine loss of self was also felt by an author whose treatment of personal relations was perhaps the most extensive within main-stream Modernism: D.H. Lawrence. His major novels (*Sons and Lovers*, 1913, *The Rainbow*, 1915, and *Women in Love*, 1920) explore the dynamism of sexual relationships, and the seemingly contradictory urges that determine the male-female polarity, that 'sort of perversity in our souls', noted by Paul Morel in *Sons and Lovers*, which 'makes us not want, get away from, the very thing we want'. Lawrence outlined the crux of the problem in an essay on Thomas Hardy, written in 1914. Men and women embody two opposing types of life force: the male proclivity to 'endless motion, endless diversity, endless change' stands at odds with the natural inclination of the female to 'infinite oneness, infinite stability'. What is required is a balance between these two principles, but one forged on the basis of a common respect for what is unique about man and woman, and not on the basis of the (feminist) desire to abolish such distinctions. This is the insight that Lawrence seems to be working towards in his major novels, most notably in *Women in Love*. Here, the two couples, Birkin and Ursula and Gerald and Gudrun, represent contrasting types of erotic engagement. Gerald and Gudrun are bonded through a reciprocated exercise of power, the exertion of will and physicality and the manipulation and control of the other's sexual need (which is, in their case, associated from the very first moment of its consummation with emptiness and 'the bitter potion of death'). In contrast, Birkin achieves a true union with Ursula; desire in their case is linked not to need, but to a mutual self-surrender to the Godhead of sexuality, whose presence dwells not within but across the libidinous pair. Their sexual bonding, depicted in one memorable scene (whose intensity strains both sense and syntax in Lawrence's writing) becomes part of a 'mysterious night, the night masculine and feminine, never to be seen with the eye, or known with the mind, only known as a palpable revelation of living otherness'.[47]

In spite of his depiction of the mystical oneness of their union, Lawrence, nevertheless, leaves the relationship between Birkin and Ursula on a note of disharmony, the former resisting the possessiveness of his partner's claims on him, the memory of his friendship with Gerald still alive. But Gerald is dead, the pure will of his self-assertiveness finding its apotheosis in the arid snow-fields of the Bavarian Alps. With his death, the opportunity for that second kind of love that Birkin had been seeking, that 'eternal union with a man', in which strength might be matched against strength, virility against virility, in an intense 'oneness of struggle' (which had briefly emerged during the 'gladiatorial' encounter between the two men earlier in the novel) has irrevocably gone. Birkin must now come to terms with the fact that his destiny lies with a woman. The clear admiration for masculinity evinced in *Women in Love* also emerges in Lawrence's next novel, *Kangaroo* (1923), but even here (in a story set amongst the male camaraderie of Australian politics), Lawrence seems reluctant to dwell upon the homo-erotic tensions between his protagonists. Other writers of the modernist period, however, most notably André Gide and Thomas Mann, were more direct in their treatment of the ambivalent nature of the masculine libido. Gide's short novel, *The Immoralist* (1902), in particular, occupies a central place in the literature devoted to the exploration of homosexuality. In his *The Notebooks of André Walter* (1891) and *Fruits of the Earth* (1897), Gide had celebrated the body culture of

the *fin de siècle* Decadent movement. In these works, Gide's homosexuality was neither clear, nor was it provided with a theoretical
justification. In *The Immoralist*, it receives both. The story tells of the
young French professor, Michel, who, during a trip to North Africa,
experiences an intense attraction for a local Arab boy. When he
returns to France, Gide's hero undergoes a personal transformation,
which takes him from his earlier Puritan 'craving for high-minded-
ness' to an amoral existentialism, and from physical weakness to
health and bodily self-confidence (achieved as his wife is going
through the reverse process). His journey ends with a second trip to
North Africa (in search of the boy), and with his decision to remain
in a land that he regards as primitive and rejuvenating, his future
committed to a further quest for those 'untouched treasures somewhere lying covered up, hidden, smothered by culture and decency
and morality'.[48]

The openness with which Gide allows Michel to confess his
newly found sexual identity was not chosen by all. For others, the
illicit, the outré, excess and transgression remained (quite literally)
unspeakable, allowed to emerge only in the margins of text and
consciousness. It is in this fashion that T.E. Lawrence deals with
sexual taboo in his *The Seven Pillars of Wisdom* (privately circulated
in 1926, and posthumously published in 1935). In the midst of his
participation in the Arab revolt during the First World War, he tells
of his capture by a contingent of Turkish troops, which includes a
notorious pederast, Hajim Bey. Lawrence's account of the episode
hovers around the subject of violation, leaving the 'delicious
warmth, probably sexual' that he experienced during his beatings
and degradation a mysterious side effect of his enforced passivity.
As Lawrence would later note, his written account arose out of a
clash between repression and confession, between the two impulses
of 'self-respect' and 'self-expression', whose unreconciled tensions
left the officer-author with a neurosis that he spent his life trying to
overcome. That psychic health requires not the evasion but the acceptance of sexual truth is the moral of Thomas Mann's novella
Death in Venice (1912). Its hero, Gustav von Aschenbach, attempts to
rid his life of the ambiguities, moral, aesthetic and sexual, with
which the artist (Mann argues, following his mentor Nietzsche)
must stay in contact as a necessary part of his vocation. Aschenbach
refuses to make the journey undertaken by Gide's hero, choosing
repression to self-analysis, and leaving the fact of his own sexual
ambiguity unrecognised. When the change does take place,

through the ageing artist's encounter with the youth Tadzio during a stay in Venice, sexual attraction is not openly admitted, as it was in Michel's case, but obfuscated, displaced, transfigured through an elaborate system of Classical allusion, which allows Aschenbach to apotheosise the loved one in terms of the latter's 'godlike beauty'. That such a process of euphemism and circumlocution must lead to the grotesque return of the repressed in sickness and death, Mann makes clear to reader and hero alike. Aschenbach, on the eve of his death, is compelled, in one final brutal dream, to recognise that he has willingly exchanged the possibility of health for the certainty of disease, balance for excess, in a process in which he has seen his much vaunted 'moral law' transformed into its opposite, an ethos of hope founded on 'the monstrous and the perverse'.[49]

If Modernism involved a liberation from conventional notions of self and from conventional categories of language and psychology, it also involved new ways of conceptualising the body and the libidinous force field of the body, whose energies slowly came to be seen as moving in an ambit between received notions of the feminine and the masculine. These more complex modes of bi- and trans-sexuality were explored by Jean Cocteau in his *The Holy Terrors* (1929). The story tells of the fluid but highly charged relationship that exists between four adolescents: the brother and sister couple, Elizabeth and Paul, and their friends, Gérard and Agatha. Inhabiting the same room, they play a multitude of games, in which roles are reversed, identities of loved ones confused and deliberately obscured, and gender stereotypes undone. Elizabeth and Paul, in particular, those 'twin halves of a single body', play the Game (as they call it) with a degree of intimacy that borders on eroticism. The desires of which they dare not speak prove incapable of resolution, and finally bring about the inevitable tragedy of the double suicide; a desperate act embraced so that they can reach a realm where 'incest lurks no more'. The violence that forms the consummation of their relationship runs like a leitmotif throughout *The Holy Terrors*, surfacing in the 'subliminal struggle' that structures the sexual subcurrents of Cocteau's text. Robert Musil, in his *Young Törless*, also explored the destructive nature of the energies released by confused and polyvalent sexualities. The journey of self-discovery that the young hero undertakes in that novel is, on one level, driven by intellectual curiosity: his need to explore the problematic status of referential language and the rationalist discourses of post-Kantian philosophy, and his desire to affirm the

tenuous nature of moral precepts, are recurrent themes within the
literature of mainstream Modernism. At the centre of these explorations lies, however, the increasingly ambiguous nature of Törless'
sexuality, which moves from the bond of sensuality that he has established with his mother (and which he later rediscovers in the
arms of the village prostitute, Bozena) to the 'sexual excitement'
that he experiences as an observer of the sadistic debasement of his
colleague, Basini. The novel concludes with Törless expelled from
school, seeking, in a return of his Electra fixation, solace on 'his
mother's corseted waist'. Whether Törless represents the revolt of
youth against patriarchal society, Musil does not make clear; but
this is exactly the theme explored by the German Expressionist
playwright, Arnolt Bronnen, in his play, *Patricide* (1922). The play
tells of a struggle between a father and his son (Walther) for authority in the family, which was a common theme in German plays
written for a post-war generation convinced of the moral bankruptcy of their elders. Bronnen also makes use of the familiar ideology of self-liberation that was at the heart of the Expressionist
ethos, but is careful to make clear that the son's real strength over
his father lies in the fluidity and potency of his sexuality. This he
demonstrates by entering into relationships with his friend, the precocious Edmund, his sister, and finally his mother. As Bronnen
makes clear, Walter's concluding words in the play: 'I am free'; 'no
one is before me, no one is beside me, no one over me: father is
dead', represent both his liberation as an individual and the
triumph of his own polymorphous sexuality.[50]

7   FRAGMENTS OF MODERNITY: MODERNIST POETRY

The Modernists focussed upon the nature of consciousness, and
upon the ways that it engaged with the world, emphasising, in
particular, the problematic nature of language, which had lost for
many its power either to express new forms of experience or
to reflect processes within the external world. Those who argued
thus received support from the writings of a number of major
linguists and philosophers of language, such as Fritz Mauthner
(*Contributions to a Critique of Language*, 1901), Ludwig Wittgenstein
(*Tractatus Logico-Philosophicus*, 1921) and Ferdinand de Saussure
(*Course in General Linguistics*, 1916). All drew attention to the non-
representational valency of language, the fact that it consists (as de

Saussure argued) of signs, which possess a meaning only in terms of the internal coherence within specific signifying systems; that (in the words of Wittgenstein) 'a proposition is a model of reality, [but only] as we imagine it'. To a large extent, these theorists of language were simply consolidating the aperçus made more than a decade earlier by poets such as Mallarmé. In his essays and letters, the great Symbolist poet had argued that the gap existing between language, self and world provided a new task for poetic agency; it would free language from simplistic denotation and open it to the infinite play of connotation. In the Modernist period, Mallarmé was followed by a generation of poets who sought, in T.S Eliot's words, to 'purify the dialect of the tribe', establishing new associations between words and concepts that had been exhausted of meaning through quotidian use. Paul Valéry was one such poet. In his major works (the extended single poem, 'The Young Fate', 1917, and the volume, *Charms*, 1922), he charted in his finely tuned style the graduations of poetic consciousness, which moves (according to Valéry, in his oft quoted 'The Graveyard by the Sea', 1920) 'between emptiness and the pure event'. Valéry's verse gives voice to an unerring feel for stasis, mood, and the passing of time, whose modulations are structured through a neo-classical control of rhythm and metre, a form which is sensitive to the flux of experience but has no place for chaos, disorder or distracting sentiment. Valéry supported his poetic output with an extensive body of theoretical work: essays such as 'Problems of Poetry' (1936), 'Poetry and Abstract Thought' (1939) and the more autobiographical 'Memoirs of a Poem' (1938). In these essays, he defined the sublime functionalism which underscored his project, elaborating upon that 'combination of ascetism and play', which was at the centre of his hermetic life and work.[51]

Valéry represented the Orphic strain in Modernist poetry. Following Mallarmé, he construed poetry as a pure product of the controlling self, and used incantatory words, multiple poetic personae and myths to capture those nuances of meaning which exist at the far reaches of hermeneutic intelligibility. The scope and intensity of Valéry's writing was matched (and possibly exceeded) by the major German-speaking poet of this period: Rainer Maria Rilke. Rilke attempted in his poetry (The *Book of Images*, 1902, *The Book of Hours*, 1905, *New Poems*, two volumes, 1907–1908, *Duino Elegies* 1912–1923, and *Sonnets to Orpheus*, 1923) to break through to increasingly more distant terrains of experience and knowledge, a process of exploration which reached its apotheosis in his *Duino*

Elegies. But even the earlier volumes contain moments when the poetic gaze approximates an intensity that borders upon the mystical. This is particularly the case in the so-called *Dinggedichte* (literally, 'thing-poems'), such as 'The Bowl of Roses' and 'The Inwardness of the Rose', from *New Poems: Second Part.* In these poems, the object-world becomes transfigured through the poet's aestheticising vision, invested, indeed, with an ontological plenitude that displays 'beyond all power of giving, presence,/ that might be ours: that might be our extreme'. The objects depicted here have attained a unity of being, a self-sufficiency that is withheld from those burdened with consciousness, those who (in the famous words of the first Duino Elegy) 'don't feel very securely at home/ in this interpreted world'. The latter must find meaning the best they can, accept the 'once and no more' of life, brute contingency and death, 'pressing on and trying to perform it,/trying to contain it within our simple hands,/in the more and more crowded gaze, in the speechless heart'. The *Duino Elegies* are a record of this process, and the poetry in that volume, with its dislocated syntax, shifting metrical forms, and abrupt changes of mood, reflects the pained terms in which the self attempts both to come to terms with existence ('Dasein'), and to achieve transcendence from it.[52]

Rilke's existentialist symbolism represented a dominant mode within the poetry of European Modernism. In Spain, poets such as Antonio Machado (*Solitudes*, 1903, *The Land of Castille*, 1912, second volume, 1917) and Juan Ramon Jiménez (*Spiritual Sonnets*, 1917, *Rock and Sky*, 1919) produced a verse that was symbolist in inspiration, but *sui generic* in its often intense mysticism; in Italy, Giuseppe Ungaretti (*Mirth of Shipwrecks*, 1919, and *Feeling of Time*, 1933), Salvatore Quasimodo (*Waters and Lands*, 1930, and *Sunken Oboe*, 1932) and Eugenio Montale (*Bones of Cuttlefish*, 1925, and *Occasions*, 1939) found inspiration from Dino Campana (*Orphic Songs*, 1914), whose famous 'The Window', with its syntactic dislocations and Symbolist epiphanies, provided one of the earliest examples of the Modernist idiom in Italian poetry. These poets converged on a style known as *Ermetismo* (hermeticism). Their poetry gives voice to a cryptically-encoded world of private associations, memories and desires, in poems in which the superfluous, the decorative, the qualifying is pared away to a radical minimalism. Noted examples include Ungaretti's two-line poem 'Morning': 'M'illumino/d'immenso' ('I am illuminated/by immensity'), and

Quasimodo's 'And suddenly it is evening', where a union of light and time is effected precisely through the audacious brevity of the poem's three-line form. Montale, in particular, made this idiom his own in his volume, *Bones of Cuttlefish*, exploring (as in the famous 'The Lemon Trees') those 'silences/in which things yield and seem/about to betray their ultimate secret'.[53]

Spanish Modernism possessed a literature of equal depth and resonance. It included the work of the playwright Ramón del Valle-Inclán, whose theory of *esperpento* (poetic de-formation), evident in plays such as *Don Friolera's Horns* (1921) and *Bohemian Lights* (1920), represents the most sophisticated theory of the Modern stage outside the epic theatre of Brecht; and the great novelist-philosopher, Miguel de Unamuno, the author of fiction such as *Mist* (1914) and *Abel Sánchez* (1917), but who is, perhaps, best remembered for his religious-existential study, *The Tragic Sense of Life* (1913). The major work of this period came, however, from the poets, Jiménez and Machado, whose deepening of the heritage of French Symbolism helped produce the finest poetry in Spain since the seventeenth century. Behind much of their writing lies a native mystical tradition, that sense of being embarked on a spiritual quest. This is evident even in the work of Machado, whose best poems, such as 'From the Road', 'Passageways', and 'From the threshold of the dream they called me ...', give voice to a determination to win through to spiritual insight even in the face of a world that is 'empty, transparent, voiceless, blind'.[54]

In Russia, the Symbolist verse of Bely and the early Blok became the critical focus of a group of young poets known as the Acmeists, who wrote between 1910 and 1922. The Russian Acmeists also wanted to move beyond the evocative musicality of the Symbolist style, hoping to create a poetic idiom that would be responsive to the emotional and spiritual needs of the poet and reader. The leading representatives of the school were Anna Akhmatova (*Evening*, 1912, *The White Flock*, 1917, and *Anno Domini MCMXXI*, 1922), Osip Mandelshtam (*Stone*, 1913, and *Tristia*, 1922) and the founder of the group (who provided its manifesto in 1913 with 'The Tradition of Symbolism and the Acmeists'), Nikolai Gumilyov (*Pearls*, 1910, *Foreign Skies*, 1912, and *Bonfire*, 1918). The Acmeists focused on matters of personal and metaphysical import: in Gumilyov's words, on 'God, sin, death, immortality'. Such concerns are evident in the poems 'July 1914' and 'Everything is Plundered ...' by Anna Akhmatova, in which the violence of history (here, the outbreak of the First World War and the ensuing Russian Revolution), is evoked through imagery of desecration and natural disaster, only to be finally (if tentatively) overcome through the symbol of the 'deep transparent skies', which represent for Akhmatova continuing life and hope. These poems give intimations of a religious faith that Akhmatova was only fully to express in *Anno Domini MCMXXI*. The poetry of Mandelshtam also looks out to history; but now the apocalyptic note is stronger, and the feeling of transcendence weaker. This is clear from a poem such as 'My Time', in which the poet evokes his age as a 'savage beast', a 'wounded animal' whose back has been broken by the impact of historical and political change. In his later poetry (much of which remained unpublished), an even deeper pessimism emerges. In poems such as 'January 1, 1924' and 'But a Sky Pregnant with the Future ...', Mandelshtam groped towards a new idiom capable of registering the changed nature of Russian society, describing a world where 'the great lime-trees smell of death', and where human aspirations must remain unfulfilled.[55]

Those who wrote within the late Symbolist idiom, such as the poets of the Hermetic school in Italy and the Acmeist school in Russia, often structured their poems around a powerfully evoked single image, which served both to organise the themes of the poem, whilst acting as a signifier of a higher, transcendent realm. In Britain, the Anglo-American Imagists, whose leading representatives were T.E. Hulme and Ezra Pound, developed this practice into a self-conscious aesthetic. For Pound the poetic image possessed an almost mystical potency: it 'presents an intellectual and emotional complex in an instant of time', offering the reader 'that sense of sudden liberation; that sense of freedom from time limits and space limits; that sense of sudden growth'. The Imagists were probably less important for their theories than for their influence upon one of the major poets of the modernist period: T.S. Eliot. His early poems, such as 'The Love Song of J. Alfred Prufrock' (1917), however, go well beyond the pointillist discourse of the Imagists; his images, unsettling but also bathetic, were part of a wider vision of the fragmented and degraded nature of modernity, the literary origins of which lay in a tradition that stretched from Baudelaire and Rimbaud, through to Corbière and Laforgue. From them, Eliot took a certain cultural pessimism (however ironically expressed), and a variety of formal procedures: the use of multiple *personae*, which allowed the poet to adopt masks and other guises in his work; a corresponding impersonality, which is the result of the abolition of the lyrical subject; extensive employment of non-poetic term-inologies; and the metrical freedom of *vers libre*. These come to the fore in Eliot's *magnum opus* of his Modernist period: *The Waste Land* (1922). Eliot invokes here past cultures of the East and West, from Dante and Shakespeare to the Upanishad, to throw into relief the shoddy materialism, gross sexuality and philistinism of the modern world. In five extended tableaux, Eliot maps out the contours of this world, through allusions, archetypes and tongue-in-cheek cita-tion. These are all framed within a narrative that enacts no general solutions to the crisis that the poem identifies; all that can be achieved (Eliot seems to suggest) is a partial and temporary re-prieve from modernity: the attainment of a cultural shelter for those who have shored up the 'fragments' of the past against the ruin of the present.[56]

The same tension, between invoked tradition and the recognition of the fragmented nature of modernity, characterises much of the poetry of this period, including that of two major Greek poets: Constantine Cavafy (whose poems, written between 1911 and 1933, did not appear in a collected edition until 1963) and George Seferis (*Turning Point*, 1931, and *Mythistorima*, 1935). They were the fore-most exponents of Modernism in their country, their reputations extending well beyond those of Kostis Palamas (*Life Immovable*, 1904) and Angelos Sikelianós (*The Light-Shadowed*, 1909), and the other Greek writers of the period. Cavafy returns to the past to speak in a language which is both conversational, and yet precise and even detached, of the ways in which ritual, ceremony, and symbolic deed are able to shape both the identity of the individual (in this case, Cavafy as poet), and the nation (and Cavafy identifies himself as a Panhellenist, writing for a people undergoing radical cultural and political change). To regain contact with this past, Cavafy employs a multiplicity of *personae*: he speaks through a Byzantine noble in exile, a sculptor in Tyana, Pharnazis, the poet, and Julian, the Roman Emperor. All emerge, through experiences, military, artistic and erotic, out of the past-as-continuing-present, to find their lyrical destination in the 'thousands of objects and faces', recreated in the mind of the poet, who is proud, like the 'mirror in the hall' (in the poem of the same name), to be able to receive unto himself 'for a few moments an image of flawless beauty'. The same dual perspective is evident in the writing of Cavafy's younger, and more self-consciously Modernist, compatriot,

George Seferis. Like so many of the other great poets of the period, such as T.S. Eliot (whose works he translated into Greek), Seferis' verse balances scepticism and irony with a desire to see patterns, morphologies and continuities working through history. As with Cavafy, Seferis seeks to regain the past for the sake of the future; but, in his often hermetic and allusive writing, this attempt involves a struggle both of imagination and interpretation. This is particularly true of his major work, *Mythistorima*. Here, Seferis undertakes a journey through Greece's recent past, 'to find again the first seed/So that the immemorial drama might begin once more'. But it is a theogony without end; its culmination lies not in resolution or in the triumph of the present, but in a grim commitment to keep alive the struggle for individual and national identity. In an otherwise pessimistic conclusion, this remains the sole positive note: the poet's exhortation to a future generation, 'those who one day shall live here where we end', that 'their dark blood should rise to overflow their memory', keeping alive the traditions of the poet and his nation, those 'strengthless souls amongst the asphodels'.[57]

A similar struggle to retain the cultural achievements of the past as a security against the fragmentation of the present takes place in the work of the great Irish poet, William Butler Yeats. Nostalgia for a past governed by 'custom and [...] ceremony', for a culture governed by 'innocence and beauty', pervades Yeats's work, particularly his early poetry such as *The Wanderings of Oisin* (1889) and *The Wind Among the Reeds* (1899). The poems in these volumes move in a pristine world of Celtic myth and arcane symbolism. Yeats was later to distance himself from the fabricated nature of this mythology, as in 'A Coat' (1914), and (with a greater sense of historical urgency) in 'Easter, 1916' and 'A Meditation in Time of War', from the collection *Michael Robartes and the Dancer* (1921). In these poems (which are part confessional, part politically analytical), Yeats gave up his early nostalgia for an increasingly frank engagement with a present dominated by anarchism and cultural decline. In his later work, the poet attempted to come to terms with this crisis through his theory of the 'gyre', outlined in his tract, *The Vision* (1925), which allowed him to argue that history was a cyclical process, constantly oscillating between 'discord' and 'concord', and that the present was simply a connecting link between the far greater realities of past and future. The transcendental quietism of the gyre theory is discernible in the poetry of this period, where a new note of irony and stoicism can be heard. It is evident throughout his later work (*The Tower*, 1928, *The Winding Stair and other Poems*, 1933, and *Last Poems and Plays*, 1940). Where once consternation and per-turbation reigned (as in 'The Second Coming'), there now comes a certain Olympian detachment, as the poet looks down on his life and history from a position that is the product of a deeply-held conviction in the continually creative, continually renewing forces of history-as-mind, particularly as they find expression in art. Yeats wrote some of his greatest poems, 'Sailing to Byzantium', 'Byzantium', and 'The Gyres' in support of that conviction, winning through to the 'tragic joy' that permitted him (in Nietzschean fashion) both to accept and to overcome the cultural pessimism that seemed inherent within the Modernist response to modernity.[58]

8   THE LITERATURE OF MODERNISM: A CHRONOLOGY

1868–1869, Lautréamont, *Les chants de Maldoror* (The Songs of Maldoror) [publ. 1874].

1869, Verlaine, *Fêtes Galantes* (Gallant Festivals).

1871, Rimbaud, '*Le Bateau ivre*' ('The Drunken Boat') [publ. in 1883].

1871, Bécquer, *Rimas* (Verse).

1872, Carroll, *Through the Looking-Glass*.

1872, Butler, *Erewhon*.

1872, Rimbaud, *Les Illuminations* (Illuminations) [publ. 1886].

1873, Rimbaud, *Un saison en enfer* (A Season in Hell).

1873, Corbière, *Les Amours jaunes* (Faded Loves).

1873, Pater, *Studies in the History of the Renaissance*.

1874, Flaubert, *La Tentation de Saint-Antoine* (The Temptation of Saint Anthony).

1874, Barbey d'Aurevilly, *Les Diaboliques* (The Diaboliques).

1875, Hopkins, 'The Wreck of the Deutschland' [publ. 1918].

1876, Mallarmé, *L'Après-midi d'un faune* (The Afternoon of a Faun).

1878, Swinburne, *Poems and Ballads*.

1879, D'Annunzio, *Primo Vere* (Early Spring).

1880, Jacobsen, *Niels Lyhne*.

1881, Verlaine, *Sagesse* (Wisdom).

1882, D'Annuzio, *Canto novo* (New Song).

1883, Villiers de l'Isle-Adam, *Contes cruels* (Cruel Tales).

1884, Huysmans, *A rebours* (Against Nature).

1884, Verlaine, *Jadis et naguère* (Of Old and Late).

1885, Pater, *Marius the Epicurean*.

1885, Laforgue, *Les Complaintes* (Complaints).

1886, Moréas, 'Manifeste du Symbolisme' ('Literary Manifesto of the Symbolist School').

1886, Stevenson, *The Strange Case of Dr Jekyll and Mr Hyde*.
1888, Verhaeran, *Les Soirs* (Evenings).
1888–1891, Barrès, *Le Culte du moi* (The Cult of Self).
1889, Yeats, *The Wanderings of Oisin*.
1890, Morris, *News from Nowhere*.
1890, Villiers de l'Isle-Adam, *Axël*.
1891, Wilde, *The Picture of Dorian Gray* .
1891, Huysmans *Là-bas* (Down There).
1891, Wedekind, *Frühlings Erwachen* (Spring's Awakening).
1892, Maeterlinck, *Pelléas et Mélisande*.
1894, D'Annunzio, *Il trionfo della morte* (The Triumph of Death).
1895, Mallarmé, 'Crise de vers' ('Crisis in Poetry').
1896, Housman, *A Shropshire Lad*.
1896, Jarry, *Ubu Roi* (King Ubu).
1897, Mallarmé, *Un Coup de dés jamais n'abolira le hasard* (A Dice Throw will Never Abolish Chance).
1897, Gide, *Les Nourritures terrestres* (Fruits of the Earth).
1897, Stoker, *Dracula*.
1898, Shaw, *Plays: Pleasant and Unpleasant*.
1900, Schnitzler, *Reigen* (Merry-Go-Round).
1900, D'Annunzio, *Il fuoco* (The Flame of Life).
1900, Conrad, *Lord Jim*.
1901, Thomas Mann, *Buddenbrooks*.
1902, Gide, *L'Immoraliste* (The Immoralist).
1902, Conrad, *Heart of Darkness*.
1902, Hofmannsthal, *Brief des Lord Chandos* (The Letter of Lord Chandos).
1903, Shaw, *Man and Superman* [perf. 1905].
1904, D'Annunzio, *Alcyone*.
1904, Blok, *Stikhi o prekrasnoy dame* (Verses about the Beautiful Lady).
1906, Ady, *Uj Versek* (New Poems).
1906, Musil, *Die Verwirrungen des Zöglings Törleß* (The Confusions of Young Törless).
1907, George, *Der siebente Ring* (The Seventh Ring).
1907, Synge, *The Playboy of the Western World*.
1907, Kokoschka, *Mörder, Hoffnung der Frauen* (Murderer, Hope of Women).
1907, Strindberg, *Spöksonaten* (Ghost Sonata).
1909, Bely, *Pepel* (Ashes).
1909, Marinetti, 'Manifesto del Futurismo' ('Manifesto of Futurism').
1910, Kuzmin, 'O prekrasnoj jasnosti' ('Concerning Beautiful Clarity').
1910, Gumilyov, *Zhemchuga* (Pearls).
1910, Rilke, *Die Aufzeichnungen des Malte Laurids Brigge* (The Notebook of Malte Laurids Brigge).
1910, Forster, *Howards End*.
1910–1933, Cavafy, *Poiemata* (Poems) [First collected edition 1963].
1911, Saint-John Perse, *Eloges* (Elegies).
1911, Hoddis, 'Weltende' ('End of the World').
1912, Pascoais, *Regresso ao Paraíso* (Return to Paradise).
1912, Benn, *Morgue und andere Gedichte* (Morgue and Other Poems).

1912, Thomas Mann, *Der Tod in Venedig* (Death in Venice).

1912, Machado, *Campos de Castilla* (The Land of Castille).

1912–1923, Rilke, *Duineser Elegien* (Duino Elegies).

1913, Gumilyov, 'Nasledie Simvolizma i Akmeizm' ('The Tradition of Symbolism and the Acmeists').

1913, Alain-Fournier, *Le Grand Meaulnes* (The Lost Domain).

1913, Apollinaire, *Alcools* (Alcohols).

1913, Martin du Gard, *Jean Barois*.

1913, Mandelshtam, *Kamen* (Stone).

1913–1927, *A la recherche du temps perdu* (In Remembrance of Things Past).

1914, Hardy, *Satires of Circumstance, Lyrics and Reveries*.

1914, George, *Der Stern des Bundes* (The Star of the Circle).

1914, Joyce, *Dubliners*.

1914, Yeats, *Responsibilities*.

1914, Campana, *Canti orfici* (Orphic Songs).

1914, Unamuno, *Niebla* (Mist).

1914, Trakl, *Sebastian im Traum* (Sebastian in a Dream). •

1915, D.H. Lawrence, *The Rainbow*.

1915, Kafka, *Der Prozeß* (The Trial) [publ. 1925].

1916, Benn, *Gehirne* (Brains).

1916, Joyce, *Portrait of the Artist as a Young Man*.

1917, T.S. Eliot, *Prufrock and Other Observations*.

1917, Valéry, *La Jeune Parque* (The Young Fate).

1917, Ball, 'Karawane'.

1917, Jiménez, *Sonetos espirituales* (Spiritual Sonnets).

1918, Blok, 'Dvenadtsat' ('The Twelve').

1918, Kaiser, *Gas*.

1918, Brecht, *Baal* [first perf. 1923].

1918, Lewis, *Tarr*.

1919, Schwitters, 'Anna Blume'.

1919, Ungaretti, *Allegria dei naufragi* (Mirth of Shipwrecks).

1920, Pinthus (ed.), *Menschheitsdämmerung* (Twilight of Mankind).

1920, Unamuno, *Tres novelas ejemplares y un prologo* (Three Exemplary Novels and a Prologue).

1920, Colette, *Chéri*.

1920, Arp, *die wolkenpumpe* (The Cloud Pump).

1920, T.S. Eliot, 'Tradition and the Individual Talent'.

1920, D.H. Lawrence, *Women in Love*.

1920, Bronnen, *Vatermord* (Patricide) [perf. 1922].

1920, Valle-Inclán, *Luces de Bohemia* (Bohemian Lights).

1921, Hofmannsthal, *Der Schwierige* (The Difficult Man).

1921, Pirandello, *Sei personaggi in cerca d'autore* (Six Characters in Search of an Author).

1922, Mandelshtam, *Tristia*.

1922, Valéry, *Charmes* (Charms).

1922, Kafka, *Das Schloß* (The Castle) [publ. 1926].

1922, Joyce, *Ulysses*.

1922, T.S. Eliot, *The Waste Land*.

1922, Akhmatova, *Anno Domini MCMXXI*.

1922, Pirandello, *Enrico IV* (Henry the Fourth).
1923, Svevo, *La coscienza di Zeno* (The Confessions of Zeno).
1923, Rilke, *Sonette an Orpheus* (Sonnets to Orpheus).
1924, Breton, 'Manifeste du Surréalisme' ('Manifesto of Surrealism').
1924, Forster, *A Passage to India*.
1924, Thomas Mann, *Der Zauberberg* (The Magic Mountain).
1925, Pessoa, *O Guardador de Rebanhos* (The Protector of the Herds).
1925, Gide, *Les Faux-Monnayeurs* (The Counterfeiters).
1925, Woolf, *Mrs Dalloway*.
1925, Montale, *Ossi di seppia* (The Bones of Cuttlefish).
1926, Aragon, *Le Paysan de Paris* (Paris Peasant).
1926, T.E. Lawrence, *Seven Pillars of Wisdom*.
1926, Benn, 'Urgesicht' ('Primal Vision').
1927, Woolf, *To the Lighthouse*.
1927, Hesse, *Der Steppenwolf*.
1928, Breton, *Nadja*.
1928, Yeats, *The Tower*.
1929, Cocteau, *Les Enfants terribles* (The Holy Terrors).
1930, Quasimodo, *Acque e terre* (Waters and Lands).
1931, Seferis, *Strophe* (Turning Point).
1932, Quasimodo, *Oboe sommerso* (The Sunken Oboe).
1933, Queneau, *Le Chiendent* (The Bark Tree).
1933, Ungaretti, *Sentimento del tempo* (Feeling of Time).
1935, Seferis, *Mythistorema*.
1936, Valéry, 'Questions de poésie' ('Problems of Poetry').
1936–1939, Montherlant, *Les Jeunes Filles* (The Girls).
1938, Artaud, *Le Théâtre et son double* (The Theatre and its Double).
1939, Yeats, *Last Poems*.
1939, Montale, *Le occasioni* (Occasions).

4

The Literature of Political Engagement

1 LITERATURE IN THE AGE OF POLITICAL COMMITMENT: THE CONTEXT

'It was in 1915 the old world ended', announced D.H. Lawrence in his novel, *Kangaroo* (1923). From that date, democratic-liberal Europe no longer possessed in the eyes of many any right to rule, its cultural and moral legitimacy nullified by the 'human ignominy' and the 'unspeakable baseness' of a war effort driven by jingoistic rhetoric and rampant xenophobia. Lawrence was not alone in viewing the Great War as a critical juncture in European history. Leonard Woolf (husband of Virginia) also saw the war as a point of no return for his generation: 'In 1914, in the background of one's life and one's mind', he later noted in his autobiography, 'there were light and hope; by 1918 one had unconsciously accepted a perpetual public menace and darkness, and had admitted into the privacy of one's mind or soul an iron fatalistic acquiescence in insecurity and barbarism.' Throughout Europe, many reached for metaphors of rupture, decline and termination in order to make sense of contemporary history. The ambit of cultural pessimism was a broad one: it ranged from the youthful radicalism of the Auden generation in England, who infused into their critique of the past a vital component of generational conflict, through the middle ground of the traditional humanism of Thomas Mann and Romain Rolland, to the more ominous anti-democratic stance embodied by the Spanish philosopher, José Ortega Y Gasset, and the German neo-nationalist writer, Ernst Jünger. In spite of differences (ideological and personal) all could agree that a fundamental and irreversible qualitative change had taken place in the political culture of the Western world, that stability had given way to uncertainty,

143

diplomacy to naked power, and the needs of the individual to the priorities of anonymous mass society.[1]

Nowhere was this pessimism more evident than in a volume whose very title seemed to sum up the secular eschatology of this period: Oswald Spengler's *Decline of the West*. Published in two volumes between 1918 and 1922, Spengler's epic work offered an overview of three thousand years of European history, from its beginnings in the 'great creations of the newly awakened dream-heavy soul' of a mythical past, to the present age, marked by crisis and confusion. Spengler saw the successive moments of this history in terms of a strict organic development, in which nations and societies were fated to pass through the inevitable stages of birth, maturity and death. European civilisation was now nearing its end, its creative energies dissipated, its will to survive against the dawning civilisations of the East broken through increasingly bloody internecine wars and through a political defeatism that Spengler graphically linked to the 'self-annihilation of democracy through money'. Teleological and deterministic, fatatalist and self-fulfilling, Spengler's historicising narrative offered neither hope nor optimism, but a craven sort of self-surrender to the forces of inexorable historical decline.[2]

And yet, Spengler's readership did not find his prognosis either too drastic or too pessimistic. Compelled to live in a post-war period characterised by rampant inflation, civil unrest and mass unemployment, in (as the noted Catholic novelist, François Mauriac explained) 'a kind of terror' that seemed unfathomable as it seemed unending, many found Spengler's angular fatalism a convincing philosophy. Much of the fiction of the 1920s and 1930s dealt with social and political dislocation. This included the epic novel sequences by Roger Martin du Gard (*The World of the Thibaults*, 8 volumes, 1922–1940), Jules Romains (*Men of Goodwill*, 27 volumes, 1932–1947), John Galsworthy (*The Forsyte Saga*, 3 volumes, 1906–1922) and Hermann Broch's *The Sleepwalkers* (3 volumes, 1930–1932). These were *Zeitromane* (novels of contemporary history), which used the experiences of representative individuals or families to explore the tensions and crises besetting a post-war Europe destabilised by class conflict, the proletarianisation of the middle classes, and female emancipation. The social focus of these novels ranged from the Galsworthy's upper bourgeoisie to Broch's proletarian agitators, but all evinced a barely containable pessimism regarding the fate of individual values and individual consciousness in the age of mass politics. Jules Romains spoke for many on this issue. As he explained in his preface to the first volume of the *Men of Goodwill* sequence (*The Sixth of October*, 1932), 'myriads of human activities are scattered in all directions by the indifferent forces of self-interest, of passion, even of crime and madness; and they proceed to destroy themselves in their clashes or lose themselves in the void – or so it seems'. As Romains explained, living in such an environment the novelist must necessarily grapple with the 'ultimate incoherence' that surrounds him, not seeking false patterns of meaning or imposing a manufactured unity (as the Modernists had tried to do), but remaining alive to the 'whole pathos of dispersion, of disappearance, in which life abounds'.[3]

For many, the confusions and dislocations of this period could be traced back to a single traumatic event, the First World War, whose repercussions only gradually came to impact upon the collective memory of the people of Europe. Its effects could still be felt well after 1918, both as a diplomatic embarrassment, and as an economic burden, but also as a powerful symbol of national unity and purpose. Assisted by the patriotic agencies of their respective governments, British and French servicemen were able to return to places of war-time tragedy, sites of despair such as Ypres, the Somme, and Passchendaele, now transformed into quasi-sacred monuments to the past. Germany cultivated its own collective memory of the war, commemorating past victories and defeats through monuments and symbols, organisations, and anniversaries such as 'The Day of Langemarck', observed on 10 November each year under the most solemn of circumstances. Celebrating that battle in a speech given almost a decade later, the German war novelist, Rudolf Binding, argued that those who died there gave their lives in an act of total idealism, upon which future Germans would forge a new sense of national identity, one that would be drawn out of the 'continuously creative, continuously rejuvenating, continuously living power of myth'. As the nationalist novelist, Franz Schauwecker noted, in a memorable formulation of this logic of compensation: 'we had to lose the war, in order to win the nation'.[4]

The war also formed the focus of a growing body of pacifist literature, which sought to strip the notion of military struggle of its heroic aura. This process of demystification had, in fact, started during the war itself, when novelists such as Henri Barbusse (*Under*

Fire, 1916) in France, and poets such as Wilfred Owen and Isaac Rosenberg in England, Giuseppe Ungaretti in Italy, and Georg Trakl and Heinrich Mann in Germany and Austria, had expressed a growing disillusionment with the conduct of the war and its aims. The general pacifist tendency of this work (inflected, it is true, through a lyrical subjectivism which stressed the pity and suffering of that conflagration, rather than its political or economic causes) was strengthened by a body of writing that appeared in the late 1920s, and which took advantage of its greater distance from events to offer a more complex perspective. With the exception of R.C. Sherriff's play, *Journey's End* (1928), the key texts were novels: Jaroslav Hašek's *The Good Soldier Schweik* (1921–1923), Arnold Zweig's *The Case for Sergeant Grischa* (1927), Edmund Blunden's *Undertones of War* (1928), Robert Graves' *Goodbye to All That* (1929), Erich Maria Remarque's *All Quiet on the Western Front* (1929) and Siegfried Sassoon's *Memoirs of an Infantry Officer* (1930). They criticised the war (and the notion of war) from varying perspectives: Sassoon's position was the closest to that of the conscientious objector; his novel (a firsthand account of his own traumatic military experiences) represented a highly personal critique of the 'political errors and insincerities for which the fighting men [had been] sacrificed'; Graves also employed the memoir form for his novel, but supplemented Sassoon's moral self-scrutiny with a more ironic, and even jocular, perspective focussed upon the quotidian details of army life: the demands of bodily function and appetite, and the mechanics of survival in a world where 'common sense' and insanity seem reversible values. The two novels that offered the greatest insight into the common man's experience of war enjoyed unsurpassed popularity in the post-war period: Hašek's *The Good Soldier Schweik* and Remarque's *All Quiet on the Western Front*. Both works attempted to give a picture of the insecurities, physical vicissitudes and sheer violence of military engagement from the point of view of the ordinary conscript. Hašek's unfinished novel provided, through the irreverent antics of its picaresque hero, a rare comic insight into war and the absurd machinations of the Austro-Hungarian war machine, whose complicated code of ethics and stultifying bureaucracy the wily Schweik manipulates to his own highly self-serving ends. Remarque's novel likewise employs the perspective of the ordinary man, but here the focus is the sheer destructiveness of war, its terrifying potential not only to maim, cripple and disfigure those involved, but also to destroy psychologically even the survivors. They are the real victims of the war experience, this lost generation, who return to civilian life 'weary, broken, burnt out, rootless, and without hope', unable to adjust to a society that wishes to forget the past.[5]

For the Western nations, the First World War culminated either in ignominious defeat or pyrrhic victory. But for Russia it ended with an event that was to transform that nation from a semi-feudal relic into one of the major world powers: the Bolshevik Revolution of October 1916. Its impact on Russian society was enormous: within a decade, first under its revolutionary leaders Lenin and Trotsky, and then, from 1924, under the more centralising influence of Stalin, the private sector was dismantled and the means of production nationalized; the agricultural sector streamlined and rationalised (and its 'inefficient' and 'selfish' *kolkhoznik* class liquidated); all cultural and educational institutions brought under a single state apparatus, controlled by a single party system, and supported by a new secret police service (the *Politburo*); and the satellite nations of the erstwhile Russia united under the control of the newly founded Union of Soviet Socialist Republics (the USSR). The ideological, if not the political, effect of the Russian Revolution was no less great in other parts of Europe. Germany had a Communist Party, founded by Karl Liebknecht and Rosa Luxemburg, by 1919, France and Britain by 1920, and Italy, under the leadership of Amadeo Bordiga (which included Antonio Gramsci), by 1921. Tied to the parent organisation in Moscow through the agency of a Communist International (Comintern), these parties sought to duplicate the success of the Bolshevik party in their own countries, hoping, ultimately, to further the interests of the World Revolution, whose advent would (it was hoped) not only free the proletariat from their economic serfdom, but, in the process, liberate all from the systems of oppression, political and ideological, that had erstwhile governed them.

The utopian dimension of the Communist vision inspired intellectuals and writers throughout Europe, many of whom (following the débâcle of the First World War) felt betrayed by the institutions, values and politicians of the liberal-democratic West. Reasons for joining the cause were diverse. The poet Stephen Spender was attracted to 'the mysterious aspect of Communism: the idea that the proletariat had some virtue whereby, when they had made the revolution, all the evils of the bourgeois class would be removed by a classless society'; whilst Arthur Koestler (future author of the famous *Darkness at Noon*, 1940) found that Communism alone had been able to purge him of that 'load of guilt' about the poor and the oppressed that he, as a member of the well-fed middle classes, would have otherwise 'carried around with him for the rest of his life'. Many of these acolytes discovered that Communism demanded much, indeed, everything, from the individual; but far from being a deterrent, this demand for total surrender to the cause proved an attraction. As Richard Crossman (journalist and British Labour politician) was later to note: 'The emotional appeal of Communism lay precisely in the sacrifices [...] which it demanded of the convert. You can call the response masochistic, or describe it as a sincere desire to serve mankind. But, whatever name you use, the idea of an active comradeship of struggle – involving personal sacrifice and abolishing differences of class and race – has had a compulsive power in every western democracy.'[6]

Above all, Communism provided a way out of the intellectual confusions and uncertainties of the Modernist period. Where writers such as Thomas Mann, Proust and Virginia Woolf had pointed to the fragmentation and rupture of modern experience, and had proffered purely subjective solutions (if any), Marxism was able to offer the individual certain fundamental and quite unquestionable truths, explaining the crisis of modernity in terms of the basic realities of imperialism, capitalist exploitation, class struggle, whilst holding out the promise of a solution to this crisis through the advent of Communist society. For a generation worried and confused by the intellectual legacy of Modernism, Communism came as a great relief. Koestler again: 'To say that one had "seen the light" is a poor description of the mental rapture which only the convert knows (regardless to what faith he has been converted). The new light seems to pour from all directions across the skull; the whole universe falls into pattern like the stray pieces of a jig-saw puzzle assembled by magic at one stroke. There is now an answer to every question; doubts and conflicts are a matter of the tortured past.'[7]

Many writers became Communist because they abhorred the past; but an equal number joined because they feared a future that was increasingly coming under the sway of the second major political force of the twentieth century: Fascism. It too arose in reaction to the radical disillusionment with the liberal-democratic tradition that was widespread after the First World War; but in the place of Communism's vision of a classless society, it celebrated the nation, state and race, and hoped to secure the victory of its cause not through social revolution but through *coup d'état* and military conquest. Fascism developed throughout Europe: in Italy, where under Mussolini it seized power in 1922; in Germany, where it agitated as a political movement under its leader, Adolf Hitler, before it finally came to power in 1933; and in Hungary, Romania, and in Spain, where through the activities of Franco's Falangist party, it initiated the most bloody civil war in modern European history. The intellectual origins of Fascism were diverse, but one contemporary source lay in the writings of the self-styled political philosopher, George Sorel. Sorel never described himself as a fascist, but in his promotion of extra-parliamentary agitation, in his advocacy of the mobilisation of the masses through myth and charismatic leadership, and in his celebration of the 'psychology of the deeper life' that is activated by political violence, he bequeathed in his seminal work, *Reflections on Violence* (1906), a constellation of anti-democratic ideas that would find further elaboration in the writings of José Primo de Rivera, in Spain, Alfred Rosenberg, in Germany, and Charles Maurras, in France. As with Communism, Fascism had its adherents amongst intellectuals and writers, many of whom were erstwhile Modernists. They included Marinetti and Pirandello, in Italy; Wyndham Lewis and D.H. Lawrence, in England; and Gottfried Benn, in Germany. They believed that Fascism offered a way back to the elemental energies and tribal solidarity of a distant past, to that 'heritage of exaltation and intoxications' that had been lost with the advent of modernity. Fascism alone (it was felt) could provide a force capable of destroying the false and superficial values of mass democracy, and of creating a new aristocratic ethos founded on 'the old, bristling, savage spirit' of our ancestors. As the French cultural critic, Julien Benda, argued in 1927, such writers were guilty of a 'spiritual betrayal' (a *trahison des clercs*), surrendering themselves to irrationalist and nihilistic philosophies whose ultimate goal was 'the intellectual organisation of political hatreds'.[8]

That the two powerful ideologies of Fascism and Communism, so similar in their totalitarian ambitions and messianic fervour, but so different in their social goals, would clash could have been predicted, although the initial site of this conflict, Spain, could not have been. The Spanish Civil War (1936–1939) permitted Europe its first sight of the Fascist militarist war machine in action. For ranged against the elected Republican government (which had come to power with a broadly-based Popular Front mandate in 1936) were not just Franco and his generals, determined to return Spain to its monarchist Catholic past, but élite divisions from Fascist Italy and from Nazi Germany, whose presence confirmed the broader European significance of the war. The plight of the Republic drew support from throughout Europe and the world, attracting individuals determined to fight for democratic government and humane values, believing themselves part of an 'international crusade' of right against wrong, the oppressed against the oppressor, of light against darkness.[9]

The Spanish Civil War was also a writer's war; and the lines here were equally clearly and equally vehemently drawn. Confronting those, such as Roy Campbell (*Flowering Rifle*, 1939) and E.E. Dwinger (*Spanish Silhouettes*, 1937), who supported Franco, came an array of writers, whose responses to the war produced some of the central texts of the inter-war period. They included André Malraux (*Days of Hope*, 1937), Georges Bernanos (*A Diary of My Times*, 1938), W.H. Auden ('Spain', 1937), Arthur Koestler (*Spanish Testament*, 1938) and George Orwell (*Homage to Catalonia*, 1938). The battle-cry was sent up by Auden in 'Spain', a poem that saw in the Spanish conflagration a pivotal moment within world history: 'Yesterday the belief in the absolute value of Greece,/The fall of the curtain upon the death of a hero;/Yesterday the prayer to the sunset/And the adoration of madmen. But to-day the struggle'. Militancy as an ethical imperative was particularly sounded by Communist poets, such as Christopher Caudwell (*Poems*, 1939) and John Cornford (*Poems from Spain*, 1936), both of whom gave their lives in the war. But it was also taken up by others such as Herbert Read (*The End of a War*, 1933) and Stephen Spender (*Poems*, 1933), who wrote poetry in honour of the soldiers of the Republic, celebrating 'the will of those who dared to move/From the furrow, their life's groove', their deeds ennobled both by the cause for which they fought and by their stoical acceptance of dying. The political necessity of self-sacrifice (both on and off the field of battle), the tensions between voluntarism and obedience, and between humanitarian sympathy and the need for military proficiency, were themes explored in one of the great novels of the war: André Malraux's, *Days of Hope*. The novel tests out the idealism and tentative optimism of which the poets spoke against a background of military and political struggle, in which atrocity and summary execution are daily realities. Within this context, order and self-discipline, technical proficiency and party unity assume the status of near-ethical priorities. As Manuel, the Communist labourer, learns, in war it is necessary to choose 'between victory and compassion', between the sacrifice of the short-term values of individual humanism, and the long-term objective, which is the defeat of Fascism. Within the bitter and confusing landscape of war, every fighter must organize 'for common action an aggregate of feelings that are often incompatible. In this case they include poverty – humiliation – Apocalyptic vision – and hope.'[10]

To many, the Spanish Civil War represented an unambiguous struggle between two divergent and quite irreconcilable political and ethical positions; but to others, such as Arthur Koestler and George Orwell, the issues were more complex. Both authors pointed to complications in the neat right wing-left wing divide, noting important cross-overs in strategy and goals, and a shared convergence on intolerance and resistance to criticism or self-scrutiny. These form the focus of Orwell's *Homage to Catalonia*. His firsthand account of the war captured not only the tactile experience of battle, that 'long nightmare of the fighting, the noise, the lack of food and sleep, the mingled strain and boredom', which was broken only by the sudden horror of random death and mutilation, but also the peculiar internecine and masochistic nature of the Republican offensive, which was marked by ineptitude, inexperience and continuing animosity between the Republicans, the Communists and the Anarchists. It is this *internal* war, conducted between supposed allies within the anti-Fascist camp, that most interests Orwell. Within their conflict the *modus operandi* of totalitarian politics became dramatically apparent: the sacrifice of individual liberties for the sake of 'higher goals'; the debasement of language through propaganda; the continual imposition of a 'me-good: you-bad' Manichean view of the world; and the emotional and psychological ambit of intellectual repression and intolerance. It is within this 'horrible atmosphere produced by fear, suspicion, hatred [and] censored newspapers' that the war claimed its greatest victim. As Orwell was later to explain in 'Looking Back on the Spanish War' (1942): the Spanish people had lost their bid for democratic self-determination, but the Western world had lost something equally vital: 'the very concept of objective truth', whose annihilation in Spain would (in the years to come) lead individuals and nations alike into the uncompromising machinations of *Realpolitik*.[11]

2   WRITERS AND POLITICS: PROGRAMME AND PRACTICE

Behind the commitment of writers such as Auden, Orwell and Malraux to the Spanish cause lay a radically new vision of the literary vocation. Writers, even those not directly involved in the fighting, had come to realise that they had become, *nolens volens*, a part of history. Stephen Spender put it simply: 'Just as the pacifist is political in refusing to participate in war, so the writer who refuses to recognise the political nature of our age must to some extent be refusing to deal with an experience in which he himself is involved.' Spain had provided the litmus test for this view of the committed writer, but it was Russia that had provided the catalyst. Under the impact of the Revolution of 1916, an entire generation of writers had come to subject their vocation to a sustained and theoretically rigorous process of scrutiny. The most polemical writer of the Revolution was the former Futurist, Vladimir Mayakovsky. His many manifestos, speeches and impromptu observations (disclaiming the value of traditional culture and extolling the poetry and art of the new Russia) were not simply extensions of the 'épater le bourgeois' philosophy of the Avant-Garde; they represented attempts to make contact with the popular voice of the revolution, and to break down the formal divisions between the arts. Mayakovsky showed the way forward in his own writing, such as in the play, *The Mystery Bouffe*, 1918, and the satirical poem, *150,000,000*, 1921, texts offered to the public (in the spirit of *Agitprop*) as 'agitational pieces and agitation on behalf of the industrial and trading establishments, i.e. advertisements'; in short, contributions towards the 'de-aestheticising of the productive arts'. Mayakovsky's work represented the most radical moment in the literature of the new Russia. The cultural goals of the Revolution were embodied both in the LEF (Left Front) organisation, whose leading members, Mayakovsky, Nikolay Aseyev and Osip Brik, sought to keep alive the populist and innovatory dynamism of the Revolution, and in the agitational movement known as *Proletkult* (Movement for Proletarian Culture), which took art directly into the streets and public places of cities and villages, in an effort to mobilise the population in the direction of the Revolution.[12]

In spite of the exuberant individualism displayed by Mayakovsky and by other early revolutionary writers such as Sergey Esenin (*Confessions of a Hooligan*, 1921), the arts in the new Russia were directly tied to the wishes of the Communist Party and its leadership.

As the Leninist guard of the first wave gave way to a new regime of consolidation and control, so experimentation and Futurist playfulness were replaced by a style and a policy that would become synonymous with Stalinist Russia: Socialist Realism. The term was not coined until 1932 and did not gain currency until 1934, when, at the First All-Union Congress of Writers, the Communist Party directed Soviet writers to produce a literature which would be Realist in form but Socialist in content, and would focus upon the positive achievements of the State, depicting 'reality in its revolutionary development'. But such a literature had existed long before this date, contending both with the continuing Avant-Garde presence of the LEF writers and with the hard-line members of RAPP (The Russian Association of Proletarian Writers), who would accept nothing other than studies of the industrial state of Russia conveyed through an almost photographic Naturalism (known in RAPP circles as 'factology'). Socialist Realism occupied the middle ground between these two extremes. Typical of the genre were the early works of Maxim Gorky: the play, *Lower Depths* (1902) and his novel, *Mother* (1907). Both are set in a working-class milieu, and both deal with characters whose optimism triumphs over material and social deprivation, and who move through diverse experiences from ignorance and isolation to a point where they understand the forward movement of history in the shape of the Socialist cause. Gorky's fiction occupies a transitional place between the literature of social protest of the Naturalist school and the more politically motivated Socialist Realism of later writers such as Dimitry Furmanov (*Chapayev*, 1923), Fyodor Gladkov (*Cement*, 1925), Alexander Fadeyev (*The Rout*, 1927) and Nikolai Ostrovsky (*The Making of a Hero*, 1934), which move almost entirely within the ambit of official Communist ideology. It is only in these novels that the classic features of the Socialist Realist style fully emerge: the absence of introspection and psychological sophistication in character construction; linear and progressive plots; and settings which are either those of recent history (*The Rout*) or the industrial present (*Cement*). Throughout all, the same spirit of political triumphalism and forced optimism reigns. These qualities are embodied in the heroes of these novels, who overcome confusion and hardship to emerge politically enlightened and vindicated by their trust in the Russian people and the Soviet state, finally joining (in a curious mixture of sentimentality and party-political pragmatism) 'the active ranks' of the future.[13]

Politicised Avant-Gardism and Socialist Realism provided the two poles around which committed literature in the post-war period revolved. The Germans also had their Communist writers, 'proletarian-revolutionary' authors such as Willi Bredel (*Machine Factory N & K*, 1930) and Ernst Ottwalt (*Law and Order*, 1929), who, affiliated with the Communist journal *Die Linkskurve* (The Left Direction), favoured the RAPP-inspired *Reportageroman* genre (the novel of documentary or 'factional' verism), rather than Socialist Realism. But the most productive committed writers of this generation gravitated either to a form of anarchist utopianism, represented in the immediate post-war period by Kurt Hiller, Walter Hasenclever and Ernst Toller, or to the more broadly based humanism of the so-called 'fellow-travellers' (*Mitläufer*), who espoused a radical socialism, but remained independent of the Communist Party. Some of the most noted fellow-travellers were Hermann Broch, Kurt Tucholsky and Heinrich Mann. All had been deeply affected by the war, and all had found an outlet for their nascent radicalism in Avant-Garde journals such as *Die Aktion* (Action), *Das Ziel* (the Goal) and *Die Erhebung* (The Uprising). Heinrich Mann was, perhaps, the best known of the group. He had begun as a *fin de siècle* aesthete in pre-war Germany, celebrating hedonism and the joys of heightened sensibility in novels such as *Cockaigne* (1900) and *Diana* (1903). But from 1910 onwards, Mann came to revise his early aestheticism, adopting a more civic and politically self-conscious stance in essays such as 'Spirit and Action' (1910) and 'Zola' (1915). Here he argued that writers should not stand apart from the issues of the day but should become 'agitators', 'aligning themselves with the people in their struggle against oppression'. Mann himself tried to do precisely this, writing novels of social conscience such as *The Important Matter* (1930) and *The Hill of Lies* (1932), where he depicted the plight of the poor and under-privileged. His example was followed by many from within the left-wing intelligentsia, from Alfred Döblin and Arnold Zweig to Kurt Tucholsky and Carl von Ossietzky, the editors of the journal *Die Weltbühne* (The Worldstage). In their consistent tirades against militarism, Fascism and the right-wing exploitation of the judicial system and the army, these writers provided a forum for political protest in the 'morally darkest years' of Germany's history.[14]

In Britain, proletarian literature moved within its own, more modest ambit. The main names here were James Hanley (*Men in Darkness*, 1931), Walter Greenwood (*Love on the Dole*, 1933) and

Hugh MacDiarmid (*First Hymn to Lenin and Other Poems*, 1931). Their work, which was associated with *The Left Review* (1934–1938) and John Lehmann's *New Writing* (1936–1939), gave expression to a vernacular style of socialism that was no less committed than its German counterpart, but was without the latter's ideological pretensions. As the contemporary Communist writer, Edgell Rickword, noted, this was a 'literature that expressed and reflected the actual struggle of the down-trodden', and 'could convey by Realistic treatment, reportage, their actual conditions of work and communicate their humanity and the plight of their position in a flourishing society'. As these writers accepted the political duties of the present, they rejected the aesthetic practices of the Modernists, whose Avant-Garde provocations and experimentations they regarded as both élitist and irrelevant in a world of mass politics. T.S. Eliot, in particular, was a favourite target. The critic, Michael Roberts, spoke for many in the famous preface to his *New Signatures* anthology (1932) (in which Auden, Spender and Day-Lewis made their first collective appearance) in describing the verse of this committed group as a 'reaction against esoteric poetry in which it is necessary for the reader to catch each recondite allusion'. In the place of what was felt to be the wilful obscurantism of the type of verse written by Eliot and others, the poets of the Auden generation sought to produce a 'popular, elegant and contemporary art', which would reach the widest readership, and bring home to it the necessity of political activism.[15]

Stephen Spender, Christopher Isherwood, Louis MacNiece and Cecil Day Lewis saw in Communism a 'faith which had the authority, the logic, the cut-and-driedness of the Roman church', an ethos, self-confident and forward-looking, which could replace that sense of moral direction that had been lost with the decline of liberal humanism. As MacNiece, the author of *Blind Fireworks* (1929) and *Poems* (1935), noted, this generation of poets was 'emotionally partisan', and fully prepared to engage with problems beyond their own private selves. These were sentiments shared by Cecil Day Lewis (*Collected Poems*, 1938), who sought to produce 'revolutionary poems', in the conviction that 'we discover reality by acting upon it, not by thinking about it'. A poetry of radical politics, however, could not simply be willed into existence, as the work of the leading representative of this generation, W.H. Auden, testifies. From his very first volume, *Poems* (1930), Auden gave evidence of a highly idiosyncratic voice, angular, obscure, oppositional and superbly tuned to a poetic idiom shot through with metaphors of intrigue, sabotage, conspiracy and transgression (see, for example, 'Missing' and 'The Secret Agent'). Auden's poetry did not acquire a clearer political trajectory until his later verse, where the poet took to task an entire generation for its lack of moral integrity and political honesty, castigating, as in 'A Communist to Others' (1933), a class to which he himself, in fact, belonged. As he explains in that poem, those who belong to the ruling caste are guilty more of mindless acquiescence in the status quo than explicit oppression, and act out of myopic self-interest, hoping 'to corner as reward/ All that the rich can here afford/Love and music and bed and board/While the world flounders'. And yet Auden's political commitment was neither permanent nor unambiguous; not only the homosexual complications of his own personal life, but also his involvement in the Spanish Civil War forced him to rethink the easy ethical judgements that had gone with his earlier political verse. After leaving Europe for America in 1939, he took stock of his past and that of his generation in one of his most anthologised poems: 'September 1, 1939'. Here in nine stanzas of conversational verse, he passes judgement on the 'low dishonest decade' of the 1930s, which had allowed personal morality to be sacrificed to political pragmatism, and the individual to the state. In the face of such collective bad faith, Auden exhorts the reader to accept one fundamental truth, reducing his earlier personal philosophy to the starkest of propositions: 'we must love one another or die'.[16]

In other parts of Europe, the literature of political commitment emerged with a greater or lesser tenacity. In spite of the theoretical initiatives made by the leader of the Italian Socialist Party, Antonio Gramsci (largely formulated during his years of imprisonment under Mussolini), there was no significant example of political literature in Italy prior to the publication of Ignazio Silone's novels, *Fontamara* (1933) and *Bread and Wine* (1936, revised 1955). The literatures of Portugal and Greece also register a similar absence, although Greece did have the remarkable early poetry of Yannis Ritsos (*Tractor*, 1934, and the celebrated *Epitaphios*, 1936). The Scandinavian countries, on the other hand, produced one of the most remarkable political writers of the age: the Danish novelist, Martin Andersen Nexø. His two epic novels, *Pelle the Conqueror* (four volumes, 1906–1910) and *Ditte: Daughter of Man* (five volumes, 1917–1921), are works of consummate early Socialist Realism, not doctrinaire but humanist in breadth, with characters who triumph over poverty and destitution through essential human strengths, rather than through political correctness. Ireland likewise produced its most popular political playwright during this period: Sean O'Casey. His major plays, the Dublin trilogy, *The Shadow of a Gunman* (1923), *Juno and the Paycock* (1924) and *The Plough and the Stars* (1926), focus upon the Easter Rebellion of 1916 and the ensuing civil war. In France, the experience of war had led many writers to a compromise between pacifism and a form of Socialist humanism. This was the ethos expounded by the Clarté movement, founded in 1919 by Henri Barbusse, which was (in the words of its mission statement) a 'league of intellectual solidarity for the triumph of the international cause'. Although the movement lasted only two years, foundering in 1921 upon internal disputes between the pacifist internationalists and a new wing, more politically self-conscious and dedicated to the class struggle, it helped to prepare the way for the markedly more successful International Writers' Congress for the Defence of Culture, founded in 1935. The organisation brought under a single rubric some of the most noted names of French literature: Louis Aragon and André Breton from the Surrealist movement; the noted Modernist novelist, André Gide; and André Malraux, who combined adventurism, epicureanism and an early version of Existentialism with a no less sincere disavowal of the imperialist polices of the West in Indo-China. In literary terms they conspicuously diverge, unlike their British and German counterparts; but what allows us to bring them together is their desperate faith in Communism, which they held with an, at times, uncritical intensity. Gide, for example, would later retract his earlier enthusiasm for the Russian model in his polemical *Return from the USSR*, 1936); but in 1932 his commitment to Soviet Communism bordered upon a religious faith. As he explained in a journal entry of that year: 'in the abominable distress of the world today, the plan of the new Russia appears to me now as salvation. There is nothing that does not convince me of it.'[17]

Political literature not only had its programme and its exponents; it also had its theory. Working along parallel lines with these committed writers was a group of literary theorists who were able to place the initiatives of the former on a more clearly adumbrated theoretical base, establishing in the process the framework for a specifically Marxist approach to literary criticism. Such an aesthetic did not, it is true, emerge *ab ovo*. Half a century earlier, Marx and Engels had both written on literature, stressing its unique ability (which they felt was particularly evident in the great Realist novels of the nineteenth century) to penetrate the real motives, values and 'illusions that govern bourgeois society'. They were followed by Lenin, who, in his essay, 'Party Organisation and Party Literature' (1905), argued that the distinction between the aesthetic and the political was illusory: there is no such thing as purely disinterested writing; all literature embodies (implicitly or explicitly) an attitude towards class, property and politics. What the progressive writer must do (Lenin insisted) is recognise this fact, abandon the myth of 'bourgeois-intellectual-individualism', and infuse into his writing 'the life stream of the living proletarian cause'. Lenin's essay was a call to arms, an exhortation to committed writers to produce a type of literature that would extol the cause of the Communist Party (*Partiinost*). But although Lenin argued for the necessity of a clear commitment to the party line he offered no indication of how literature (conceived of as a specific form of *artistic* activity) could meet these demands. That lacuna was filled by a work that was to become one of the seminal texts of Marxist literary criticism: Leon Trotsky's *Literature and Revolution* (1924). Trotsky attempted here to answer a number of questions that Marx, Engels and Lenin had left in the margins of their work: Should politics be explicit in a text? (Engels had answered in the negative, Lenin in the affirmative); Should revolutionary politics have a revolutionary form? Must writers follow the party line? Is all 'bourgeois' literature necessarily politically reactionary? Can genuine Socialist art be created before the advent of universal socialism? Trotsky framed his questions within a broad analysis of contemporary Russian literature, which ranged from the mystical work of Alexander Blok through to Avant-Garde groups such as the Futurists and the Constructivists. And behind his analysis lay not only a sharp perception of the relationship between cultural policy and political strategy, but also a broad, almost utopian vision of what culture can help achieve: the classless society of the Socialist state, and a new man, a 'higher social biologic type', who, freed from material want and political exploitation, will mutate into the future, capable of raising 'his instincts to the heights of consciousness'.[18]

The classical tradition of Marxist literary criticism provided the parameters within which subsequent theoreticians in this field would move. These included Christopher Caudwell (*Illusion and Reality*, 1937), Walter Benjamin (*The Work of Art in the Age of Mechanical Reproduction*, 1936), Ernst Bloch (*Heritage of Our Times*,

1934), Georg Lukács (*Essays on Realism*, 1948) and Jean-Paul Sartre (*What is Literature?*, 1948). Although the point of contact between these theorists was often oblique, collectively they produced, nevertheless, a model of literary analysis that, for the first time in European literature, opened up the process of writing to the priorities of political and ideological engagement. In his works, Caudwell sought to explicate what he termed 'the destructive illness' that was besetting 'bourgeois culture' in the twentieth century. He meant by this not only the objective circumstances of its decline (which he believed to be evident in the increase of imperialist expansion, poverty and militarism), but the ideological and artistic attempts to dissimulate that crisis, the 'illusions' and the myths of political liberty that many still adhered to in democratic nations. Lukács was equally critical of what he termed late-capitalist society, and likewise worked with a model of terminal decline; but behind his analysis lay a deep desire to restore totality in the face of the fragmentation and dissolution that, as he had argued in his *Theory of the Novel* (1920), characterised the decline of bourgeois society. Lukács conducted his struggle on two fronts: he rejected the idea that literature should be simply propaganda, arguing in a series of important essays published between 1930 and 1933 in *The Left Direction* that only a complete, epic account of the present, one capable of integrating individual political fate into the collective movement of history, as the Realist novelists of the nineteenth century had done (albeit, in an apolitical fashion) could produce 'the great proletarian work of art'. For that reason, Lukács found the Modernists' preoccupation with subjectivity and psychology unacceptable, and their pessimistic attitude to the possibility of social change and to history unnecessarily fatalistic. As he wrote in the German *émigré* journal based in Moscow, *Das Wort* (The Word), the Modernists, and, in particular, the German Expressionists, by tying their representation of the world to the experience of individual consciousness, had offered a picture of society that remained 'opaque, fragmentary, chaotic and uncomprehended'. At a historical juncture, where clarity of analysis and coherent political purpose were necessary in the struggle against Fascism, the Modernist perspective was not only erroneous in itself; it also served 'to discourage rather than promote the process of revolutionary clarification amongst its followers', travestying in the process 'the great social mission of literature'.[19]

In spite of his open espousal of a revolutionary art of the working class, Lukács was both conservative and uncompromisingly élitist in his cultural inclinations. Walter Benjamin arrived at a similar commitment to Marxism, but from a position that was more alive to the politically dynamic textures and energies of Modernist culture. Benjamin was particularly attracted to the dramaturgy of Bertolt Brecht, whose epic theatre seemed to him to embody the 'destructive, cathartic aspect, that is, the liquidation of the traditional value (Benjamin termed it 'aura') of the cultural heritage', without which the formal apparatus of bourgeois culture could not be undone. The writer and artist, argued Benjamin in his most influential work, *The Work of Art in the Age of Mechanical Reproduction*, must seize the technical means of aesthetic production, distance the consumer of culture from the origins of the artistic experience in ritual, and replace that experience by the process of political education. Only through such means could the masses be brought 'face to face with themselves', and helped to an understanding of their essential role as agents of revolutionary change. It was, above all, through Benjamin's insights, less systematically theorised than Lukács' and less empirically grounded than those of Adorno, that Marxism regained contact with the revolutionary energies of the European Avant-Garde.[20]

3   THE POLITICISATION OF MODERNISM: BETWEEN EXPRESSIONISM AND *NEUE SACHLICHKEIT*

That tension between Avant-Garde experimentation and political commitment that Lukács had brought to light in his sustained critique of the German Expressionists had been anticipated by many from within that movement itself, by writers and artists long aware of the problems involved in translating radical aesthetics into progressive politics. Following 1918, these tensions helped cause a fragmentation of that movement, whose erstwhile members moved off in heterogenous directions. Some sought a surrogate destiny for their utopian goals by joining the nationalist cause, for example Hanns Johst, who celebrated what he regarded as its youthful idealism in the proto-Nazi play *Schlageter* (1930); others, impatient with the contradictions within politicised Avant-Gardism, reached out to a fully unambiguous party-political Marxism, as found in the poetry of J.R. Becher (*To All!*, 1919, and *Machine Rhythms*, 1926);

whilst others still, such as the dramatists Walter Hasenclever (*The Saviour*, 1919, and *Beyond*, 1920) and Ernst Toller (*The Luddites*, 1922) translated the utopianism evident in their early work into revolutionary fantasies of struggle and resistance.

The most important voice in this process of political adaptation, the figure who acted as a fulcrum for the increasingly committed writers of this generation in Germany and elsewhere, was the play-wright and poet, Bertolt Brecht. He had begun life with the play *Baal* (1918, published 1922), in which he had celebrated the raw vi-tality and animalist hedonism of his amoral hero, who consumes others and himself in an unbridled process of sensual exploitation. Some of these errant energies found their way into Brecht's first po-litical plays – *Drums in the Night* (1922) and *In the Jungle of the Cities* (1923) – both of which deal with topical themes, but from a per-spective that construes political behaviour as a confused mixture of self-seeking careerism, ignorance and (as Brecht later admitted) a 'pure delight in fighting'. These plays capture the cynicism and earthy pragmatism of German society in the early years of the Weimar Republic, qualities that Brecht further intensified in his bawdy *Threepenny Opera* (1928). The greater perspective was not to come until the late 1920s, with a series of so-called didactic plays (*Lehrstücke*): *The Measures Taken* (1930), *The Exception and the Rule* (1930) and *Saint Joan of the Stockyards* (1932). Here, under the influ-ence of a newly-found Marxism (and the more immediate presence of the innovating dramaturgist, Erwin Piscator), Brecht dramatised the necessity of transforming liberal humanism into a more self-reflective, and more politically viable ethos, one capable of judging the predicament and values of individuals in terms of the higher goals of the world revolution. Underscoring these plays lay a new vision of a political stage, the 'epic theatre'. Brecht outlined the model for this new dramaturgy in his *Little Organum for the Theatre* (1949), but its defining features had already been sketched in notes to his musical drama *Rise and Fall of the City of Mahagonny* (1930). Here he condemned the 'dramatic form of the theatre' (elsewhere called 'Aristotelian', but clearly that of the Realist-Naturalist stage of the late nineteenth century), because it stupefies the critical facul-ties of the audience, and encourages it, through empathy, suspense and other techniques, to identify with, and uncritically accept, the actions represented on stage. Such a theatre presupposes (Brecht argued) an unchanging model of human nature, existing beyond history and impervious to political change. Epic theatre, for its part,

seeks to challenge the reactionary, and purely reactive, nature of
traditional drama by distancing the audience from the action
through 'alienation devices' (*Verfremdung* or *V-Effekten*). It forces it,
thus, to view the dramatic events as fictional allegories, open to
analysis and discussion, in a process of critical confrontation,
whose aim is the creation of a 'quite definite practical attitude, directed towards changing the world'.[21]

Brecht's epic theatre represented the fruits of a political optimism
hard won in the teeth of a natural pessimism regarding the existence
of ideals and values in a world that had become, as he wryly noted
in his famous poem 'The tale of poor B.B.', from his *Manual of Piety*
(1927), 'mistrustful, and idle, and self-satisfied'. But there were other
writers of this generation who could not, or would not follow Brecht
down the road of political activism, but preferred to meet this world
head on, eschewing future visions, and ethical or political impera-
tives. The culture that they produced was called *Neue Sachlichkeit*
(New Functionalism). Politically aware, but uncommitted, the exponents of New Functionalism celebrated the machine, speed, technology, and all the other epiphenomena of modern urban existence,
with its sharp and brittle mass culture. In literature, a new realism
or pragmatism installed itself in the 'functional poetry'
(*Gebrauchslyrik*) penned by Walter Mehring (*Arche Noah SOS*, 1930)
and Erich Kästner (*Honest to Truth*, 1928, and *A Man gives
Information*, 1930); in the novels of social crisis produced by Hans
Fallada (*Little Man, What Now?* 1932); and in the wry satirical studies
of provincial *mores* evident in the plays of Ödön von Horváth
(*Italian Nights* and *Tales from the Vienna Woods*, both 1931). This was
a literature that dealt with characters caught between the extremes
of political activism, forced into quizzical passivity, ultimately
unable, like the hero of Kästner's popular novel, *Fabian: The Story of
a Moralist* (1930), to free themselves from the 'hopeless, pitiless
labyrinth' of German history on the eve of Hitler's Third Reich.[22]

The spirit of the New Functionalism manifested itself in a trio of
remarkable novels published at this time, all of which gave voice to
the same post-Expressionist, post-Avant-Garde mood of quietism
and political disillusionment: Alfred Döblin's *Berlin Alexanderplatz*
(1929), Elias Canetti's *Auto-da-Fé* (1935) and Robert Musil's *The Man
without Qualities* (three volumes, 1930–1943). Musil's novel (left unfinished at his death in 1942) is the most epic and the most philosophical of these. Through the story of the free-wheeling Ulrich,

who moves in a half-hearted fashion between the different professional and personal spheres in a semi-picaresque voyage of self-discovery, Musil subjects the coherence of categories such as causality, historical progress and personal identity to sustained sceptical comment. As Ulrich discovers through his many experiences, neither the 'interior space' of the self, nor the larger space of contemporary history seem to possess an inherent logic or direction. In the age of modernity, one can only be 'negatively free, constantly aware of the inadequate grounds for one's own existence', and compelled to choose irony and intellectual distance as modes of survival. Canetti's novel likewise focusses upon an individual's attempts to come to terms with the chaos and confusion of mass society. The story centres on the élitist bibliophile, Peter Kien, who uses his library as a mental and cultural barricade against the 'angular, painful, biting multifariousness' of the society that surrounds him. Canetti's hero ends up, paradoxically, internalising some of the worst aspects of this society: its anonymity, its lack of respect for others, and its destructive irrationalism. Kien is brought close to madness before surrendering himself, in an act of desperation and protest, to a funeral pyre made from his own books, an act which objectivises the apocalyptic pessimism that runs throughout Canetti's novel. A similar prescience of impending catastrophe pervades Döblin's *Berlin Alexanderplatz*. His novel moves within the same world of violence, criminality and brutal materialism explored by Canetti; but this time the values of mass society are viewed not through the superior narrative perspective used by Canetti, but through the limited point of view of the ex-criminal and denizen of the Berlin *demi-monde*, Franz Biberkopf. A victim of life, persecuted by erstwhile friends and present foes, Biberkopf's unsure grasp on the world (the product of an urban consciousness that is both fragmented and anomic) is reconstructed by Döblin through a stylistic register that moves between the Joycean interior monologue, Expressionistic subjectivism and the neo-naturalistic 'faction' techniques of the *Reportageroman*. Döblin's hero spends the entire novel trapped within a world that he never really understands, struggling 'against something fortuitous, something unaccountable, something that looks like fate'. At the end of his story, Döblin leaves Biberkopf (as he leaves the reader) caught between a vague optimism in collective action and a vision of a future, 'red of night and red of day', leading 'deathward'.[23]

Post-Expressionist developments in German literature may well have culminated in a political *impasse*, but they produced, in the process, a spectrum of writing that warrants serious attention. The Surrealist movement in France, however, trod a more barren path from Avant-Garde experimentation to political radicalism. Its moment of truth came in 1926. In that year a junior member of the group, Pierre Naville, published a tract, *The Revolution and the Intellectuals: What can the Surrealists do?* Naville argued that the Surrealist attempt to overturn the bourgeois social order through anarchic individualism had been a failure from the start. Its outrageous antics and public demonstrations, its provocative use of nonsense texts and techniques, its irreverent stance towards the institutions of bourgeois society had simply been assimilated by a public increasingly inured to the excesses of the Avant-Garde. An effective challenge to the status quo could only be launched on the basis of a revolutionary understanding of class warfare, and through an open adherence to the Communist Party. Naville's strictures brought to the surface the central contradiction within the Surrealist project: its desire to transform the real world through purely aesthetic methods, and effectively split the movement. In spite of the 'Second Manifesto of Surrealism' of 1930, which included an open acceptance of the class struggle and of 'allegiance to the principle of historical materialism' (yoked in an unconvincing way to the familiar discourse of dream cultivation, automatic writing and eroticism) the movement was irrevocably split. After 1927, Aragon and Breton (the two presiding spirits of the movement) went their separate ways: the former towards the Communist Party, and to the polemical *Treatise on Style* (1928), and eventually to the full-blown Socialist triumphalism of the novelistic series, *The Real World* (1933–1944), whilst Breton wrote the diary-novel, *Nadja* (1928), whose gentle eroticism and narrative surrender to 'the demon of analogy' represented a continuation of his earlier Surrealist aesthetics. It was not until Aragon's *The Eyes of Elsa* (1942), written in the midst of the German occupation of France, that Surrealism was able to find a median point between the attractions of fantasy and the demands of political conscience.[24]

In Spain, however, Communism and Surrealism were seen not as antinomies, but as complementary positions on the spectrum of political radicalism. Surrealism flowered in the work of a group of poets who rank amongst the outstanding voices of twentieth

century European poetry: Rafael Alberti, Luis Cernuda and
Federico García Lorca. They wrote in the period between 1928 and
1933, exactly at that point when writers throughout Europe were
discovering Communism. It was a happy coincidence, for the extravagant dislocation of grammar and syntax that was a product of
the Surrealist recovery of the logic of the dream world is given momentum in the work of these poets by a pointed and at times pas-
sionate statement of political protest. As Alberti noted, this was a
poetry written in periods of anger and outrage, when 'electricity
runs through my skeleton and blood tastes to me of cataclysm'.
This note of protest is heard throughout the work of the Spanish
Surrealists, from Cernuda's *Forbidden Pleasures* (1931) and *Where
Forgetfulness Dwells* (1933), and Alberti's *Concerning the Angels*
(1929) and, with a greater topical focus, *From one Moment to the
Next: Poetry and History* (1937), through to the writing of Lorca. In
his poetry, *Songs* (1927), *Gipsy Ballads* (1928) and *A Poet in New York*
(written 1929–1930), and in his plays, particularly *Blood Wedding*
(1933), the subconscious emerges through the imagery of aggression and fear, to be organised by sentiments that are invariably political. This is the case in the ironically entitled 'Romance of the
Spanish Civil Guard' (1927). The poem tells of the extermination of
a gipsy camp by a contingent of local police. Lorca uses the traditional ballad form, but combines religious iconography with
Surrealist symbolism to recreate a landscape of sheer violence,
where 'tender and naked the imagination burns out'. The an-
guished nature of Lorca's politically sensitive surrealism reached
its most heightened form in *A Poet in New York*. Here, the sufferings of the marginalised blacks and poor are depicted in imagery
which is grotesque and unsettling. Lorca's poetry in this volume
possesses, at times, a disturbingly elemental quality, frequently
rising (as in his description of the sufferings of the negroes of
Haarlem) to the level of ritualistic insistence: 'Blood has no doors in
your upturned night./There is no flush of blood. Blood raging
under the skins,/living in the thorn of the dagger and in the heart
of landscapes,/under the pincers and genistas of the celestial moon
of cancer.' Lorca's *A Poet in New York* remained unpublished during
his lifetime. In the second month of the Spanish Civil War, in
August 1936, the poet was forced to pay both for his political convictions and for the provocative nature of his literary genius, murdered by the supporters of Franco at the height of his achievement
and reputation.[25]

4   THE IMPERATIVE OF COMMITMENT: THE LITERATURE OF RADICAL HUMANISM

The literature of political engagement raised a number of fundamental issues relating to the political and ethical responsibilities of the writer; questions such as: What is the nature of political commitment? Is motivation the result of rational choice, or are there other factors involved? To what extent should private ethical criteria be suspended for the sake of greater political goals? Is a belief in individualism tolerable in an age in which the collective good is the overriding desideratum? Is honesty a precondition for political judgment or a secondary factor? To what extent can politics satisfy spiritual needs? And how can we explain the willingness of civilised people to embrace nihilistic political programmes? These questions had been posed, implicitly, at least, by previous writers of social conscience in the nineteenth century, but left largely answered. The literature of political engagement written in the 1920s and 1930s moved these questions from the margins of literary consciousness to its centre. Even a work such as Brecht's famous *Lehrstück, The Measures Taken* (1930), written in defence of the notion of party discipline, ultimately resolves itself into a set of *ethical* issues, offering in the place of traditional notions of personal compassion a new ethos of moral activism to which everything, even assassination, is permitted in the service of revolutionary agitation, that 'inflexible will to change the world'.[26]

Brecht's elevation of the principle of party expediency into a law of political pragmatism was intended to provide a general set of criteria against which all individual actions might be judged. It was a principle that constituted (however paradoxical this may seem) a Marxist version of the Kantian categorical imperative. But for other writers of the period, the conflict between ethical norms and revolutionary strategy, between conscience and duty, self-determination and subservience to the party line, could not be resolved so easily. In this category, come three writers of particular note: Ignazio Silone, André Malraux and Thomas Mann. All explored the intellectual parameters of political commitment, hedging their acceptance of the necessity for political struggle with caveats concerning the ethical implications (for individuals and societies alike) of such struggles, and all converged on a radical humanism, which was sympathetic to, but ultimately critical of, the inhibiting and debilitating strictures of party politics. Silone wrote three major novels: *Fontamara* (1933), *Bread and Wine* (1937) and *The Seed Beneath the Snow* (1941). They deal with the class nature of society in Southern Italy, and with confrontations between peasants and the landowning class, which Silone describes against the backdrop of the rise of Fascism. In spite of Silone's early adherence to Communism, these novels reveal a scepticism regarding the relevance of Communist Party activities and policies. The central figure of *Bread and Wine*, the fugitive Pietro Spina, for example, finds that his increasing contact with the peasantry, and the elemental nature of their existence, forces him to abandon his doctrinaire Marxism in favour a more pragmatic Christian socialism, capable of uniting (as in the symbolic imagery of the title) religious faith and bodily need. The novel, *Fontamara*, lacks any single hero; its focus is upon a collectivity, and upon its attempts to resist 'the living dead': the blackshirts of Mussolini, who lend support to the landowners in their expropriation of peasant lands. The struggle of the village people is inhibited by illiteracy and by a traditional acceptance of adversity. But even here, where class consciousness cannot hope to flourish, the basis of opposition slowly emerges, on the back of continual suffering and through a growing feeling (however incoherently held) of the necessity of establishing natural justice. The final pages adumbrate a crucial turn towards political self-consciousness amongst the peasants, which is the more convincing for having its origins in (as Silone was later to note concerning his own development) their willingness to extend 'the ethical impulse from the restricted individual and family sphere to the whole domain of human activity', in full recognition of the 'need for effective brotherhood'.[27]

The disjunction between radical politics and ethical idealism is also explored by André Malraux in his novels; but now the focus is not upon peasant communities, caught within political ideologies that they dimly understand and only imperfectly resist, but upon self-confident and articulate intellectuals, who embrace revolutionary activity in order to give a higher purpose to their lives. The urgency of this personal need for political engagement is explored by Malraux in *The Conquerors* (1928), *Man's Estate* (1933), *Days of Contempt* (1935) and *Days of Hope* (1938). The novels set up quite specific historical contexts to lay bare those mechanisms (emotional and intellectual) by which people come to sacrifice themselves to the cause of radical politics. Malraux drew upon the experiences that he had gathered in Indo-China in the mid-1920s, where he acted as editor of the anti-imperialist journal, *Indo-China Enchained*, and in Spain, where he commanded a pro-Republican air force during the 1936–1939 civil war. All of his novels deal with revolutionary situations, and with characters who embody the full range of ideological positions open to the agitator during periods of radical change: in *The Conquerors*, Garine and Borodine represent militant individualism and Comintern pragmatism; in *Days of Hope*, Lopez and Manuel incline towards anarchism and a strict doctrinaire Communism, whilst the semi-autobiographical Magnin is a revolutionary Socialist, and a technician with ideals; and in *Man's Estate*, a medley of characters appear, ranging from the terrorist Chen and Vologuin, the party functionary, through to the insurrectionist leader, Kyo Gisors and his wife, May, whose fraught relationship with her husband lends to the work a component of sexual and even feminist politics that is missing from the author's other novels.

The focus of *Man's Estate* is upon the revolt of the local Chinese against their Imperialist overseers in Shanghai in March 1927. Malraux gives substance to the major issues with great historical verisimilitude. He outlines in impressive detail the uneasy *détente* between the newly formed Chinese Communist Party and the Nationalists (the Kuomintang) under Chiang Kai Shek, who form a strategic alliance only for the latter to liquidate the former in the final stages of the struggle; the cynical but ultimately ineffectual policies pursued by Moscow; and the exploitative and intransigent nature of the foreign occupying powers. Such detail convinced his contemporaries that the author had experienced the upheavals at first hand, a perception that helped the novel to win the prestigious Prix Goncourt, and its author to a reputation as the foremost representative of the literary left in France. But Malraux's main interest lay (as the author argued in reply to Trotsky's critical review of *The Conquerors*) in examining 'the relationship between individual and collective action and not [...] collective action alone'. The same is true of *Man's Estate*. Its real focus is not the Chinese masses and their struggle, but the individual protagonists, who, like the decadent aristocrat, Baron de Clappique, see in the revolutionary experience a 'new frightful sense of liberty', an occasion for self-realisation. The terrorist Chen exemplifies their predicament. He is a man of the people, part of the anonymous, oppressed masses; yet he too is haunted by an existential need for personal legitimacy, being determined through his actions to enter that 'timeless world' of 'exaltation' that comes with the act of assassination. Chen is an extreme example of the voluntarism that is implicit in the behaviour and motives of the other characters in Malraux's novel: Kyo, who views self-sacrifice as a necessary step in investing human affairs with a moral idealism; Gisors, who believes that the foundation of the self can be reached only by suffering; and even Ferral (the cynical capitalist and misogynist), who argues that 'man is the sum-total of his actions, of the things he has *done*'. In the final analysis, it is these values that the novel returns to time and time again, expanding the activity of political commitment into a metaphor for that 'mystic faith', which (Malraux argues) can alone 'couple fool and universe together'.[28]

In his writing after 1939, Malraux sought to put himself beyond the emotional pull of 'collective passions' to which he had at one time been prey, and renounced his early internationalism in favour of a commitment to an 'organic culture' rooted in the French nation. It is only an apparent paradox that Malraux was to end where Thomas Mann had begun; in a celebration of the traditional culture of Europe and in a rejection of the materialist civilisation of America. For what had led Mann in the 1920s to abandon his earlier conservative position, which he had memorably formulated in the lengthy politico-cultural tract, *The Reflections of a Nonpolitical Man* (1918), was precisely the same perception of cultural and political crisis that Malraux was responding to under different circumstances in the devastation of post-war Europe. In Mann's case, the transition had been effected by one episode in particular: the assassination of the Jewish foreign minister, Walter Rathenau, in 1922 by a group of nationalist radicals. Rathenau was a friend of Mann, and one of the most gifted Republican statesmen of the period. Abandoning his former role as a *Vernunftrepublikaner* (a reluctant supporter of democratic politics), Mann now became convinced that writers were inextricably a part of the public realm. As he argued in a famous essay written just after Hitler's election successes in 1930, the artist's traditional 'immersion in the eternal-human predicament' had become an 'intellectual impossibility' for those forced to witness the new barbarism of Fascist mobilisation and what was clearly widespread preparation for a second, and possibly even bloodier, world war.[29]

Mann had already anticipated his political awakening in the novella, *Mario and the Magician* (1929). The story tells of a German family on holiday in Italy, who stumble into the performance of an expert hypnotist. Mann uses the experience of the family (and that of the local community, who are likewise drawn to the 'magician'), as the basis for a parable on the dangers of the seduction of fascism. Mann focusses upon those elements that had permitted Fascism to exert its power over successive electorates in Italy and Germany: the mystique of the charismatic leader; its exploitation of the need of the majority to be led and guided; and its cynical stage-management of collective euphoria. Even the narrator (a respectable *pater familias* from the German *Bürgertum*) comes under the magician's spell; but not before he registers the key insight of the novella: that simply rejecting a political phenomenon such as Fascism can not provide the basis for adequate opposition; if the individual is to resist such ideologies, he or she must grasp a clearly felt alternative position, because 'between not willing a certain thing and not willing at all [...] there may lie too small a space for the idea of freedom to squeeze into'.[30]

The focus of *Mario and the Magician* is upon individual psychology, and upon those aspects of the mind that are susceptible to charismatic personalities and vitalistic politics. In his last major novel, *Doctor Faustus* (1947), Mann moved from a personal to a national perspective, and to an examination of those broader irrationalist ideologies that had allowed so many Germans to embrace political nihilism. He was joined here by other *émigré* writers fleeing from Hitler, who likewise sought to explicate the intellectual and moral origins of the evil embraced by their homeland. They included writers such as Klaus Mann (*Mephisto*, 1936), Heinrich Mann (*Henry the Fourth of France*, two volumes, 1935 and 1938), and Anna Seghers (*The Seventh Cross*, 1942). They all wrote important novels, but few possess the intellectual complexity and the broad humanist scope of Mann's *Doctor Faustus*. In this novel, Mann attempts to reconstruct, through a fictional biography of the composer, Adrian Leverkühn, nothing less than the intellectual history of his country, focussing upon those elements in its cultural past that have brought it into the camp of Hitler's National Socialism. In his brief life, Leverkühn rehearses in symbolic form the key moments of the German ideology: the penchant for the irrational that emerged during a medieval period dominated by 'fantastic and mystical folk-movements'; the spiritual fanaticism of Luther; the quest for the absolute that characterises the late music of Beethoven; that desire to renew Western music by returning to the 'elemental, the primitive, the primeval', which Mann identified with the music of Wagner; the misplaced patriotic idealism of the *Wandervögel*; and, finally, that sustained intellectual reaction against the Western liberal tradition known as the Conservative Revolution, whose exponents sought to replace the liberal institutions of the West with a more typically Germanic People's Community, united by racial ties and charismatic leadership. Leverkühn's personality and music reflect in diverse ways these aspects of the Germanic ideology, as does the central deed of the novel: his pact with the devil, made to enable the faltering composer to achieve a break-through to a new musical idiom. But what composer and nation achieve (Mann suggests towards the end of his epic novel) is not transcendence, nor the heroic transfiguration of modernity, nor even a lasting contribution to the future, but unimaginable horror. It is a burden of guilt that all must share, even the well-meaning narrator and Leverkühn's *confidant*, Zeitblom. As the extermination camps are opened to reveal the charred remains of those victimised by the Nazi regime, the gentle scholar must join the ranks of his countrymen, to witness the consequences of a politics conducted without compassion or minimal humanism, 'standing wild-eyed in face of the void', in a belated recognition of the horror of the Nazi cause.[31]

5   'THE GOD THAT FAILED': DISILLUSION/DYSTOPIA

Writers joined the Communist Party (or allied themselves with its policies) because they saw in Communism the only way of keeping alive humane values in a world threatened by unfeeling capitalism and, even worse, rampant Fascism. But once they had become members, they soon discovered that at the heart of its ethos lay an insidious and nihilistic logic, which sought to destroy the present for the sake of the future, individual rights for the sake of a classless society. Communism, in Arthur Koestler's words, encouraged its followers to accept 'the necessary lie, the necessary slander; the necessary intimidation of the masses to preserve them from shortsighted errors; the necessary liquidation of opposition groups and hostile classes; the necessary sacrifice of a whole generation in the interest of the next'. Disillusionment with the Communist cause became widespread during the Spanish Civil War, where Orwell, Spender and Koestler were able to witness at first hand the manipulative tactics of the Party and its uncompromising use of *force majeure* through which it imposed its hegemony on the broadly based Popular Front alliance. The credibility of the Soviet model took a further blow during the Moscow show trials of 1935–1937. Here, in what was evidently a systematic miscarriage of justice, Stalin sought to rid himself of the old wing of the Party, those who had helped carry through the October Revolution of 1916, people like Bukharin, Zinoviev and Kamenev. Both the way the trials were conducted, their use of fabricated confessions and intimidation, and the many blatant impingements upon the basic rights of the accused, who were tortured and brain-washed, and deprived of legal representation, shocked the Western world, and left many (as the English radical, George Woodcock, would later note) 'disillusioned [...] with the orthodox Communism that [had] beguiled our predecessors'.[32]

A similar revision of allegiances was registered in the literature of the period, most memorably in Arthur Koestler's *Darkness at Noon*. Written in German in 1939 (and published the following year in English), Koestler's novel became the key anti-Communist document of its generation. Set in the era of the show trials, *Darkness at Noon* tells of the experiences of the old Bolshevik, Rubashov, who has been arrested and held in custody on suspicion of crimes against the state. During his incarceration, he takes the opportunity, in the periods between his interrogations, to analyse himself and his original reasons for joining the Communist Party. The latter had offered, in the face of the bankruptcy of nineteenth-century liberal ethics, both moral credibility and the promise of a classless society. By helping to achieve that goal, Rubashov had sought an identity beyond personal volition, beyond those values that emerge from the little world of the self. As he explains at one point in the story: 'For us [the true believers in Communism] the question of subjective good faith is of no interest. He who is in the wrong must pay; he who is in the right will be absolved. That is the law of historical credit: it was our law'. To achieve the ultimate goal all is permissible: 'history has taught us that often lies serve better than the truth', 'virtue does not matter to history'. In the final analysis, it is not individuals but the party which embodies the will of history: the self, the 'I', is a 'grammatical fiction', a provisional entity when set beside the greater reality of class and Party. Against the consequential logic of this secularised credo, Rubashov (during his many moments of introspection) painstakingly reconstructs the premises of a new faith in human nature and a new argument in defence of individualism, which he seeks to justify both to himself and to his two inquisitors, the sympathetic Ivanov, and the new man, the peasant functionary, Gletkin. Rubashov meets his end before resolving his political and ethical impasse, caught between an ideology that he has helped create, and a premonition of a new ethical faith that is still beyond his reach. His life expires on a note of almost mystical quiescence, as he greets the single pistol shot from his executioner with a 'shrug of eternity'. It was left to Koestler himself to give shape to the more positive ethos towards which his hero falteringly moves, sketching out in *The God that failed* the modest assumptions of a new humanism. It includes the conviction 'that man is a reality, mankind an abstraction; that men cannot be treated as units in operations of political arithmetic because they behave like the symbols for zero and the infinite, which dislocate all mathematical operations; that the end justifies the means only within very narrow limits; that ethics is not a function of social utility, and charity is not a petty-bourgeois sentiment but the gravitational force which keeps civilisation in orbit'.[33]

With such sentiments Koestler ended his association with Communism. In subsequent novels and essays, such as *Arrival and Departure* (1943) and *The Yogi and the Commissar* (1945), he went into further detail regarding the logic of duplicity and the moral pitfalls endemic to revolutionary politics. In spite of their undeniable originality, these works can best be seen as examples of a widespread disillusionment with the Soviet state, which had set in as early as the 1920s. This was the period (in the years following Stalin's assumption of power in 1922) which saw the optimism and idealism exhibited by young writers such as Vladimir Mayakovsky, Sergei Esenin and Eugene Zamytin turn into sober vigilance, cynicism, and, finally, despair. By the time of the show trials in 1935, many writers in Russia had already distanced themselves from Communism, hoping to keep alive humanist values within the most inhospitable of landscapes. Such writers included Isaak Babel (*The Red Cavalry*, 1926), Ilya Erenburg (*The Extraordinary Adventures of Julio Jurenito*, 1922), Mikhail Bulgakov (*The Master and Margarita*, 1940) and Mikhail Sholokhov (*And Quiet Flows the Don*, published in three volumes between 1928 and 1940). All reach out to a broader European tradition of humanist affirmation and political pluralism, and either ignore the politics of the regime or treat it with irony. Concrete opportunities for protest were limited, but two works did emerge to speak for a generation now thoroughly alienated from the rhetoric of revolutionary socialism: Mayakovsky's play *The Bedbug*, written in 1929, shortly before his suicide the following year, and Zamytin's bleak vision of totalitarianism, the novel *We* (1924). *The Bedbug* is a satire upon the principle of collectivisation which has succeeded in reducing those who do not fit into Socialist society (represented in the play by the gross ex-Communist, Prisypkin) to the level of 'parasites' and 'insects', capable only of zoological classification. Satire is similarly evident in Zamytin's *We*, but here it is framed within an extended political allegory. Set in an indefinite future, the novel focusses upon the centrally planned United States, whose citizens (identified simply as he or she numbers) have surrendered the right to self-determination in return for social order and the guarantee of material happiness. In this dystopian vision, the most restrictive and dehumanising regulations and practices are presented by the narrator as unambiguously progressive measures; even individual death, an increasing occurrence as the tentative spirit of protest begins to emerge in some quarters, can be dismissed as mathematically irrelevant: 'practically considered, it is an infinitesimal of the third order. Only the ancients were prone to arithmetically illiterate pity; to us it is ridiculous.' This is a system that has replaced participation with directives, ideals with brutal pragmatism, the individual with the state, which takes upon itself the right to liquidate all who stand in the way, those 'enemies of happiness', who do not or will not accept the irrevocable march of history.[34]

Zamytin's *We* had, however, a much broader target than that of Soviet Russia. Its critical animus was directed not at specific governments as such, but at principles and forms of political organisation, which, irrespective of their ideological content, had converged in their use of technology to control both the social and personal spheres. In this respect, Zamytin was aligning himself with the dystopian tradition in literature, which had emerged in England in the late nineteenth century, finding its most persuasive exponent in H.G. Wells. Like Zamytin, Wells also, in novels such as *The Time Machine* (1895) and *War of the Worlds* (1898), had harboured a fundamental mistrust of the mechanistic-scientific ethos, which recognises only quantitative not qualitative change, and sets no moral limits to their expansion. The result of the victory of the technocratic mind-set was not the best but the worst of all possible worlds: dystopia not utopia. As the Czech dystopian science fiction writer, Karel Čapek, made clear in his novels, *The Absolute at Large* (1922) and the trilogy, *Hordubal* (1933), *Meteor* (1935) and *An Ordinary Life* (1936), and in his plays, such as *R.U.R.: Rossum's*

Universal Robots (1920), one of the most disturbing aspects of the march of the technological spirit was that the majority (depreciatively designated throughout the 1920s and 1930s as 'the masses') were eager, as developments in Germany and Russia were demonstrating, to embrace these changes, irrespective of their consequences. Political subjugation seemed now to be a matter of an inner surrender of values rather than of external compulsion, with electorates throughout Europe showing themselves more interested in order and consensus than free speech or democracy. This paradox formed the central theme of Aldous Huxley's novel, *Brave New World* (1932). Set in 'the year of stability', 632 After Ford, the novel depicts a world in which individuals have been reduced to automata, and personal values to functional reflexes installed by an omniscient and omnipotent World Controller. *Brave New World* is a memorable statement of the key components of the dystopian nightmare: the centralised control of the individual, and the absorption of the latter into a community ethos; the deadening of consciousness through emotive symbolism; and the omnipresence of technology as the means through which both hierarchy and the acceptance of hierarchy are assured. Huxley added to this picture the notion of genetic engineering, parodying the eugenicist preoccupations of Fascist governments, and a highly contemporary understanding of the role of state-administered narcotics in stilling potential points of friction between the individual and system through 'chemically induced happiness'. What disrupts the oppressive coherence of this society is not politics but sex, and a residual anarchism of spirit which allows the single aberrant unit of this world, the enigmatic John 'Savage', not only to demand 'danger', 'freedom' and 'goodness', but to claim the right to resolve the impasse of his own life through suicide.[35]

The dystopian novel moved in the realm of endless possibilities, its hypothetical nature deliberately left open so that its grim vision would be relevant to the future, as it was to the present. But that such novels had a more immediate context in the political cataclysms of the early to mid-twentieth century, in an era that witnessed the transition from liberal democracy to totalitarianism in so many European countries, was clear, and most notably from the work of George Orwell. He had been one of the first in Europe to lose his illusions regarding the Soviet State. In his *Homage to Catalonia*, he had disclosed the ruthless means by which the Soviet government attempted to control the Republican cause during the

Spanish Civil War; whilst in *The Road to Wigan Pier* (1937) (a hybrid mixture of journalism and autobiography), he had firmly rejected the 'materialistic Utopia' promised by the Communists: it could only come into existence by dint of a machine logic and a ruthless functionalism 'that would make fully human life impossible'. During the following decade, Orwell deepened these insights into a systematic critique of Communism, which he now saw largely as a variant of the totalitarianism practised by the Fascist states. The result was a series of searching essays such as 'Inside the Whale' (1940), 'Politics v. Literature' (1946), and novels such as *Animal Farm* (1945) and *1984* (1949). The former novel is unashamedly di-dactic, a piece of political satire in the Swiftian mode, a fairy story in which human vices are brought out through animal personae. The novel is also a precise *roman à clef* : the fate of the farm after the overthrow of the 'bourgeois' human owner mirrors in miniature the historical development of the Soviet Union, from the heady days of the Revolution inspired by Lenin and Trotsky (here Old Major and Snowball) to its consolidation as a state power under Stalin (here Napoleon). Not only the grim events of that regime: the establishment of a police state, the liquidation of opponents and erstwhile supporters, but also the perverse system of logic and ar-gumentation used by the regime ('All animals are equal. But some animals are more equal than others') form the focus of Orwell's parable, as does the paradoxical circularity of the story, which sees the animals at the end of the story returned to the servitude from which they had originally liberated themselves.[36]

The psychological mechanisms that allow such duplicity to func-tion are further explored in *1984*, but here they are anchored in human suffering and in the pain of failed protest. The moral of the novel is that knowledge is power, and total knowledge is total power. The coercion that the hero of the novel, Winston Smith, must undergo is not primarily centred upon the body (although the torture scenes in the novel are amongst the most vivid in the dystopian genre), but upon the mind. Here, in the London of 1984, consciousness has become a site of struggle between the anony-mous (but omnivideant) gaze of Big Brother, on the one hand, and rare individuals such as Smith, on the other. The latter survives only by practising 'doublethink', a mental set which allows Orwell's hero both 'to know and not to know, to be conscious of complete truthfulness while telling carefully constructed lies [...] to use logic against logic [and] to repudiate morality while laying claim to it'. 'Double think' encompasses everything: history, political identities, and even the details of geography are all written and rewritten to serve the needs of the regime. Truth is a matter of political expediency. In *1984*, we have reached the furthest point from the political idealism and ethical goals that motivated an entire generation in the inter-war period; what Orwell's pessimistic vision leaves us with is an image of a state dedicated, not to the fullest development of the individual freed from class and economic restrictions, but purely to its self-preservation and continuing hegemony over a population caught in the eternal moment of the manipulated present, without a sense of the past, or hope for the future.[37]

6   THE ATTRACTIONS OF FASCISM: THE LITERATURE OF THE CONSERVATIVE REVOLUTION

The literature of political commitment came not only from the Left. In every European nation, there existed writers who viewed the crisis of liberal humanism and the emergence of mass industrial society with the same distrust and concern as left-wing writers, but sought a solution to this crisis not in class warfare or the creation of a Socialist society, but in the promotion of national consciousness and racial identity. These writers viewed Communism, not as a solution to, but as a continuation of the mechanistic, materialist and utilitarian philosophies of nineteenth-century liberalism. Such views were held by Oswald Spengler and José Ortega Y Gasset, two of the foremost conservative philosophers of the early years of the twentieth century. Both saw the modern period as the 'progressive triumph of the pseudo-intellectual, unqualified, unqualifiable' masses, whose presence had come to dominate in all political and cultural spheres. Spengler's *Decline of the West*, in particular, found a powerful resonance amongst those who were emotionally and intellectually alienated from the social and political forces of modernity. For here Spengler prophesied the advent of a new Caesarism, a radical conservative force that would break 'the dictatorship of money and its political weapon democracy', and return society to a more elemental reality, creating in the process an authoritarian political state, which would govern on the basis of a 'stronger, fuller, and more self-assured life'.[38]

Spengler and Ortega Y Gasset were part of a widespread movement that attracted, and was given a popular political resonance by, many writers in Europe. They included Pierre Drieu la Rochelle and Robert Brasillach, in France; Ernst Jünger, in Germany; Knut Hamsun, in Norway; and Gabriele D'Annunzio, in Italy. Radical conservatism also attracted figures who had made an important contribution to the Modernist movement in literature, such as Gottfried Benn, in Germany, and D.H. Lawrence and Wyndham Lewis in England. As the 1920s gave way to the 1930s, these figures came increasingly under the sway of dynamic right-wing theories and even, eventually, of Fascism. They hoped that Fascism would undo the social and cultural consequences of mass society, the commercialisation of modern life, and the growing influence of America, which they held responsible for (in the words of Gottfried Benn) the 'obliteration of the aristocratic principle of form [and] suppression of the inclination to cultivation and style'.[39]

The solutions that these reactionary modernists offered to the impingements of mass society were diverse. The Swedish writer, Verner von Heidenstam (*The Tree of the Folkungs*, 1905–1907), the Norwegian writer, Knut Hamsun (*Growth of the Soil*, 1917), and the German novelist, Hans Grimm (*A People without Living Space*, 1926), took their cue from the *Heimatkunst* (Rural Art) movement of the late nineteenth century. They looked to the land and its customs, and to the *mores* of peasant life, in which they hoped to find the stability, order and consensus so conspicuously missing in a modern urban culture dominated by material self-interest. The literature of Grimm, Hamsun and the other exponents of rural life found a particular resonance amongst the conservative middle-classes in the inter-war period, who viewed the rampant inflation and continually changing governments that characterised that period as an 'unfathomable chaos'; it is a 'mystery', as Hermann Stehr (another best-selling author of peasant fiction) noted, 'that we are forced to endure without ever understanding its causes'. This style of writing found less favour, however, amongst the radical youth of those nations. They did not share the nostalgia and rural fixations of the *Heimatkunst* group, but identified themselves with a new breed of political activist, whose nationalism was energetic, radical and populist. In Germany, their spokesman was Ernst Jünger, a veteran of the First World War. In his major works, *The Storm of Steel* (1920), *War as an Inner Experience* (1922), and *Fire and Blood* (1925), Jünger evoked war as a highly personal, almost existential experience; in a world without values, it alone could provide a test of the worth of man and nation. Throughout his writings, Jünger sang the praises of the Storm Troopers, those frontline soldiers who had managed to survive the horror and impersonality of artillery warfare by developing a feeling of comradeship, selfless idealism and a sense of national purpose. Such qualities, (Jünger argued) were precisely the values that could provide the base for a new type of political governance, whose values would be 'national, social, militant and authoritarian'.[40]

These exponents of the conservative revolution in Germany had a quite specific agenda: they wished to see the complex social and personal relations of an urban culture returned to a simpler model, intellect and rational theorising replaced by intuition, individualism by collective identity, and the evils of a liberal, pluralistic and alien modern state swept away in favour of a community, hierarchally organized and based on obedience and consensus. Their writing was a response to a series of social, political and economic factors that were unique to that nation: the rapid pace of industrialisation and urbanisation that the country had undergone in the late nineteenth century, with its attendant traumatic social dislocations; the harsh terms of the Versailles Treaty; the absence of firm democratic institutions and liberal values, and corresponding support for the traditional power élites of the monarchy and the army; and the vulnerability of Germany in central Europe. France and Italy, on the whole, did not share these problems, and consequently produced a conservative literature that was both less ideologically based and more individualistic. Italian Fascism, in particular, proved capable of exploiting talents as diverse as those of the Italian *fin de siècle* Nietzschen poet, Gabriele D'Annunzio, and the idiosyncratic Futurist, Filippo Marinetti, who happily lent his Avant-Garde energies to the service of the 'aesthetic and social dynamism' of an emerging Fascist Italy.[41]

In France, the *éminence grise* of the neo-nationalist movement was Maurice Barrès. Years earlier, he had sought in his *The Cult of the Self* trilogy – *Beneath the Gaze of the Barbarians* (1888), *A Free Man* (1889) and *The Garden of Berenice* (1891) – and in a later trilogy which included the famous *The Uprooted* (1897), as well as *Appeal to the Soldier* (1900) and *Their Figures* (1902), to inject a Nietzschean individualism and self-assertiveness into a new patriotic ethos founded on racial solidarity and nationalism. Barrès' influence on subsequent French writers, such as Pierre Drieu la Rochelle and Robert Brasillach, was immense. Like him, they felt that France had become a decadent nation, devoid of heroic and martial values, and corrupt with hedonism and petty materialism. That is the image that emerges from Drieu la Rochelle's fiction, notably the stories collected in *The Farce at Charleroi* (1934) and the novel *Gilles* (1939), and from Brasillach's novel, *The Seven Colours* (1939). Both writers deplored the defeatism, mediocrity and self-seeking nature of 'modern man, urban man', and set against the image of a modern France 'trapped in its negligence and its empty pride', a more authentic world redeemed through 'exuberance, exultation, culmination', where the individual feels himself part of a greater totality. For these young exponents of the conservative revolution, Fascism alone was able to provide a source of values capable of wrenching the individual into the higher realm of national purpose and historical destiny. A different type of radical militancy comes to the fore in the work of Louis-Ferdinand Céline. His fiction registers the shadow world of the Fascist mentality: those darker energies of misanthropy and nihilism that festered beneath the rhetoric of individual enthusiasm and collective action cultivated by youthful writers such as Ernst Jünger and Drieu la Rochelle. The political implications of Céline's will to destruction did not appear until the mid-1930s, when he published *Bagatelles for a Massacre* (1937) and *School for Cadavers* (1938), where he gave expression to his vehement anti-Semitism and anti-Communism. But the premises of Céline's world-view were apparent from his first and most famous novel, *Journey to the End of the Night* (1932). The work is an elaborate picaresque tale, which gives voice through the views and experiences of its central character, Ferdinand Bardamu, to a bleak, nihilistic vision of contemporary life. The novel contains little explicit politics; but in its insistence upon the inherent worthlessness of modern urban existence, in its valorisation of irrationalism and violence, and its feeling for an apocalyptic resolution to the impasse of modernity, it betrays parallels with many of the key texts of the conservative revolution, whose authors likewise believed that the present was moving inexorably toward a future of 'war and disease, those two infinities of nightmare'.[42]

Many intellectuals were attracted to Fascism less by its policies than by the style with which it promoted itself, drawn to the aggressive self-confidence and energetic machismo exhibited by its leaders, and to its talent for organising the body through uniform and ritual, and impressed by its ability to mobilise the masses through manipulation and civic ceremony. Fascism was construed as part of a new discovery of the irrational and the primitive; it was the political medium through which man (and sometimes woman) could be put back in touch with instinctual drives and energies that had too long been repressed by a civilisation based on narrow rationality and mechanistic principles. Accordingly, Fascism brought within its ambit a number of modernist writers who sought, in the wake of Nietzsche, Freud and Jung, to explore those deeper realms of the psychic self that lie beyond linguistic and social convention. Two such explorers of the irrational were Gottfried Benn and D.H. Lawrence. In the 1920s, both began to extol the value of primitivist and vitalistic ideas, arguing for their relevance to the social and political spheres: Lawrence in theoretical works such as *Psychoanalysis and the Unconscious* (1921), *Fantasia of the Unconscious* (1922) and the novel, *Kangaroo* (1923), and Benn in essayistic prose-poems such as 'Primal Vision' (1926). Typical of the tenor of their work were the sentiments expressed by Lawrence in the foreword to *Fantasia*. Here we learn that our 'mistaken democracy' has produced a 'mechanistic' civilisation, which no longer has room for the deeper wisdom conveyed through 'ritual, gesture and myth-story'. 'It has all gone grey and opaque'. We must, Lawrence argues, 'rip the old veil of vision across', and allow the 'renewed chaos' of those continually self-creating, unbridled life forces, with which our ancestors were in touch, to inform our lives. Lawrence developed his analysis further in *Kangaroo*, where he expressed (through the autobiographical figure of Somers) his 'dread, almost horror, of democratic society, the mob'. The latter is the product of a shoddy superficial culture that has long lost any feeling for the 'great living darkness' which lies beneath the veneer of civilisation. In order to regain contact with this deeper force, Somers goes to the Australian Bush, as Lawrence would go to Mexico, and write *The Plumed Serpent* (1926). Both become in the process converts to a new religion, whose faith lies in that 'instinctive passional self' that is only accessible to those who return to the 'old dark gods', and to an ethos that is both pre-Christian and pre-Humanist.[43]

It is here that Lawrence joined in spirit the pundits of the conservative revolution: not in his explicit politics (for like Somers, Lawrence disdainfully stood apart from party ideologies of any kind), but in his model of human nature, which is both élitist and regressive. Where Lawrence's irrationalist ethos might have led him is demonstrated by the case of Gottfried Benn. He too had extolled those 'chthonian powers' which lie deeper than wisdom, belonging to the primitive unconscious that Benn attempted to give voice to in his poetry. In Benn's poetry, reaching such depths through linguistic exploration produced at best metaphoric insight, at worst poetic obscurantism; but in the realm of politics, such quests led Benn to embrace the most virulent and most nihilistic of the reactionary philosophies of his age: Hitler's National Socialism. As the Weimar Republic hastened to its end in 1933 (sinking under the burden of increasing political infighting and economic disaster), the poet saw in the victory of Nazism the beginning of a new era in German history. Gone, he argued in essays such as 'The New State and the Intellectuals' (1934), were the weak and vacillating policies of liberal democracy. They had been replaced by a radically new style of politics, whose mission lay in the creation of a more ele-mental state of civic being, where public life would be informed by the rejuvenating power of myth and ritual. For all who had longed for a conservative revolution, the time had come: 'to surrender the self to the community, to the state, to one's race, to the immanent, in this turn from the economic to the mythic collective', in a process that would finally free individual and nation alike from the confu-sions and confines of modernity.[44]

7   THE LEAP OF FAITH: THE LITERATURE OF THE CATHOLIC REVIVAL AND EXISTENTIALISM

Writing in the same year in which Orwell published his *1984*, the ex-Communist critic, George Woodcock, argued that the committed writer, 'to display the truth, even a limited aspect of the truth' had necessarily to embrace a 'criterion against which falsehood must be judged and condemned'. For, as Woodcock explained, 'by express-ing an independent standard of values he attacks the principle of authority; by portraying the truth according to his own vision he attacks the factual manifestations of authority'. But in an age of moral relativism and political *Realpolitik* where should the writer look for values that he or she might set against the systematic falsifications of governments and rulers? The answers had been tentatively provided well before 1945 by a number of writers who had retained faith in religion and, more specifically, in Catholic or-thodoxy. France, in particular, had cultivated this tradition, pro-ducing successive generations of writers from Paul Claudel (*The Five Great Odes*, 1910) and Charles Péguy (*Eve*, 1913) through to

Georges Bernanos (*Beneath the Sun of Satan*, 1926, and *Diary of a Country Priest*, 1936) and François Mauriac (*Thérèse Desqueyroux*, 1927, *The Knot of Vipers*, 1932, *The Frontenac Mystery*, 1933, and *The Unknown Sea*, 1939), who had made it their mission to find spiritual integrity in the modern world. Mauriac was, perhaps, the most noted Catholic writer of this generation. At the centre of his work lies the driving conviction that 'even the genuinely good cannot, unaided, learn to love. To penetrate beyond the absurdities, the vices, and above all, the stupidities of human creatures, one must possess the secret of a love which the world has now forgotten'. Mauriac brings his characters to find that secret in different ways; Alain discovers his religious vocation in *That Which was Lost* (1930), in the face of the moral dissolution of his family; the *pater familias* in *The Knot of Vipers* learns to transcend his hatred for his avaricious children, reaching a state of forgiveness and charity just before his death; the *roué*, Pierre, in *The Unknown Sea* discovers faith amidst death and financial corruption in Paris. All bear testimony (as Mauriac noted in a discussion of the work of Graham Greene) to 'the hidden presence of God in an atheistic world'.[45]

In Bernanos' fiction the struggle is not to attain, but to retain faith, and to convey it to others in the direst moments of their need. In *Beneath the Sun of Satan*, Abbé Donissan must attempt to save the soul of the murderess, Mouchette, whose exploitation and abuse by successive lovers has reduced her to mocking and callous indifference towards herself and others. Donissan must conduct a struggle against both the provincial and duplicitous world which he serves as a priest, and against an inner recognition of the power of evil in human nature, anthropomorphised as Satan, that 'incomparably subtle and stubborn creature', whose existence, paradoxically, seems a precondition for the attainment of grace. In *Diary of a Country Priest*, Bernanos explores the modest terrain on which spiritual realisation must (on a daily basis) be attained. The moral idealism that motivated many amongst Bernanos' generation to embrace revolutionary politics for the sake of a utopian future has no place here in the diary of a humble provincial priest. 'To accept and partake in the shame of another's sin', as the latter defines his task, requires both an intellectual modesty and a concern for the many small rituals and acts of service and kindness that constitute pastoral care. But it is in this modest terrain that sanctity can form a part of human reality, becoming accessible to those for whom doubt is a precondition of moral sympathy, and who can, like

Bernanos' priest, open their 'eyes to death in all the simplicity of surrender, yet with no secret wish to soften or disarm it'.[46]

Religion inspired other major European writers during this period. In Norway, Sigrid Undset (*The Wild Orchid*, 1929, and *The Burning Bush*, 1930), in Sweden, Pär Lagerkvist (*The Dwarf*, 1944, and *Barabbas*, 1950), and in Greece, Nikos Kazantzákis (*Zorba the Greek*, 1946, and *Christ Recrucified*, 1954), engage with the difficulties of spiritual witness in an era of rampant and apparently inexorable scepticism. In England, two writers arrived at a literature of religious faith from entirely different directions: Graham Greene and T.S. Eliot. Although Greene had begun as a writer of the Left, he soon developed into one of the major Catholic novelists of his generation with *Brighton Rock* (1938), *The Power and the Glory* (1940) and *The Heart of the Matter* (1948). All explore the difficulty of witnessing, of retaining or achieving religious faith against prevailing attitudes, often to the detriment of personal self-interest. Certainly, in *Brighton Rock*, the possibility of salvation is only ambiguously nurtured in the main character, Pinkie, a small time hoodlum who has cheated and murdered his way through life, driven by social resentment and a sense of injustice. And yet even here a strange inverted religious sense is present ('Heaven was a word: hell was something he could trust'). What Pinkie only distantly gleans is held with greater determination by his girlfriend, Rose. In spite of the shoddy and violent nature of her companion, she wins through to the realisation (in the final scene of the novel) that hope and forgiveness remain open to all, in spite of the sins of the past. In *Brighton Rock*, the issue of salvation is a purely personal one, connected to the spiritual survival of the individual in an environment of urban anomie. But in *The Power and the Glory* (set in the politically unstable Mexico of the late 1930s) the parameters are far broader. The novel is structured around a clash between two irreconcilable forces: a revolutionary government intent on modernising peasant Mexico at any costs (represented in the novel by the young lieutenant), and a pastoral Catholicism, morally committed to the same peasantry, but concerned for their salvation in a state that has outlawed the Church in its fight against superstition and ignorance. The struggle is an unequal one; but it is precisely the hopelessness of the Church's position that calls forth the most unlikely hero in Greene's work: an unnamed drunken whisky priest. With a loose grip on conventional morality and unsure in his ministering of rite and ceremony, he is elevated above his shortcomings by his capacity for self-sacrifice, and by a determination to serve and continue serving his flock, knowing that he will pay for this solicitation with his life. It is in the priest's actions that (as Greene argued elsewhere) the bedrock of real idealism is laid; not in the grandiose projects of utopian politicians, who are prepared to destroy the present for the sake of the future, but amongst those, humble in spirit, who may (like Greene's unlikely hero on the eve of his execution) regard themselves with 'grotesque unimportance', but nevertheless maintain a militancy of outlook, and remain fully mindful of their duty to the spiritual needs of the present.[47]

T.S. Eliot's *The Four Quartets* (a series of four connecting poems written between 1935 and 1943) represented the culmination of a gathering religious component in Eliot's work, which began with the poems 'Ash Wednesday' (1930), and the *Ariel* sequence (1927–1930), to reach an important climax in the play, *Murder in the Cathedral* (1935). In these works, the iconoclastic Modernist idiom that Eliot had exploited in *The Waste Land* (1922) is abandoned in favour of a new vision of the ethical importance of human action and ideals, the intellectual roots of which lay in Eliot's conversion to Anglo-Catholicism. In *The Four Quartets*, much of Eliot's religious thinking is distilled into what borders upon a mystical reading of the mutability of self. In them, experience of place and time is now fashioned into an ornately wrought formal pattern based on circularity and repetition, in a developing structure that seems propelled by a spiritual need to achieve that 'inner freedom from the practical desire,/The release from action and suffering, release from the inner/And outer compulsion'.[48]

And yet even here, in what seems to be a realm of pure transcendence, the traces of a consciousness inflected against certain formations within contemporary history are discernible. They do not, it is true, possess the political moment that is evident in the work of Graham Greene, whose advocacy of the claims of religious sanctity, made, for example, in *The Power and the Glory*, was intended to be read as a critique of the totalitarian ethos espoused by many nations in the age of Fascism. Eliot's concern lies not with politics *per se*, but with those homogenising and levelling processes that emanate from a world moving 'in appetency, on its metalled ways', caring nothing for spiritual values and insensitive to subtle modulations of feeling and intellect. All who wish to survive the encroachments of modernity must confront the 'mental emptiness' that surrounds them, and which is evident (above all, for the poet) in the debasement of language, that 'shabby equipment always deteriorating/In the general mess of imprecision of feeling'. Eliot struggles against these limitations, formulating a counter-ethos that will be alive to the transcendent nature of experience, forever aware that it is only through communal discourse that the fleeting insight into a world transfigured can be caught. It is only here that poetry and religious sentiment can join; in those moments of heightened subjectivity made possible through a purified language, 'where every word is at home', and where 'the fire and the rose are one'.[49]

Writing in the midst of the Second World War, George Bernanos committed himself to defending 'that interior life against which conspires our inhuman civilisation with its delirious activity' of utopian politics and totalitarian menace. His words reflected an ethical militancy that underscored his religious world-view; but they also anticipated the next and, perhaps, final stage in that ethos of personal and political commitment that stamped its mark upon the literature of the inter-war period: Existentialism. Its exponents were the French writers Jean-Paul Sartre and Albert Camus. Like the religious writers before them, they, too, sought a source of ethical criteria beyond both the conventional wisdom of the liberal-humanist tradition and the totalitarian ideologies of Communism and Fascism. Camus put his position succinctly in an interview given in 1953: 'I am arguing in favour of a true realism against a mythology that is both illogical and deadly, and against romantic nihilism whether it be bourgeois or allegedly revolutionary.' These words charted his own personal path between Marxism and Humanism, paradigms of engagement whose competing claims would continue to dominate his life and his work until his death in 1960. Those who belonged to the Existentialist school, and they included some of the foremost thinkers of the age, such as Martin Heidegger and Jacques Merleu-Ponty, were concerned to find a point of personal authenticity beyond the false ideologies, role playing and special pleading (in Sartre's language, 'bad faith') that they saw as endemic in modern mass society. Camus anchored his philosophy in the notion of the Absurd, a category that drew upon the Nietzschean notion of the eternal return and the Heideggerian imperative of the gratuitous act. In his extended essay, *The Myth of Sisyphus* (1942), he sketched out his philosophy, invoking the travails of Sisyphus, a legendary figure, who resolutely accepts his part in a never-ending task, which he carries out with resolution and pride, in spite of the hopelessness of his situation. Even without faith in absolute values, modern man (argues Camus) can be like Sisyphus, prepared to greet even the most pointless and cruel of acts, 'convinced of the wholly human origin of all that is human', and seeing simply in the struggle for meaning a sufficient reason for existence.[50]

In literature, the existentialist initiative had already manifested itself in Sartre's *Nausea* (1938), in Camus' own *The Outsider* (1942), and perhaps even earlier in Raymond Queneau's *The Bark Tree* (1933), and Rilke's study of urban alienation, *The Notebook of Malte Laurids Brigge* (1910). In Sartre's novel, Antoine Roquentin undergoes a crisis of identity brought about by his realisation that names (indeed all conceptual categories) are simply empty abstractions used to dissimulate the essential emptiness of the world, to hide the fact that 'everything is gratuitous'. Sartre added a sharper historical focus to this ethos in his trilogy, *The Roads to Freedom* (*The Age of Reason*, 1945, *The Reprieve*, 1945, and *Iron in the Soul*, 1949), but it was his first novel, with its introspective intensity and analytical impersonality, which gave the most persuasive inflection to Sartre's Existentialism. Camus employed a similar focus in his *The Outsider*, but dispensed with the elaborate philosophical import of Sartre's novel. The uncomplicated hedonism of the novel's hero, Meursault, sketches a form of personal authenticity that cannot be approached in terms of conventional notions of motivation, duty and guilt. He awaits his execution, for the crime of murder, not only with a newly-won understanding of the 'benign indifference of the universe' but also (and the paradox was central to Camus' theory of the Absurd) with a heightened conviction of the inextinguishable value of life.[51]

As both Sartre and Camus had consistently argued, the ultimate reference point of Existentialism was not consciousness but the world. Accordingly, in their later work, both moved towards a greater sense of the applicability of their respective positions to real situations: Sartre in his plays *The Flies* (1943), *Men without Shadows* (1946) and *Crime Passionnel* (1948); and Camus in his novel, *The Plague* (1947), and in his plays, notably *Caligula* (1944) and *The Just* (1950). All explore what Sartre termed 'being-in-the-world', where the individual recognises the necessity, indeed, inevitability, of commitment as a precondition of liberty. The question that these texts pose is: To what extent can we serve others without embracing the utopian wish-fulfilment which lay at the heart of the political ideologies of the 1920s and 1930s? Camus offers a tentative answer in *The Plague* (1947). Here, in the midst of an outbreak of bubonic plague (which is possibly to be interpreted as a symbol of the German occupation of France in the Second World War) a group of characters finds itself trapped in a small town in Northern Africa. In the face of the imperious advance of the plague, many of them strike postures either of passive acquiescence or of futile heroism, all caught between the imperative of self-survival and care for a community, between despondency and heroic self-sacrifice, and between idealism and practical solicitation. Rieux, the doctor (and narrator of the story) alone chooses the middle path of 'common decency'. In his words, but above all, in his deeds, he embodies a modest humanism, the sources of which lie not in an abstract code of morals, but in a concrete sense of duty that is supported by a pragmatic understanding of immediate and local exigency.[52]

The limitations of political heroism are also explored in Sartre's play, *Crime Passionnel*. Its hero, Hugo, comes at the end of a long line of political activists in modern European literature stretching from the rebel personae of the Romantics through to the three comrades in Brecht's *The Measures Taken*, and Chen in Malraux's *Man's Estate*. Like them, Hugo is infused with the logic of dialectical materialism, which permits short-term injustices (here the assassination of the lapsed party boss, Hoederer) for the sake of long-term strategic objectives. Sartre explores in his play the applicability of that logic, showing through Hugo's jealousy of Hoederer how political judgements are influenced by those mechanisms of the self that are irredeemably apolitical. As Hugo himself comes to realise, the links between a consciously held ideology and an unconsciously motivated action are complex and fraught: he has liquidated his victim, not because he felt himself the impersonal tool of world history, but because he needed to prove his manhood, both to his peers, and to his wife, whose sexual seduction by Hoederer provides the real catalyst for his action. Hugo cannot undo his deed; but by distancing himself in the final act of the play from those who style themselves masters of history, 'the toughs, the conquerors, the leaders', and by willingly giving himself over to the Party's executioners, he seeks, in one final act, both to redeem the inauthentic act that he has committed and the integrity of the man that he has killed.[53]

8 LITERATURE IN THE AGE OF POLITICAL COMMITMENT: A CHRONOLOGY

1902, Maxim Gorky, *Na dne* (The Lower Depths).
1906–1910, Nexø, *Pelle Erobreren* (Pelle the Conqueror).
1906–1922, Galsworthy, *The Forsyte Saga*.
1907, Gorky, *Mat* (Mother).
1916, Barbusse, *Le Feu* (Under Fire).
1917–1921, Nexø, *Ditte Menneskebarn* (Ditte: Daughter of Man).
1917, Hamsun, *Markens grøde* (The Growth of the Soil).
1918, Mayakovsky, *Misterriya-buff* (The Mystery Bouffe).
1918, Heinrich Mann, *Der Untertan* (Man of Straw).
1919, Silanpää, *Hurskas Kurjuus* (Meek Heritage)
1920, Toller, *Masse-Mensch* (Mass Man).
1920, Jünger, *In Stahlgewittern* (The Storm of Steel).
1920, Zamyatin, *My* (We) [publ. 1924].
1921, Esenin, *Ispoved Khuligana* (Confessions of a Hooligan).
1921–1923, Hašek, *Osudy dobrého vojáka Šejka za světové války* (The Good Soldier Schweik).
1922, Brecht, *Trommeln in der Nacht* (Drums in the Night).
1922, Erenburg, *Neobychayynye pokhozhdeniya Khulio Khurenito* (The Extraordinary Adventures of Julio Jurenito).
1922, Jünger, *Der Kampf als inneres Erlebnis* (War as an Inner Experience).
1922–1940, Martin du Gard, *Les Thibault* (The World of the Thibaults).
1923, D.H. Lawrence, *Kangaroo*.
1923, O'Casey, *The Shadow of a Gunman*.
1924, Trotsky, *Literatura i Revolutionya* (Literature and Revolution).
1925, Gladkov, *Zement* (Cement).
1926, Bernanos, *Sous le soleil de Satan* (Beneath the Sun of Satan).
1926, George, *Das neue Reich* (The New Empire).
1926, Babel, *Konarmiya* (Red Cavalry).
1926, Grimm, *Volk ohne Raum* (A People without Land).
1926, Becher, *Maschinenrhythmen* (Machine Rhythms).
1926, Naville, 'La Révolution et les intellectuels' ('The Revolution and the Intellectuals').
1927, García Lorca, *Canciones* (Songs).
1927, Toller, *Hoppla, wir leben!* (Hurray! We're alive!).
1927, Fadeyev, *Razgrom* (The Rout).
1927, Brecht, *Die Hauspostille* (Manual of Piety).
1928–1940, Sholokhov, *Tikhiy Don* (And Quiet Flows the Don).
1928, Seghers, *Der Aufstand der Fischer von St Barbara* (The Revolt of the Fishermen of St Barbara).
1928, Malraux, *Les Conquérants* (The Conquerors).
1928, García Lorca, *Romancero gitano* (Gypsy Ballads).
1929, Thomas Mann, *Mario und der Zauberer* (Mario and the Magician).
1929, Graves, *Goodbye to All That*.
1929, Remarque, *Im Westen nichts Neues* (All Quiet on the Western Front).
1929, Mayakovsky, *Klop* (The Bedbug).

1929, Döblin, *Berlin Alexanderplatz*.

1929, Ottwalt, *Ruhe und Ordnung* (Law and Order).

1929, Alberti, *Sobre los angeles* (Concerning the Angels).

1929, Undset, *Gymnadenia* (The Wild Orchid).

1929, József, *Nincsen apám, se anyám* (I Have neither Father nor Mother)

1929–1930, García Lorca, *Poeta en Nueva York* (A Poet in New York) [publ. 1940].

1930, Auden, *Poems*.

1930, Bredel, *Maschinenfabrik N & K* (Machine Factory N & K).

1930–1943, Musil, *Der Mann ohne Eigenschaften* (The Man without Qualities).

1930, Brecht, *Die Maßnahmen* (The Measures Taken).

1931, Horváth, *Geschichten aus dem Wienerwald* (Tales from the Vienna Woods).

1931, MacDiarmid, *First Hymn to Lenin and Other Poems*.

1931, Cernuda, *Los placeres prohibidos* (Forbidden Pleasures).

1932, Heinrich Mann, *Ein ernstes Leben* (The Hill of Lies).

1932, Huxley, *Brave New World*.

1932–1947, Romains, *Les Hommes de bonne volonté* (Men of Goodwill).

1932, Hermann Broch, *Die Schlafwandler* (The Sleepwalkers).

1932, Céline, *Voyage au bout de la nuit* (Journey to the End of the Night).

1932, Fallada, *Kleiner Mann, was nun ?* (Little Man, What Now?).

1932, Mauriac, *Le Noeud de vipères* (The Knot of Vipers).

1934, Ostrovsky, *Kak zakalyalas' stal'* (The Making of a Hero).

1933, Cernuda, *Donde habite el olvido* (Where Forgetfulness Dwells).

1933, Johst, *Schlageter*.

1933, Greenwood, *Love on the Dole*.

1933, Malraux, *La Condition humaine* (Man's Estate).

1933, Silone, *Fontamara*.

1933, Spender, *Poems*.

1933, Mauriac, *Le Mystère Frontenac* (The Frontenac Mystery).

1934, Bloch, *Die Erbschaft dieser Zeit* (Heritage of Our Times).

1934, Aragon, *Les Cloches de Bâle* (The Bells of Basle).

1934, Drieu de la Rochelle, *La Comédie de Charleroi* (The Farce at Charleroi).

1934–1935, Laxness, *Sjalfstaettfolk* (Independent People).

1935, Eliot, *Murder in the Cathedral*.

1935, Heinrich Mann, *Die Jugend des Königs Henri Quartre* (Young Henry of Navarre).

1935, Canetti, *Die Blendung* (Auto-da-Fé).

1935, Gide, *Les Nouvelles nourritures* (New Nourishment).

1935, Aleixandre, *La destrucción o el amor* (Destruction and Love).

1935–1943, Eliot, *The Four Quartets*.

1936, Benjamin, *Das Kunstwerk im Zeitalter seiner technischen Reproduzierbarkeit* (The Work of Art in the Age of Mechanical Reproduction).

1936, Klaus Mann, *Mephisto*.

1936, Bernanos, *Journal d'un curé de campagne* (The Diary of a Country Priest).

1937, Silone, *Pane e vino* (Bread and Wine).

1937, Orwell, *The Road to Wigan Pier*.

1937, Alberti, *De un momento a otro: poesía e historia* (From one Moment to the Next: Poetry and History).
1937, Caudwell, *Illusion and Reality.*
1937, Hernández, *Viento del Pueblo* (The Wind of the People).
1938, Orwell, *Homage to Catalonia.*
1938, Koestler, *Ein spanisches Testament* (Spanish Testament).
1938, Malraux, *L'Espoir* (Days of Hope).
1938, Bernanos, *Les Grands Cimetières sous la lune* (A Diary of My Times).
1938, Greene, *Brighton Rock.*
1938, Heinrich Mann, *Die Vollendung des Königs Henri Quartre* (Henry, King of France).
1938, Sartre, *La Nausée* (Nausea).
1939, Drieu la Rochelle, *Gilles.*
1939, Brasillach, *Les Sept Couleurs* (The Seven Colours).
1939, Isherwood, *Goodbye to Berlin.*
1940, Bulgakov, *Master i Margarita* (The Master and Margarita) [publ. 1967].
1940, Koestler, *Sonnenfinsternis* (Darkness at Noon).
1940, Greene, *The Power and the Glory.*
1941, Brecht, *Mutter Courage und ihre Kinder* (Mother Courage and her Children).
1942, Seghers, *Das siebte Kreuz* (The Seventh Cross).
1942, Camus, *L'Etranger* (The Outsider).
1942, Aragon, *Les Yeux d'Elsa* (The Eyes of Elsa).
1942, Eluard, *Poésie et Vérité 1942* (Poetry and Truth, 1942).
1943, Sartre, *Les Mouches* (The Flies).
1944, Lagerkvist, *Dvärgen* (The Dwarf).
1945, Wiechert, *Der Totenwald* (The Forest of the Dead).
1945, Orwell, *Animal Farm.*
1945, Andrić, *Na Drini ćuprija* (The Bridge on the Drina).
1945–1949, Sartre, *Les Chemins de la liberté* (The Roads to Freedom).
1946, Kazantzákis, *Víos kai politía tou Aléxi Zormpá* (Zorba the Greek).
1946, Orwell, 'Politics v. Literature'.
1947, Thomas Mann, *Doktor Faustus* (Doctor Faustus).
1947, Camus, *La Peste* (The Plague).
1948, Lukács, *Probleme des Realismus* (Essays on Realism).
1948, Sartre, *Les Mains sales* (Crime Passionnel).
1948, Sartre, *Qu'est-ce que la littérature?* (What is Literature?).
1949, Brecht, *Kleines Organon für das Theater* (A Little Organum for the Theatre).
1949, Orwell, *1984.*
1950, Lagerkvist, *Barabbas.*

5

Postmodernism

1   AFTER ALL: THE CONTEXT OF EUROPEAN POSTMODERNISM

Literature in Europe after 1945 was dominated by the moral and material legacy of the Second World War. Not only had a major part of the continent been destroyed, its land pillaged and its economies ruined, but the war had culminated in two events that were to remain as open wounds within the collective consciousness of the peoples of Europe: the sickening disclosures of the extermination camps at Auschwitz and Treblinka in March 1945, and the dropping of atomic bombs on Hiroshima and Nagasake six months later. Arthur Koestler was later to view the dropping of the Bomb as the 'single most important date in the history of the human race'. It was the day on which humanity was confronted with 'the prospect of its extinction as a *species*'. André Malraux was equally pessimistic. As he gloomily observed in 1948: 'Europe's current drama is the death of man. With the atom bomb [...], we came to realise that what the nineteenth century called "progress" had extorted a heavy ransom. We realised that the world had become dualistic again, and that man's immense, unmortgaged hope for the future was no longer valid.' Not fear but collective shame, and an inkling of a complicity that was to be felt well beyond Germany, attended the liberation of the extermination camps. The moral outrage and horror to which they gave rise was to affect an entire generation. As the French novelist, Jean Cayrol, noted in 1950: 'the emotional shock grows with the years, with whiffs from that extreme of misery finding their way even into the most hidden corners of peace: the smell of the concentration camp is stronger than ever'. In England, George Orwell sought to remind his readership of the continuing prejudice against Jews in Britain; whilst the French Existentialist (now turned radical politician), Jean-Paul

Sartre, made resistance to antisemitism the test of a writer's political credibility in his *What is Literature?* (1948). Was the horror of Auschwitz too momentous to discuss in civilised language? The German literary theoretician and cultural critic, Theodor Adorno, thought it was, believing that literature should simply fall silent in the face of such an outrage. As he uncompromisingly argued: 'to write poetry after Auschwitz is barbaric'. German writers, in particular, from Heinrich Böll and Paul Celan to Rolf Hochhuth and the Swiss writer, Max Frisch, entered upon a painful confrontation with their past (a process called in German *Vergangenheitsbewältigung*), seeking to account for the involvement (or at least the complicity) of an entire nation in the attempted extermination of the Jewish people. All would have accepted as self-evident the words of Günter Grass, who wrote, thirty years after a disbelieving world first learnt of the horror of the camps, that for the Germans of the post-war period no amount of economic prosperity could conceal 'the moral vacuum engendered by their incomparable guilt'.[1]

The legacy of the Second World War produced amongst many writers of this period a radical mistrust of political ideologies, irrespective of whether they were liberal, socialist or nationalist in nature, and a scepticism regarding notions such as civilisation and progress. The mood was well captured by the first novels of two English writers: Malcolm Lowry and William Golding. Lowry's visionary (if over-encoded novel) *Under the Volcano* (1947) captured the widespread moral disillusionment of the post-war generation. Set in the 1930s, in a politically unstable South America, it dramatises the predicament of a group of cynical, world-weary characters, wavering between a commitment to politics (the Spanish Civil War is raging in Europe), and the easier solutions of alcoholism and suicide. In spite of their differing personal philosophies, they are all engaged in a studied flight from the 'horrors of the present'. A similar pessimism regarding the sustainability of ideals in the modern world is evident in William Golding's *Lord of the Flies* (1954). The story tells of a group of English schoolboys who, stranded on a desert island, gradually give themselves over to barbaric customs and murderous deeds. The novel is a succinct parable on the precarious and superficial nature of civilised morality which (as the Fascist experience in Europe showed) is often unable to resist the call of the wild, irresistibily drawn to a world where no moral voice is heard, 'no words, and no movements but the tearing of teeth and claws'.[2]

The novels of Lowry and Golding gave literary shape to a distinctive end-game mentality, a mood of termination, of arrival without further departure, which was widespread throughout the literature of the immediate post-war period. It was particularly prevalent in German and Italian writing. In the former country, it was discernible in novels such as Hans Erich Nossack's *Interview with Death* (1948), Wolfgang Koeppen's *Doves in the Grass* (1951) and Gerd Gaiser's *Final Ball* (1958), all of which deal with characters who are both alienated from the past and uneasy about the future. This was, in the words of their most famous representative, Heinrich Böll, a 'literature of war, of homecoming and of rubble', written in the 'Zero Hour' (*Nullpunkt*) of German history. Böll's own novels, *The Train Was on Time* (1949), *Tomorrow and Yesterday* (1954) and *The Bread of our Early Years* (1955), were central texts in this genre. Their focus is not upon triumph but upon survival, not upon actions which follow pre-existing value structures, but upon individuals living, however precariously, with compromise, indecision and defeat, working 'out of fear and desperation', and forced to exchange ideals for sustenance. In all of Böll's novels (including the later *Billiards at Half-past Nine*, 1959, and *The Clown*, 1963, which target in a more consistent way the emerging political inequalities of West Germany, and criticise an establishment preoccupied with power, self-publicity and wealth) the past looms as a presence that has not been (and perhaps cannot be) fully exorcised. The conduct of the war, its loss, and its morality, was further explored in Alfred Andersch's *Flight to Afar* (1957) and Siegfried Lenz's *The German Lesson* (1968), both of which speak of the psychological impediments to a retrospective understanding of collective guilt.[3]

Italian writers were likewise forced to come to terms with the moral and political bankruptcy of their nation, 'having' (as the novelist, Italo Calvino, described it) 'emerged from an experience, a war and a civil war that had spared no one'. Like their German counterparts, the Italians moved towards a neo-realist style in their writing. Some of leading names here were Cesare Pavese, Vasco Pratolini, Leonardo Sciascia, Franco Fortini, Paolo Volponi and Elio Vittorini. Grouped around the journal *Il Politecnico*, founded by Vittorini in 1945, the neo-realists, exponents of *verismo*, rejected the hermetic style that had been dominant in Italy prior to the war, wishing to see in its place a type of literature that would be historical, political, and would deal with the issues of the day. There were, certainly, exceptions to this general trend. One of the most popular novels of post-war Italy was Giuseppe Tomasi di Lampedusa's *The Leopard* (1958), which conjures up, sometimes with nostalgia, sometimes with realism, the travails of a family during the period of the *Risorgimento*. But it was the present, not the past, that preoccupied the great majority of writers of this generation. Some focussed upon the peasant south, with its backwardness, misery, political and religious contradictions (tensions well captured in Sciascia's *Salt in the Wound*, 1956), whilst others wrote about northern urban Italy, dominated by increasing mechanisation, industrial conflict, and the easy temptations of a new consumerist society. This is the type of society that is depicted in the industrial novels of the late 1950s and early 1960s, notably in Volponi's *My Troubles Began* (1962), Goffredo Parise's *The Boss* (1965) and Pasolini's *A Violent Life* (1959), which took as its context the harsh world of Rome's *Lumpenproletariat*. Like their German counterparts, the Italian neo-realists also wrote about the war; but in their case moral guilt was balanced by a positive assessment of the part played by the resistance in its struggle against fascism. Some of the most noted novels here were Vittorini's *Men or Not* (1945), Calvino's *The Path to the Nest of Spiders* (1947) and (with an intent to complicate the picture somewhat) Pavese's *The House on the Hill* (1949). The plight of those victimised by the fascist regime, forced into inner emigration and exiled, formed the focus of Carlo Levi's *Christ stopped at Eboli* (1945); whilst the complex motives that gave rise to the fascist mentality in Italy were treated by Alberto Moravia in his *The Conformist* (1951). Finally, the literature of neo-realism engaged with both the Italian and German treatment of the Jews, in Primo Levi's moving account of his experiences in Auschwitz, *If this is a Man* (1947), and (with greater distance) by Giorgio Bassani, *The Garden of the Finzi Continis* (1962). Even the noted hermetic poet, Salvadore Quasimodo, felt the need to abandon his earlier cryptic symbolism to write poems such as 'Auschwitz' (1954), giving voice in his later verse to that 'limp/pain that memory leaves/to its silence without irony or anger'.[4]

In the immediate post-war period, there were many who deliberately remained aloof from the social and political issues of the day (the catch-phrases were *qualunquismo* in Italy, and *ohne mich* in Germany). Particularly in the late 1940s and 1950s, this retreat from the public realm seemed to be encouraged by successive conservative governments in Britain, France and Germany, who sought to win over the electorate through a mixture of welfare state legislation and the stimulation of consumer consumption. Helped by the Marshall plan of 1948, Germany, in particular, experienced a so-called *Wirtschaftswunder* (economic miracle). The success of that nation (and of others, such as Italy) seemed to suggest that capitalist society was able to solve the kinds of political problems that had almost destroyed it in the inter-war period. The revolutionary politics of those days were now no longer: transition not revolution, pragmatism not idealism, were the policies promoted by early postwar governments throughout Europe. The result was a culture that many found to be parochial and self-satisfied, and permeated, as John Osborne (author of the iconoclastic play, *Look Back in Anger*, 1956), wryly noted, with 'the odour of anaemic self-righteousness, the lifeless whine, the lack of rigour or gift of even petty decision'. In England, literary manifestos such as Robert Conquest's introduction to his anthology, *New Lines* (1956), advertised their work as being 'free from mystical and logical compulsions', and committed to 'real rather than ideological honesty'. As Karl Miller observed in his retrospective anthology of English literature of this period (published in 1968), the writers of post-war sobriety 'were tired of the international, experimental avant-garde and of mandatory modernity; they were tired of romantic individualism, the religiosity, the martyred sensitiveness that had been favoured by writers during the war; they were sceptics; and they were democrats'. This was a literature of bathos, less politically self-conscious and lacking the moral anxiety of contemporary German and Italian writing, but working, nevertheless, within the same minimalist ethos that grew out of the political and economic realism of postwar Europe. It is represented by novels such as Alan Sillitoe's *Saturday Night and Sunday Morning* (1958) and *The Loneliness of the Long Distance Runner* (1959), David Storey's *This Sporting Life* (1960), John Braine's *Room at the Top* (1957) and Stan Barstow's *A Kind of Loving* (1960); by plays such as Arnold Wesker's *Chips with Everything* (1962) and Shelagh Delaney's *A Taste of Honey* (1959); and by the poetry of the Movement group, best represented by Philip Larkin (*The Whitsun Weddings*, 1964). Set in working- or lower middle-class milieux (often in the north of England), and dealing with individuals struggling against the machinations of family life and class prejudice, the new British Realism offered a literature without illusions and political bias, but also without visions and blue-prints for the future: the self-confidence and energy expressed by the heroes of this literature cannot hide the fatalism and quietism that resides beneath the surface of their lives. Larkin put their predicament succinctly in his poem 'Wants' (1955): 'despite the artful tensions of the calender/The life insurance, the tabled fertility rites,/The costly aversion of the eyes from death –/Beneath it all, desire of oblivion runs'.[5]

To a large extent, this rediscovery of the parochial was a consequence of the loss of world-power status that many European countries suffered in the period between 1945 and 1970. During this time, France lost control over Indo-China, in 1954, and Algeria, in 1962; Great Britain granted independence to India, in 1947, and Nigeria, in 1963; Belgium, the Congo, in 1960; and Portugal, Goa, in 1961. Such changes to the colonial hegemony of Europe reflected the new global order that had emerged out of the Second World War, whose precarious fulcrum was a hostile balance between the Western Allies (now clearly led by the United States) and the Soviet Union, the ideological differences between whom formed, in the words of Churchill's famous speech of March 1946, an 'Iron Curtain'. Countries such as Hungary, Czechoslovakia and Poland, which had been liberated in 1945 from one totalitarian neighbour, now found themselves consigned to the dependency of even more powerful one, which was equally uncompromising in its denial of basic human rights, political liberty and freedom of speech. Soviet Imperialism, which appeared at its most blatant in the suppression of popular uprisings in Hungary in 1956, East Germany in 1961 and Czechoslovakia in 1968, compelled many former adherents of Communism, such as Ignazio Silone, Stephen Spender and André Malraux, to revise their long-held allegiances. They now concluded that Communism and the hope for Socialism in Europe was, in the words of Richard Crossman's famous volume, a God that had failed. It had been a Utopian movement, which artists and writers had joined out of social despair, moral guilt, or intellectual *naïveté*, hoping, by aligning themselves in an 'active comradeship of struggle' with the working classes, to become part of the forward march of history. The sight of the tanks of the Soviet Union on the streets of Berlin and Budapest had brought, as Günter Grass noted, that 'dream of Socialism' to an abrupt end.[6]

Acts of resistance to the military hegemony in Eastern Europe of the Soviet State were supported, even from within that nation, by attacks against its moral credibility. In 1962, Alexander Solzhenitsyn published his *One Day in the Life of Ivan Denisovich*, which became, after Pasternak's *Doctor Zhivago* (1957), the single most influential Russian novel of the post-war period. Solzhenitsyn's novel (describing a single day in the life of a political prisoner in a Siberian prison camp under Stalin) takes place in a closed society dominated by cruelty and torture, but also by a regime of custom and ritual which deadens the senses and destroys the spirit. It is a world without transcendence, populated by those who survive simply because they have abandoned all ideals, and who have given up believing 'in paradise or in hell'. The moral minimalism and quiet despair to which Solzhenitsyn's novel gives voice links it to the *Nullpunkt* literature written elsewhere in Europe. But the novel, written in the brief period of cultural liberalisation that set in between the death of Stalin in 1953 and the resumption of state control over the arts initiated by the Brezhnev era ten years later, can also be seen as an act of protest, a gesture of defiance against a political regime responsible for perpetuating the misery of concentration camp life even as it denied its existence. As such, it took its place beside a growing genre of oppositional literature in Russia, which included Ilya Erenburg's *The Thaw* (1954), Vladimir Dudintsev's *Not by Bread Alone* (1957) and the poetry of Yevgeny Yevtushenko, particularly his 'Babi Yar' sequence of 1961. Elsewhere in Eastern Europe, the same will to self-expression and the same creative circumnavigation of political despotism gave rise to an impressive literature of protest and inner emigration. Poland, for example, was able to produce not only the novels of Marek Hłasko, such as *The Graveyard* (1958), and Witold Gombrowicz, *Pornography* (1960), and Tadeusz Borowski's concentration camp stories (*Farewell to Maria* and *The World of Stone*, both 1948), but also the poetry of the Nobel Prize-winning Czesław Miłosz and Zbigniew Herbert, and the drama of the Absurdists, such as Slawomir Mrożek and Tadeusz Różewicz; whilst in Czechoslovakia, the fiction of Ladislav Mňačko, *The Taste of Power* (1967), and the early fiction of Milan Kundera could appear, as could the plays of Václav Havel and Josef Topol (*The End of the Carnival*, 1965). Collectively, these writers helped bring into existence a body of writing that sought to merge the sense of moral seriousness characteristic of the politically engaged writers of the 1920s and 1930s, with a Postmodern openness towards the fantastic and the surreal. They created in the process often highly personal modes of literary statement able to withstand that 'distorted rationality' which underscored the 'compulsory duties, evasions and concessions' (intellectual and political alike), which dominated life in the Eastern Bloc for most of the post-war period.[7]

The major Communist parties of Western Europe were deeply affected by the declining status of the Soviet Union. By the time of his death in 1964, Togliatti had steered the Italian Communist Party away from its Stalinist past and into a future of electoral responsibility, seeking to reach, in the words of its subsequent leader, Enrico Berlinguer, an 'historical compromise' (*compromesso historico*) with the new priorities of a rapidly modernising Italy. Communist parties throughout Europe now surrendered their radical initiative to Maoist, Trotskyist and anarchist groups, who worked largely beyond the party system. It was these groups who provided the dynamo for the events that took place in Germany, Italy, England and, above all, in France in May 1968, where workers, students and intellectuals combined in an attempt to destabilise the state. In the final analysis, the politics of these oppositional forces were inherently unstable and strategically naive; in the face of the tear gas of the CRS and the strong-arm tactics of Europe's para-military police forces, the revolutionary agenda of this generation disappeared, forced to give way to a course of European politics that in the governance of Margaret Thatcher (1979–1990), Helmut Kohl (1982–) and François Mitterand (1981–1993), restored conservatism to power with an even more trenchant right-wing bias. It was precisely the failure of the events of May '68 that forced a fundamental re-think amongst oppositional groups in Europe. After that date (as the English dramatist, David Edgar, later noted), 'revolutionary politics was seen as being much less about the organisation of the working class at the point of production, and much more about the disruption of bourgeois ideology at the point of consumption'. Radical politics now took two diverging directions: towards terrorism, with the Baader-Meinhof group in Germany, and the Red Brigade in Italy; and towards collaborative-parliamentarian politics, which was the path adopted by the Green movement and by many Feminists. These groups acted according to a new definition of the political, one that remained inherently suspicious of all master narratives and '-isms', whether from the Right or the Left. Such groups also evinced a greater awareness of the symbolic forms through which power is exercised, and of the cultural channels through which consciousness is formed (and de-formed). They drew here upon cultural commentators such Theodor Adorno and Hans Magnus Enzensberger (in Germany), Richard Hoggart and Raymond Williams (in England), and Pierre Bourdieu and Louis Althusser (in France). Neo-Marxist (or Marxist-revisionist) in the main, these cultural critics viewed power as something that is not only *produced* by economic and class realities, but also *reproduced* by institutions such as the media and education. To effect lasting political change, it was necessary to intervene into those linguistic and symbolic structures which secure the ideological hegemony of the ruling class. This was the thesis developed, for example, by Enzensberger in his seminal essay 'The Industrialisation of the Mind' (1962), where he argued that the structures of capitalist society perpetuated themselves through the manufacture of consciousness, interpellating even the supposed watchdogs of the cultural system, intellectuals and artists, as 'accomplice[s] of a huge industrial complex'.[8]

Many writers had arrived at the same insights, but through different routes. In the theatre, in particular, dramatists such as Peter Weiss (*The Persecution and Assassination of Marat*, 1964), Peter Handke (*Offending the Audience*, 1966), Dario Fo (*Accidental Death of an Anarchist*, 1970), Edward Bond (*Lear*, 1971) and Heiner Müller (*The Hamlet Machine*, 1977) focussed on the personal politics of power, showing how dominance and submission, control and exploitation, were inscribed into the theatricality, into the rituals and ceremonies of everyday life. Such plays also embodied an awareness of the institutional parameters in which politics imposes itself upon culture: the nature of the audience, the ownership of the theatre, the controlling presence of censor and state. It was a perception which encouraged many playwrights into a form of 'constructive sabotage' of the system. As Heiner Müller argued, the stage should be a 'laboratory of social fantasy', a context in which to experiment with possibilities for concrete change. His words sum up not just the political content of the Postmodern position, but also its *attitude* to politics. In this respect, he spoke for many of his East German compatriots, such as Johannes Bobrowski, Stefan Heym, Ulrich Plenzdorf, Christa Wolf and Christoph Hein, who likewise charted a course between inner emigration and cultural revolt, producing in the process a body of writing whose province was not high-moral seriousness but deflationary intellectualising, not ideological rigour but playful irony, not spiritual abstinence but consumption and *jouissance*.[9]

The waiting game that these writers and others throughout the Eastern Bloc played in the post-war period finally brought results in the late 1980s, when rigid structure gave way to movement, intellectually, diplomatically and physically, across the numerous frontiers of central Europe. Talk was now of *perestroika* and *glasnost* rather than imperialism or state control. The most tangible symbol of this process of political liberation was the destruction of the Berlin Wall in 1989. Its dismantlement, engineered by a populace intoxicated by the sudden advent of liberalisation throughout Eastern Europe, was greeted by many who witnessed the event, novelists such as Christoph Hein (*The Foreign Friend*, 1982, and *The Last Days of Horn*, 1985) and Stefan Heym (*The King David Report*, 1972, and *Ahasver*, 1981) as the first step in the 'transformation' of German society. But for Europe, as a whole, the event was equally significant. Forty years earlier, the Polish poet, Czesław Miłosz had exclaimed in his 'Child of Europe' (1946): 'The voice of passion is better than the voice of reason/The passionless cannot change history', condemning the quietism of many of his contemporaries faced with the political status quo in Europe. Now those passions (in spite of their inchoate nature) had reasserted themselves, had helped dismantle those monolithic structures that had grimly oppressed so many people since the end of World War Two. What the demolition of the Wall (carried out in a spirit of almost carnival abandon) seemed to indicate was that European history, after almost half a century of moving around a fixed point of moral and political anguish, had finally given way to energies and values that were genuinely populist in their origins, and which were phrased, not in the language of guilt and recrimination but in that of optimism and confidence, and which spoke not of the past but of the future.[10]

2   POSTMODERNISM: A THEORETICAL PROJECT

The literature of post-war Europe was characterised by a multiplicity of styles, schools and genres. They ranged from the Magic Realism of writers such as Günter Grass and Salman Rushdie, through to the Theatre of the Absurd of Eugène Ionesco and Jean Genet, and the literature of political protest written by writers in Eastern Bloc countries, such as Milan Kundera, Václav Havel and Zbigniew Herbert. In spite of evident differences in intent and theme, this literature converged upon a shared literary strategy and a common aesthetic that came to be known as Postmodernism. The term first made its appearance not in Europe but in the United States, amongst a group of critics attempting to demarcate the lines between the high-culture of Modernism, and the more experimentalist, minimalist, self-reflexive aesthetic of the contemporary period. The main voices here were Ihab Hassan, Leslie Fiedler, John Barth and Irving Howe. They observed that much contemporary American fiction, such as William Burroughs' *The Naked Lunch* (1959), Thomas Pynchon's *The Crying of Lot 49* (1966), Richard Brautigan's *Trout Fishing in America* (1967) and Kurt Vonnegut's *Slaughterhouse-Five* (1969), broke both with the epic narratives of nineteenth-century Realism (which sought to totalise experience and assert closure), and with the Modernist revalorisation of individual agency and the subjectivist workings of the mind, which was so evident in the stream of consciousness techniques used by Virginia Woolf and James Joyce. In spite of their different perspectives, both Realism and Modernism assumed that human experience (however orderly or disorderly it might appear), could be made to reveal its inherent structure through the productive agency of language. The literature addressed by the theorists of Postmodernism, on the contrary, resisted any notions of aethetic order, preferring fragmented structures, disconnected and episodic narratives, and forms of characterisation that dispensed with psychological coherence and rounded personalities. It was a literature without illusions, which proclaimed its proximity to the terminal state of Western high-culture, positively cultivating (in Barth's words) 'an apocalyptic ambience'. 'Waste', 'exhaustion', 'silence' were amongst the critical metaphors used to appropriate such literature, productive negativities that also opened on to 'self-parody, self-subversion, and self-transcendence'.[11]

In establishing the intellectual parameters of Postmodernist literature, the American theorists were able to draw upon the writings of a body of European philosophers, cultural theorists, literary critics and linguists, such as Roland Barthes, Jacques Derrida and Jean Baudrillard. Their work (deepened through the influence of the philosophies of Nietzsche and Heidegger) articulated a number of issues central to the Postmodern mentality, issues relating to the abolition of distinctions between high and popular culture, to the non-sustainable nature of Enlightenment models of universalist reason and logo-centric thinking, and to the problematic relationship between individual intentionality and the determining discourses of language and ideology. This was a set of issues addressed as early as the 1950s by the French Structuralists. The latter traced their project back to the linguistic theories of Ferdinand de Saussure

(*Course in General Linguistics*, 1916), who had foregrounded in his work the conventional, non-representational nature of language. In works such as Roland Barthes' *Writing Degree Zero* (1953) and *Mythologies* (1957), Gerard Genette's *Figures* (3 vols, 1966–1972), Tzvetan Todorov's *Literature and Signification* (1967), A-J Greimas' *Structural Semantics* (1966) and Julia Kristeva's *Semiotics* (1969), the Structuralists attempted to apply de Saussure's insights to areas as diverse as semiotics, the poetics of narrative and discourse theory. As Roland Barthes explained, Structuralism was 'not a school nor even a movement', but an 'activity', a form of textual analysis which 'takes the real, decomposes it, then recomposes it', in an attempt to uncover those conventions that exist behind the signifying processes that we use to make sense of the world.[12]

The Structuralists sought to raise awareness about the agency of language, and about the relationship between literature and its readership, actual and imagined. Their initiative was most notably taken up by the proponents of the New French Novel (*Nouveau Roman*), such as Alain Robbe-Grillet, Nathalie Sarraute, Michel Butor and (with a greater sense of the political implications of this methodology) Philippe Sollers (editor of the innovative journal *Tel Quel*). But Structuralism also influenced the work of Italian novelists and theorists, particularly those, such as Umberto Eco and Renato Barilli, the founders of Group '63. The Structuralist view that language is never naive but always inscribed with certain ideological values was also adhered to by Magic Realist writers, such as Günter Grass, Salman Rushdie and Milan Kundera, and by a generation of feminist authors, from Simone de Beauvoir to Doris Lessing, Angela Carter and Hélène Cixous. In spite of obvious differences in their methodologies and political priorities, these writers shared a common set of assumptions about the relationship between literature and the world. They all rejected the idea that language could simply re-present external reality; few, if any, believed in the possibility of transcendence in a world without God (or even Marx); all viewed individual subjectivity as something problematic, a torn entity, which finds itself formed and deformed (the current term was 'decentred') by conflicting semiotic systems; and all, particularly the feminists (but also Grass), sought to uncover the inherent repressiveness of master narratives, which exclude women, ethnic minorities and other groups from involvement in the processes of cultural self-definition.

That coming to terms with such issues required a framework broader than the purely literary was obvious to all. As Milan

Kundera, the author of *Life is Elsewhere* (1973), attested, literature had to remain open to the 'historical dimension of human existence'. With this new sense of historical responsibility came a new definition of the political, one that would have been unrecognisable to the majority of the writers of the 1920s and 1930s. The Post-modernists rejected the doctrinaire nature of the ideologies espoused by that earlier generation, remaining suspicious (as Harold Pinter put it) of the 'warnings, sermons, admonitions, ideological exhortations, moral judgements [and] defined problems with built-in solutions' favoured by the committed Left (and Right) during that time. Writers in the Postmodern period, feminist writers in particular, moved well beyond the nineteenth-century identification of politics with party factionalism or policy, to focus upon the personal realm, upon the mechanics of desire, aiming (in Carter's case) to demystify the clichés surrounding sexual relations, which prevent the 'real relations between man and his kind' being understood. D.M. Thomas (*The White Hotel*, 1981), Christa Wolf (*Cassandra*, 1983) and Milan Kundera (*The Unbearable Lightness of Being*, 1984) followed a similar trajectory. They too explore the complex relationship between personal desire and political agency, working towards (what we might call) an historical anthropology. In their fiction, power is seen not as some foreign agency imposing itself from without, but as a set of psychic dispositions, which are articulated wherever notions of individual identity and self-hood are being asserted or contested, defined or marginalised.[13]

These initiatives took the literature of Postmodernism away from the largely linguistic focus of Structuralism and into the ambit of its successor: Post-structuralism. The intellectual parameters of that movement were broad: it included the later work of Roland Barthes (*S/Z*, 1970, *The Pleasure of the Text*, 1973, and *Camera Lucida*, 1980), the Freudian revisionist psychoanalysis of Jacques Lacan (*Writings*, 1966) and, above all, the deconstructionism of Jacques Derrida (*Writing and Difference*, 1967). Where the Structuralists of the 1960s had looked for the systemic patterns (narrative and generic) which govern the production of meaning within texts and assure their comprehensibility, the Post-structuralists focussed upon the aporia, indeterminacies and radical ambiguities that they saw as endemic within all attempts to articulate meaning. Pierre Macherey (*A Theory of Literary Production*, 1966) and Julia Kristeva ('The System and the Speaking Subject', 1973) argued from their different points of view against the homogenising notion of structure favoured by the Structuralists, and against the latter's overly classificatory approach to literature, which (they argued) forecloses avenues to the irrational, and to those formally and politically indeterminate qualities within texts. Correspondingly, the Post-structuralists emphasised not discourse, but the spaces between discourse, not semantic clarity, but those elements of meaning that exist in the margins of a text, that 'real and necessary discontinuity' which reveals the ruptures and dislocations of consciousness (individual and collective) that are always at play in the literary process. And to the critique of metaphysical presence undertaken by Derrida and others, the French philosopher, Michel Foucault, added an important historicising perspective, mapping out in his *The Archaeology of Knowledge* (1969), *Discipline and Punish* (1975) and *The History of Sexuality* (3 volumes, 1976–1984) both the conceptual and the institutional terrain upon which knowledge and power have traditionally been maintained.[14]

Postmodernism was represented in different European countries in different ways. In Sweden (the most cosmopolitan of the Scandinavian nations during this period), major literature came from the poets Gunnar Ekelöf (*Ferry Song*, 1941, and *Guide to the Underworld*, 1967) and Erik Lindegren (*The Man without a Way*, 1942, and *Winter Sacrifice*, 1954), and from Stig Dagerman (the stories, *Games of the Night*, 1947, and the novel, *A Burnt Child*, 1948). In spite of Lindegren's moments of visionary insight, and Ekelöf's mysticism, these are works of dark introspection, which cultivate a minimalist aesthetic that brings such literature close to the end-game mentality of Beckett and others. Historical factors inhibited the development of a distinctively Postmodern literature in Portugal or in Spain, which remained under the dictatorship of Franco until 1975, where, with the work of Rafael Sánchez Ferlosio (*The One Day of the Week*, 1956) and Juan Goytisolo (*The Assassins*, 1954), a modernised form of urban Realism (close to the Italian *verismo*) reigned. Scope for formal experimentation was not great. Nevertheless, novelists such as Camilo José Cela (*The Hive*, 1951), Luis Martín-Santos (*The Time of Silence*, 1962) and Miguel Delibes (*Parable of the Shipwrecked Man*, 1969), showed that they had learnt much from the narrative techniques of Joyce and Döblin. Similar political obstacles existed for writers in post-war Greece, which was forced to sustain the political rule of military regimes between 1936 and 1952, and again between 1967 and 1975. But it was precisely such conditions that helped produce the work of a trio of remarkable poets: Odysseus Elytis (*Axion Esti*, 1960), Nanos Valaoritis (*Central Stoa*, 1958) and, above all, Yannis Ritsos (*Pitcher*, 1957, *The Prison Tree and the Women*, 1963, and *Fourth Dimension*, 1977). Ritsos' work, in particular, successfully fuses native Greek traditions and iconography with a distinctly Postmodern idiom. His poetry registers the pressures of political and historical change upon the individual, in a language (as he notes in his poem 'The Meaning is one', 1970) that seeks to be 'dense, determined/vague, insistent, simple, suspicious', because these are the only values that can keep consciousness alive in an unliberated world.[15]

It is, perhaps, in this concern with the political and historical parameters of individual experience that European Postmodernism differs most conspicuously from its North American counterpart. In works such as Don DeLillo's *White Noise* (1985) and Kathy Acker's *Don Quixote which Was a Dream* (1986), and in the cut-ups of William Burroughs, American Postmodernist writing has become increasingly preoccupied with the media-technological paradigm that is all-pervasive in American culture. These novels and others draw our attention to the capability of the media to fashion and refashion personal identity, as it dispenses with notions of authenticity in favour of radical chic and the ever-repeating simulacrum. The theorist of this obsession with the media image is Jean Baudrillard. In his many theoretical pronouncements, such as *Simulations* (1981), he has argued that we are now the victims of an aesthetic overdeterminsm, a totalising ambit of media aestheticism, which sees everything as text: history, politics, the body, psychology, and notions of the self; they are all 'simulacra', images worked and reworked through other images, which refer to nothing other than themselves. As Baudrillard explains: in Postmodernist culture 'it is no longer a question of imitation, nor of reduplication, nor even of parody. It is rather a question of substituting signs of the real for the real itself.'[16]

Postmodernism in Europe has taken such insights to heart, as it has the ludic and relativistic mode of American Postmodernism. But it has also registered a greater critical distance from the celebration of the surface that such an aesthetic implies. The difference lies in an attitude to time, temporality and history; Postmodern culture in America is the product of the philosophy and life-style of 'nowism', locked, as Jean-François Lyotard (one of the earliest observers of the movement) has noted, into the 'paradox of the future (post) anterior (modo)', in which past and future are bracketed out so that the texture of the present may emerge in its distinctive grain. The major writers of European Postmodernism – novelists such as Günter Grass, Milan Kundera and Christa Wolf, playwrights such as Heiner Müller and Edward Bond, and poets such as Paul Celan, Zbigniew Herbert and Vasko Popa – embody the same disregard for master narratives and the same suspicion of the totalising frameworks of the past, but anchor that disregard and suspicion within a broader historical context, one that allows notions of memory and identity, love, loss and death, to be treated as continuing realities. This larger framework is evident in the work of Kundera, who argues that 'history itself must be understood and analysed as an existential situation', which is, in the age of Postmodernism, a 'period of terminal paradoxes'. These European writers refuse to abandon ethical seriousness, that 'feeling of responsibility for the condition of people's consciences', maintaining faith (in the words of Wolf) with that 'urge to go forward into those still uncharted regions in which the structure of the moral world of man living in society is open to question'. It is here that the distinctive contribution to European Postmodernism lies: in the work of a generation of writers determined to merge the open possibilities of the Postmodernist text with the positive values of a post-war (and post-Cold War) humanism.[17]

3 THE SELF-CONSCIOUS TEXT: FROM THE *NOUVEAU ROMAN* TO METAFICTION

In many respects, Postmodernist fiction begins with James Joyce's prodigious novel, *Finnegan's Wake* (1939). In its playful intertextuality and semantic profusions (that 'savage economy of hieroglyphics' praised by Samuel Beckett), and in its aleatory monumentalism, Joyce's vast novel opened up new possibilities of writing for an entire generation. Its influence is evident in the novels of Arno Schmidt, whose *The Republic of Savants* (1957), *KAFF, or Mare Crisium* (1960) and *Bottom's Dream* (1970) extend Joyce's technique through experimentation with phonemes, morphemes and syntagms, and in the work of the Italian writer, Carlo Emilio Gadda, author of *That Awful Mess on Via Merulana* (1957). The latter novel structures its narrative around a complex web of archaisms, neologisms, word-play, technical and obsolete vocabulary, slang, puns, and lexical obscurities, in striking anticipation of the 'multi-lingualism' approach (*plurilinguismo*) that Gadda's compatriot, Sebastiano Vassalli, was to use in his novel *Narcissus* (1968). In Britain, Christine Brooke-Rose used typographical diversification in her novel, *Between* (1968), Anthony Burgess invented a *sui generic* Russified English in *A Clockwork Orange* (1962), whilst B.S. Johnson experimented with different linguistic registers in his *Albert Angelo* (1964) and *Trawl* (1966), 'inventing, borrowing, stealing or cobbling from other media forms which will more or less satisfactorily contain an ever-changing reality'.[18]

Literary self-consciousness was most systematically explored by a group of French novelists who produced a fictional genre known as the *Nouveau Roman* (New French Novel). They included Alain Robbe-Grillet, Natalie Sarraute, Michel Butor and Claude Simon. The took as their starting-point a repudiation of the nineteenth-century Realist novel, particularly as it was written by Balzac in his *The Human Comedy*. The writers of the *Nouveau Roman* rejected both the totalising effect of Balzac's fiction (the fact that it draws protagonists and reader alike into a realm of all-inclusive energy), and the intellectual assumptions upon which it was based: a belief in the objective status of the real world, and its independence from a viewing subject; the conviction that language can unproblematically transcribe reality; a belief in the centrality and individuality of human experience (which they saw inscribed into the Realist's concern for character and character development); and a confidence in the teleological shape of experience (reflected in the linearity and closed nature of the typical Realist narrative). As Robbe-Grillet (the leading theoretician of the movement) explained in his treatise, *For a New Novel* (1963), such assumptions had no place in the Postmodern period; they were part of 'the fixed significations, the ready-made meanings which afforded man the old divine order, and subsequently the rationalist order of the nineteenth century', and (as such) had to be rejected on both literary and political grounds.[19]

In the place of such fiction, the writers of the *Nouveau Roman* posited a new type of writing, which would accommodate both the aleatory nature of human experience (its essential randomness), and its lack of metaphysical depth. In their novels, the techniques that had prevailed for a century and more were replaced by an alternative aesthetic: the omniscient narrator of the Realist novel forced to give way to viewing positions which were often limited, internally incoherent and mysterious in their origin (see, for example, Robbe-Grillet's *The Voyeur*, 1955); the notion of character deprived of psychological depth and reconstituted as something impressionistic and fragmented (as in Sarraute's *The Planetarium*, 1959), or, even more minimally, reduced to pure nominalism (as in Robbe-Grillet's *Jealousy*, 1957); and the relationship between narrative and causal time uncoupled, so that events come to be repeated, narrated out of order and left incomplete (Simon's *The Flanders Road*, 1960, and Butor's *Passing Time*, 1956, are the most memorable examples of this technique). Even the plots of these novels resist easy interpretation, often centring on a paradox, an enigma, or some other unresolved issue. This is the case with the detective story in Robbe-Grillet's *The Erasers* (1953), where false clues are fed to the reader; and the novel within a novel in Sarraute's *The Golden Fruits* (1963), whose content is never revealed. These devices and others help create a world whose ultimate purpose and meaning remain for characters and reader alike ultimately unfathomable. Faced with pure enigma, the reader is forced out of passivity into activity, into a practical collaboration with the text, participating in the 'invention of the world and of man, constant invention and perpetual interrogation', a process that is, as Robbe-Grillet argues, a *sine qua non* for both aesthetic and personal freedom.[20]

The *Nouveau Roman* drew attention to itself as a practice of writing not simply by removing omniscient narration, or obscuring and problematising sources of perspective, but also by incorporating the poetic itself as a function within the text (as Robbe-Grillet does with the native songs in *Jealousy*, or Sarraute with her imaginary novel in *The Golden Fruits*.) By using such devices, these novels were effectively offering themselves as 'meta-texts', as texts about texts, as statements on the rules of literary writing, and even upon the conventionality and artificiality of language, *per se*. Metafiction became one of the major trends within the fiction of the Postmodern period. Examples include John Fowles' novel, *The French Lieutenant's Woman* (1969), in which the narrator interrupts the otherwise Realist narrative to proclaim that his story is perhaps a 'game', the work of an author who is no longer 'omniscient and decreeing', and concerned 'with freedom (as) our first principle, not authority'. Metafiction appears as a sharp moment of self-reflexivity in Fowles' novel, allowing the reader to return to the main story-line sceptical of the sweeping generalisations and totalising vision of the narrator. Similar devices were also used by Julian Barnes in *Flaubert's Parrot* (1984) (where fact and mythology combine to produce an image of an author, who may or may not be real); by Umberto Eco in his playful and semiotically self-conscious *The Name of the Rose* (1980); and by Georges Perec in his compendious *Life, A User's Manual* (1978). This is a work which includes (in its complex panorama of a day in the life of a Parisian apartment block) literary puzzles and allusions, radio transcriptions, restaurant menus and acrostics, celebrating, as Perec's cryptic preface to the novel indicates, the dialectic between 'the organised, coherent, structured signifying space of the picture, and the 'inert, formless elements' that characterise real life. These novels are also supreme examples of the novel as 'intertext', a term coined by Julia Kristeva to describe those works of fiction that are made up of 'a mosaic of quotations' drawn from a multitude of secondary texts, echoes, transpositions, and parodies. It was intertextuality that allowed the Postmodernist novel to obtain that richness of detail and that polyphonic perspectivism that the Realist novel had achieved in the nineteenth century through the creation of multiple characters.[21]

That metafiction could accommodate both the humanist concerns of traditional fiction and the self-conscious formalism of Postmodernist writing was demonstrated in Italo Calvino's intriguing novel, *If on a Winter's Night a Traveller*. Published in 1979, Calvino's novel came towards the end of a body of writing which had been largely devoted to exploring the relationship between text and world. As he explained in the 1967 preface to his first novel: 'Reading and experience of life are not two universes, but one. Every experience of life, in order to be interpreted, calls on certain readings and is fused with them. The fact that books are always born from other books is a truth, and only apparently in contradiction with that other truth: that books are born from practical life and from relationships with human beings'. Calvino's fiction, from the early *The Path to the Spiders' Nest* (1947) to his last work, *Mr Palomar* (1983), gives shape to this position, moving between neo-realism and science fiction, parodies of medieval literature and futuristic travelogues, as in the trilogy, *The Cloven Viscount* (1952), *The Baron in the Trees* (1957) and *The Non-existent Knight* (1959). The later *Cosmicomics* (1965) and *t zero* (1967) are works of pure fantasy, which complete Calvino's break with the traditions of European Realism. All of these novels problematise the categories and codes by which we perceive (visually and cognitively) the world, in order to provide (as with the cities visited by Marco Polo in the intriguing *Invisible Cities*, 1972) that 'catalogue of forms' that constitutes the world, and which is inexhaustible but, ultimately, unnamable.[22]

Calvino's semiotic self-consciousness found its fullest expression in his novel, *If on a Winter's Night a Traveller*. Its subject is the Book, as a creative artefact, as a tool, as an object of desire, as a stimulus, as merchandise, as a sham and as a piece of cultural capital. At the centre of the novel is the Reader, a directly-invoked 'you', whose task it is to track down the real *If on a Winter's Night a Traveller* in the midst of a multitude of novels and genres (from detective fiction to Japanese pornography) that masquerade as Calvino's original text. The novel plays, thus, with all the conventions of the discourse of fiction: psychological characterisation, linear narratives, the assumption of a real world that is being transcribed. All are abandoned in favour of a pure playfulness, which is manifested through the novel's fusion of 'real' and imagined scenes, its false correspondences, its microscopic depiction of objects and bodily gesture, and its leitmotific, almost musical narrative structure. And yet behind these small fictions lie the bigger 'fictions' of everyday life, those existential patterns that manifest themselves in 'the continuity of life, the inevitability of death'. These are revealed through the gentle humanism of Calvino's novel, and through a perspective that remains (in spite of its endemic formalism,) supremely alive to the open nature of experience and to the invigorating banalities of ordinary life.[23]

4   THE POLITICS OF RITUAL: THE THEATRE OF THE ABSURD

Roland Barthes saw the New French Novelist as a revolutionary figure, who had rewritten the rhetorical rules of literary expression. As Barthes explained in his essay 'Objective Literature' (1954): 'Robbe-Grillet's importance is that he has attacked the last bastion of our traditional art of writing: the organisation of literary space. His endeavour is equal in importance to that of surrealism against rationality, or that of the Avant-Garde theatre (Beckett, Ionesco, Adamov) against the bourgeois stage.' Barthes' parallels were well chosen. The plays of Beckett, Ionesco, and Adamov did indeed take up the aesthetic of the *Nouveau Roman*, retaining its critical impetus, and transposing it to a realm where its implications for larger metaphysical questions would become apparent. These dramatists took their cue from the Existentialist philosophy of Albert Camus, theo-retician of the absurd. In his *Myth of Sisyphus* (1942), Camus had observed that 'in a universe suddenly divested of illusions and of light, man feels an alien, a stranger. His exile is without remedy, since he is deprived of the memory of a lost home or the hope of a promised land. This divorce between man and his life, the actor and his setting, is properly the feeling of absurdity'. Dramatists such as Eugène Ionesco, Ferdinand Arrabal and Jean Genet (the French school of Absurdist drama) endeavoured to make their readers recognise this existential fact, seeking to give voice to what the Romanian-French writer, Eugène Ionesco, has called the 'malaise of existence', 'an experience of the 'strangeness of the uni-verse, the banality of ordinary life shot through by horror'. As Ionesco explained in his essay 'Experience of the Theatre': 'We need to be virtually bludgeoned into detachment from our daily lives, our habits and mental laziness, which conceal from us the strange-ness of the world [...] The real must be in a way dislocated, before it can be reintegrated.' Ionesco, accordingly, structured his plays around grotesque images that attain absurdity by being framed within the discourse of normalcy. In *The Lesson* (1951), an otherwise innocuous tutorial between a professor and his student becomes the context for a murder, whilst in *The Bald Prima-Donna* (1950), social roles are reduced to linguistic clichés. In his most famous play, *The Rhinoceros* (1959), Ionesco described a society that has, through the gathering momentum of collective opinion, decided to turn itself into a community of rhinoceros. The target of the play is the ethos of consensus, whether that emanates from the common sense convictions of normal life or the explicitly totalitarian ones of Fascism and Communism. Ionesco seeks here to demystify all ideo-logies that seek to obliterate the distinction between individual dis-cernment and collective belonging. His ultimate goal was to make visible (as he later noted in an essay) the 'collective hysteria' that lurks beneath the surface of reason.[24]

Lacking the recognisable social context of Ionesco's plays, but with a greater sense for the metaphysical import of Absurdist themes, is Samuel Beckett's *Waiting for Godot* (1953). On a formal level, Beckett's play is paradigmatic of the non-representational and non-psychological trajectory of Absurdist drama: it posits action not as linear but as circular; character not as psychological but as emblematic; and the stage not as a simulation of an external reality but as a space for fantasy. The orgins of the play lie not in the theatrical gravitas of main-stream European drama, but in clowning and slapstick, mime, verbal gaming, and other tricks drawn from boulevard theatre. Like other Absurdist plays, *Waiting for Godot*, with its slender plot (structured around the confrontation between the two tramps, Estragon and Vladimir, and two other characters, the master and his slave, Pozzo and Lucky) is domi- nated by a mood of uncertainty and circularity: 'Nothing happens, nobody comes, nobody goes, it's awful.' The characters (the op- pressed and oppressors alike) are caught between an unspecified past and a perpetually postponed future, living out their lives through comic and sinister rituals, trapped (as Robbe-Grillet noted in an early review of the play) on the 'frontiers of dissolution', in a world of suggestive negativity where *'less than nothing'* happens.[25]

In his later plays, Beckett moved towards an ever greater reduc- tion of action and human agency in *Endgame* (1957), *Krapp's Last Tape* (1958) and *Happy Days* (1961), plays which explore blindness, permanent immobility and the inability of memory to restore iden- tity and sense of self. The sombre undertones of Beckett's plays, his characters' often cruel exercise of power over one another and their desire to subjugate and be subjugated, is heightened into ritualistic violence in the work of other Absurdist playwrights, such as Fernando Arrabal and Jean Genet. The latter had already antici- pated such themes in his novels, *Miracle of the Rose* (1946) and *Our Lady of the Flowers* (1944), which fuse erotic fantasy and violence in their explorations of the homosexual and transsexual world of the Parisian *demi-monde*. But it was in his plays, *The Maids* (1947), *The Balcony* (1957) and *The Blacks* (1959), that the ritualistic element in Genet's treatment of power and eroticism emerged most clearly. As the author himself has explained, these plays take place 'in a realm where morality is replaced by the aesthetics of the stage'; absurdity is here not simply an existential fact, an irrevocable part of the human condition, or the consequence of the loss of religious tran- scendence; it is intimately connected to the artificial ways that per- sonal identity is made and unmade in the social process; it is part of the theatricality of self. Whether it is the temporary exercise of power in *The Maids*, the assumption of revolutionary political in- tegrity in *The Balcony*, or slaves dissimulating confrontation with their white masters in *The Blacks*, individual attempts at self-asser- tion and personal autonomy in Genet's plays are seen to be purely theatrical gestures, requiring the gaze of the other for their legitima- tion, and hence affirming the code of repression that the protagonists wish to accept, even as they seemingly revolt against it. It is a world where identity and ceremony, character and role, are linked, often through rituals that involve violence, pain and bodily mutilation. In this respect, Genet's 'theatre of cruelty' was close to the work of the Spanish Absurdist, Fernando Arrabal, whose main plays, *Picnic on the Battlefield* (1952), *Fando and Lis* (1955), *The Two Executioners* (1956) and *The Car Cemetery* (1958), transpose the melo-dramatic element of Genet's treatment of ritual onto a terrain that is at once more impersonal and more surreal. Like Ionesco before him, Arrabal seeks to bring to the surface the cruelty and violence that he sees as part of the exercise of conventional morality. He brings the two realms together in characters such as François in *The Two Executioners*, and Fando in *Fando and Lis*, who regard the torture they inflict upon their respective spouses as necessary components of filial duty. Arrabal's later work, such as *The Architect and the Emperor of Assyria* (1967), is characterised by a dream logic that seeks to act out and give objective representation to the phobias and com-plexes that dominate the subconscious self.[26]

The Theatre of the Absurd found a broad echo throughout Europe. In England, Harold Pinter explored the countless rituals and customs, gestures and acts of phatic-communion with which we seek to impose coherence upon the incoherent, emphasising the potential for violence that exists beneath the surface of quotidian intercourse in *The Birthday Party* (1957), *The Dumb Waiter* and *The Caretaker* (both 1960); Brendan Behan dealt with the powerlessness of the social outsider in *The Quare Fellow* (1954) and *The Hostage* (1958); Joe Orton the susceptibility of individuals to erotic manipu-lation in *Entertaining Mr Sloane* (1964) and *Loot* (1966); and Tom Stoppard, the inherent theatricality of all behaviour and the cen-trality of role-playing to social life in *Rosencrantz and Guildenstern are dead* (1966), *Jumpers* (1972) and (with a sharper historical focus) *Travesties* (1974). Collapsing the distinction between dream and reality, conventional morality and criminality, role-playing and au-thenticity, and foregoing the conventional stage in favour of one that combined the circus, puppet show and religious ceremony, was a trajectory followed by dramatists throughout Europe in the Postmodern period. It is evident in authors as diverse as the German playwright, Wolfgang Hildesheimer (see his collection *Plays in which Darkness Falls*, 1958), the German-Swiss author, Max Frisch (*The Fire-raisers*, 1958), the French playwrights, Jean Tardieu (*Chamber Theatre*, 1955) and Boris Vian (*The Empire Builders*, 1959), and the Italian, Dino Buzzati (*A Clinical Case*, 1953). Even in Eastern Europe, where Stalin's death in 1953 had opened up possibilities for new literary forms, Absurd theatre flourished. In Poland, the main names were Slawomir Mrożek (*The Police*, 1958, and *Tango*, 1964), and Tadeusz Różewicz (*The Card Index*, 1960, and *The Witnesses*, 1962); whilst in Czechoslovakia, Václav Havel emerged as the most avant-garde playwright of his generation with *The Garden Party* (1963) and *The Memorandum* (1965). These exponents of the Absurd were able to draw upon a rich vein of indigenous mime and popular carnivalism, which was consciously revived in the slap-stick boulevard antics of Jerzy Afanasjew's 'Green Goose' Theatre. To this tradition and to that of the French school of Absurdists, plays written in the Eastern Bloc added a deep mistrust of abstractions, ideologies and principles, and a Kafkaesque focus upon the arbitrary nature of power and justice as exercised by the state and its anonymous bureaucracy. After 1968, when the thaw gave way to a new ice age of Soviet dominance, such plays could only be circulated in clandestine form as *samizdat* writing, their oppositional fervour and challenging Absurdism forced underground in a totalitarian society that was becoming (in the words of Havel, compelled into internal exile and then prison) increasingly 'merciless, gloomily serious, Asiatic, hard'.[27]

In Western Europe, the political potential of Absurdist drama was exploited with greater freedom, by, for example, Peter Handke, in Austria, and Dario Fo, in Italy. The latter's early work has clear affinities with the popular tradition of mime and circus favoured by Polish and Czech dramatists of the Absurd. Plays such as *Archangels Don't Play Pinball* (1959), *He Had Two Guns with Black and White Eyes* (1960) and *He who Steals a Foot is Lucky in Love* (1961) are iconoclastic, parodistic and irreverent, targeting institutions such as the Church, the State and the Media. The formal qualities of such plays, their impromptu textual status, their widespread use (as Fo himself has explained it) of that 'rich cultural heritage of popular culture, satire and grotesque farce', mark them as comedies. But with his most famous play, *The Accidental Death of an Anarchist* (1970) (which deals with the framing and likely defenestration by the police of an anarchist suspected of complicity in a bombing incident), the political implications of Fo's absurdist mode became apparent. The details of the anarchist's crime are reconstructed within the play by a confidence man, whose own investigations into the case reveal a legal system that is founded on deception and self-deception. Fo's later plays, *We Can't Pay, We Won't Pay* and *Fanfani Kidnapped* (both 1974), are clearly indebted to the *agitprop* tactics of the 1920s, although they retain elements from the Theatre of the Absurd.[28]

Fo's iconoclasm is also evident in the plays of Peter Handke, but the ironising anarchism of the former's work is replaced here by a more theoretically sophisticated and less populist re-configuration of the relationship between the theatre and its public. In his essay, 'Literature is Romantic' (1966), Handke advanced a new definition of politicised writing, one which eschewed the priorities of traditional committed theatre for a literature of direct intervention which would use the streets, factories and offices as the places for its performances. He called the plays that he wrote in the spirit of this theory 'speak-ins' (*Sprechstücke*), arguing that, in them, the plot and character of the traditional stage would be replaced by a discourse that makes use 'of swearing, of self-indictment, of confession, of testimony, of interrogation, of justification, of evasion, of prophecy, of calls for help'. Handke's most famous play, *Offending the Audience* (1966), for example, contains neither dramatic action nor *dramatis personae*, but structures its minimalist progress around a verbal confrontation between the 'actors' on the stage and the audience, who are made the subject of a process of accelerating vilification. Handke's plays are didactic, but they possess no clear message. His goal was (as he says in his preface to *Offending the Audience*) 'not to revolutionise the audience but to make it aware', conscious of itself as an ideological construct. This goal is also evident in Handke's subsequent plays, such as *Cries for Help* (1967) and the famous *Kaspar* (1968), which likewise focus upon the complex relationship between knowledge and power, demonstrating how definitions of the self come through the understanding and manipulation of language.[29]

More recent drama in Europe has combined the gestural politics of Fo and Handke with the Absurdist exploitation of the ritualistic and the surreal, producing in the process a complex body of work that both raises important issues of a social and existential nature, while problematising the conventions of the stage and its relationship to the public. This trajectory is evident in the work of the Germans Heiner Müller (*Germania: Death in Berlin* and *The Hamlet Machine*, both 1977), Botho Strauss (*Rendezvous Trilogy*, 1976, and *Kalldewey. Farce*, 1981) and Tankred Dorst (*Toller*, 1968, and *Ice Age*, 1973); in British playwrights such as Edward Bond (*Lear*, 1971),

Trevor Griffith (*The Comedians*, 1975), David Edgar (*The Shape of the Table*, 1990) and David Hare (*Plenty*, 1978); and in France in the plays of Michel Deutsch (*Sunday*, 1974), Jean-Claude Grumberg (*Dreyfus*, 1974, and *The Atelier*, 1979) and Michel Vinaver (*Iphigénie Hotel*, 1977, and *Flight into the Andies*, 1983). All take eclectically from the themes and techniques of Absurdist and post-Absurdist drama, but combine them with a revitalised theatre of political engagement, seeking to demonstrate (in Edward Bond's words) how 'knowledge and experience of the real world illuminate and reform subjective individuality'.[30]

5   SELF, HISTORY, MYTH: THE LITERATURE OF MAGIC REALISM

Roland Barthes, the *nouveau romancier*, had achieved a conceptual *tour de force*. He had broken not only with the literary sensibility of our 'ancestral reflexes', but also with the conceptual categories of time, space and causality that had been current since Kant and even Newton. Authors like Robbe-Grillet (Barthes argued) have successfully de-anthropomorphised the object-world, and opened up a literary space in which a 'new structure of matter and movement' can emerge. The phenomenological project outlined here by Barthes, which sought to deny any absolute distinctions between surface and depth, object and subject, was brought to fruition by a body of novelists whose style came to be characterised as 'Magic Realist'. They included some of the most productive figures in Postmodernist literature: Günter Grass, Italo Calvino, Salman Rushdie, J.G. Ballard, Thomas Bernhard, Michel Tournier and D.M. Thomas. As a genre, Magic Realism had its origins in South America, in a body of writing that sought to locate notions of unreality and surreality within the texture of everyday social life. Its seminal texts included Alejo Carpentier, *The Lost Steps* (1953), Carlos Fuentes, *Where the Air is Clear* (1958), Jorge Luis Borges, *Fictions* (1962), and Gabriel García Márquez, *One Hundred Years of Solitude* (1967). Salman Rushdie defined Magic Realism as a 'development out of Surrealism that expresses a genuinely 'Third World' consciousness', reminding us not only that the style has its origins in South American literature, but that it embodies that feeling of otherness that many ethnic minorities and other groups marginalised by the Western intellectual tradition have experienced.

The French author, Michel Tournier, has offered a broader, more metaphysical definition. He characterised his writing as a 'cosmic' comedy, which knows that 'the real world, rife with contradictions and bristling with absurdities, is a fabric full of holes', a porous weave that can only be stopped through the agency of the active imagination. Such sentiments were shared by Italo Calvino, who described his own 'phenomenological' approach as the result of a desire 'to break through the screen of words and concepts and see the world as if it appeared for the first time to our sight'. In textual terms, the magic realist novel retained both the representational import of Realism and its humanist focus upon suffering, moral choice and historical tragedy; but refracted these concerns through such Postmodernist techniques as the self-conscious narrator, the abandonment of linear narrative and the drawing of apsychological characters. Above all, the magic realist novel collapsed traditional distinctions between the fantastic and the normal, the supernatural and the natural, the objective and the subjective, in an attempt to demonstrate, using myths and recurrent symbols, how these spheres interact to determine private lives and national destinies.[31]

Magic Realism did not, however, emerge *ab ovo*. A tradition of fabulation and fantasy had long existed in European literature, in the Gothic fiction of the late eighteenth and nineteenth centuries, which ran from Horace Walpole's *The Castle of Otranto* (1764) and Mary Shelley's *Frankenstein* (1818), through to Bram Stoker's *Dracula* (1897) and the science fiction of H.G. Wells and Zamyatin. This tradition re-emerged in the Postmodern period. It is evident in the hallucinogenic novels of Aldous Huxley (*Island*, 1962), in the neo-medieval cultism of Tolkien's *Lord of the Rings* (1954–1955), in Doris Lessing's psychiatric explorations (such as her *Briefing for a Descent into Hell*, 1971), and in the work of new-age science-fictionists, such as J.G. Ballard (*The Atrocity Exhibition*, 1970, *Crash*, 1973, and *Myths of the Near Future*, 1982) and the Polish writer, Stanislaw Lem (*Solaris*, 1961, *The Cyberiad*, 1965, and *Imaginary Magnitude*, 1984). Typical of much literature written in the Postmodern age, these novels make the cross-over between high and popular culture, using contemporary scientific theory to form a bridge between the two realms. Ballard, in particular, frames his project within the context of philosophical challenges to the status of the stable mechanical world. As the author has noted: 'We live inside an enormous novel. For the writer, in particular, it is less and less necessary for him to invent the fictional content of his novel. The fiction is already there. The writer's task is to invent reality'. That these realities are polymorphous as well as ontologically ambiguous is clear from the contexts of Ballard's own fiction, which moves between the urban tribalism and motorised manias of the modern city (in *High Rise*, 1976), through the timeless seascape of *The Drowned World* (1962), to Ballard's autobiographical account of his childhood in war-torn China, in his best known novel, *Empire of the Sun* (1984). Throughout these discrete worlds runs an apocalyptic mood that avoids fatalism only by invoking the possibility of escape through technology, creative fantasy and 'the dream's awareness of its own identity'.[32]

The ambit of Magic Realism was broad. It included writers as diverse as Italo Calvino (*The Cloven Viscount*, 1952, *The Baron in the Trees*, 1957, and *The Non-existent Knight*, 1959), Miguel Delibes (*Parable of the Shipwrecked Man*, 1969), Salman Rushdie (*Midnight's Children*, 1981, and *Shame*, 1983), Thomas Bernhard (*The Gargoyles*, 1967, and *Auslöschung*, 1986), Michel Tournier (*The Erl King*, 1970, and *Gemini*, 1975), D.M. Thomas (*The White Hotel*, 1981), Jeanette Winterson (*The Passion*, 1987, and *Sexing the Cherry*, 1989) and the prolific output of Günter Grass. Magic Realism brought the mythopoetic logic of fantasy into worlds that were historically and socially recognisable, such as Grass' Third Reich in his *Tin Drum*, and Rushdie's Pakistan in his *Midnight's Children*. In these novels, the moral, social and political shortcomings of these societies are exposed through the perspectives of quasi fairy-tale figures, such as the ogre in Tournier's *The Erl-King*, the boy-dwarf, Oskar, in Grass' *The Tin Drum*, or the nun in Calvino's *The Non-existent Knight*. Such characters are empowered with magical gifts that allow them to impose their fantasies upon the real world. The narratives that they produce conflate memory and desire, and use shifting and contradictory points of view, circular and repetitive time scales, labyrinthine plots, the doubling of events and the use of the *Doppelgänger* motif (as in the mirror-protagonists of Tournier's *Gemini*) to conjure up worlds where rationality is replaced by the deeper logic of dream and fantasy. As Rushdie noted with respect to his own novel, the material world appears here in fantastic guises; 'trivial things seem like symbols, and the mundane acquires numinous qualities'. They are symbols for a people 'obsessed with correspondences'.[33]

In spite of their insistence upon the importance of subjective myth-making, the exponents of Magic Realism were, nevertheless, committed to a recognisable 'historical project', to a 'confrontation with history', of the immediate past but also of the present. The political objectives of the Magic Realist school are most evident in the writings of Günter Grass. His early 'Danzig trilogy' – *The Tin Drum* (1959), *Cat and Mouse*, (1961) and *Dog Years* (1963) – was set in the Third Reich, and dealt with the values, rituals and absurdities of National Socialist ideology, and their impingement on everyday life. In his more recent fiction, most notably *Local Anaesthetic* (1969), *The Flounder* (1977), *From the Diary of a Snail* (1972) and *Headbirths, or the Germans are Dying out* (1980), Grass applies the techniques of Magic Realism to the issues of the present. The contemporary world may be less under threat from totalitarian politics, but it is, nevertheless, in danger of becoming a victim of new obsessions, new irrationalities, every bit as dangerous as National Socialism: 'technological mysticism, aggressions spawned by the mass media, terrorism, productivity [and] the parallel increase of pollution and prosperity'. Grass' opposition to such threats is unambiguously resolute. And yet, in spite of their avowal of democratic-socialist, feminist and ecological points of view, these novels evince a more pessimistic and even apocalyptic tone, which is a product of the author's perception of a future, which he sees 'altogether shrouded in mist, open at most to speculation'.[34]

Grass' later work seeks to demonstrate that individuals are irrevocably embroiled in the public sphere of politics even when they believe themselves defined through the purely personal realm of dream and sexual fantasy. It is precisely this relationship between private fantasy and historical nightmare that D.M. Thomas explores in his remarkable novel, *The White Hotel* (1981). The story tells of the opera singer, Lisa Erdman, of her career, her personal life, and her extended psycho-analytic treatment by Freud. Lisa is a two-fold victim: as a Jew, she suffers under the Nazi occupancy of Russia, dying at Babi Yar; but as a patient of Freud, she undergoes an uncovering of the self that is equally barbaric, being subject to practices that were (according to the author) 'pathetic metaphors of the *real* hallucinations of an event such as Babi Yar'. Thomas attempts to link the personal and political realms by combining fictionalised private journals, reports from psychiatric doctors, with Freud's non-fictional case studies and letters, and poetry. The result is a novel that gives shape to a notion of self that is both inherently complex and historically conditioned, a product of that collective 'libidinous fantasy' with which Thomas, and Magic Realist novelists in general, sought to bring their readers into contact.[35]

6 STRUCTURES OF SUBJECTIVITY: POSTMODERNISM AND THE POETIC TEXT

The bond between poetry and the Romantic notion of poetic creativity had already been severed in the Modernist period, by poets such as Paul Valéry and Gottfried Benn, who refused to see their work as simple expressions of the creative self, agreeing with T.S. Eliot that the poetic act represented an 'escape from personality'. In a period endemically suspicious of all humanist paradigms, these tendencies were intensified and put on a theoretical basis by French Structuralists such as Roland Barthes ('The Death of the Author', 1968) and Michel Foucault ('What is an Author?', 1969), who subjected notions such as authorial intentionality and artistic expressivity to a sustained critique. The notion of 'the author', they argued, was simply a convenient construct, produced by literary critics seeking to reduce complicated patterns of meaning to unambiguous authorial intention; the real author of texts (called by Barthes a 'scriptor') was, on the contrary, part of a subtle linguistic process whose ambit was the 'eternally written here and now', and whose product was the book as a polysemic entity that resisted ultimate interpretation, being a 'tissue of signs, an imitation that is lost, infinitely deferred'.[36]

For many poets in the Postmodern period, this problematisation of the Romantic notion of subjectivity closed down certain avenues of writing, as it opened up others. The Italian poet and film-maker, Pier Paolo Pasolini, for example, embraced the dissolution of the authorial subject, but sought its reconstitution through the agency of language. As he noted in his essay 'From the laboratory' (1965): 'I, by speaking – in the pure and simple act of speaking – live a structure that is in the process of being structured: I myself contribute to such a structuration, and I know it, but I don't know what it is founded on, and what it will be.' His own poetry (*Gramsci's Ashes*, 1957, *The Religion of my Age*, 1961, and *Poetry in the form of a Rose*, 1964) is firmer in voice than this statement would suggest; nevertheless Pasolini's idiom reflects the self-removal of the artistic subject, which seemed to him to be the precondition for that stark, impersonal language, which alone was capable of capturing (as in 'The Ditch Digger's Tears', 1957), the 'humble/sordid, confused, immense reality', swarming in the slums of a swiftly urbanising Italy.[37]

For other poets, the surrender of subjectivity entailed a near mystical dissolution of the self in the phenomenal world. This was the case with the most important French poet of this period, Yves Bonnefoy. In his major works (*On the Motion and the Immobility of Douve*, 1953, *In Yesterday's Desert Dominion*, 1958, *Words in Stone*, 1965, and *The Lure of the Threshold*, 1975), Bonnefoy attempted to realise the Symbolist dream of returning the world to magic by purifying language of its quotidian banalities. As the poet argued in an essay of 1977, words must be made to 'detach themselves, as words of communion, of meaning, from the web of concepts'; this alone permits the 'advent of being in its own absoluteness'. The volume, *The Lure of the Threshold*, in particular, charts this struggle to make language transparent with the radiance of the object-world, containing poems which are self-contained verbal icons, poems dislocated from syntax and linearity. One such text is 'The Clouds', the concluding words of which point both to the defeat and the triumph of Bonnefoy's vision: 'Here is the task/I cannot finish. Here, the words/I will not speak./Here, the black/Pool, in the storm-cloud/Here, the blind spot/In the glance of an eye'.[38]

Hermetic, paradoxical and quasi-surreal, Bonnefoy's poetry tried to capture modulations of self and identity barely accessible to consciousness. A similar trajectory was followed by the Jewish Rumanian-German writer, Paul Celan. His poetry, published in volumes such as *Poppy and Memory* (1952), *From Threshold to Threshold* (1955) and *The Gates of Language* (1959), is both exhortation and lament, a complex emotional position that seeks to keep the memory of the Holocaust alive, not directly but through powerfully charged allegory, as in the famous, 'Fugue of Death' (1952). Celan described his work as 'language actualised, set free under the sign of a radical individuation which, however, remains as aware of the limits drawn by language as of the possibilities it opens'. This is a poetry which speaks, but remains aware of the impossibility of full speech. Celan called the gap between the assertion of the poetic statement and its withholding through insecurity or incomprehensibility 'the turning-point of breath' (*Atemwende*). The exhortation made in the poem 'Speak, you also' (1955): 'Speak −/But keep yes and no unsplit,/And give your say this meaning:/Give it the shade', was one that he himself followed throughout a body of work committed to areas of experience, (personal and historical) that must necessarily remain beyond the easy grasp of intelligibility.[39]

Celan's influence was immense. It is evident in the work of the Egyptian-French writer (of Jewish descent), Edmond Jabès (*The Questions*, 1963–1973), as it is in the sombre, understated verse of the Austrian poet, Ingeborg Bachmann (*Time Suspended*, 1953, and *Invocation of the Great Bear*, 1956), and in the work of the East German, Johannes Bobrowski (*Sarmatian Time*, 1961, and *Sign of the Approaching Storm*, 1966). The difficulty of witnessing, the loss of language through emigration, the problem of speaking of the suffering of self without pathos, are also themes explored by the Russian Nobel prize-winning poet, Joseph Brodsky. Castigated as a 'social parasite' in his native country, Brodsky was forced into American exile in 1972, from where he published some of his most important poems. In his major work, poems such as 'Elegy for John Donne' (1963), 'Verses on T.S. Eliot' (1965) and 'Nature Morte' (1971), Brodsky explored the relationship between language, exile and identity, those 'borderline situations' that exist for the *émigré* between assimilation and alienation. The stoicism (but also the residual optimism) that displacement gives rise to is evident throughout his verse, such as the autobiographical poem 'May 24, 1980' (1980): 'Now I am forty./What should I say about life? That it's long and abhors transparence./Broken eggs make me grieve; the omelette, though, makes me vomit./Yet until brown clay has been crammed down my larynx,/Only gratitude will be gushing from it'. In the final analysis, Brodsky's poetry can be read (as Brodsky noted with respect to the poetry of Marina Tsvetaeva) as a 'plea for the cause [of those condemned to experience] existence on the edge'.[40]

A similar perspective is evident in poets writing in the Eastern Bloc countries. Polish poets, in particular, such as Tadeusz Różewicz (*Anxiety*, 1947, *The Red Glove*, 1948, and *Faces of Anxiety*, 1969), the Nobel Prize-winner Czesław Miłosz (*City without a Name*, 1969, *Hymn of the Pearl*, 1983, and *Unattainable Earth*, 1984) and Zbigniew Herbert (*Chord of Light*, 1956, *A Study of the Object*, 1961, and *Pan cogito* 1974) attempted to find an idiom that could register the pain of their predicament without dissolving into self-pity. In a context in which self-expression was a political (but, often, politically impossible) act, these poets of internal exile look ironically upon heroic constructions of the artistic subject. As Herbert confides in the poem 'The Knocker' (1957): 'my imagination/is a piece of board/and to complete the instrument/I have a wooden stick/I strike the board/and it answers/yes – yes/no – no'. But Herbert's board was heard by many who were aware of the menace, fear and moral turpitude that surrounded them, and who, like the poet, also chose to 'obey the counsels of the inner eye/[and] admit no one'.[41]

Elsewhere in Europe, poets tried to win through to a deeper notion of personal identity, evoking in the process atavistic or mythic notions of the self. Representative of this trend were Ted Hughes and Seamus Heaney, in England and Ireland, László Nagy, in Hungary, and Vaska Popa, in Serbia. In their work, Hughes and Heaney had the example of the great Welsh poet, Dylan Thomas, before them. Thomas's early poems, 'The force that drives the green fuse drives the flower', 'And death shall have no dominion' (both 1933), 'Poem in October' (1944) and 'A Refusal to Mourn the Death, by Fire, of a Child in London' (1945) possess a strikingly elemental quality, which derives from the poet's faith in the continually re-newing, continually regenerating power of spirit in nature. Hughes (*Hawk in the Rain*, 1957, and *Lupercal*, 1960) and Heaney (*Death of a Naturalist*, 1966, *Door into the Dark*, 1969, *Wintering Out*, 1972, and *North*, 1975), also look to nature as a source of authenticity; but here there is a more sober articulation of the relationship between mankind and the phenomenal world. Hughes, in particular, grants a special autonomy to the brute facticity of the animal kingdom, celebrating in poems such as 'The Hawk in the Rain' (1957) and 'The Otter' (1960) the raw vitality of the animal spirit, as if it alone is able to achieve unity of self in a Post-modern age marked by doubt and confusion. Hughes deepened this position into a virtual animism in *Crow* (1970), whose central character (half animal, half myth) articulates his uncompromising philosophy of the world 'from a buried cell of bloody blackness'. These poems constitute a paean upon the raw energies of nature, in which procreation and death, renewal and destruction inextricably belong (in Hughes' thinking) to the same amoral universe.[42]

In his poetry, the Hungarian, László Nagy (*The Bride of the Sun*, 1954, and *Hymn for Anytime*, 1965), finds a perspective upon the troubles of his contemporary Hungary by identifying himself with those rituals and customs that inform the popular mind, and help make sense of life in periods of confusing historical change. His outlook is at its most genial (almost Larkinesque) in 'Pleasuring Sunday' (1955) and 'Wedding' (1964), which celebrate the 'sudden urge to create anew' (biologically and culturally) amidst the 'stone scriptures' of the past and present. The poet Vasko Popa (*Bark*, 1953, and *The Unrest Field*, 1956) also attempts to link the personal and the historical, in his case by grafting the symbolism and iconography of his native Serbia onto a highly personal cosmography. As Ted Hughes notes, in Popa's poetry 'heads, tongues, spirits, hands, flames, magically vitalised wandering objects, such as apples and moons, present themselves, animated with strange but strangely familiar destinies'. Popa's object-world is a hieroglyphic system, the key to which is now personal, now historical, as in the 'Song of the Tower of Skulls' (from the volume *Earth Erect*, 1972), which begins: 'For the great-eyed sunflower you gave us/Blind stone your unface/And what now monster./You made us one with yourself/With the emptiness in your empty poison-tooth/With your dock-tailed eternity/Is that all your secret?'. Often without punctuation, diacritics or familiar syntax, Popa's poetry hovers between statement and question, focussing upon archetypal images of birth and destruction, as if his goal is to reach the source of the collective unconscious of his people, and (indeed) of human kind, in general.[43]

There were poets, however, who granted neither history nor nature a determining presence in their poetic discourses, but language itself, conceived of in its pure materiality, as a textual reality on the page. The French poet, Francis Ponge, was one such poet. His writing, over a period of half a century, consistently accorded a unique respect to the typographical dimensions of the poetic utterance. Ponge believed that the poem was not a finished object, a verbal icon, but simply one point in an ongoing process of writing, an evolving intertext. His publications, *Taking the Side of Things* (1942), *Proêmes* (1948) and *The Making of the Pré* (1971), are, consequently, largely revisions and commentaries on an *Urtext* that does not (and possibly, never will) exist. *The Making of the Pré* is typical of his work. Around a central poetic narrative, Ponge structures a diary account of the genesis of the poem, speculations regarding the etymology of its key terms, quotations from linguistic philosophers, photographs, drawings and paintings. All of which are interwoven in an elaborate textual process, which is given structure by a continuous system of punning on the two meanings of 'pré' in the title (meaning both 'before' and 'meadow'). The result is both a Postmodern version of the *Dinggedicht* (favoured by Modernist poets such as Rilke), and a gentle paean to the 'marvelously tedious/ Monotony and variety of the world,/In short, its perpetuity'.[44]

Ponge's *The Making of the Pré* was, in many respects, a supreme example of one of the most popular genres within Postmodern versification: concrete poetry. The genre attracted some of the most linguistically creative minds of this generation: Ernst Jandl in Austria; Ian Hamilton Finlay in Britain; Lamberto Pignotti and Nanni Balestrini in Italy; Helmut Heissenbüttel and Max Bense in Germany; and Eugen Gomringer in Switzerland. These were persuasive advocates of their discipline. Gomringer described concrete poetry as a 'reality in itself, not a poem about something or other', a definition expanded by Bense who typified it as a 'style of material poetry', which was 'not subject to the conventional rules of grammar and syntax', but was ruled by 'unique visually and structurally oriented models'. These goals seem realised in *Occasional Poems and Blurbs* (1973) and *The Splitting of the Cabbage* (1974) by Heissenbüttel. Both volumes include poems of autotelic formalism, texts constructed, for example, around the repetition of key words, and formed into a series without punctuation or syntax (the so-called *perpetuum mobile*). Bereft of conventional stanza encasement, such poems become free-floating semantic units, creative possibilities rather than finally formed utterances, whose sheer indeterminacy forces the reader into entirely new ways of reading and interpreting.[45]

Heissenbüttel believed that the stark and confusing form of his poetry contained a necessary political moment; dislocating expectations of form and structure it could be seen as a 'demonstration' against those normalising ideologies that foreclose analysis and action. The Italian poets, Alfredo Giuliani (*Poor Juliet and Other Poetry*, 1965) and Nanni Balestrini (*Other Procedures*, 1966) (members of the 1960 'novissimi' group), and Lamberto Pignotti (founding member of Gruppo '63), foregrounded the political implications of this textual interrogation. Pignotti (*The Provocative Nude*, 1965, and *A Form of Lottery*, 1967), in particular, sought to create not only a different type of poetry, but also a different space for what he termed 'seen poetry' (*poesia visiva*). Its publication would not be through the traditional channels of book and journal, but through the juke-box, advertising hoardings, loudspeakers at sporting events and even matchboxes. The poetry of Hans Magnus Enzensberger is less radical in its formal procedures, but he too writes anti-poetry that is critical of consumer society and technological civilisation. His most important work, *In Defence of Wolves*

(1957), *Native Speech* (1960), *Braille* (1964) and *Disappearing Furies* (1980), is both politically committed and simultaneously conversational in tone and terminology. Not poetic transport, but the refusal of flight, not intoxication, but sobriety, not the loss of critical acumen, but its sharpening through ideological and linguistic vigilance is the goal of this verse. Such concerns are evident in his best-known poems, such as 'In a Textbook for the Twelfth Form', 'Social Partners in the Armaments' Industry' (both 1957), 'Portrait of a Pimp' (1964), 'Song of those for whom everything is relevant and who know everything already' (1967) and 'The Shits' (1971), whose very titles indicate both the controlled anger of Enzensberger's verse and its rejection of traditional poetic themes. The Postmodernist direction of Enzensberger's writing is most evident in *The Sinking of the Titanic* (1978), an extended narrative on the sinking of the famous ship, which includes not only an account of the genesis of the poem, but also theoretical meditations about that narrative, as well as upon literature, history and historiography. The poet's disclosure, 'it is my pleasure to recover a text/that probably never existed. I fake my own work', draws our attention to the purely fabulatory status of Enzensberger's project. It is a gesture of honesty that might be read in sharp contrast to the elaborate process of self-deception and self-aggrandisement that surrounded the public promotion of the unsinkability of the Titanic three-quarters of a century earlier.[46]

7 WRITTEN AS THE BODY: FEMINIST WRITING AND POSTMODERNISM

Postmodernism was not simply a literary movement or category of scholarly classification; it was also a complex philosophical and cultural movement that sought to explicate and re-define notions of political agency and subjectivity. In the immediate post-war period, the terms of this process of definition were largely Marxist, the product of a rediscovery of the work of Walter Benjamin, Georg Lukács and Theodor Adorno. These were sophisticated theorists of the Left, who refracted their analysis of the classic tropes of Marxist analysis, categories such as class, ideology and false consciousness, through an awareness of the determining influence of aesthetic and symbolic forms. Their work was further developed by neo-Marxists such as Louis Althusser (*For Marx*, 1969), and by post-Marxists such as Michel Foucault (*Discipline and Punish*, 1975), who emphasised the local technologies of power, 'how things work at the level of on-going subjugation, at the level of those continuous and uninter-rupted processes which subject our bodies, govern our gestures, dictate our behaviours'.[47]

This inter-relationship between politics in the public sphere and the exercise of power in the private was also explored by writers in the Postmodernist period, such as the Czech novelist, Milan Kundera. His novels, *The Joke* (1967), *Life is Elsewhere* (1973) and *The Book of Laughter and Forgetting* (1979), deal with the tensions between private morality and public definitions of the truth in po-litical states that are closed to flexibility and inquiry. That govern-ments in such societies exercise their control over individuals through the manipulation of the inner lives of people as much as through direct force is the theme of Kundera's most famous work, *The Unbearable Lightness of Being*, published in 1984. The novel con-stitutes a meditation upon the relationship between the private sphere (here love between a man and a woman), and historical change (the Soviet invasion of Czechoslovakia), describing charac-ters who move back and forth between living for themselves (light-ness), and a commitment to higher moral and political choices (weight). Like the nations of which they are a part, these individu-als must establish their place in a world that remains both ener-gised but also, in a strange way, terrorised by that infinite 'realm of possibility' that is history.[48]

The most systematic and, perhaps, the most ethically persuasive exploration of this relationship between personal and political power was, however, undertaken by a generation of women writers working in Europe and, most notably, in France. Some of the major figures here were Simone de Beauvoir, Julia Kristeva, Luce Irigaray, and Hélène Cixous. Supported by initiatives from within the Anglo-American women's movement, represented by seminal texts such as Betty Friedan's *The Feminine Mystique* (1963), Kate Millett's *Sexual Politics* and Germaine Greer's *The Female Eunuch* (both 1970), these feminist theorists sought to make visible the otherwise excluded presence of women in history and society. In the process, they gave a central place in their thinking to the concept of 'Otherness', which they identified with those disruptive energies that resist assimilation into the ordered systems of phallocentric thought that have traditionally governed Western thinking. The major statements of European feminism include Beauvoir's *The Second Sex* (1949), Irigaray's *Speculum of the Other Woman* (1974), Leclerc's *Word of Woman* (1974), Cixous' 'The Laugh of the Medusa' (1975) and Kristeva's *Polylogue* (1977). These studies move between analysis and critique, empirical classification (Beauvoir) and post-structuralist speculation (Irigaray), giving particular weight to the agency of language, which is held to work largely at the level of the unconscious, in positioning and defining female (and male) subjectivity. In the work of these writers, the body is lent a particular potency, visceral, productive (and sometimes) irrational. Recuperating this realm is both a social and ecological necessity. Cisoux puts their message in her characteristically imperative mode: 'write your self. Your body must be heard. Only then will the immense resources of the unconscious spring forth.' On the back of this theoretical re-valorisation of gender identity, what has been traditionally conceived of as alien otherness, and located to that 'place reserved for the guilty', can now be rearticulated as 'native strength', as a speech that opens into a new vision of that which can be.[49]

Given the diversity and complexity of the feminist movement, it is not surprising women writers engaged with this agenda in different ways. In England, Iris Murdoch took up philosophical themes in *Under the Net* (1954), *The Bell* (1958) and *The Sea, the Sea* (1978), which largely derived from her interest in Existentialism and the writings of Jean-Paul Sartre; whilst Muriel Spark, the author of *Momento Mori* (1959) and *The Prime of Miss Jean Brodie* (1961), added to Murdoch's concern with the dangers of false orders a theological focus on guilt and retribution. Female characters figure prominently in such novels, but the problems they encounter are not specifically women's issues, as they are in the novels of Edna O'Brien (*The Country Girls*, 1960, and *The Girl with Green Eyes*, 1962) and Margaret Drabble (*Jerusalem the Golden*, 1967, and *The Ice Age*, 1977), who frequently explore the tension between female self-assertion and the confinements of the patriarchal family and prescribed female roles. Similar themes were taken up by the French writer Françoise Sagan in her best-selling *Bonjour Tristesse* (1954), and by the Italian writer, Natalia Ginzburg, in her autobiographical *Family Sayings* (1963). Another Italian writer, Elsa Morante, paints on a broader canvas, positioning her women within the sweep of contemporary history, in novels such as *House of Liars* (1948), *Arturo's Island* (1957) and, particularly, *History: A Novel* (1974). Morante's novels give voice to a form of humanism that emerges through a feminine, but not necessarily feminist, perspective. The same might be said of the fiction of Doris Lessing, whose novels, from *The Grass is Singing* (1950) and *The Children of Violence* sequence (published between 1952 and 1969), through to *Briefing for a Descent into Hell* (1971) and *The Diaries of Jane Somers* (1984), work through insights gleaned from a number of contexts, political, post-colonial and psychoanalytic. The central text of Lessing's corpus, *The Golden Notebook* (1962), brings these diverse concerns together in the figure of Anna Wulf. Her search for womanhood is at the same time a search for artistic and personal self-fulfilment, which she achieves, moving from self-destructive emotions, such as anger and resentment, to a more positive welcoming of experience, arriving at that 'delight one feels at whatever is alive, the delight of recognition'.[50]

Feminist literature in Europe may have lacked the programmatic force of American feminist fiction in this period, as evident, for example, in Marge Piercy's *Woman on the Edge of Time* (1976), or Marilyn French's *The Women's Room* (1977), in which women are seen as victims of a hostile male world resistant to change and accommodation. Nevertheless, European writers, such as Marguerite Duras in France, Christa Wolf in Germany, Elsa Morante in Italy, Gert Brantenberg in Norway, Montserrat Roig in Spain, and Angela Carter in England, did take up issues that were both theoretically complex and socially urgent, issues relating to the politics of eroticism and pornography, the commercialisation of the female body, and the problem of bi- and trans-sexuality. Duras' work, in particular, from *The Square* (1955), *Moderato Cantabile* (1958) and the film script *Hiroshima, mon amour* (1959) through to *The Lover* (1984), opened a space for a uniquely female voice in literature, for a style of writing, a 'feminist literature' (*écriture feminine*), that was (as Duras explained) 'translated from blackness, from the unknown, like a new way of communicating rather than an already formed language'. *The Lover* bears witness to this new style: hovering ambiguously between autobiography and fictional narrative, between confession and analysis, it forms its account of the formation of female subjectivity within the bourgeois family through a *bricolage* of images, memories, and descriptions of feelings that engage directly with Oedipal complexes, incest taboos and inter-racial relationships. Duras' aim in her novel was to deconstruct the myth of heterosexuality, to free those who are caught within its confines both from their utopian longing for the 'perfect duality of desire', but also from an endemic role-playing that requires a violence to the self (and to others) for such a myth to be maintained. The contribution of image and self-image to the exercise of sexual power is also a theme of much of Angela Carter's fiction, most notably *The Magic Toyshop* (1967), *The Infernal Desire Machines of Doctor Hoffman* (1972), *The Bloody Chamber* (1979) and *Wise Children* (1991). Throughout Carter's corpus runs the concern to break with essentialist notions of femininity, and with systems of social classification that allocate women to a narrow range of biologically-fixed roles, such as the protectress, the helper, the wife, seductress or mother. In *The Bloody Chamber*, Carter re-writes fairy stories such as 'Little Red Riding Hood' and 'Beauty and the Beast', transforming them into parables of sexual conflict and transgression; whilst in *The Magic Toyshop*, familial relationships are posited as the sources for control and definition of gender. In these works and others, women are installed as 'beings of power', as active agents in the imaginary worlds that govern sexual and political discourses, alike.[51]

That resistance to patriarchy will involve active struggle is a premiss accepted by every feminist writer, from Duras to Christa Wolf. As a militant philosophy, it is stated in its most radical form by the French writer (resident in America), Monique Wittig. Wittig espouses what she calls a 'materialist lesbianism' which has as its motivating energy the desire to 'destroy politically, philosophically, and symbolically the categories of "men" and "women" '. As such, she makes cause with the other feminist writers who view sexuality not as a fixed grid but as a fluid reality, a spectrum on which individuals are located between the artificial poles of masculinity and femininity. It is a vision of gender beyond biological determinism. In her two works of fiction (*The Warriors*, 1969, and *The Lesbian Body*, 1973), Wittig dramatically reverses those phallocentric paradigms which juxtapose woman as the Other, as Unreason, as Darkness, to the 'parameter of the One, of Male, of Light'. In *The Warriors*, Wittig celebrates the militancy and resourcefulness of her Amazonian heroines, whilst in *The Lesbian Body*, it is the female form itself (for so long purely the object of male discourse) which comes to the fore, transformed into virtually a speaking subject in its own right, with its unique syntax and grammar. In the former text, masculinity is openly destroyed; in the latter it is actively transcended, displaced by a vision of a new society that will merge the 'fictional, symbolic and the actual' on the basis of a shared lesbian communality.[52]

The German feminist, Christa Wolf, on the other hand, seeks to keep a dialogue between men and women open, not for sentimental or romantic reasons (although there is no refusal of heterosexuality in her work), but from a pressing recognition that *Realpolitik* (the exercise of political and military power by men) is a reality that women must learn to understand and come to terms with. This concern (it is true) is not directly evident in Wolf's early novels (*The Quest for Christa T.*, 1968, and *A Model Childhood*, 1976), although both works explore the connections between the evolution of their heroines and patriarchal political systems: East German Communism in the former work, and Nazism in the latter. These novels are certainly written from a distinctive female perspective, but it was only in *Cassandra* (1983) that a clear statement in defence of feminist politics emerged. The novel combines a fictional account of the tribulations of the Trojan priestess, gifted with foresight, but shunned by her countrymen, with an extended autobiographical account of how Wolf chose and developed her theme during a visit to Greece. Around this complex weaving of fact and fiction, Wolf develops a sophisticated critique of the scientific, rationalist, utilitarian, mechanistic 'hierarchal male reality principle' that the author (in common with many feminists) holds responsible for that 'leaning toward self-destruction' that is a characteristic of patriarchal power. Castigated as an eccentric, her prophecies deprecated and neglected, Cassandra fails to steer the community of which she is a part away from military catastrophe. Her fate, Wolf argues, must not be shared by the women of today, many of whom likewise find themselves witnesses of ecological ruin and impending nuclear disaster. Patriarchal discourse must be opened, its terms of reference re-written, alternative sources of self-assertion and legitimation created, both for men and women alike, and grandiose dreams of militarist expansion elided in favour of those more modest satisfactions which centre on the 'inconspicuous, the precious everyday, the concrete'. Upon this basis (the novel argues) a new humanism is possible, one which will not only retain matriarchal values (rather than banning them into an alien otherness), but will also prove capable of absorbing the workings of difference/

différance, political, sexual and linguistic, into a serviceable strategy for survival.[53]

8   THE LITERATURE OF POSTMODERNISM:
A CHRONOLOGY

1938, Beckett, *Murphy*.
1939, Joyce, *Finnegan's Wake*.
1940, Buzzati, *Il Deserto dei Tartari* (The Tartar Steppe).
1942, Camus, *Le Mythe de Sisyphe* (The Myth of Sisyphus).
1944, Genet, *Notre-Dame-des-fleurs* (Our Lady of the Flowers).
1944, Malaparte, *Kaputt*.
1945, Broch, *Der Tod des Vergil* (The Death of Vergil).
1945, Carlo Levi, *Cristo si è fermato a Eboli* (Christ Stopped at Eboli).
1946, Thomas, *Deaths and Entrances*.
1947, Lowry, *Under the Volcano*.
1947, Genet, *Les Bonnes* (The Maids).
1947, Primo Levi, *Se questo è un uomo* (If this is a Man).
1947, Rózêwicz, *Niepokój* (Anxiety).
1948, Sarraute, *Portrait d'un inconnu* (Portrait of a Stranger).
1948, Nossack, *Interview mit dem Tode* (Interview with Death).
1949, Beauvoir, *Le Deuxième Sexe* (The Second Sex).
1950, Pavese, *La luna e i falò* (The Moon and the Bonfire).
1951, Moravia, *Il conformista* (The Conformist).
1951, Cela, *La colmena* (The Hive).
1952, Arrabal, *Pique-nique en campagne* (Picnic on the Battlefield).
1952, Ionesco, *Les Chaises* (The Chairs).
1952, Celan, *Mohn und Gedächtnis* (Poppy and Memory).
1952, Ginzburg, *Tutti i nostri ieri* (All our Yesterdays).
1953, Popa, *Kora* (Bark).
1953, Barthes, *Le Degré Zéro de l'écriture* (Writing Degree Zero).
1953, Beckett, *En attendant Godot* (Waiting for Godot).
1953, Bachmann, *Die gestundete Zeit* (Time Suspended).
1953, Böll, *Und sagte kein einziges Wort* (Acquainted with the Night).
1954, Frisch, *Stiller* (I am not Stiller).
1954, Golding, *Lord of the Flies*.
1954, Beauvoir, *Les Mandarins* (The Mandarins).
1954, Erenburg, *Ottepel* (The Thaw).
1954, Murdoch, *Under the Net* .
1954, Behan, *The Quare Fellow*.
1954, Juan Goytisolo, *Juegos de manos* (The Assassins).
1955, Adamov, *Le Ping-Pong* (Ping Pong).
1955, Robbe-Grillet, *Le Voyeur* (The Voyeur).
1956, Butor, *L'Emploi du temps* (Passing Time).
1956, Genet, *Le Balcon* (The Balcony).
1956, Sarraute, *L'Ere du soupçon* (The Age of Suspicion).
1956, Herbert, *Struna światła* (A Chord of Light).

1956–1958, Vestdijk, *Symphonie van Victor Slingeland* (Victor Slingeland Symphony).

1957, Gadda, *Quer pasticciaccio brutto de Via Merulana* (That Awful Mess on Via Merulana).

1957, Schmidt, *Die Gelehrtenrepublik* (The Republic of Savants).

1957, Beckett, *Fin de partie* (Endgame).

1957, Butor, *La Modification* (A Change of Heart).

1957, Robbe-Grillet, *La Jalousie* (Jealousy).

1957, Pasolini, *Le ceneri de Gramsci* (Gramsci's Ashes).

1957, Pinter, *The Birthday Party*.

1957, Enzensberger, *Verteidigung der Wölfe* (In Defence of Wolves).

1958, Arrabal, *Le Cimetière des voitures* (The Car Cemetery).

1958, Duras, *Moderato cantabile*.

1958, Tomasi di Lampedusa, *Il gattopardo* (The Leopard).

1958, Valaoritis, *Kentriki Stoa* (Central Stoa).

1958, Škorecký, *Zbabělci* (The Cowards).

1959, Böll, *Billiard um Halbzehn* (Billards at Half-past Nine).

1959, Sillitoe, *The Loneliness of the Long Distance Runner*.

1959, Grass, *Die Blechtrommel* (The Tin Drum).

1959, Ionesco, *Le Rhinocéros* (Rhinoceros).

1959, Sarraute, *Le Planétarium* (The Planetarium).

1959, Pasolini, *Una vita violenta* (A Violent Life).

1959, Johnson, *Mutmaßungen über Jakob* (Speculations about Jacob).

1960, Elytis, *Axion Esti*.

1960–1982, Sollers (ed.), *Tel Quel* (As is).

1960, Gombrowicz, *Pornografia* (Pornography).

1960, Różewicz, *Kartoteka* (The Card Index).

1960, Simon, *La Route des Flandres* (The Flanders Road).

1961, Spark, *The Prime of Miss Jean Brodie*.

1961, Johnson, *Das dritte Buch über Achim* (The Third Book about Achim).

1962, Volponi, *Memoriale* (My Troubles Began).

1962, Lessing, *The Golden Notebook*.

1962, Burgess, *A Clockwork Orange*.

1962, Solzhenitsyn, *Odin den' Ivana Densisovicha* (One Day in the Life of Ivan Denisovich).

1962, Bassani, *Il giardino dei Finzi-Contini* (The Garden of the Finzi Continis).

1962, Wesker, *Chips with Everything*.

1962, Martín-Santos, *Tiempo del silencio* (Time of Silence).

1963, Robbe-Grillet, *Pour un nouveau roman* (For a New Novel).

1963, Havel, *Zahradní slavnost* (The Garden Party).

1963, Ritsos, *Tis Fylakis Kai I Gynaikes* (The Prison Tree and the Women).

1964, Larkin, *The Whitsun Weddings*.

1964, Sartre, *Les Mots* (Words).

1964,Weiss, *Die Verfolgung und Ermordung Jean Paul Marats* (The Persecution and Assassination of Marat).

1964, Leduc, *La Bâtarde* (The Bastard).

1964, Kluge, *Schlachtbeschreibung* (Description of a Battle).

1965, Hrabal, *Ostře sledované vlaky* (Closely Watched Trains).

1965, Perec, *Les Choses* (Things).
1966, Handke, *Publikumsbeschimpfung* (Offending the Audience).
1966, Fowles, *The Magus* [revised 1977].
1966, Stoppard, *Rosencrantz and Guildenstern are Dead.*
1966, Vaculík, *Sekyra* (The Axe).
1967, Kundera, *Žert* (The Joke)
1967, Mňačko, *Ako chutí moc* (The Taste of Power).
1967, Carter, *The Magic Toyshop.*
1967, Bernhard, *Verstörung* (Gargoyles).
1967, Ekelöf, *Vägvisare till underjorden* (Guide to the Underworld).
1968, Sollers, *Nombres* (Numbers).
1968, Lenz, *Deutschstunde* (The German Lesson).
1968, Wolf, *Nachdenken über Christa T.* (The Quest for Christa T.).
1969, Fowles, *The French Lieutenant's Woman.*
1969, Delibes, *Parábola del náufrago* (Parable of the Shipwrecked Man).
1969, Wittig, *Les Guérillères* (The Warriors).
1969, Milosz, *Miasto bez imienia* (City without a Name).
1970, Tournier, *Le Roi des Aulnes* (The Erl King).
1970, Fo, *Morte accidentale di un anarchico* (The Accidental Death of an Anarchist).
1970, Hughes, *Crow.*
1971, Ponge, *La Fabrique du 'Pré'* (Making of the Pré).
1971, Lessing, *Briefing for a Descent into Hell.*
1971, Bond, *Lear.*
1972, Calvino, *Le città invisibili* (Invisible Cities).
1972, Weöres, *Psyché.*
1973, Kundera, *Život je jinde* (Life is Elsewhere).
1973, Barthes, *Le Plaisir du texte* (The Pleasure of the Text).
1973, Heissenbüttel, *Gelegenheitsgedichte und Klappentexte* (Occasional Poems and Blurbs).
1974, Leclerc, *'Parole de femme'* ('Word of Woman').
1974, Morante, *La storia: Romanzo* (History: A Novel).
1975, Bonnefoy, *Dans le leurre du seuil* (In the Lure of the Threshold).
1975, Heaney, *North.*
1976, Zinoviev, *Ziyayushchiye Vysoty* (The Yawning Heights)
1977, Irigaray, *'Ce sexe qui n'en est pas un'* ('This Sex which is not One').
1977, Brodsky, *Chast' rechi* (A Part of Speech).
1977, Müller, *Hamletmaschine* (The Hamlet Machine).
1978, Perec, *La Vie, mode d'emploi* (Life, A User's Manual).
1978, Enzensberger, *Der Untergang der Titanic* (The Sinking of the Titanic).
1978, Bitov, *Puskinskii Dom* (Pushkin House).
1979, Calvino, *Se una notte d'inverno un viaggiatore* (If on a Winter's Night a Traveller).
1979, Kundera, *Kniha smíchu a zapomnění* (The Book of Laughter and Forgetting).
1980, Eco, *Il nome della rosa* (The Name of the Rose).
1981, D.M. Thomas, *The White Hotel.*
1981, Rushdie, *Midnight's Children.*
1981, Heym, *Ahasver.*

1983, Hein, *Drachenblut* (Dragon's Blood)

1983, Wolf, *Kassandra*.

1984, Ballard, *Empire of the Sun*.

1984, Kundera, *Nesnesitelná lehkost byti* (The Unbearable Lightness of Being).

1984, Duras, *L'Amant* (The Lover).

1984, Barnes, *Flaubert's Parrot*.

1985, Patrick Mondiano, *Quartier Perdu* (Out-of-the-Way-District).

1985, Winterson, *Oranges are not the Only Fruit*.

1985, Klima, *Má veselá jitra* (My Merry Mornings).

1985, Busi, *Vita standard di un venditore provvisorio di collant* (The Standard Life of a Temporary Pantyhose Salesman).

1988, Juan Goytisolo, *Las virtudes del pájaro solitario* (The Virtues of the Solitary Bird).

1988, Duras, *La Vie materielle* (Practicalities).

1989, Kónrad, *Kerti mulatság* (A Feast in the Garden).

1989, Perec, *53 jours* (53 Days).

1990, Byatt, *Possession*.

From Romanticism
to Postmodernism: An
Annotated Bibliography

1 ROMANTICISM

The term 'Romanticism' first appeared in Germany in 1802, France in 1816, Italy in 1818, and England in 1823, and in other European countries after that date (Wellek, 1963, p. 151). Its emergence as a concept within the culture of this period is charted by Lilian Furst in her short study, *Romanticism* (London: Methuen, 1976, pp. 6–14), by the contributors to *'Romantic' and its Cognates: The European History of the Word*, ed. Hans Eichner (Toronto: University of Toronto Press, 1972), and with a greater sense for the contested meaning of the notion, for its problematic status within literary history, by René Wellek, in his 'The Concept of Romanticism in Literary History' (first published in 1949, and republished in *Concepts of Criticism* (New Haven: Yale University Press, 1963, pp. 128–98). Wellek takes issue there with scholars such as A.O. Lovejoy, who, in his 'On the Discrimination of Romanticisms' (first published in 1924, and reprinted in Robert F. Gleckner and Gerald D. Enscoe's *Romanticism: Points of View*, New York: Prentice-Hall, 1962, and in a second, heavily revised edition, 1970, pp. 66–81) argued that the term Romanticism reflects a 'confusion of terms, and of ideas', and describes a movement without a 'common denominator' (Gleckner and Enscoe, 1970, pp. 66 and 69). Wellek, however, draws the movement together by stressing the Romantics' shared acceptance of certain key tropes: 'imagination for the view of poetry, nature for the view of the world, and symbol and myth for poetic style', to which Wellek adds that 'concern for the reconciliation of subject and object, man and nature, consciousness and unconsciousness' that formed the greater philosophical goal of the Romantic project (Wellek, 1963, pp. 161 and 218). The wider ambience of Romanticism within recent scholarship is documented by Anthony Thorlby in his *The Romantic Movement* (London: Longmans, 1966), and by John B. Halsted in his *Romanticism: Problems of Definition, Explanation and Evaluation* (Boston: Heath, 1965).

Romanticism was perhaps the most philosophically sophisticated and theoretically pointed of all the movements in modern European literature. Writers were able to draw upon the work of seminal thinkers such as Kant, Schelling and Schleiermacher to give depth and complexity to their personal poetic visions. The major study of the Romantic aesthetic remains M.H. Abrams' *The Mirror and the Lamp: Romantic Theory and the Critical Tradition* (Oxford: Oxford University Press, 1953), which shows how theories of artistic expressivity (the 'lamp' archetype), came to dominate the imagination of the European (but particularly) English Romantics. Finally,

Lilian Furst, in her bi-lingual anthology, *European Romanticism: Self-definition* (London: Methuen, 1980) offers a selection of primary texts drawn from Romantic manifestos and essays.

An overview of the major trends within European Romanticism is provided by H.H.H. Remak in his 'West European Romanticism: Definition and Scope', reprinted in *Comparative Literature: Method and Perspective*, edited by Newton P. Stallknecht and Horst Frenz (Carbondale: Southern Illinois Press, 1971, pp. 275–311), and by H.G. Schenk in his *The Mind of the European Romantics: An Essay in Cultural History* (London: Constable, 1966). A country-by-country account of the Romantic movement is offered in Roy Porter and Mikulas Teich (eds), *Romanticism in national Context* (Cambridge: Cambridge University Press, 1988), but it is regrettable that important works such as Paul van Tieghem's *Le Romantisme dans la littérature européenne* (Paris: Michel, 1948, second edition 1969), and Ernst Behler i.a., *Die Europäische Romantik* (Frankfurt am Main: Athenäum, 1972), remain untranslated.

These works help frame the more targeted studies of European Romanticism, whose major titles include M.H. Abrams, *Natural Supernaturalism: Tradition and Revolution in Romantic Literature* (New York: Norton, 1971), Morse Peckham, *The Birth of Romanticism, 1790–1815* (Greenwood: Penkevill, 1986), Lilian Furst, *Romanticism in Perspective: A Comparative Study of Aspects of the Romantic Movement in England, France and Germany* (London: Macmillan; 1969), and her *The Contours of European Romanticism* (Lincoln: University of Nebraska Press, 1979), and Maurice Cranston, *The Romantic Movement* (Oxford: Basil Blackwell, 1994). These studies read the Romantic project largely out of its own self-image, focussing upon the positive aspects of the Romantic discourse, which include the primacy of feeling, individualism, freedom of the imagination, the cult of originality, the importance of dream and mystery and a belief in the sacred seriousness of art (Furst, 1979, p. xii). More critical in its focus is the work of the American deconstructivist, Paul de Man, whose *The Rhetoric of Romanticism* (New York: Columbia University Press, 1984), possibly influenced by Harold Bloom's epoch-making studies of English Romanticism, draws attention to the linguistic self-consciousness of the Romantic poetic text. A darker side of the Romantic mind is traced in Mario Praz's seminal study, *The Romantic Agony* (Oxford: Oxford University Press, 1970), first published in Italian in 1930 with the more revealing title *Flesh, Death and the Devil in Romantic Literature*. Romantic subjectivity is viewed here as a form of 'erotic sensibility' (Praz, 1970, p. xv), which manifested itself in a penchant for excess, for the taboo, for the darker side of the sexual impulse. Praz's influence is evident in subsequent studies of Romanticism, such as David Punter's illuminating *The Romantic Unconscious: A Study in Narcissism and Patriarchy* (Hemel Hempstead: Harvester Wheatsheaf, 1989), which seeks to establish the 'common psycho-social root' that links Romanticism with other forms of narcissistic self-empowerment (Punter, p. x).

Finally, Romantic literature is brought into alignment with its historical context in R.B. Mowat's *The Romantic Age: Europe in the early Nineteenth Century* (London: Harrap, 1937), Howard Mumford Jones' *Revolution and Romanticism* (Cambridge, Mass.: Harvard University Press, 1974), J.L.

Talmon's *Romanticism and Revolt: Europe 1815–1848* (New York: Norton, 1967), and, through an extensive use of primary materials, John B. Halsted's *Romanticism* (London: Macmillan, 1969).

2 REALISM AND NATURALISM

Realism lacked both the Messianic fervour and the philosophical impetus of the Romantic movement. The term first appeared, in France, in 1856, where it was used by Edmond Duranty in his review *Réalisme*, and then by the critic Champfleury in his book *Le Réalisme* in 1857, to describe (and defend) the style of the painter, Gustave Courbet, and then as a way of characterising the writing of Balzac, Flaubert and others. The term was first used in Germany in 1856 (albeit with reference to the hybrid genre of Poetic Realism), in England in 1858, and in Italy in 1878. Its emergence is described by René Wellek in his 'The Concept of Realism in Literary Scholarship' in *Concepts of Criticism* (New Haven: Yale University Press, 1963, pp. 222–55), by E.B.O. Borgerhoff in his '*Réalisme* and Kindred Words (*PMLA* 53, 1938, 837–43), and by Bernard Weinberg, *French Realism: The Critical Reaction, 1830–1870* (London: Oxford University Press, 1937). A invaluable selection of primary documentation, manifestos, essays and reviews, is provided by George J. Becker in his *Documents of Modern Literary Realism* (Princeton: Princeton University Press, 1963).

There are a number of excellent introductions to Realism and its kindred movement, Naturalism. They include Damian Grant's *Realism* (London: Methuen, 1970), and Lilian Furst's *Naturalism* (London: Methuen, 1971), although both focus upon the theoretical parameters of the movement rather than upon its literature; George J. Becker's *Master European Realists of the Nineteenth Century* (New York: Ungar, 1982), the essays collected in F.W.J. Hemmings' edited volume, *The Age of Realism* (Harmondsworth: Penguin, 1978); those in a similar volume edited by D.A. Williams, *The Monster in the Mirror: Studies in Nineteenth Century Realism* (Oxford: Oxford University Press, 1978); and, with a greater degree of theoretical self-reflexivity, the essays collected in *Realism in European Literature*, edited by Nicholas Boyle and Martin Swales (Cambridge: Cambridge University Press, 1986). The last volume was written in honour of J.P Stern, whose study, *On Realism* (London: Routledge, 1973), captures the Janus face of the Realist aesthetic, the fact that it can be seen both 'as a liberation and an emblem of the riches of the world [and], at other times, as a restriction and a prison-house' (Stern, 1973, p. 32). In his *Man and Society in Nineteenth Century Realism: Determinism and Literature* (London: Macmillan, 1977), Maurice Larkin focusses upon the intellectual origins of the Realist aesthetic, stressing (as many Realist writers themselves did) the relevance of contemporary scientific theory to their work. Larkin's approach might be read as a sober counterpart to Erich Auerbach's *Mimesis: The Representation of Reality in Western Literature* (Princeton: Princeton University Press, 1953). Written in German in 1946, and published in English in 1953, Auerbach's epic study ranges over two thousand years of European literature, from

Homer to James Joyce. Its focus is upon those writers who have dealt with 'individuals from daily life in their dependence upon current historical circumstances and made them the subjects of serious, problematic, and even tragic representation' (Auerbach, p. 554). Auerbach's work is perhaps too inclusive (Realism seems to describe all that is positive in Western literature), but his chapter on Stendhal, Balzac, and Flaubert (pp. 454–524) does take up many of the themes and preoccupations that characterised nineteenth-century Realism and Naturalism. Equally humanistic in its inspiration is the excellent study by Harry Levin, *The Gates of Horn: A Study of Five French Realists* (Oxford: Oxford University Press, 1966), although its focus is exclusively upon French fiction. With insight and scholarship, Levin offers convincing readings of some of the great novels of the Realist movement, those 'monumental glories' of the nineteenth century, which (Levin argues) were written as a critique of the societies from which they came, but also, in a strange way, to honour them (Levin, 1966, p. 471).

It was precisely the residual humanism evident in the great Realist novels that attracted the distinguished Hungarian Marxist, Georg Lukács. His engagement with the Realist aesthetic comes towards the end of a long tradition which began with the seminal theorists of Communism, Marx and Engels. Engels, in particular, praised the ability of the Realist writer to capture the forward momentum of history, who often went, as Balzac did, 'against his own class sympathies and political prejudices' in order to provide an accurate picture of his times (Engels in Becker, 1963, p. 485). In his own appropriation of the Realist tradition, Georg Lukács followed his mentors, elaborating their insights into a full-blown and finely accented assessment of the nineteenth-century Realist novel. In his essays, 'Reportage or Portrayal? Critical Remarks a propos a Novel by [Ernst] Ottwalt', and ' 'Tendency' or Partisanship?' (both 1932, and republished in *Essays on Realism*, edited by Rodney Livingstone (Cambridge, Mass.: MIT Press, 1981), and in 'Realism in the Balance' (written in 1938, and republished in *Aesthetics and Politics*, edited by Ronald Taylor, London: Verso, 1980), Lukács defended Realism both against the proletarian-propaganda *Reportage* novels of writers such as Ernst Ottwalt and Willi Bredel, and against the Avant-Garde experimentations of, for example, German Expressionism. In his later works, *Studies in European Realism* (London: Merlin Press, 1950, originally in German in 1948), and *The Historical Novel* (London: Merlin Press, 1962, German edition, 1955), he allocated to the Realist tradition a central position in European literature between the mystical excesses of Romanticism and the studied disfigurations of Modernism. The Realist novel alone (he argues here) proved capable of capturing the totality of life in nineteenth-century bourgeois society, of mediating between the personal and the public realms, between the individual and history, capturing in the process the 'three-dimensionality' that is a part of the dialectic of historical change (Lukács, 1950, p. 6).

In contrast to the almost emotive defence of Realism by Marxist critics, recent British and French Structuralists and Post-structuralists have subjected the Realist aesthetic to a sustained critique, criticising both its lack of theoretical self-reflexivity and its essentialist reading of history and human nature. The seminal works are Roland Barthes' *Writing Degree Zero*

(London: Jonathan Cape, 1967, but first published in French in 1953), and his *S/Z* (New York: Hill and Wang, 1974, first published in French in 1970). In the latter work, Barthes established the distinction between the 'readerly' and the 'writerly' text. As Barthes' English disciple, Stephen Heath, explained in his *The Nouveau Roman: A Study in the Practice of Writing* (London: Elek, 1972), the former type of writing finds its paradigm in the Realist novel, in a style that seeks to obscure all traces of its fictionality. In Heath's words: 'its function is the naturalisation of that reality articulated by a society as *the* 'Reality''. The Realist novel articulates a 'certain social seeing', constructing social forms and values that must be 'learned, repeated and consumed' by the reader (Heath, 1972, pp. 20 and 21). How this process takes place is analysed by Colin MacCabe in his *James Joyce and the Revolution of the Word* (London: Macmillan, 1978). MacCabe attempts here to establish a paradigm for the Classic Realist text (the CRT), using novels such as George Eliot's *Middlemarch* to show how the reader is manipulated through narrative devices into accepting the 'self-evident reality' of the author's world-view (MacCabe, 1978, p. 18). Within this Post-structuralist paradigm, Realism loses the emancipatory function that Auerbach, Lukács and others saw in the genre, and assumes the status of a 'practical ideology', a negative totality which, through its very self-seeming naturalness, holds the reader in perpetual captivity (Heath, 1972, p. 20).

3   MODERNISM

'Modernism' is a relatively recent term in literary history, the result of attempts to bring the heterogeneous literary movements and writers of the period between 1890 and 1925 under a single rubric. When contemporary critics of this period used the epithet 'modern' to describe their contemporary literature, as Georg Brandes does in his *The Men of the Modern Breakthrough* (first published in Danish in 1883), Samuel Lublinski in his *Assessing the Moderns* (first published in German in 1904), and T.E. Hulme in his lecture 'Modern Poetry' (1914), they often had in mind the dissolving and challenging ethos of late Realist and Naturalist writers, rather than those whom we now regard as 'Modernist'. The ambit of the term 'modern' in late nineteenth- and early twentieth-century literature is charted by Monroe K. Spears in his *Dionysus and the City: Modernism in Twentieth-Century Poetry* (New York: Oxford University Press, 1970, pp. 3–34). The importance of the term within literary history is examined by Douwe W. Fokkema in his *Literary History, Modernism, and Postmodernism* (Philadelphia: John Benjamins, 1984). Fokkema draws here upon Harry Levin's seminal 'What was Modernism?', first published in 1960, and reprinted in *Refractions: Essays in Comparative Literature* (New York: Oxford University Press, 1966), and David Lodge, *The Modes of Modern Writing: Metaphor, Metonymy, and the Typology of Modern Literature* (London: Arnold, 1977) in establishing the central features of the Modernist aesthetic: its valorisation of the incomplete or fragmented text; its scepticism regarding veristic notions of representation; its use of metalingual devices; and its

refusal to give guidance to the reader (Fokkema, 1984, p. 19). Other import-
ant discussions of the Modernist typology include Joseph Chiari's *The
Aesthetics of Modernism* (London: Vision, 1970), Peter Faulkner's *Modernism*
(London: Methuen, 1977), Ricardo J. Quinones' *Mapping Literary Modernism:
Time and Development* (Princeton: Princeton University Press, 1985), and
Astradur Eysteinsson's *The Concept of Modernism* (Ithaca: Cornell University
Press, 1990).

Most scholars regard Symbolism as the first movement within literary
Modernism. In English, two near-contemporary studies are of particular
importance: Arthur Symons, *The Symbolist Movement in Literature* (London:
William Heineman, 1899), and Holbrook Jackson's *The Eighteen Nineties*
(first published in 1913, and reprinted in 1972, Alfred Knopf, New York).
To their work must be added the seminal study of Edmund Wilson, *Axël's
Castle: A Study in the Imaginative Literature of 1870–1930* (London: Fontana,
1961, but first published in 1931), which stresses the 'revolutionising'
impact of Symbolism, the way that it 'indicates relations which, recently
perceived for the first time, cut through or underlie those in terms of which
we have been in the habit of thinking' (Wilson, 1961, p. 234). Subsequent
studies of Symbolism (with a understandable French focus) include:
A.E. Carter, *The Idea of Decadence in French Literature, 1830–1900* (Toronto:
Toronto University Press, 1958), A.G. Lehmann, *The Symbolist Aesthetic in
France, 1885–1895* (Oxford: Basil Blackwell, 1950), and Henri Peyre, *What is
Symbolism?* (Alabama: University of Alabama Press, 1980). With a broader
focus upon European literature are John Porter Houston, *French Symbolism
and the Modernist Movement: A Study of Poetic Structures* (Baton Rouge:
Louisiana State University Press, 1980), and *The Symbolist Movement in the
Literature of European Languages*, edited by Anna Balakian (Budapest:
Akadémiai Kiadó, 1982).

In their studied rejection of the cultural norms of bourgeois society, and
in their elevation of the role of the artist and artistic practice to an autotelic
creed, the Symbolists (and their *confrères*, the Romantic Decadents) anticipated the full-blown oppositionalism that later groups such as the
Dadaists, Futurists, Surrealists, Expressionists and others were to cultivate
in the years immediately prior to and following the First World War. This
radical wing of the Modernist movement is conventionally approached
under the rubric of the Avant-Garde. Major studies of this movement
include Renato Poggioli, *The Theory of the Avant-Garde* (Cambridge Mass.:
Belknap Press, 1968), Peter Bürger, *Theory of the Avant-Garde* (Manchester:
Manchester University Press, 1984), Matei Calinescu, *Faces of Modernity:
Avant-Garde, Decadence, Kitsch* (Bloomington: Indiana University Press,
1977), Charles Russell, *Poets, Prophets and Revolutionaries: The Literary
Avant-Garde from Rimbaud through Postmodernism* (Oxford: Oxford
University Press, 1985), and Peter Nicholls, *Modernisms: A Literary Guide*
(London: Macmillan, 1995).

The literature of main-stream writers such as Proust, Gide, Joyce, Woolf,
Kafka and Thomas Mann continues to receive the closest focus in the scholarship on European Modernism. Some of the major titles include the anthology *Modernism, 1890–1930*, edited by Malcolm Bradbury and James
McFarlane (Harmondsworth: Penguin, 1976), Marshall Berman, *All that is

Solid Melts into Air: The Experience of Modernity (London: Verso, 1983), *Modernism and the European Unconscious*, edited by Peter Collier and Judy Davies (New York: St. Martin's Press, 1990), and, with reference to the powerful influences of Nietzsche and Freud respectively, John Burt Forster, *Heirs to Dionysus: A Nietzschean Current in Literary Modernism* (Princeton: Princeton University Press, 1981), and Judith Ryan, *The Vanishing Subject: Early Psychology and Literary Modernism* (Chicago: University of Chicago Press, 1991). In spite of differences in emphasis and methodology, all of these studies view the Modernist aesthetic as a response to the experience of 'modernity', an articulation of that feeling of being poured into a 'maelstrom of perpetual disintegration and renewal, of struggle and contradiction, of ambiguity and anguish', which Berman sees throughout the literature of this period (Berman, 1983, p. 15). The intellectual, political and socio-economic parameters of that condition have been variously mapped, as has its relationship to the literatures of the modern period. Recent works include David Frisby, *Fragments of Modernity: Theories of Modernity in the Work of Simmel, Kracauer and Benjamin* (Cambridge: Polity Press, 1985), Robert Pippin, *Modernism as a Philosophical Problem: On the Dissatisfactions of European High Culture* (Oxford: Basil Blackwell, 1991), and, with a greater sense for the impact of modernity upon specific texts and authors, the essays by Steve Giles and Richard Sheppard, collected in *Theorizing Modernism: Essays in Critical Theory*, edited by Steve Giles (London: Routledge, 1993). These studies and others collectively designate the paradoxical nature of the Modernist project: the fact that its writers helped give voice to a widespread process of change and disruption that they came increasingly (and T.S. Eliot comes to mind) to despise, and which they sought to overcome through integrating aesthetic structures, creating, as in the great novels of Proust, Mann and Joyce, a 'unity of disunity' that was only achievable at the level of text, but rarely at the level of historical or personal experience (Berman, 1983, p. 15).

4   THE LITERATURE OF POLITICAL COMMITMENT

That politicised literature is not the exclusive property of twentieth century authors is demonstrated by Irving Howe in his seminal *Politics and the Novel* (New York: Horizon Press, 1955), and by Renee Winegarten, *Writers and Revolution: The Fatal Lure of Action* (New York: Franklin Watts, 1974). Both discuss a tradition that extends as far back as Romanticism (Blake and Stendhal come in for particular attention), and even further. Judged, however, as a conscious strategy, underpinned by a coherent political philosophy, the literature of political engagement did not reach maturity until the 1920s and 1930s. The major studies of the writing of this period include George Woodcock, *Writers and Politics* (London: Porcupine Press, 1948), John Mander, *The Writer and Commitment* (London: Secker and Warburg, 1961), Jürgen Rühle, *Literature and Revolution: A Critical Study of the Writer and Communism in the Twentieth Century* (Pall Mall Press: London, 1969), Alan Swingewood, *The Novel and Revolution* (London: Macmillan, 1975),

George A. Panichas (ed), *The Politics of Twentieth Century Novelists* (New York: Hawthorn Books, 1971), Charles I. Glicksberg, *The Literature of Commitment* (Lewisburg: Bucknell University Press, 1976), and the six volumes in *The Writers and Politics* series, edited by John Flower (London: Hodder and Stoughton, 1977–1978). Written largely from political positions sympathetic to the literature of political engagement, from a 'humane socialism' (Rühle, 1969, p. viii), these studies nevertheless chart the many personal confusions and disappointments experienced by this generation, as its initial uncritical enthusiasm for the ideology and realities of revolutionary Communism gradually gave way to reservation and finally apostasy.

Radical politics during this period came, however, not only from the Left but from the Right; and just as Fascist radicals offered their own solutions to the crisis of parliamentary democracy in the West, so too did writers and philosophers sympathetic to that particular ideology. Aligning major Modernist figures such as D.H. Lawrence, Luigi Pirandello and Gottfried Benn with the racist and nationalist policies of Hitler and Musolini will always be controversial; but both John Harrison, in his *The Reactionaries* (London: Gollanncz, 1967), and Alastair Hamilton, *The Appeal of Fascism: A Study of Intellectuals and Fascism, 1919–1945* (London: Blond, 1971) approach their writers with understanding and, at times, sympathy, in an attempt to explain how so many noted figures could embrace such an anti-democratic, anti-humanist credo. Broader in scope than these two studies are many of the essays collected in *The Attractions of Fascism: Social Psychology and Aesthetics of the 'Triumph of the Right'*, edited by John Milfull (New York and Oxford: Berg, 1990), which seek to understand (on its own terms) the compulsive nature of the Fascist experience.

Two of the major historical events of this period: the First World War and the Spanish Civil War, generated not only political and military activity, but also a body of writing that has remained of interest to subsequent generations. *The First World War in Fiction*, edited by Holger Klein (London: Macmillan, 1976), includes essays on the major war novels of the period, whilst Frank Field's *British and French Writers of the First World War: Comparative Studies in Cultural History* (Cambridge: Cambridge University Press, 1991), offers an in-depth discussion of British and French writing on the war, in an attempt to identify those 'similarities of approach that transcend national boundaries' (Field, p. 3). The literature of the Spanish Civil War has been well covered, most notably by Frederick Benson, *Writers in Arms: The Literary Impact of the Spanish Civil War* (London: University of London Press, 1968), Stanley Weintraub, *The Last Great Cause: The Intellectuals and the Spanish Civil War* (London: W.H. Allen, 1968), and Peter Monteath, *Writing the Good Fight: Political Commitment in the International Literature of the Spanish War* (Westport: Greenwood, 1994).

The most clearly defined doctrine of committed literature promulgated in the inter-war period was Socialist Realism. Formulated in 1934 by the Russian Communist, Andrey Zhdanov, it became an orthodoxy for an entire generation of writers in the Soviet Union and elsewhere, who felt compelled (or were compelled) to produce a type of literature which eschewed all Modernist techniques to extol the achievements of the workers' state. The goals and programme of Socialist Realism have been well documented by

C. Vaughan James, *Soviet Socialist Realism: Origins and Theory* (London: Macmillan, 1973), Herman Ermolaev, *Soviet Literary Theories, 1917–1934* (New York: Octagon Books, 1977, first published 1963), and George Bisztray, *Marxist Models of Literary Realism* (New York: Columbia University Press, 1978). The effect of the doctrine upon the literature of the period is described by Marc Slonim in his *Soviet Russian Literature: Writers and Problems, 1917–1977* (Oxford: Oxford University Press, 1977), Gleb Struve in *Russian Literature under Lenin and Stalin, 1917–1953* (Norman: University of Okalahoma, 1971), and Katerina Clark in her *The Soviet Novel: History as Ritual* (Chicago: University of Chicago Press, 1981).

Not all Marxists were Socialist Realists. Georg Lukács, for example, took his models not from contemporary Soviet theory but from the great Realist novelists of the nineteenth century. Lukács' extended debate with Brecht, conducted in the 1930s, largely in the pages of the *émigré* journal, *Das Wort* (The Word), provides one of the most sustained and theoretically sophisticated dialectics between Marxist literary theorists in this period. Documentation of this dispute (which also involved Ernst Bloch and Walter Benjamin) is provided, together with an excellent commentary by Rodney Livingstone, Perry Anderson and Francis Mulhern, in *Aesthetics and Politics*, edited by Ronald Taylor (London: Verso, 1980). The broader theoretical ambit of the debate is analysed by Frederic Jameson in his *Marxism and Form: Twentieth Century Dialectical Theories of Literature* (Princeton: Princeton University Press, 1971). The tradition of Marxist literary criticism, as a whole, is documented in *Marxists on Literature: An Anthology* edited by David Craig (Harmondsworth: Penguin, 1975).

The religious revivalism evident in the work of Bernanos, Greene and T.S. Eliot forms the focus of works such as Georg M.A. Gaston's *The Pursuit of Salvation: A Critical Guide to the Novels of Graham Greene* (New York: Whitston Publishing Company, 1984,) and (on Eliot) Frank Burch Brown's *Transfiguration: Poetic Metaphor and the Languages of Religious Belief* (Chapel Hill: University of North Carolina Press, 1983). The bigger picture is provided by Eugene Webb in his *The Dark Dove: The Sacred and the Secular in Modern Literature* (Seattle: University of Washington Press, 1975), and by many of the contributors to the anthology *Religion and Modern Literature: Essays in Theory and Criticism*, edited by G.B. Tennyson and Edward E. Ericson (Michigan: Eerdmans, 1975), works which seek to address (in the words of Nathan A. Scott Jr,) the 'problem of understanding the stratagems that become inevitable for the artist when history commits him to the practice of his vocation in a vacuum of belief' (Tennyson and Ericson, 1975, p. 125). These studies, and others, such as Nathan A. Scott's *Rehearsals of Discomposure: Alienation and Reconciliation in Modern Literature: Franz Kafka, Ignazio Silone, D.H. Lawrence, T.S. Eliot* (London: Lehmann, 1952), are largely written from a Christian perspective, but retain, nevertheless, a concern for the intellectual integrity of the authors and texts under discussion. The state of scholarship in this area is reviewed in *Religion in Contemporary Fiction: Criticism from 1945 to the Present*, compiled by George N. Boyd and Louis A. Boyd (San Antonio: Trinity University Press, 1973).

Individual studies of Camus, Sartre, de Beauvoir and other Existentialist writers abound, but there are relatively few which offer a comparative reading of their literature. Hazel E. Barnes does this in her *The Literature of Possibility: A Study in Humanistic Existentialism* (Lincoln: University of Nebraska Press, 1959), as does Sarah N. Lawall, *Critics of Consciousness: The Existential Structures of Literature* (Cambridge, Mass.: Harvard University Press, 1968), and, with a feel for the broader tradition of Existentialist thought, Edith Kern, *Existential Thought and Fictional Technique: Kierkegaard, Sartre, Beckett* (New Haven: Yale University Press, 1970).

5 POSTMODERNISM

Postmodernism is a concept, complex, amorphous and, for many, replete with internal contradictions, its creative writing 'quarrelsome, abundant, various' (Hassan, 1970, p. 248); yet it has come to provide both the dominant paradigm within contemporary cultural theory, and the most important conceptual framework for our understanding of recent literature. The term was first used by a group of American critics seeking to demarcate new writing in North and South America from the dominant tradition of European Modernism. The major texts in this re-evaluation were Irving Howe's essay 'Mass Society and Post-Modern Fiction' (which first appeared in *Partisan Review* in 1959, and is reprinted in *Decline of the New*, New York: Harcourt Brace, 1970, pp. 190–207); Harry Levin's 'What was Modernism?', in *Refractions* (New York: Oxford University Press, 1966), pp. 271–95; Leslie Fiedler's, 'Cross the Border – Close the Gap: Post-Modernism', published in *The Collected Essays of Leslie Fiedler*, 2 vols (New York: Stein and Day, 1971), vol. 1, pp. 461–85; Susan Sontag's, *Against Interpretation* (New York: Farrar, Strauss and Giroux, 1966); John Barth's, 'The Literature of Exhaustion' (in *The Atlantic Monthly*, August 1967, pp. 29–34); and Frank Kermode's 'The Modern' in *Continuities* (London: Routledge, 1968, pp. 1–32). What these critics were trying to identify was not only an original type of literature, but a new attitude to literary culture, one that rejected, as Fiedler explained in his 1965 essay 'The New Mutants' (in Fiedler, 1971, vol 2, pp. 379–400), notions such as 'cultural continuity and progress', indeed the entire 'bourgeois-Protestant version of Humanism' (Fiedler, pp. 383 and 385). In its place, young American writers (Fiedler mentions John Barth, Ken Kesey and Thomas Berger), are seeking to produce a type of work which is, as Howe argues in 'The New York Intellectuals' (in Howe, 1970, pp. 211–65) 'forceful, healthy, untangled', a literature which 'chooses surfaces against relationships, the skim of texture rather than the weaving of pattern', and which seeks to 'collapse aesthetic distance on behalf of touch and frenzy' (Howe, pp. 254 and 256).

But that such literature possessed its own intellectual tradition was demonstrated by Ihab Hassan, who gave, in his *The Dismemberment of Orpheus: Towards a Postmodern Literature* (New York: Oxford University Press, 1971), the Postmodern aesthetic a lineage (and a largely European one), which ran from the Marquis de Sade to Kafka, Genet and Beckett. For Hassan, Postmodernist literature centres on 'the two accents of silence': 'the negative echo of language, autodestructive, demonic, nihilist' [and] its positive stillness, self-transcendent, sacramental, plenary' (p. 248). In his subsequent *Paracriticisms: Seven Speculations of the Times* (Urbana: University of Illinois Press, 1975), the American critic worked up a typology of the Postmodern, describing an art which 'cancels itself', 'deprecates itself', 'becomes a self-reflexive game', 'orders itself loosely, even at random', and 'refuses interpretation. Fancy pretends to be fact. And vice versa'. For Hassan, the Postmodern represents an extension of the techniques and interests of Modernism; it is a more playful, self-conscious and minimalist exploration of the tropes of urbanism, primitivism, technologism and eroticism that underscored that earlier aesthetic. As Hassan explains: 'Postmodernism may be a response, direct or oblique, to the Unimaginable which Modernism glimpsed only in its most prophetic moments.' He adds: 'Modernism does not suddenly cease so that Postmodernism may begin: they now *coexist*.' 'Post', in Hassan's scheme of things, suggests a certain qualitative change in the identity of contemporary culture rather than a simple chronological development (Hassan, pp. 21, 53 and 47).

In these seminal studies, literary theory, philosophy and aesthetics enter into a relationship that is often exhilarating, at other times unconvincing. But that Postmodernism represents a fundamental break not only with Modernism, but with the Humanist tradition in general, is undeniable. The major study of the epistemological consequences of this break is Jean-François Lyotard's highly influential *La Condition postmoderne* (published in 1979, and translated into English as *The Postmodern Condition*, in 1985). Lyotard defined Postmodernism as 'an incredulity towards meta-narratives', those systems of explanation, which range from Kantian Idealism to Marxism, that seek to make sense of human behaviour in terms of a single, monolithic methodology. In the Postmodern period, in societies dominated by fragmentation of discourse, the de-centring of subjectivity, and the proliferation of (manipulated) aesthetic forms, such systems have lost both their intellectual credibility and their hermeneutic validity (Lyotard, 1985, p. xxiv). Lyotard's position has been rejected as unnecessarily fatalistic by many, including neo-Marxist critics such as Frederic Jameson, in his *Postmodernism, or, the Cultural Logic of Late Capitalism* (Durham: Duke University Press, 1991), and by Terry Eagleton, who argues, in his 'Capitalism, Modernism and Postmodernism' (in *New Left Review*, 152 (1985), pp. 60–73), that Lyotard is simply granting an ontological status to the fetishised culture of consumer capitalist society. Similar criticisms have been made (but from an essentially neo-Humanist ethical perspective) by Jürgen Habermas in his 'Modernity versus Postmodernity', *New German Critique*, 22 (1981), pp. 3–14, and in *The Philosophical Discourse of Modernity* (Cambridge: Polity Press, 1987), in which he insists upon the unfinished 'project of modernity', which aims at 'an undifferentiated relinking of modern culture with an everyday praxis that still depends on vital heritages' (Habermas, 1981, pp. 12–13). The debate between Lyotard and Habermas has been joined from a philosophical direction by Richard Rorty, most notably in his *Contingency, Irony, and Solidarity* (New York: Cambridge University Press, 1989), and, with a greater sense of the social implications of the issues at stake, by Anthony Giddens, in his *Modernity and Self-Identity: Self and Society in the late Modern Age* (Cambridge: Polity

Press, 1991), and by Ulrich Beck and Scott Lash, *Reflexive Modernisation: Politics, Tradition and Aesthetics in the Modern Social Order* (Cambridge: Polity Press, 1994). The terms of reference of this debate are well-documented in Patricia Waugh's *Postmodernism: A Reader* (London: Edward Arnold, 1992), and Thomas Docherty's, *Postmodernism: A Reader* (New York: Columbia University Press, 1993).

Postmodernism acted both as an imperative and an analytical category. Those who most enthusiastically formulated its aesthetic argued for the abolition of distinctions between high and popular literature, foregrounding, as in Andreas Huyssen's *After the Great Divide: Modernism, Mass Culture, Postmodernism* (Bloomington: Indiana University Press, 1986), the centrality of film, television, pop music and street art to contemporary culture. As a specifically literary category, Postmodernism has received widespread treatment by scholars moving across the related terrains of Anglo-American and European culture. Those with a conspicuous European focus include Christopher Butler, *After the Wake: An Essay on the Contemporary Avant-Garde* (Oxford: Oxford University Press, 1980); Matei Calinescu and Douwe Fokkema (eds.), *Exploring Postmodernism* (Amsterdam: John Benjamins, 1987); Colin Falck, *Myth, Truth and Literature: Towards a True Post-Modernism* (Cambridge: Cambridge University Press, 1989); Linda Hutcheon, *A Poetics of Postmodernism: History, Theory, Fiction* (London: Routledge, 1988); Richard Kearney, *The Wake of Imagination: Towards a Postmodern Culture* (Minneapolis: Minnesota University Press, 1988); Brian McHale, *Postmodernist Fiction* (London: Methuen, 1987); Edmund J. Smyth (ed), *Postmodernism and Contemporary Fiction* (London: Batsford, 1991); Alan Wilde, *Horizons of Assent: Modernism, Postmodernism, and the Ironic Imagination* (Baltimore: John Hopkins, 1981) and Nicholas Zurbrugg, *The Parameters of Postmodernism* (London: Routledge, 1993). In spite of differences of approach and methodology, these works converge upon a common aesthetic, one that is suspicious of unreflective representationalism, master narratives and of all discourses that seek to foreclose the free play of subjectivity and the unpredictable trajectories of desire. For, in the final analysis, Postmodernism was, even in its most pointedly political form, essentially a ludic movement. Its province was not high-moral seriousness but deflationary critique, not cultural capital but forms of literary fabulation that played, often in a highly self-conscious way, with the very notion of serious literature. These are values and attitudes which energise the present as they hold open avenues to the future.

Notes

1 Romanticism

1 Southey, letter to Caroline Bowles, 13 February 1824, in *The Correspondence of Robert Southey with Caroline Bowles*, ed. E. Dowden (Dublin: Hodges and Figgis, 1881), p. 52; and William Godwin, *Caleb Williams* [1794] (London: New English Library, 1966), p. 5.

2 Wordsworth, *Poetical Works*, ed. Thomas Hutchinson, and newly revised by Ernest de Selincourt (Oxford: Oxford University Press, 1969), p. 570; Schlegel, *Schriften und Fragmente*, ed. Ernst Behler (Stuttgart: Kröner, 1956), pp. 104 and 97; Wieland, 'Unparteiische Betrachtungen über die dermalige Staatsrevolution in Frankreich' [1790], in *Werke*, ed. Hans Böhm, 4 vols (Berlin: Aubau Verlag, 1969), vol. 4, p. 206; and Heine, 'Über Ludwig Börne' [1840], in Heine, *Werke*, ed. M. Greiner, 2 vols (Cologne: Kiepenheuer and Witsch, 1962), vol. 2, p. 779.

3 De Quincey, *The Collected Writings*, ed. David Masson, 13 vols (Edinburgh: Adam Charles and Black, 1890), vol. 10, p. 138; and Robespierre, in *Robespierre*, ed. George Rudé (New York: Prentice-Hall; 1967), p. 72.

4 Byron, *Poetical Works*, ed. Frederick Page, corrected by John Jump (London: Oxford University Press, 1970), p. 240; and Wordsworth to William Mathews, 8 June 1792, in *Letters of William Wordsworth: A New Selection*, ed. by Alan G. Hill (Oxford: Oxford University Press, 1984), p. 15.

5 Napoleon, *The Mind of Napoleon: A Selection from his written and spoken Words*, trans. J. Christopher Herold (New York: Columbia University Press, 1953), p. 73; Chateaubriand, *Memoirs*, trans. Robert Baldick (Harmondsworth: Penguin, 1961), p. 329; and Hegel to Niethammer, 13 October 1806, in *Briefe*, ed. Joseph Hoffmeister, 4 vols (Hamburg: Felix Meiner, 1961), vol. 1, p. 120.

6 Stendhal, *Vie de Napoléon* [1828], in *Oeuvres complètes*, ed. Victor Del Litto and Ernest Abravanel, 50 vols (Paris: Librairie Ancienne Honoré Champion, 1970), vol. 39, pp. 75–6; Lamartine from 'Bonaparte' [1823], in *Oeuvres poétiques*, ed. Marius-François Guyard, (Paris: Gallimard, 1963), p. 120; and Hazlitt, *Complete Works*, ed. P.P. Howe, 21 vols (London: Dent, 1931), vol. 13, p. ix.

7 Novalis, *Werke und Briefe*, ed. Alfred Kelletat (Munich: Winkler Verlag, 1953), p. 367; Burke, *Reflections on the Revolution in France* (Harmondsworth: Penguin, 1968), p. 91; and Coleridge, *Biographia Literaria*, ed. George Watson (London: Dent, 1965), p, 103.

8 Johann Peter Eckermann, *Conversations with Goethe*, trans. John Oxenford (London: Dent 1930), p. 246.

9 Schleiermacher, *On Religion: Speeches to its Cultured Despisers* [1799], trans. John Oman (New York: Harper, 1958), p. 10; Kleist, *Werke und Briefe*, ed. Siegfried Streller, 4 vols (Berlin: Aufbau Verlag, 1978),

vol. 2, p. 271; Fichte, *Addresses to the German Nation*, newly ed. George Armstrong Kelly (New York: Harper and Row, 1968), p. 215; and Eichendorff, *Sämmtliche Werke. Historisch-Kritische Ausgabe*, ed. Wilhelm Kosch and August Sauer, 24 vols (Regensburg: Josef Habbel, 1908–13), vol. 10, pp. 159–60.

10   Runeberg, *The Tales of Ensign Stål*, trans. Charles Wharton Stork (Princeton: Princeton University Press, 1938), p. 19; Lönnrot, *Kalevala: The Land of Heroes*, trans. W.F. Kirby, 2 vols (London: Dent, 1907), vol. 1, p. 2.

11   Eckermann, *Conversations with Goethe*, p. 394; and Scott, *Waverley* (Harmondsworth: Penguin, 1972), pp. 478 and 415.

12   Diderot, preface to his *Le Père de famille*, in *Oeuvres choisies*, ed. François Tulou, 2 vols (Paris: Garnier, 1901), vol. 2, p. 111.

13   Samuel Johnson, preface to Father Jerome Lobo's *A Voyage to Abyssinia* [1735] (London: Elliot and Kay, 1789), p. 11; and Stendhal, *Oeuvres complètes*, vol. 37, p. 72.

14   Wordsworth, *Poetical Works*, p. 734.

15   Mme de Staël-Holstein, *Oeuvres Complètes*, 3 vols (Paris: Firmin Didot, 1871), vol. 1, pp. 252–3; Friederich Schlegel, 'Dialogue on Poetry' [1800], in *Dialogue on Poetry* and *Literary Aphorisms*, trans. Ernst Behler and Roman Struc (Pennsylvania: Pennsylvania University Press, 1968), p. 101; and Mme de Staël-Holstein, *Oeuvres Complètes*, vol. 1, p. 257.

16   Macpherson, *The Poems of Ossian*, 2 vols (London: Cadell, 1807), vol. 1, pp. v and 74.

17   Young, *The Complete Works*, ed. James Nichol [1854] (Hildesheim: Georg Olms, 1968), pp. 557 and 554; and Shelley, *Complete Works*, ed. Roger Ingpen and Walter E. Peck, 10 vols (New York: Gordian Press, 1965), vol. 7, pp. 138 and 140.

18   Wordsworth, *Poetical Works*, p. 585; Wordsworth to Walter Savage Landor, 21 January 1824, *Letters*, p. 222; and Coleridge, *Biographia Literaria*, p. 167.

19   Schlegel, *Schriften und Fragmente*, p. 98; Novalis, *Werke und Briefe*, p, 439; and Blake, *Poetry and Prose*, ed. Geoffrey Keynes (London: Nonesuch Press, 1946), p. 187.

20   Wordsworth, *Poetical Works*, p. 735; Keats to George and Tom Keats, 27 December 1817, *Letters of John Keats*, ed. Robert Gittings (Oxford; Oxford University Press, 1970), p. 43; and Shelley, *Complete Works*, vol. 7, p. 135.

21   Schiller, *Naive and Sentimental Poetry*, trans. Julias A. Elias (New York: Frederick Ungar Press, 1966), p. 85; and Kleist 'On the Marionette Theatre', trans. Christian-Albrecht Gollub, in *The German Mind of the Nineteenth Century: A Literary and Historical Anthology*, ed. Hermann Glaser (New York; Continuum, 1981), p. 90.

22   Rousseau, *The Reveries of a Solitary*, trans. John Gould Fletcher (New York: Burt Franklin, 1927), p. 37; and Sand, *George Sand in her own words*, trans. and ed. Joseph Barry (New York: Doubleday, 1979), p. 8.

23   Carlyle, 'On Goethe' [1828], in *Critical and Miscellaneous Essays*, 5 vols (London: Chapman and Hall, 1905), vol. 1, p. 217.

24 Chateaubriand, *René*, trans. Walter J. Cobb (New York: Signet, 1962), p. 106; and Constant, *Adolphe* (London: Hamish Hamilton, 1959), p. 169.
25 Byron, *Poetical Works*, pp. 307, 651 and 112.
26 Pushkin, *Selected Verse*, trans. John Fennell (Harmondsworth: Penguin, 1964), p. 196.
27 Pushkin, *Selected Verse*, pp. 145–6; and Lermontov, *A Hero of our Times*, trans. Paul Foote (Harmondsworth: Penguin, 1966), pp. 93–4, and 157.
28 Lermontov, *A Hero of our Times*, pp. 126–7 and 100; and Nietzsche, *Beyond Good and Evil: Prelude to a Philosophy of the Future* [1886], trans. R.J. Hollingdale (Harmondsworth: Penguin, 1973), p, 39.
29 Blake, *Poetry and Prose*, p. 375; and Shelley, *Complete Works*, vol. 2, p. 196.
30 Lenz, *Werke und Schriften*, ed. Britta Titel and Hellmut Haug, 2 vols (Stuttgart: Goverts Verlag, 1966), vol. 1, p. 379; Lenz, *The Soldiers*, trans. William E. Yuill (Chicago: University of Chicago Press, 1972), p. 119; and Beaumarchais, *La Trilogie de Figaro* (Paris: Gallimard, 1966), p. 137.
31 Adolf Freiherr von Knigge in *Schiller: Zeitgenossen aller Epochen*, ed. Norbert Oellers (Frankfurt am Main: Athenäum Verlag, 1970), p. 57; Schiller, *The Robbers*, trans. F.J. Lamport (Harmondsworth: Penguin, 1979), p. 48; and *Mary Stuart*, in *Five German Tragedies*, trans. F.J. Lamport (Harmondsworth: Penguin, 1969), p. 316.
32 Goethe, *Egmont*, in *Five German Tragedies*, p. 137.
33 Goethe, *Faust: Part One*, trans. Philip Wayne (Harmondsworth, Penguin: 1949), pp. 44 and 89.
34 Kleist to Wilhelmine von Zenge, 21 May 1801, in *Werke und Briefe*, vol. 4, p. 218; and *Penthesilea*, in Heinrich von Kleist, *Five Plays*, trans. Martin Greenberg (New Haven: Yale U.P, 1988), p. 265.
35 Hugo, 'Préface de *Cromwell*', in *Théâtre Complet*, ed. J-J Thierry and Josette Mélèze, 2 vols (Paris: Gallimard, 1963), vol. 1, p. 422; and Hugo, *Hernani* in *Théâtre Complet*, vol. 1, p. 1288.
36 Solomos, *Apanta*, ed. Linos Polites, 2 vols (Athens: Ikaros, 1948–1960), vol. 1, p. 237.
37 Nerval, *Selected Writings*, trans. Geoffrey Wagner (London: Panther Books, 1968), p. 170.
38 Blake to Dr Trusler, 23 August 1799, in *Poetry and Prose*, p. 835; Bernadin Saint Pierre, *Paul and Virginia* (New York: Burt, no date), p. 26; and Leopardi, *Selected Prose and Poetry*, trans. Iris Origo and John Heath-Stubbs (Oxford: Oxford University Press, 1966), p. 213.
39 Lamartine, *Oeuvres Poétiques*, p. 20; and Schleiermacher, *On Religion*, p. 84.
40 Shelley, *Complete Works*, vol. 1, p. 230; Coleridge, *Complete Poetic Works*, ed. Ernest Hartley Coleridge, 2 vols (Oxford; Clarendon Press, 1912), vol.1, p. 102.
41 Burns, *Poems and Songs*, ed. James Kinsley (London: Oxford University Press, 1969), p. 101.
42 Ruskin, *Modern Painters*, 5 vols (London: George Allen, 1904), vol 3, pp. 161–177; and Wordsworth, *Poetical Works*, p. 164.
43 Wordsworth, *Poetical Works*, pp. 587 and 585–6.

44 Coleridge, *Complete Poetical Works*, p. 208; and Coleridge, *Biographia Literaria*, p. 168.
45 Novalis, *Werke und Briefe*, p. 532; and Hoffmann, *Tales of Hoffmann*, trans. R.J. Hollingdale (Penguin: Harmondsworth, 1982), p. 96.
46 Tieck, 'Blond Eckbert' in Four Romantic Tales from 19th Century Germany, trans. Helen Scher (New York: Ungar, 1975), p. 20.
47 Jane Austen, *Northanger Abbey* (Harmondsworth: Penguin, 1972), pp. 175 and 202; and Bedford, *Vathek* in *Three Gothic Novels*, ed. Peter Fairclough (Harmondsworth: Penguin, 1968), pp. 254–5.
48 Shelley, *Poetical Works*, vol. 1, p. 67, and vol 2, p. 180; Byron, *Poetical Works*, p. 260; Keats, *The Complete Poems*, ed. John Barnard (Harmondsworth: Penguin, 1973), p. 335; and Blake, *Poetry and Prose*, p. 531.
49 Schlegel, *Lucinde* (Stuttgart: Reclam, 1964), pp. 7 and 107.
50 Mary Shelley, *Frankenstein*, in *Three Gothic Novels*, ed. Peter Fairclough (Harmondsworth: Penguin, 1968), pp. 263, 313, 312, 318, 319 and 338.
51 Shelley, *Frankenstein*, pp. 493 and 494.
52 Blake, *Poetry and Prose*, p. 118; Leopardi, *Selected Prose and Poetry*, pp. 213 and 307; and Solomos, *Apanta*, vol. 1, p. 255.
53 Novalis, *Werke und Briefe*, pp. 52 and 48–9.
54 Senancour, *Obermann*, 2 vols (Paris: Arthaud, 1947), vol. 1, p. 150; and De Quincey, *Confessions of an English Opium-Eater* (London: Dent, 1960), p. 246.
55 Nerval, *Selected Writings*, p. 227; Nerval, letter to Madame Alexander Dumas, 9 November 1841, in *Oeuvres*, ed. Albert Béguin and Jean Richer (Paris: Gallimard, 1952), p. 853.
56 Nerval, 'Aurelia' in *Selected Writings*, pp. 119, 181, 171, and 151.

2 Realism and Naturalism

1 Wordsworth, *Poetical Works*, p. 385; and Heine, *The Poetry and Prose*, ed. Frederic Ewen (New York: Citadel Press, 1948), p. 725.
2 Burke, *Reflections on the Revolution in France*, p. 193; and Ludwig Büchner, *Kraft und Stoff* (Leipzig: Kröner, 1855).
3 *Clausewitz on War*, ed. Anatol Rapoport (Harmondsworth: Penguin, 1968), p. 119; and Treitschke, *History of Germany in the Nineteenth Century* [1879], trans. Eden and Cedar Paul, 7 vols (London: Jarrold, 1915), vol. 1, p. ix.
4 Manzoni, *The Betrothed*, trans. Bruce Penman (Harmondsworth: Penguin, 1972), p. 720.
5 Stendhal, *The Charterhouse of Parma*, trans. C.K. Scott Moncrieff (London: Chatto and Windus, 1962), p. 146; and Tolstoy, second epilogue to *War and Peace*, trans. Louise and Aylmer Maude (London: Oxford University Press, 1941), p. 537.
6 Dickens, *Our Mutual Friend* (Harmondsworth: Penguin, 1971), p. 146; and Karl Marx and Friedrich Engels, *Selected Works in one Volume* (London: Lawrence and Wishart, 1968), p. 38.

7   Smiles, *Self-Help* (London: John Murray, 1892), p. 94; Spencer, *Principles of Sociology*, 3 vols (London: Williams and Northgate, 1897–1906), vol. 2, p. 241; and Spencer, *Principles of Biology*, 2 vols (London: Williams and Northgate, 1884), vol. 1, p. 444.

8   Robert Southey, *Letters from England by Don Manuel Alvarez Espriella*, 3 vols (London: Longman, Hurst et al., 1808), vol. 2, p. 57; and Jaurès, 'Idealism in History' [1895], in *Socialist Thought: A Documentary History*, ed. Albert Fried and Ronald Sanders (New York: Anchor Books, 1964), p. 407.

9   Gaskell, *Mary Barton* (Harmondsworth: Penguin, 1970), p. 38.

10   Morris, letter of 5 September 1883 to Andreas Scheu, in *William Morris: Selected Writings and Designs*, ed. Asa Briggs (Harmondsworth: Penguin, 1962), p. 32; and Gautier, *Mademoiselle de Maupin*, trans. Joanna Richardson (Harmondsworth: Penguin, 1981), p. 49.

11   Baudelaire, *The Flowers of Evil*, trans. Richard Howard (Boston: Godine, 1982), pp. 94 and 155.

12   Sainte-Beuve, *Selected Essays*, trans. Francis Steegmuller (New York: Anchor Books, 1964), p. 276; and Balzac, *Old Goriot*, trans. Ellen Marriage (London: Everyman, 1907), p. 2.

13   Eliot, *Adam Bede* (Harmondsworth: Penguin, 1980), p. 221; Trollope, *An Autobiography* (Oxford: Oxford University Press, 1953), p. 196; Stendhal, *Scarlet and Black*, trans. Margaret R.B. Shaw (Harmondsworth: Penguin, 1953), p. 365; and Sand, *George Sand in her own words*, ed. Joseph Barry (New York: Doubleday, 1979), p. 5.

14   Brandes, *Creative Spirits of the Nineteenth Century* [1886], trans. Rasmus B. Anderson (New York: Books for Libraries Press, 1923), p. 347; and Brandes, *Henrik Ibsen: A Critical Study*, trans. Jessie Muir, revised by William Archer (London: Macmillan, 1899), pp. 56 and 79.

15   Eliot, 'Worldliness and Other-Worldliness: the Poet Young' [1857], in *Essays of George Eliot*, ed. Thomas Pinney (New York: Columbia University Press, 1963), pp. 370, 385 and 375; and Balzac, *Old Goriot*, p. 2.

16   Eliot, in *Westminster Review*, 65 (April 1856), p. 626; Galdós, 'Contemporary Society as Novelistic Material' [1897], in *Documents of Modern Literary Realism*, ed. George J. Becker (Princeton: Princeton University Press, 1963), p. 153; and Hardy, 'The Profitable Reading of Fiction' [1888], in *Thomas Hardy's Personal Writings: Prefaces, Literary Opinions, Reminiscences*, ed. Harold Orel (London: Macmillan, 1967), p. 118.

17   See Champfleury 'Lettre à Madame Sand sur M. Courbet', in *Le Réalisme* (Geneva: Slatkine Reprints, 1967), p. 279.

18   Letter to Turgenev, 8 November 1877, in *The Letters of Gustave Flaubert, 1857–1880* trans. Francis Steegmuller (Cambridge, Mass.: Harvard University Press, 1982), p. 242; Baudelaire, *Selected Critical Studies of Baudelaire*, ed. D. Parmée (Cambridge: Cambridge University Press, 1949), pp. 72–3; and Edmond and Jules Goncourt, preface to *Germinie Lacerteux* [1865] (Paris: Charpentier, 1901), p. vii.

19   *The Essential Comte: Selected from 'Cours de Philosophie Positive'*, trans. Margaret Clarke (London: Croom Helm, 1974), p. 24; and Taine, *History of English Literature*, 4 vols (New York: Ungar, 1965), vol. 1, p. 17.

20 Balzac, preface to *The Human Comedy* [1848] in *The Works of Honoré de Balzac*, 18 vols (Philadelphia: Avil Publishing Company, 1901), vol. 1, pp. liv and lviii.

21 Eliot, 'The Progress of the Intellect' [1851, in *Essays of George Eliot*, p. 31; Feuerbach, *The Essence of Christianity*, trans. Marian Evans (London: Trübner, 1881), p. ix; and Turgenev, *Literary Reminiscences and Autobiographical Fragments*, trans. David Magarshack (London: Faber, 1958), p. 121.

22 Bernard, *An Introduction to the Study of Experimental Medicine*, trans. Henry Copley Greene (New York: Henry Schuman, 1949), p. 1; and Zola, 'The Experimental Novel', in Becker, *Documents of Literary Realism*, p. 167.

23 Strindberg, 'Naturalism in the Theatre' [1892], in Becker, *Documents of Literary Realism*, p. 398.

24 Balzac, *Old Goriot*, p. 308; Dostoyevsky, *Letters from the Underworld* [1864], trans. C.J. Hogarth (London: Everyman's Library, 1913), p. 9; Dickens, *Dombey and Son* [1848] (Harmondsworth: Penguin, 1970), p. 121; and Fontane, *Effi Briest*, trans. Douglas Parmée (Harmondsworth: Penguin, 1967), p. 87.

25 Dickens, *Miscellaneous Papers* (Oxford: Clarendon Press, 1958), p. 105; and Dickens, *Hard Times* (Harmondsworth: Penguin, 1969), pp. 127 and 145.

26 Dickens, *Dombey and Son* (Harmondsworth: Penguin, 1972), p. 290.

27 Edmund and Jules Goncourt, *Journal*, 4 vols (Paris: Flammarion, 1956), vol. 1, p. 398.

28 Engels to Mary Harkness, April 1888, in *Marx, Engels, Lenin: Über Kultur, Ästhetik, Literatur*, ed. Hans Koch (Leipzig: Reclam, 1973), p. 436; and Balzac, *Old Goriot*, pp. 121 and 308 (my translation).

29 Baudelaire, *Paris Spleen*, trans. Louise Varèse (New York: New Directions, 1947), p. 116.

30 Turgenev, *Fathers and Sons*, p. 30; Gogol, *Diary of a Madman and other Stories*, trans. Ronald Wilks (Harmondsworth: Penguin, 1972), pp. 22 and 93.

31 Dostoyevsky, *Letters from the Underworld*, pp. 7, 20 and 15.

32 Dostoyevsky, *Letters from the Underworld*, pp. 46–7; and *Crime and Punishment*, trans. Ernest J. Simmons (New York: Dell Publishing, 1959), p. 576.

33 Stendhal, *Scarlet and Black*, trans. by Margaret R.B. Shaw (Harmondsworth: Penguin, 1953), p. 451.

34 Stendhal, *Scarlet and Black*, p. 452.

35 Stendhal, *Scarlet and Black*, p. 497; Stendhal, *Love* [1822], trans. Gilbert and Suzanne Sale (Harmondsworth: Penguin, 1957), pp. 193 and 195; and Sand, *George Sand In Her Own Words*, pp. 219 and 8.

36 Charlotte Brontë, *Jane Eyre* (Harmondsworth: Penguin, 1966), p. 476; and Peréz Galdós, *Fortunata and Jacinta*, trans. Agnes Moncy Gullón (Harmondsworth: Penguin, 1986), p. 816.

37 Fontane, *Effi Briest*, pp. 43 and 215; and Tolstoy, *Anna Karenina*, trans. Rosemary Edmonds (Harmondsworth: Penguin, 1954), p. 796.

38 Flaubert, *Madame Bovary*, trans. Alan Russell (Harmondsworth: Penguin, 1950), pp. 79 and 145.

39 Fontane, *Effi Briest*, p. 215; Freytag, 'Neue deutsche Romane' [1853], in *Realismus und Gründerzeit: Manifeste und Dokumente zur deutschen Literatur, 1848–1880*, ed. i.a. Max Bucher, 2 vols (Stuttgart: Metzler, 1975), vol. 2, p. 72.

40 Mörike, *Sämtliche Werke*, 2 vols ed. Helga Unger (Munich: Winkler, 1967), vol. 1, p. 735.

41 Dilthey, *Poetry and Experience*, trans. Rudolf A Makkreel and Frithjof Rodi (Princeton: Princeton University Press, 1985), p. 336; and Goethe, *Wilhelm Meister's Travels*, trans. Edward Bell (London: Bell, 1911), p. 421.

42 Stifter, *Gesammelte Werke*, 6 vols (Frankfurt am Main: Insel, 1959), vol. 3, p. 10; and Stifter, *Der Nachsommer* (Augsburg: Kraft, 1954), p. 213.

43 Keller, *Der grüne Heinrich*, second edition (Munich: Goldmann, 1974), pp. 262 and 585.

44 Austen, *Mansfield Park* (Harmondsworth: Penguin, 1966), pp. 384, 244 and 381.

45 Eliot, *Mill on the Floss* (Oxford: Clarendon Press, 1980), p. 238; and Eliot, *Middlemarch* (Harmondsworth: Penguin, 1965), p. 896.

46 Grillparzer, *Sämtliche Werke*, ed. Peter Frank and Karl Pörnbacher, 4 vols (Munich: Hanser, 1961), vol. 2, p. 342; Hebbel, 'A Word about the Drama', in *Masterpieces of the Modern German Theatre*, ed. Robert W. Corrigan (New York: Collier Books, 1967), p. 71; and Hebbel, *Maria Magdalena*, trans. Carl Richard Mueller, in Corrigan, pp. 87, 120 and 130.

47 Büchner, letter to Minna Jaeglé, 10 March 1834, in *Complete Plays, 'Lenz' and Other Writings*, trans. and ed. John Reddick (Harmondsworth: Penguin, 1993), pp. 195–6; and *Danton's Death*, in *Complete Plays*, p. 69.

48 Büchner, *Complete Plays*, p. 128.

49 Büchner, *Complete Plays*, p. 205; Ibsen, *Ghosts and other Plays*, trans. Peter Watts (Harmondsworth: Penguin, 1964), p. 61; and Ibsen, *When We Dead Wake*, in *Ghosts and other Plays*, pp. 229 and 259.

50 Chekhov, *Three Sisters*, in *Plays*, trans. Elisaveta Fen (Harmondsworth: Penguin, 1959), p. 253; and Chekhov, *The Cherry Orchard*, in *Plays*, p. 386.

51 Zola, *Thérèse Raquin*, trans. Leonard Tancock (Harmondsworth: Penguin, 1962), pp. 22, 26 and 25.

52 Zola, *L'Assommoir*, trans. Margaret Mauldon (Oxford: Oxford University Press, 1995), p. 3; and Zola, *Nana*, trans. Victor Plarr (London: Elek Books, 1957), pp. 206–7 and 446.

53 Tennyson, 'Locksley Hall: Sixty Years After', in *Poems and Plays* (London: Oxford University Press, 1968), p. 524; Verga, *I Malavoglia* (Manchester: Manchester University Press, 1972), p. 4; Holz, *Die Kunst: Ihr Wesen und ihre Gesetze* [1891], in *Literarische Manifeste des Naturalismus, 1880–1892*, ed. Erich Ruprecht (Stuttgart: Metzler, 1962), p. 210; and Conrad, in preface to Holz and Schlaf, *Papa Hamlet* (Stuttgart: Reclam, 1977), p. 12.

54 Hauptmann, *Before Sunrise*, trans. James Joyce (Marino: Huntington Library, 1978), p. 124; and Hauptmann, *The Weavers*, in *Three Plays*, trans. Horst Frenz (New York: Ungar, 1977), p. 92.

55 Strindberg, preface to *Miss Julie*, in Becker, *Documents of Literary Realism*, p. 396; and Strindberg, *The Father*, in *Three Plays*, trans. Peter Watts (Harmondsworth: Penguin, 1958), p. 63.

56   Strindberg, *The Father*, pp. 69 and 56; and Strindberg, *Miss Julie*, in
     Three Plays, p. 97.

3   Modernism

1   Kingsley, *Letters and Memories* [1876], ed. Fanny Kingsley (London:
     Macmillan, 1890), p. 113; and Coleridge, *On the Constitution of the
     Church and State* [1830] (London: Hurst and Chance, 1839), p. 63.
2   Zola, 'J'accuse' [1898], in *Oeuvres Complètes*, ed. Henri Mitterand, 15
     vols (Paris: Cercle du Livre Précieux, 1970), vol. 14, p. 929.
3   Buchan, *Prester John* (Nelson: London, 1910), p. 276; and Conrad, *Heart
     of Darkness* (New York: Bantam, 1971), p. 25.
4   Carlyle, 'Signs of the Times' [1829], in *Selected Writings*, ed. Alan
     Shelston (Harmondsworth: Penguin, 1971), p. 72; and Shaw, preface
     to *Plays Pleasant and Unpleasant* [1898] (Harmondsworth: Penguin,
     1946), p. xxiv.
5   Forster, *Two Cheers for Democracy* (New York: Harcourt, Brace and
     World, 1951), p. 57; and Forster, *Howards End* (Harmondsworth:
     Penguin, 1975), pp. 184 and 329.
6   Tönnies, *Community and Society*, trans. Charles P. Loomis (New York:
     Harper Row, 1963), p. 35; Durkheim, *Suicide*, trans. John A. Spaulding
     and George Simpson (New York: The Free Press, 1951), p. 255; and
     Weber, *The Protestant Ethic and the Spirit of Capitalism*, trans. Talcott
     Parsons (New York: Scribner, 1958), pp. 182 and 181.
7   Mann, *Buddenbrooks*, trans. H.T. Lowe-Porter (Harmondsworth:
     Penguin, 1957), p. 315; Rilke, *The Notebook of Malte Laurids Brigge*,
     trans. John Linton (London: Hogarth Press, 1969), p. 70; and Hesse,
     Steppenwolf, trans. Basil Creighton, and revised by Walter Sorrell
     (Harmondsworth: Penguin, 1965), p. 252.
8   Zweig, *The World of Yesterday: An Autobiography* (London: Cassell,
     1943), p. 155.
9   Housman, *A Shropshire Lad* (London: Richards, 1896), p. 57; and
     Mann, *Death in Venice*, trans. H.T. Lowe-Porter (Harmondsworth:
     Penguin, 1955), p. 7.
10   Nietzsche, *The Case of Wagner* [1888], trans. Walter Kaufman (New
     York: Vintage Books, 1967); Heym, 'War', in *Twentieth-Century German
     Verse*, trans. Patrick Bridgwater (Harmondsworth: Penguin, 1963),
     p. 106; Marinetti in *Futurist Manifestos*, trans. Robert Brain et al, and
     ed. Umbro Apollonio (New York: The Viking Press, 1973). p. 22; and
     Marinetti, *Selected Writings*, ed. R.W. Flint (London: Secker and
     Warburg, 1972), p. 85.
11   Bergson, *Matter and Memory*, trans. Nancy Margaret Paul and W. Scott
     Palmer (London: Allen and Unwin, 1911), p. 276.
12   Lewis, *Time and Western Man* (London: Chatto and Windus, 1927),
     p. 102; and Laura Riding and Robert Graves (eds), *A Survey of
     Modernist Poetry* (London: Heineman, 1927), p. 9.
13   Hardekopf in *Expressionismus: Literatur und Kunst, 1910–1923*, ed.
     Bernhard Zeller (Marbach: Deutsches Literaturarchiv, 1960), p. 125;

and Tzara, *Seven Dada Manifestos and Lampisteries*, trans. Barbara Wright (London: John Calder, 1977), pp. 8 and 112.

14 Benn, *Primal Vision: Selected Writings*, trans. E.B. Ashton (New York: New Directions, 1971), p. 37; Flake in *Expressionismus: Der Kampf um eine literarische Bewegnung*, ed. Paul Raabe (Munich: dtv, 1965), p. 65; Edschmid, 'Über den dichterischen Expressionismus' [1917], in Edschmid, *Frühe Manifeste* (Hamburg: Christian Wegner, 1957), p. 32.

15 Lewis, *Blasting and Bombadiering: An Autobiography, 1914–1926* [1937] (London: Caldar and Boyers, 1967), p. 41; and Lewis, *Wyndham Lewis the Artist: From 'Blast' to Burlington House* [1939] (New York: Haskell House, 1971), p. 128.

16 Breton, *Manifestos of Surrealism*, trans. Richard Seaver and Helen R. Lane (Ann Arbor: University of Michigan Press, 1969), p. 26; Breton, 'What is Surrealism?' [1934] in *Theories of Modern Art*, ed. Herschel B. Chipp (Berkeley: University of California Press, 1968), p. 414; and Queneau, *The Bark Tree*, trans. Barbara Wright (London: Caldar and Boyars, 1968), p. 59.

17 Aragon, *Paris Peasant*, trans. Simon Watson Taylor (London: Jonathan Cape, 1971), p. 24; and Artaud, *The Theatre and its Double*, trans. Mary Caroline Richards (New York: Grove Press, 1958), pp. 8, 89 and 86.

18 Marinetti, 'Destruction of Syntax – Imagination without Strings- Words in Freedom', in *Futurist Manifestos*, pp. 105 and 95; Schwitters, 'Konsequente Dichtung', in *Das literarische Werk*, ed. Friedhelm Lach, 5 vols (Cologne: DuMont, 1981), vol. 5, p. 191.

19 Woolf, 'Mr Bennett and Mrs Brown' [1924], in *Collected Essays*, 4 vols (London: The Hogarth Press, 1971), vol. 1, pp. 320 and 334; and Eliot, in *Selected Prose*, ed. Frank Kermode (London: Faber and Faber, 1975), pp. 44 and 39.

20 Brod, *Franz Kafka: A Biography* [1937] (New York: Schocken Books, 1960), p. 195; and Woolf, 'Modern Fiction' [1919], in *Collected Essays*, vol. 2, p. 106.

21 Symons, *The Symbolist Movement in Literature* (London: William Heineman, 1899), p. 10; Baudelaire, 'Since it is a Question of Realism' [1855], in *Baudelaire as a Literary Critic: Selected Essays*, trans. Lois Boe Hyslop and Francis E. Hyslop, Jr. (Pennsylvania: Pennsylvania State University Press, 1964), p. 86; and Flaubert, letter to Turgenev, 8 November 1877, in *The Letters of Gustave Flaubert, 1857–1880*, trans. Francis Steegmuller (Cambridge, Mass.: Harvard University Press, 1982), p. 242.

22 Lautréamont, *Les Chants de Maldoror*, ed. Daniel Oster (Paris: Presses de la Renaissance, 1977), p. 6; Rimbaud, letter to Georges Izambard, 13 May 1871, in *Rimbaud: Collected Poems*, trans. Oliver Bernard (Harmondsworth: Penguin, 1962), p. 6; and Rimbaud, *A Season in Hell*, in *Collected Poems*, pp. 309 and 317.

23 Huysmans, *Against Nature*, trans. Robert Baldick (Harmondsworth: Penguin, 1959), pp. 63 and 65.

24 Symons in 'The Decadent Movement in Literature' [1893], as quoted by his contemporary, Holbrook Jackson, in *The Eighteen Nineties* [1913] (New York: Alfred Knopf, 1972), p. 55; Gautier, preface to Baudelaire,

Les Fleurs Du Mal (Paris: (Calmann-Lévy, 1868), p. 17. Pater, *The Renaissance: Studies in Art and Poetry* (London: Collins, 1961), p. 222; Wilde, *The Picture of Dorian Gray* [1891] (New York: Lamb Publishing, 1919), pp. 47; and Wilde, preface to *The Picture of Dorian Gray*, p. 6.

25 Mallarmé, 'Crisis in Poetry' [1895], in Mallarmé, *Selected Prose Poems, Essays and Letters*, trans. Bradford Cook (Baltimore: John Hopkins, 1956), pp. 40 and 41.

26 From 'The Evolution of Literature' [1891], in Mallarmé, *Selected Prose Poems, Essays and Letters*, p. 21; and Mallarmé, *Selected Poems*, trans. Anthony Hartley (Harmondsworth: Penguin, 1965), p. 52.

27 Pater, *Marius the Epicurean* (New York: Boni and Liveright, no date), p. 380; and Hopkins, letter to Coventry Patmore, 24 September 1883, in *Further Letters of Gerard Manley Hopkins*, ed. Claude Colleer Abbott (Oxford: Oxford University Press, 1956), p. 306.

28 George, *Werke*, 2 vols (Munich and Düsseldorf: Helmut Küpper, 1958), vol. 1, p. 418.

29 Laforgue, *Poésies*, ed. Claude Pichois (Paris: Armand Colin, 1959), p. 264; Rimbaud, letter to George Izambard, 13 May 1871, in *Rimbaud: Collected Poems*, p. 6; and Lawrence, letter to Edward Garnett, 5 June 1914, in *The Letters of D.H. Lawrence*, ed. George J. Zytaruk and James T. Boulton, 7 vols (Cambridge: Cambridge University Press, Cambridge, 1981), vol. 2, p. 183.

30 Nietzsche, *The Birth of Tragedy* [1871], trans. Francis Golffing (New York: Doubleday Anchor, 1956), pp. 8 and 19; and Freud, *New Introductory Lectures on Psychoanalysis* [1933], trans. James Strachey (Harmondsworth: Penguin, 1973), pp. 105–6.

31 Stevenson, *Dr Jekyll and Mr Hyde* (London: Dent, 1968), p. 56.

32 Stevenson, *Dr Jekyll and Mr Hyde* p. 50; and Conrad, *Heart of Darkness* (New York: Bantam Books, 1969), pp. 50, 112.

33 Conrad, *Heart of Darkness*, p. 132; and Musil, *Young Törless*, trans. Eithne Wilkins and Ernst Kaiser (London: Granada, 1971), pp. 61–62.

34 Benn, *Gesammelte Werke*, ed. Dieter Wellershoff, 4 vols (Wiesbaden: Limes Verlag, 1961), vol. 1, p. 436; and Benn, *Primal Vision*, p. 9 [my translation].

35 Pirandello, preface to *Six Characters in Search of an Author*, in *Naked Masks: Five Plays by Luigi Pirandello*, ed. Eric Bentley (New York: Dutton, 1952), p. 367; Pirandello, *Henry IV*, in *Naked Masks*, p. 206; and Pirandello, *Six Characters in Search of an Author*, in *Naked Masks* p. 217.

36 Kafka, *The Complete Stories*, ed. Nahum N. Glatzer [various translators] (New York: Schocken Books, 1972), pp. 144 and 122.

37 Kafka, *The Trial*, trans. Willa and Edwin Muir (Harmondsworth: Penguin, 1953), pp. 18 and 250.

38 Musil, *Young Törless*, p. 86; Hofmannsthal, *Selected Prose*, trans. Mary Hottinger and Tania and James Stern (New York: Pantheon Books, 1952), pp. 134–5; and Kafka, letter to Ottla Kafka, 10 July 1914, in *Letters to Friends, Family, and Editors*, trans. Richard and Clara Winston (New York: Schocken Books, 1977), p. 109.

39 Woolf, 'Modern Fiction', in *Collected Essays*, vol. 2, pp. 106 and 107; Leonard Woolf, quoted from *The Diary of Virginia Woolf*, ed. Anne

Olivier Bell, 3 vols (London: Hogarth Press, 1980), vol. 3, p. 59; and Woolf, *To the Lighthouse* (Harmondsworth: Penguin, 1964), pp. 121 and 237.

40   Leonard Woolf, quoted in *The Diary of Virginia Woolf*, vol. 3, p. 123; Svevo, *Confessions of Zeno*, trans. Beryl de Zoete (Harmondsworth: Penguin, 1964), p. 25; and Mann, *The Magic Mountain*, trans. H.T. Lowe-Porter (Harmondsworth: Penguin, 1960), p. 477.

41   Proust, *Swann's Way*, trans. C.K. Scott Moncrieff (London: Chatto and Windus, 1973), p. 61; and Proust, *Time Regained*, trans. Andreas Mayor (London: Chatto and Windus; 1972), p. 451.

42   Joyce, *Ulysses* (Harmondsworth: Penguin, 1969), p. 42.

43   Joyce, *Ulysses*, p. 704.

44   Schnitzler, *Merry-Go-Round*, trans. Frank and Jacqueline Marcus (London: Weidenfeld and Nicolson, 1953), p. 38.

45   Kokoschka, *Murderer, The Women's Hope*, trans. Michael Hamburger, in *Anthology of German Expressionist Drama*, ed. Walter H. Sokel (New York: Doubleday, 1963), p. 19.

46   Colette, *Chéri*, trans. Roger Senhouse (Harmondsworth: Penguin, 1954), p. 29; and Montherlant, *The Girls*, a tetralogy in two volumes, trans. Terence Kilmartin (London: Weidenfeld and Nicolson, 1968), vol. 1, pp. 45 and 111.

47   Lawrence, *Sons and Lovers* (Harmondsworth: Penguin, 1948), p. 345; Lawrence, *Selected Literary Criticism*, ed. Anthony Beal (London: Heinemann, 1955), p. 68; and Lawrence, *Women in Love* (Harmondsworth: Penguin, 1960), pp. 388 and 361.

48   Lawrence, *Women in Love*, pp. 541 and 305; and Gide, *The Immoralist*, trans. Dorothy Bussy (Harmondsworth: Penguin, 1960), pp. 15 and 137.

49   T.E. Lawrence, *Seven Pillars of Wisdom* (Harmondsworth: Penguin, 1962), p. 454; Lawrence, letter to Charlotte Shaw, 26 December 1925, in T.E. Lawrence, British Museum Additional Manuscripts, 45903; and Mann, *Death in Venice*, pp. 34 and 77.

50   Cocteau, *The Holy Terrors*, trans. Rosamond Lehmann (New York: New Directions Books, 1957), pp. 40, 181 and 64; Musil, *Young Törless*, pp. 94 and 189; and Bronnen, *Vatermord* in *Stücke* (Kronberg: Athenäum, 1977), p. 53.

51   Wittgenstein, *Tractatus Logico-Philosophicus*, trans. D.F. Pears and B.F. McGuinness (London: Routledge, 1961), p. 37; Eliot, *Collected Poems, 1909–1962* (London: Faber and Faber, 1963), p. 218; Valéry, *Poems*, trans. James R. Lawler (Princeton: Princeton University Press, 1971), p. 215; and Valéry, *The Art of Poetry*, trans. Denise Folliot (New York: Pantheon Books, 1958), p. 108.

52   Rilke, *Selected Works*, 2 vols, trans. J.B. Leishman (London: Hogarth Press, 1967), vol. 2, pp. 195, 225 and 244.

53   Ungaretti, *Selected Poetry*, trans. Patrick Creagh (Harmondsworth: Penguin, 1971), p. 9; and Montale, *Selected Poems*, trans. Ben Belitt i.a. (New York: New Directions, 1965), p. 3.

54   Machado, *Selected Poems*, trans. Alan S. Trueblood (Cambridge Mass.: Harvard University Press, 1982), p. 163.

55 Gumilyov, 'Acmeism and the Legacy of Symbolism' [1913], in *Selected Works*, trans. Burton Raffel and Alla Burago (Albany: State University of New York Press, 1972), p. 248; Akhmatova, *Poems*, trans. Stanley Kunitz and Max Hayward (Boston: Little, Brown and Company, 1973), p. 73; and Mandelstam, *Complete Poetry*, trans. Burton Raffel (Albany: State University of New York Press, 1973), pp. 130–1 and 297.

56 Pound, *Literary Essays*, ed. T.S. Eliot (London: Faber and Faber, 1960), p. 4; and Eliot, *Collected Poems*, p. 79.

57 Cavafy, *Complete Poems*, trans. Rae Dalven (London: Hogarth Press, 1961), p. 165; and Seferis, *Poems*, trans. Rex Warner (Boston: Little, Brown and Company, 1960), pp. 11 and 31.

58 Yeats, *Collected Poems* (London: Macmillan, 1950), p. 214; Yeats, *A Vision* (London: Macmillan, 1956), p. 68; and Yeats, *Collected Poems*, p. 337.

4 The Literature of Political Engagement

1 Lawrence, *Kangaroo* (Harmondsworth: Penguin, 1950), pp. 240–1; and Woolf, *Downhill All the Way: An Autobiography of the Years, 1919–1939* (London: Hogarth Press, 1968), p. 9.

2 Spengler, *Decline of the West*, trans. Charles Francis Atkinson, 2 vols (London: Allen and Unwin, 1932), vol, 1, Table. 1, and vol. 2, Contents, p. 2.

3 Mauriac, *The Inner Presence: Recollections of My Spiritual Life*, trans. Herma Briffault (New York: Bobbs-Merrill, 1968), p. 116; and Romains, *The Sixth of October*, trans. Warre B. Wells (London: Lovat Dickson, 1933), p. 12.

4 Binding, 'Deutsche Jugend vor den Toten des Krieges' in *Grundschriften der deutschen Jugendbewegung*, ed. Werner Kindt (Düsseldorf: Diederichs, 1963), p. 431; and Schauwecker, *Der Aufbruch der Nation* (Berlin: Frundsberg, 1930), p. 403.

5 Sassoon, *Memoirs of an Infantry Officer* (London: Faber and Faber, 1965), p. 218; Graves, *Goodbye to All That* (Penguin; Harmondsworth, 1960), p. 215; and Remarque, *All Quiet on the Western Front*, trans. A.W. Wheen (London: Putnam, 1929), pp. 317–18.

6 Spender, *World Within World* (Berkeley: University of California Press, 1966), p. 305; and Koestler in *The God that Failed: Six Studies in Communism*, ed. Richard Crossman (London: Harper and Row, 1950), p. 28; and Crossman, *The God that Failed*, p. 11.

7 Koestler in Crossman, *The God that Failed*, p. 32.

8 Sorel, *Reflections on Violence*, trans. T.E. Hulme and J. Roth (New York: Collier Books, 1961), p. 48; Benn, 'Primal Vision' [1927], in *Primal Vision: Selected Writings*, trans. E.B. Ashton (London: Bodley Head, 1961), p. 36; Lawrence, 'A Letter from Germany' [1924], in *Essays* (Harmondsworth: Penguin, 1950), p. 177; and Benda, *The Great Betrayal*, trans. Richard Aldington (London: Routledge, 1928), p. 21.

9 John Lehmann, *The Whispering Gallery* (London: Longmans, Green and Co., 1955), p. 275.

10 Auden, 'Spain', and Spender, 'At Castellon' [1938], in *The Penguin Book of Spanish Civil War Verse*, ed. Valentine Cunningham (Harmondsworth:

Penguin, 1980), pp. 97 and p. 135; and Malraux, *Days of Hope*, trans. Stuart Gilbert and Alastair Macdonald (Harmondsworth: Penguin, 1970), pp. 354 and 355.

11 Orwell, *Homage to Catalonia* (Harmondsworth: Penguin, 1966), pp. 141 and 142 and 235.

12 Spender, *World Within World*, p. 249; and Mayakovsky, *Mayakovsky*, trans. Herbert Marshall (London: Denis Dobson, 1965), p. 90.

13 Andrey Zhdanov i.a., *Problems of Soviet Literature: Reports amd Speeches at the First Soviet Writers' Congress* (Moscow: Co-operative Publishing Society, 1935), p. 21; and Ostrovsky, *The Making of a Hero*, trans. Alec Brown (London: Secker and Warburg, 1937), p. 440.

14 Mann, 'Geist und Tat', in *Politische Essays* (Frankfurt am Main: Suhrkamp, 1970), p. 13; and Ossietzky, *Rechenschaft: Publizistik aus den Jahren 1913–1933* (Frankfurt am Main: Fischer, 1972), p. 188.

15 Rickword in interview with John Lucas, in *The 1930s: A Challenge to Orthodoxy*, ed. John Lucas (Harvester Press: Sussex, 1978), p. 5; and Roberts, *New Signatures* (London: Hogarth Press, 1932), pp. 11–12.

16 Day Lewis, *The Buried Day* (London: Chatto and Windus, 1969), pp. 211 and 212; MacNeice, *Modern Poetry* [1938] (Oxford, Oxford University Press, 1968), p. 25; and Auden, in *Poetry of the Thirties*, ed. Robin Skelton (Harmondsworth: Penguin, 1964), pp. 56, 280 and 283.

17 Gide, *Journal*, 2 vols (Paris: Pléiade, 1948), vol. 1, p. 1126.

18 Engels, letter to Minna Kautsky, 26 November 1885, in *Marx, Engels, Lenin: Über Kultur, Ästhetik, Literatur*, ed. Hans Koch (Leipzig: Reclam, 1973), p. 433; Lenin, *Collected Works*, 44 vols (Moscow: Foreign Languages Publishing House, 1960), vol. 10, p. 46; and Trotsky, *Literature and Revolution*, trans. Rose Strunsky (Michigan: University of Michigan Press, 1960), pp. 256 and 255.

19 Caudwell, *Studies in a Dying Culture*, (MR Books: New York, 1971), p. xx; Lukács, 'Aus der Not ein Tugend' [1932], in Lukács, *Schriften zur Literatursoziologie*, ed. Peter Ludz (Neuwied: Luchterhand, 1961), p. 145; and Lukács in *Aesthetics and Politics: Debates between Bloch, Lukács, Brecht, Benjamin, Adorno*, tr. and ed. Ronald Taylor (London: Verso, 1977), pp. 39, 52 and 57.

20 Benjamin, 'The Work of Art in the Age of Mechnical Reproduction', in Benjamin, *Illuminations*, ed. Hannah Arendt (London. Fontana, 1973), pp. 223 and 253.

21 Brecht, 'Bei Durchsicht meiner ersten Stücke' [1954], in *Frühe Stücke* (Frankfurt am Main: Suhrkamp, 1973), p. 11; and *Brecht on Theatre*, ed. John Willett (Methuen: London, 1964), p. 57.

22 Brecht, *Manual of Piety*, trans. Eric Bentley (New York: Grove Press, 1966), p. 247 [my translation]; and Kästner, *Fabian: Die Geschichte eines Moralisten* [1931] (Frankfurt am Main: Ullstein, 1975), p. 124.

23 Musil, *The Man without Qualities*, trans. Eithne Wilkins and Ernst Kaizer, 3 vols (London: Panther, 1968), vol. 1, pp. 68 and 69; Canetti, *Auto-da-Fé*, trans. C.V. Wedgwood (London: Pan Books, 1978), p. 366; and Döblin, *Berlin Alexanderplatz*, trans. Eugene Jolas (Harmondsworth: Penguin, 1978), pp. 7 and 478.

24   Breton, *Manifestos of Surrealism*, trans. Richard Seaver and Helen R. Lane (Ann Arbor: University of Michigan Press, 1969), p. 142; and Breton, *Nadja*, trans. Richard Howard (New York: Grove Press, 1960), p. 111.

25   Alberti, *Poesias Completas* (Buenos Aires: Editorial Losada, 1961), p. 308; and Lorca, *Selected Poems*, trans. J.L. Gili (Harmondsworth: Penguin, 1960), pp. 63 and 72.

26   Brecht, *Measures Taken*, trans. Carl R. Mueller (London: Methuen, 1977), p. 33.

27   Silone, *Fontamara*, trans. Eric Mosbacher (London: Dent, 1985), p. 48; and Silone in Crossman, *The God that failed*, p. 119.

28   Malraux, `Reply to Trotsky' [1931], in *Malraux*, ed. R.W.B. Lewis (New York: Prentice Hall, 1964), p. 21; and Malraux, *Man's Estate*, trans. Alastair Macdonald (Harmondsworth: Penguin, 1961), pp. 240, 11–12, 215, 219, and 316.

29   Malraux, `Afterword' [1947] to *The Conquerors*, trans. Stephen Becker (New York: Holt, Rinehart and Winston, 1976), pp. 189 and 183; and Mann, `Deutsche Ansprache', in *Essays*, ed. Hermann Kurzke, 3 vols (Frankfurt am Main: Fischer, 1977), vol. 2, p. 110.

30   Mann, *Mario and the Magician*, trans. H.T. Lowe-Porter (Harmondsworth: Penguin, 1975), p. 150.

31   Mann, *Doctor Faustus*, trans. H.T. Lowe-Porter (Harmondsworth: Penguin, 1968), pp. 39, 64 and 462.

32   Koestler, in Crossman, *The God that Failed*, p. 69; and Woodcock, *Writers and Politics* [1948] (Montreal: Black Rose Books, 1990), p. 6.

33   Koestler, *Darkness at Noon*, trans. Daphne Hardy (Harmondsworth: Penguin, 1964), pp. 82, 83, 172 and 211; and in Crossman, *The God that Failed*, p. 76.

34   Mayakovsky, *The Bedbug and Selected Poetry*, trans. Max Hayward and George Reavey and ed. Patricia Blake (New York: World Publishing, 1960), pp. 300 and 303; and Zamytin, *We*, trans. Mirra Ginsburg (New York: The Viking Press, 1972), pp. 95 and 130.

35   Huxley, *Brave New World* (New York: Perennial Library, 1969), p. 2; Huxley, *Brave New World Revisited* (New York: Harper Row, 1958), p. 3; and Huxley, *Brave New World*, p. 163.

36   Orwell, *The Road to Wigan Pier* (Harmondsworth: Pennguin, 1962), pp. 188 and 167; and Orwell, *Animal Farm: A Fairy Story* (London: Secker and Warburg, 1971), p. 99.

37   Orwell, *1984* (Harmondsworth: Penguin, 1954), p. 31.

38   Ortega Y Gasset, *The Revolt of the Masses* [1930] (London: Allen and Unwin, 1961), p. 13; and Spengler, *The Decline of the West*, vol. 2, pp. 506 and 507.

39   Benn, 'Lebensweg eines Intellektualisten' [1934], in *Gesammelte Werke*, 4 vols. ed. Dieter Wellershoff (Wiesbaden: Limes Verlag, 1961), vol. 4, p. 56.

40   Stehr, 'Das neue Evangelium', in *Stundenglas: Schriften, Reden, Tagebücher*, (Leipzig: List, 1936), p. 165; and Jünger, preface to *Feuer und Blut* (Berlin: Mittler, 1925).

41   Marinetti, 'Beyond Communism' [1920], in *Selected Writings* (New York: Farrar, Straus and Giroux, 1971), p. 148.

42 Drieu la Rochelle, *The Comedy of Charleroi*, trans. Douglas Gallagher (Cambridge: Rivers Press, 1973), pp. 17, 14 and 44; and Céline, *Voyage au bout de la nuit* (Paris: Gallimard, 1962), p. 407.

43 Lawrence, *Fantasia of the Unconscious* (Harmondsworth: Penguin, 1971), pp. 11, 12, 13 and 16; and *Kangaroo* (Harmondsworth: Penguin, 1950), pp. 287, 289 and 294.

44 Gottfried Benn, *Werke*, vol. 2, p. 117, and vol. 1, p. 440.

45 Woodcock, *Writer and Politics*, p. 18; Mauriac, *The Knot of Vipers*, trans. Gerard Hopkins (Harmondsworth: Penguin, 1985), p. 185; and Mauriac, 'Graham Greene', from *Men I Hold Great* (New York: Philosophical Library, 1951), pp. 124–8.

46 Bernanos, *Sous le soleil de Satan* (Paris: Plon, 1926), pp. 286–7; and Bernanos, *The Diary of a Country Priest*, trans. Pamela Morris (New York: Macmillan, 1962), pp. 139 and 251.

47 Greene, *Brighton Rock* (London: William Heineman, 1970), p. 284; and *The Power and the Glory* (London: William Heineman, 1971), p. 253.

48 Eliot, *The Four Quartets* (London: Faber and Faber, 1959), p. 16.

49 Eliot, *The Four Quartets*, pp. 18, 28, 31, 58 and 59.

50 Bernanos, *La Liberté, pour quoi faire?* [1942] (Paris: Gallimard, 1953), pp. 287–8; and Camus, 'The Artist and his Time', in *The Myth of Sisyphus*, trans. Justin O'Brien (New York: Alfred Knopf, 1955), p. 148.

51 Sartre, *Nausea*, trans. Robert Baldick (Harmondsworth: Penguin, 1965), p. 188; and Camus, *The Outsider*, trans. Stuart Gilbert (Harmondsworth: Penguin, 1961), p. 120.

52 Camus, *The Plague*, trans. Stuart Gilbert (New York: The Modern Library, 1948), p. 150.

53 Sartre, *Crime Passionnel*, trans. Kitty Black (London: Methuen, 1961), p. 118.

5 Postmodernism

1 Koestler, *Bricks to Babel: A Selection from 50 Years of his Writings* (New York: Random House, 1980), p. 507; Malraux, afterword to *The Conquerors* [1949], trans. Stephen Becker (New York: Holt, Rinehart and Winston, 1976), p. 188; Cayrol, 'Pour un romanesque lazaréen' in *Les Corps étrangers* (Paris: Éditions du Seuil, 1964), p. 201; Adorno, *Prisms* (London: Neville Spearman, 1967), p. 34; and Grass, 'What shall we tell our children?' [1979], in *On Writing and Politics, 1967–1983* (Harmondsworth: Penguin, 1987), p. 76.

2 Lowry, *Under the Volcano* (Harmondsworth: Penguin, 1963), p. 11; and Golding, *Lord of the Flies* (London: Faber and Faber, 1962), p. 188.

3 Böll, 'In Defense of Rubble Literature' [1952] in *Missing Persons and other Essays*, trans. Leila Vennewitz (New York: McGraw-Hill Book Company, 1977), p. 127; and Böll, 'Number Seven, Hülchrather Street' [1971], in *Missing Persons*, p. 16.

4 Calvino, *The Path to the Nest of Spiders*, trans. Archibald Colquhoun (New York: Ecco Press, 1976), p. v; and Quasimodo, *Selected Poems*, trans. Jack Bevan (Harmondsworth: Penguin, 1965), p. 102.

5   Osborne, *A Better Class of Person: An Autobiography, 1929–1956* (Harmondsworth: Penguin, 1982), p. 168; Conquest, *New Lines: An Anthology* (London: Macmillan, 1956), p. xv; Miller, *Writing in England Today: The last Fifteen Years* (Harmondsworth: Penguin, 1968), p. 13; and Larkin, *Collected Poems* (London: Faber and Faber, 1988), p. 42.

6   Crossman, in *The God that failed*, ed. Richard Crossman (London: Hamilton, 1949), p. 11; and Grass, 'Open Letter to Anna Seghers' [1961], reprinted in Grass, *Two States – One Nation?* (London: Harcourt Brace 1990), p. 93.

7   Solzhenitsyn, *One Day in the Life of Ivan Denisovich*, trans. Ralph Parker (Harmondsworth: Penguin, 1963), p. 139; and Havel, 'On Evasive Thinking' [1965], in *Open Letters: Selected Prose, 1965–1990* (London: Faber and Faber, 1991), pp. 16 and 17.

8   Edgar, 'Ten Years of Political Theatre, 1968–1978', in *The Second Time as Farce: Reflections on the Drama of Mean Times* (London: Lawrence and Wishart, 1988), p. 26; and Enzensberger, *The Consciousness Industry: On Literature, Politics and the Media* (New York: Seabury Press, 1974), p. 15.

9   Müller, 'Ein Brief', in *Theater-Arbeit* (Berlin: Rotbuch Verlag, 1975), p. 121; and Müller, 'Ein Brief', in *Theater-Arbeit*, p. 126.

10   Hein and Heym in *'Wir sind das Volk': Flugschriften, Aufrufe und Texte einer deutschen Revolution*, ed. Charles Schüddekopf (Reinbek: Rowohlt, 1990), p. 207; and Milosz, *Collected Poems (1931–1987)*, (Harmondsworth: Penguin, 1988), p. 88.

11   Barth, 'The Literature of Exhaustion', *The Atlantic Monthly* , vol. 220, no. 1 (August 1967), 33; and Hassan, *The Dismemberment of Orpheus : Towards a Postmodern Literature* (New York: Oxford University Press, 1971), p. 258.

12   Barthes, 'The Structuralist Activity' [1963], in *Critical Essays*, (Evanston: Northwestern University Press, 1972), pp. 213 and 215.

13   Kundera, 'Dialogue on the art of the novel' [1983], in *The Art of the Novel* (London: Faber and Faber, 1988), p. 36; Pinter, *Plays*, 3 vols (London: Eyre Methuen, 1976), vol. 1, p. 12.; and Angela Carter, *The Sadeian Women: An Exercise in Cultural History* (London: Virago, 1979), p. 19.

14   Machery, *A Theory of Literary Production*, trans. Geoffrey Wall (London: Routledge, 1978), p. 122.

15   Ritsos, *Selected Poems*, trans. Nikos Stangos (Penguin: Harmondsworth, 1974), p. 168.

16   Baudrillard, *Simulations* (New York: Semiotext(e), 1983), p. 4.

17   Jean-Francois Lyotard, *The Postmodern Condition: A Report on Knowledge* [1979] (Manchester: Manchester University Press, 1984), p. 81; Kundera, 'Dialogue on the art of the novel', p. 41; Herbert 'Why the Classics?' [1967], in *The Poetry of Survival: Post-war Poets of Central and Eastern Europe*, ed. Daniel Weissbort (Harmondsworth: Penguin, 1991), p. 332; and Wolf, 'The Reader and the Writer', in *The Reader and the Writer: Essays, Sketches, Memories* (Berlin: Seven Seas, 1977), p. 200.

18   Beckett, 'Dante...Bruno. Vico...Joyce', *in Our Exagmination round his Factification for Incamination of Work in Progress* [1929] (New York: New Directions Books, 1972), p. 15; and Johnson, *Aren't you rather young to be writing Your Memoirs?* (London; Hutchinson, 1973), pp. 16–17.

19   Robbe-Grillet, *For a New Novel: Essays on Fiction*, trans. Richard Howard (New York: Grove Press, 1965), p. 141.
20   Robbe-Grillet, *For a New Novel*, p. 161.
21   Fowles, *The French Lieutenant's Woman* (London: Panther, 1977), p. 86; Perec, *Life, A User's Manual*, trans. David Bellos (London: Collins Harvil, 1987), p. xvii; and Kristeva, 'Word, Dialogue and Novel [1966], in *Desire and Language: A Semiotic Approach to Literature and Art* (New York: Columbia U.P, 1980), p. 66.
22   Calvino, Preface to *The Path to the Nest of Spiders*, p. xvi; and Calvino, *Invisible Cities*, trans. William Weaver (New York: Harcourt Brace, 1974), p. 139.
23   Calvino, *If on a Winter's Night a Traveller* (London: Picador, 1982), p. 204.
24   Barthes, 'Objective Literature', in *Critical Essays*, p. 23; Camus, *The Myth of Sisyphus*, trans. Justin O'Brien (New York: Signet, 1955), p. 5; Ionesco, *Fragments of a Journal*, trans. Jean Stewart (New York: Grove Press, 1969), p. 19; and Ionesco, *Notes and Counter Notes*, trans. Donald Watson (London: John Calder, 1964), p. 206.
25   Beckett, *Waiting for Godot* (London: Faber and Faber, 1959), p. 41; and Robbe-Grillet, 'Samuel Becket, or Presence on the Stage' [1953], in *For a New Novel*, p. 116.
26   Genet, 'Letters to Roger Blin' [1966], in *Reflections on the Theatre*, trans. Richard Seaver (London: Faber and Faber, 1972), p. 20.
27   Vaclav Havel, 'Second Wind' [1977], in *Open Letters*, p. 9.
28   Fo, Introduction to *Knock, Knock! Who's There? Police!* in *File on Dario Fo*, ed. Tony Mitchell (London: Methuen, 1989), p. 45.
29   Handke, Author's note to *Self-Accusation and Offending the Audience*, trans. Michael Roloff (London: Methuen, 1971), p. 7.
30   Bond, 'If we were here', in *The Worlds* with *The Activist Papers* (London: Methuen, 1980), p. 142.
31   Barthes, 'Objective Literature' [1954], in *Critical Essays*, p. 23; Rushdie, *Imaginary Homelands: Essays and Criticism, 1981–1991* (London: Granta Press, 1991), p. 301; Tournier, *The Wind Spirit: An Autobiography* [1977] (Boston: Beacon Books, 1988), p. 164 and 129; and Calvino, 'The Written and the Unwritten Word', *New York Review of Books*, 12 May 1983, 38–9.
32   Ballard, Introduction to *Crash* [1973] (London: Granada, 1985), p. 8; and Ballard, 'The Overloaded Man [1961], in *The Best Short Stories of J.G. Ballard* (New York: Holt, Rinehart and Winston 1978), p. 123.
33   Rushdie, *Imaginary Homelands*, p. 12; and Rushdie, *Midnight's Children* (London: Jonathan Cape, 1981), p. 300.
34   Rushdie and Grass, 'Fictions are lies that tell the truth', *The Listener*, 27 June 1985, 14–15; Grass, 'Writers and the Trade Unions', in *On Writing and Politics*, p. 116; Grass, *Headbirths, or the Germans are dying out* (London: Secker and Warburg, 1982), p. 135.
35   Thomas, *Memories and Hallucinations: A Memoir* (New York: Viking Press, 1988), p. 40; and Thomas, *The White Hotel* (London: Victor Gollancz, 1981), p. 13.
36   'Tradition and the Individual Talent' [1919] in T.S. Eliot, *Selected Essays* (London: Faber and Faber, 1932), p. 21; and Barthes, in *Image, Music, Text*, ed. Stephen Heath (London: Fontana, 1977), pp. 145 and 147.

37   Pasolini, *Heretical Empiricism* (Bloomington: Indiana Press, 1988), p. 71;
      and Pasolini, *Poems*, trans. Norman Macafee (New York: Random
      House, 1982), p. 31.

38   Bonnefoy, *Le Nuage Rouge: Essais sur la poétique* (Paris: Mercure de
      France, 1977), p. 279; and Bonnefoy, *Poems, 1959–1975*, trans. Richard
      Pevear (New York: Random House, 1985), p. 145.

39   Celan, 'The Meridian' [1960], in *Collected Prose*, trans. Rosemarie
      Waldrop (Manchester: Carcanet Press, 1986), pp. 49 and 47; and
      Celan, *Selected Poems* trans. Michael Hamburger and Christopher
      Middleton (Harmondsworth: Penguin, 1972), p. 43.

40   Brodsky, *To Urania : Selected Poems, 1965–1985* (New York: Farrar,
      Straus, Giroux, 1987), p. 3; and Brodsky, 'A Poet and Prose', in *Less than
      one: Selected Essays* (New York: Farrar, Straus, Giroux, 1986), p. 188.

41   Herbert, 'Knocker' in *The New Polish Poetry*, ed. Milne Holton and
      Paul Vangelisti (Pittsburgh: University of Pittsburgh Press, 1978), p. 9;
      and Herbert, 'Study of the Object' [1961], from *Post-War Polish Poetry*,
      trans. Czeslaw Milosz (Harmondsworth: Penguin, 1970), p. 113.

42   Hughes, 'Crow Hears Fate Knock on the Door', in *Crow: From the Life
      and Songs of the Crow* (London: Faber and Faber, 1972), p. 23.

43   Nagy, *Love of the Scorching Wind: Selected Poems, 1953–1971*, trans.
      Tony Connor and Kenneth McRobbie (London: Oxford University
      Press, 1973), pp. 54 and 53; and Popa, *Collected Poems, 1943–1976*,
      trans. Anne Pennington (Manchester: Carcanet, 1978), pp. 4 and 117.

44   Ponge, *The Making of the Pré* [1971], trans. Lee Fahnestock (Columbia:
      University of Missouri Press, 1979), p. 228.

45   Gomringer, 'From Line to Constellation' [1954], in *Concrete Poetry: A
      World View*, ed. Mary Ellen Solt (Bloomington: Indiana University
      Press, 1968), p 67; and Bense, 'Concrete Poetry' [1965], in Solt, p. 73.

46   Heissenbüttel, 'Über den Einfall', in *Über Literatur: Aufsätze und
      Frankfurter Vorlesungen* (Munich: dtv, 1966), p. 215; and Enzensberger,
      The Sinking of the Titanic: A Poem, trans. by author (Boston: Houghton
      Mifflin, 1980), p 18.

47   Foucault, *Power/Knowledge: Selected Interviews and other Writings,
      1972–1977*, ed. Colin Gordon (Brighton: Harvester Press, 1980), p. 97.

48   Kundera, *The Unbearable Lightness of Being* (Harmondsworth: Penguin,
      1984), p. 34.

49   Cixous, 'The Laugh of the Medusa', in *Signs: Journal of Women in
      Culture and Society* (Summer 1976), p. 880.

50   Lessing, *The Golden Notebook* (New York: Simon & Schuster, 1962),
      p. 488.

51   Susan Husserl-Kapit, 'An Interview with Marguerite Duras', *Signs:
      Journal of Women in Culture and Society*, (Winter 1975), p. 425; Duras,
      Practicalities: Marguerite Duras speaks to Jérôme Beaujour [1987], (New
      York: Grove Weidenfeld, 1990), p. 35; and Carter, *The Sadeian Women:
      An Exercise in Cultural History* (London: Virago, 1979), p. 36.

52   Wittig, preface to *The Straight Mind and other Essays* (New York:
      Beacon Press, 1992), pp. xiii–xiv; Wittig, *The Straight Mind*, p. 56; and
      Wittig, *The Lesbian Body* [1973] (Boston: Beacon Press, 1975), p. 9.

53   Wolf, *Cassandra: A Novel and four Essays*, trans. Jan van Heurck
      (London: Virago, 1984), pp. 257, 258 and 270.

Index

Sanctis, Francesco de, 87
Sand, George (French, 1804–76), 17, 35, 55, 71
Sartre, Jean-Paul (French, 1905–80), 159, 186–8, 193, 229
Sassoon, Siegfried (English, 1886–1967), 146
Saussure, Ferdinand de, 132, 202–3
Say, J.B., 50
Schauwecker, Franz, 145
Schelling, Friedrich, 59
Schickelé, René (German, 1885–1940), 102
Schiller, Friedrich (German, 1759–1805), 12, 15, 17, 21, 22–3, 25, 45, 81
Schlaf, Johannes (German, 1862–1941), 87–8
Schlegel, August Wilhelm von (German, 1767–1845), ix, 10, 12
Schlegel, Friedrich von (German, 1772–1829), ix, 2, 10, 12, 14, 35
Schleiermacher, Friedrich, 7, 29, 59
Schmidt, Arno (German, 1914–79), 207
Schnitzler, Arthur (Austrian, 1862–1931), 127
Schopenhauer, Arthur, 107
Schwitters, Kurt (German, 1887–1941), 106
Sciascia, Leonardo (Italian, 1921–89), 194, 195
Scott, Walter (Scottish, 1771–1832), 8, 47
Scribe, Eugène (French, 1791–1861), 80
Seferis, George (Greek, 1900–71), 137–8
Seghers, Anna (German, 1900–83), 170
Sehnsucht (Romantic longing), 35, 38
Sekundenstil, 87
Sénancour, Etienne (French, 1770–1846), 38
sensibility (*Empfindsamkeit*), 9–10
Shakespeare, William (English, 1564–1616), 8, 12, 25, 137

Shaw, George Bernard (Irish, 1856–1950), 95–6
Shelley, Mary (English, 1797–1851), 10, 11, 17, 34–6, 45, 218
Shelley, Percy Bysshe (English, 1792–1822), 1, 13, 15, 21, 29
Sherriff, R.C. (English, 1896–1975), 146
Sholokhov, Mikhail (Russian, 1905–84), 173
show trials (Moscow), 172–3
Sikelianos, Angelos (Greek, 1884–1951), 137
Sillitoe, Alan (English, 1928–), 196
Silone, Ignazio (Italian, 1900–78), 156, 166–7, 197
Simon, Claude (French, 1913–), 208–9
Slowacki, Juliusz (Polish, 1809–49), 26
Smiles, Samuel, 50
social Darwinism, 62, 89, 98
Socialist Realism, 153–5, 156
Sollers, Philippe, 203
Solomos, Dionysios (Greek, 1798–1857), ix, 27, 37
Solzhenitsyn, Alexander (Russian, 1918–), 197–8
Sorel, George, 149
Soupault, Philippe (French, 1897–1990), 104
Southey, Robert (English, 1774–1843), 1, 45, 51
Spanish Civil War, 149–51, 152, 165, 168, 171, 176, 193
Spark, Muriel (English, 1918–), 229
Spencer, Herbert, 50–1
Spender, Stephen (1909–95), 147, 150, 152, 155, 171, 176, 193
Spengler, Oswald, 144, 177, 178
Spitta, Karl (German, 1801–59), 73
Staël, Madame de (French, 1766–1817), 10, 12–13, 35
Stalin, Joseph, 147, 153, 172, 173, 176, 198, 199, 215
Stehr, Hermann (German, 1864–1940), 178